"Abigail Rian Evans is one of the leading voices in the interplay of theology, medicine, and health. This book of hers is magisterial in scope and insight. Evans covers the whole range of issues in medical ethics and pastoral care related to issues of death and dying. This text belongs on the bookshelf of hospital chaplains, pastors, bioethicists, theologians, and health-care providers. Comprehensive and evenhanded, *Is God Still at the Bedside?* describes the main issues facing patients and their families and those who care for them medically and spiritually. Essential reading for anyone concerned with death and dying, medical ethics, and pastoral care from a Christian perspective."

— Bruce Epperly
Lancaster Theological Seminary
author of *God's Touch: Faith, Wholeness, and the Healing Miracles of Jesus*

"Many readers will appreciate the comprehensive approach that Evans takes to the challenging topic of death and dying. . . . An insightful and enlivening book."

— C. George Fitzgerald
Director, Spiritual Care Service,
Stanford University Medical Center

"The most comprehensive study of end-of-life issues that I have seen. . . . *Is God Still at the Bedside?* is a lucid, timely, and enormously relevant book that combines religious knowledge, excellent scholarship, and practical guidance. I am happy to recommend this book with enthusiasm."

— Raymond A. Dunmyer
St. Thomas the Apostle Catholic Church,
Montevallo, Alabama

D0962662

Is God Still at the Bedside?

THE MEDICAL, ETHICAL, AND PASTORAL ISSUES OF DEATH AND DYING

Abigail Rian Evans

LIBRARY
ARAPAHOE COMMUNITY COLLEGE
5900 SOUTH SANTA FE DRIVE
P.O. BOX 9002
LITTLETON, CO 80160-900

WILLIAM B. EERDMANS PUBLISHING COMPANY
GRAND RAPIDS, MICHIGAN / CAMBRIDGE, U.K.

© 2011 Abigail Rian Evans

All rights reserved

Published 2011 by

Wm. B. Eerdmans Publishing Co.

2140 Oak Industrial Drive N.E., Grand Rapids, Michigan 49505 /

P.O. Box 163, Cambridge CB3 9PU U.K.

Printed in the United States of America

16 15 14 13 12 11   7 6 5 4 3 2 1

Library of Congress Cataloging-in-Publication Data

Evans, Abigail Rian.

    Is God still at the bedside?: the medical, ethical, and pastoral issues of death and dying /
Abigail Rian Evans.

        p.   cm.

    Includes bibliographical references and index.

    ISBN 978-0-8028-2723-4 (pbk.: alk. paper)

    1. Death — Religious aspects — Christianity.   2. Death — Moral and ethical aspects.
3. Death. I. Title. II. Title: Medical, ethical, and pastoral issues of death and dying.

BT825.E93   2011

236′.1 — dc22

2010034597

www.eerdmans.com

This book is dedicated to my sister Roanne Rian Pulliam
(January 24, 1930–August 24, 2008) and her children —
Brian, Gay, and Claire — whose collective bravery
and love triumphed over the sadness of her death.
Her strong faith was reflected in her choice of
Tennyson for the scattering of her ashes:

> Sunset and evening star,
> And one clear call for me!
> And may there be no moaning of the bar,
> When I put out to sea,
>
> But such a tide as moving seems asleep,
> Too full for sound and foam,
> When that which drew from out the boundless deep
> Turns again home.
>
> Twilight and evening bell,
> And after that the dark!
> And may there be no sadness of farewell,
> When I embark;
>
> For tho' from out our bourne of Time and Place
> The flood may bear me far,
> I hope to see my Pilot face to face
> When I have crossed the bar.

Alfred, Lord Tennyson (1809-1892), "Crossing the Bar"

NOV 1 5 2011

MOA-12 504

Contents

Acknowledgments

An author is always indebted to many people in the research and writing of a book. First, I would like to thank Princeton Theological Seminary for a year's sabbatical, which enabled me to go deeply into my research and writing on a subject I have pursued for many years.

I would like to especially recognize the outstanding work of Janice Miller, my Princeton Theological Seminary assistant for fifteen years, whose unfailing support, competence, and patience through dozens of drafts of this book, and so many other projects, has made it possible for me to accomplish whatever I have. Also, my thanks to Michael Davis, adjunct professor at Westminster Choir College at Rider University, whose able assistance at the end of this project helped to pull the book together into a coherent whole; and to Jan Jacewicz, whose editorial suggestions, as always, have clarified parts of this book tremendously.

Through the years I have been blessed with the assistance of so many outstanding Princeton Theological Seminary MDiv and PhD student research assistants. For this project they are Anna Kate Ellerman Shurley, Philip Helsel, Luiz Nascimento, Anita Wright, and especially Miriam Diephouse McMillan, whose skill in finding obscure information and giving editorial assistance greatly enhanced this book. Those who reviewed specific parts of my manuscript were Gerald Rupp, Esq., Dr. Lawrence Stratton, and Sr. Mary Louise Wessell. Kudos!

The nature of this book required interviewing those with firsthand experience at the bedside. I am most grateful to the following pastors, chaplains, and health care professionals who gave of their time and insights, which added reality and depth to this difficult subject of death and dying. They include Cindy Alloway, Graham Bardsley, David Barile, Karen Else

Cambria, Deborah Davis, C. George Fitzgerald, Laura Gronberg, Andrea Heinlein, Robin Bacon Hoffman, Marc Peloquin, and Diane Smith.

In addition, due to the dynamic and evolving status of the Faith Community Nurse specialty, interviewing leaders in this field was imperative. My deep gratitude goes to Sharon Stanton, Norma Small, Peggy Matteson, and Nancy Durbin for their knowledge and clarification of this emerging field.

Praise God from whom all blessings flow. Amen.

Preface

Why write a book on death and dying? Because death will come to everyone and often will be accompanied by painful and difficult choices. As we struggle with these choices, we look for guidance, hope, and insight as we walk through the valley of the shadow of death. This book attempts to provide an overview of the issues surrounding death and dying. In twenty-five years of teaching death and dying courses, I have discovered that most books in this field are collections of single-subject essays by various authors gathered and edited in a single volume. While these are valuable works that contribute significantly to the literature, a single-author text that draws on a variety of disciplines may lend more of a cogency and coherence to the analysis of these issues.

We begin with a tour of the medical, ethical, theological, pastoral, and legal landscape that relates to end-of-life issues; this will provide a foundation for the current complexities in addressing the needs and concerns of the dying. Such an overview will also help the reader understand the interrelatedness of each of these various topics. These perspectives will be placed within the realities of contemporary society — a society that is supporting a rapidly aging population — by providing basic facts and statistics about our social and economic situation. I hope that this material will invite further in-depth reading and research on the part of the reader.

I wrote this book for a diverse readership. First, it can be used as a textbook for courses on death and dying, bioethics, and other disciplines that address end-of-life issues. Second, physicians, nurses, Faith Community Nurses, clergy, and those in related professions may find this book useful for understanding the range of issues for those in ministry to the dying and their families. Third, it can be used by individuals and their families as a source of information with specific guidelines for making end-of-life decisions. Testimonies from those who are walking the difficult last journey of this life will demonstrate the critical importance of faith. This book can be a helpful tool for navigating the rough waters stirred up in an era often charged with controversial emotional, medical, and spiritual decisions that literally can have life-and-death consequences.

My perspective is that of a Christian bioethicist and a Presbyterian pastor who has worked within ecumenical and interfaith contexts with clergy, family members, and patients as well as with medical professionals who are addressing the needs of those dealing with death and dying. It is clear that no one religious or faith perspective has a corner on the truth concerning end-of-life issues. As we navigate what can often be the rocky terrain of pain, suffering, and dying, we need all the brilliance, insight, and experience of people from a large variety of cultures, backgrounds, and faiths. This is a universal experience that touches every person: illness and death are shared by all humanity. As we face this ultimate mystery, we trust ourselves to God, who has conquered death and is the source of our hope and new life. I invite you to walk this journey with me through the pages of this book.

Introduction

There are two bookends to human life: birth and death. What is the meaning of them? How do we understand these realities? Death cannot be understood or accepted until we have learned to live and savor the preciousness of life. We can talk about life because we are experiencing it, but death is the great unknown. For this reason, without faith in a future life we may do anything to stave it off. We have tried to domesticate death, but sometimes it seems to be a wild beast devouring us and all we hold dear. At other times it can be a welcome release from pain and suffering. When confronted with the loss of a loved one, grief may overwhelm us. But we can know joy in that mourning in the sure hope that God is the Lord of life and death — the alpha and the omega.

Medicine is a gift from God and has done much to alleviate suffering, increase our longevity, and provide previously unimagined cures. However, the deeper questions of the meaning of why we die — and what will happen after we die — remain unanswered. These are the questions religion wrestles with. This book seeks to address those existential questions of the meaning of life and death and how Christian faith and theology respond to this question: Is God still at the bedside?

> When we deal with death and dying issues, we are immediately confronted with our world views and hence theology. Definitions of death, judgments about treatment termination or futility, and moral arguments surrounding euthanasia are deeply intertwined with our theological assumptions. It is nearly impossible to grapple with these ethical issues without significant engagement in matters such as: the nature of life, the nature of death, the meaning of suffering, the meaning and the limits of human agency, and the nature of actions of

God. . . . When we begin to construct a theology for ethical issues of death and dying, one is struck by the paucity of theological engagement with death.[1]

This book's structure reflects its theses that the complexity of death demands an interdisciplinary approach that examines both metaquestions and quandary issues. I have written the chapters in several different styles to fit the content of each: firsthand experiences, great literature, scientific treatises, legal rulings, and philosophical, theological, and biblical texts, all of which require various styles of expression.

Part I, the prologue, will begin with an exploration of our understanding of life and of death. Part II, "Negotiated Death," will move the discussion to the modern experience of dying as seen in debates about euthanasia, physician-assisted suicide, organ donation, and, in many instances, our failure to resolve these issues, driving us to the courts, which in turn have created rulings and precedent cases.

Technological advances have allowed us to extend our dying as well as our living. This is the phenomenon of negotiated death, where to some it may appear that we are playing God, or at minimum making God redundant. Has technological medicine pushed God aside? Americans often appear to be less concerned with God and more with freedom of choice. We prize autonomy above all else, and autonomy includes, when possible, making a choice about how and when to die. However, when we enter the medical machine we may not be given the opportunity to make decisions that are consistent with our values.

Part III, "The Experience of Dying," will explore the realities of loss, grief, bereavement, mourning, pain, and suffering — areas about which medicine has little to say. However, there are health care professionals who are especially equipped to address these issues, such as those working in hospice and other palliative-care settings.

Part IV, "God at the Bedside," will discuss the role of the clergy as especially important, particularly in pastors' work with the faith community and the faith community nurses. Here we see God most vividly at the bedside. Understanding the best way to comfort and care for the dying person and her family will lead to a funeral based on strong Christian faith and God's presence, which will reinforce how God has been present through-

1. Dennis Hollinger, "Theological Foundations for Death and Dying Issues," *Ethics and Medicine* 12, no. 3 (1996): 60.

out the journey. However, this book is especially meant to serve as a wake-up call for clergy who often find themselves ill equipped to deal with death and dying.

> Many Americans want spiritual comfort in their final days, but only about one-third think clergy would be very helpful in providing it, a Gallup Institute poll shows.
>
> Among the highlights of the 1,200 polled:
>
> - Half of those polled consider prayer important at life's end and fear they'll die feeling cut off from a higher power.
> - 56% are concerned they won't be forgiven by God or reconciled with others.
> - 36% say clergy would be comforting in many ways, compared with 81% who cite family and 81% friends.
>
> "Clergymen are seen as ministers of religion — boxed in by creeds and dogmas," says theological historian Robert Webber. "But most people don't want religion, they want spirituality." In addition, with the mobility of our society, not only do people lack a church home, but they might not know the pastor or rabbi very well. "You don't start breaking the ice when you're dying. You want someone who knows you well and accepts you totally."[2]

Studies have revealed that spirituality is important.

- Intrinsic religiousness is positively associated with spiritual well-being and hope among patients regardless of their level of physical well-being.
- Dying patients have more death anxiety than healthy patients. Religious meaning and the strength of one's religious beliefs play an important role in one's not being afraid to die.
- Religiosity was significantly and positively related to greater beliefs in afterlife and reduced death anxiety among a group of undergraduates.
- Spirituality can be a helpful source of comfort in time of overwhelming stress.
- Parents whose children died found comfort in their religious beliefs and used those beliefs to give meaning to their suffering.

2. Marilyn Elias, "Few would turn to clergy for help if they were dying," *USA Today,* December 9, 1997, p. 1A.

- Existential and religious well-being is associated with a lower state of anxiety among patients with cancer who are dying.
- Religious activism and connections are associated with greater well-being and lower levels of pain among patients with advanced cancer.
- Religious involvement is associated with hopefulness and general life satisfaction.[3]

These realities about the importance of religion and spirituality call us to consider that, if we are courageous and faithful to God in our everyday life, this is likely to influence our dying. Learning how to live helps us learn how to die. The irony is that the richer our life is — within God's will, living life abundantly — the more ready we may be for death, that is, we have no regrets. Understanding life as a gift from God is the foundation of facing our death and dying. Furthermore, Christians begin to see glimpses of eternity this side of the grave, and although loving life more, we long, as did the apostle Paul, to be fully present with God. However, that does not in any way lessen our grief at the loss of a loved one, because it is precisely that loss — our loss, not theirs — that is the occasion of our sorrow. Death is the event from which the truth emerges that we are not in control, which is why serious illness and a slow dying process frighten us. The greatest fear of the frail elderly is loss of control.

Death is, to Christians, the entrance into eternal life, though some would argue that how we *live* will determine if we make that journey. Some of the choices we make about how we live while dying have both ethical and theological components and consequences. Central to my analysis in this book is a theology of life and death that provides the framework in which we make these choices.

In order to develop a Christian theology of death, we need to analyze how pastoral care and ethics intersect in end-of-life decision-making, and we need to find ways for pastors and churches to work collaboratively with doctors to bring about healing in the face of sickness, suffering, bereavement, and death. A collaborative approach to the care of the dying entails a cooperative model that will involve clergy, physicians, nurses, family, friends, and the patient him- or herself.

The question of this book's title, Is God still at the bedside? will accompany us throughout these various chapters. This is not simply a ques-

3. "Spirituality Plays Important Role in Chronic Illness and Dying," *Faith and Medicine Connection* 2, no. 4 (Summer 1998).

tion about God's existence, but also about God's role in our everyday lives, especially at life's end. There are many people who believe in God, but when they address serious illness or death, they turn solely to the medical profession and do not try to understand how God is involved (though 92 percent of Americans say they believe in God, and many pray for healing).[4] The tension for many people is between aggressively pursuing medical treatment to stave off death at any cost and turning the dying process over to God, or choosing how or when to die. This may be a false tension, since medical resources are also gifts of God; but it is their trumping of everything else that I am calling into question. These are the tensions, challenges, and issues with which this book will wrestle.

4. Adelle M. Banks, "Think You Know What Americans Believe About Religion? You Might Want to Think Again," *Religion News,* The Pew Forum on Religion and Public Life, June 23, 2008: http://pewforum.org/news/display.php?NewsID=15907 (accessed June 18, 2009). And 60 percent say they pray. "CBS Poll: Prayer Can Heal," *CBS News.com online,* 1998: http://www.cbsnews.com/stories/1998/04/29/opinion/main8285.shtml (accessed Sept. 14, 2007).

I. PROLOGUE

1. Reflections on Human Life

LIFE

LIFE, believe, is not a dream
So dark as sages say;
Oft a little morning rain
Foretells a pleasant day.
Sometimes there are clouds of gloom,
But these are transient all;
If the shower will make the roses bloom,
O why lament its fall?

Rapidly, merrily,
Life's sunny hours flit by,
Gratefully, cheerily
Enjoy them as they fly!

What though Death at times steps in,
And calls our Best away?
What though sorrow seems to win,
O'er hope, a heavy sway?
Yet Hope again elastic springs,
Unconquered, though she fell;
Still buoyant are her golden wings,
Still strong to bear us well.
Manfully, fearlessly,
The day of trial bear,

> For gloriously, victoriously,
> Can courage quell despair!
>
> Charlotte Brontë (1816-1855)

Introduction

Before we address the topic of death, we need to reflect on life. Some say the specter of death gives life its meaning. William Coffin in *Credo* wrote the following: "Without death, we'd never live. Without discovering the limits of our talents, we'd never discover who we are. And, finally, hard choices have a potential for riches beyond any reckoning, 'for eye hath not seen nor ear heard nor the heart of man perceived the good things that God hath prepared for those who love him.'"[1] Authors such as Dorothee Sölle write that we learn about death through the death of another.[2] "The great use of life is to spend it for something that outlasts it."[3] For the Christian, what outlasts our physical life is love of God and others; that is, our view of life is from the perspective of eternity.

Perspectives on Life

We will examine three general perspectives on life: vitalism, instrumentalism, and conditionalism. *Vitalism* is the belief that pure biological human life is a good no matter what the quality. Life has value in all its forms — animal, vegetable, or human. From a theological perspective, life's value stems from its being created by God.[4] However, physical life is not an absolute value, but a primary one. One may be called to sacrifice one's own life to save the life of another — or for a higher ideal. But life is considered an intrinsic good, like happiness, truth, freedom, or justice.[5] This view is usu-

---

1. William Sloane Coffin, *Credo* (Louisville: Westminster John Knox Press, 2004), p. 167.

2. Dorothee Sölle, *The Mystery of Death* (Minneapolis: Fortress Press, 2007).

3. Attributed to William James (1842-1910), American psychologist and philosopher.

4. Stated Clerk of the Presbyterian Church in the United States, "The Nature and Value of Human Life," a paper adopted by the 121st General Assembly and Commended to the Church for Study, publication no. 8984 (Atlanta: Presbyterian Church USA, 1981).

5. Robert Veatch, *Death, Dying, and the Biological Revolution: Our Last Quest for Responsibility*, rev. ed. (New Haven: Yale University Press, 1989), p. 235.

ally coupled with an appeal to the sixth commandment, which prohibits killing. This is a difficult position to defend since exceptions are usually made for war, capital punishment, and self-defense. In some cases there may be overriding values, such as the protection of one's country or punishment for a crime, which may trump the value of life.

Instrumentalism is a moderate position that holds that life is a good to be preserved as a condition of other values. When other values can no longer be realized, then it no longer needs to be continued. Richard McCormick, when he refers to the struggle to survive, or the undue or unending effort to live, reflects this position. This position also regards life as meaningful and not absurd, a gift to be treasured. In other words, life is a *prima facie* good. However, life can be laid aside for higher values, for example, the duty to relieve others of the burdens produced by my life, or a heroic self-sacrifice to save a person or defend a cause. In other words, being alive enables us to fulfill other values, such as loving: that is, it is simply an instrumental value.[6]

The third position, *conditionalism,* argues that life is only worth living as long as it meets certain established levels, criteria, or quality. (The story of *Whose Life Is It Anyway?* addresses this perspective. Originally a BBC documentary, a play (1972), and later a film (1981), it is the story of a quadriplegic who could no longer make love and sculpt, hence wanted to leave the hospital so he could die; it posed in dramatic form the issue of whether humans should be able to make their own choices about dying.) Here we begin to move into the areas of taste and preferences: what is acceptable to some people would not be tolerated by others. The difficulty with "quality of life" definitions are their misuse; they are open to all kinds of connotations. Some may judge the relative worth of a person based on diminishing humanhood, degree of suffering, or mental and physical prowess. The criteria used to establish quality of life generally fall into four categories: (1) The presence of incapacitating pain. Here there is nothing but misery and uncontrollable suffering. John Fletcher adopts this standard for the ending of life. (2) The standard of awareness — when the patient is unconscious or unaware of her surroundings with no prospect of change in the quality of life. This could include Paul Ramsey's category of those "beyond the reach of care" (Lynsch-Nylan), or the never-alive-in-the-first-place group, as with the anencephalic infant. (This is an infant born without a brain, but the distinction that such infants "were never

6. Veatch, *Death, Dying,* p. 235.

alive in the first place" no longer applies, given current scientific advances that enable them to live longer and longer.)[7] (3) Potential for relationships: life still has value but this value cannot be realized in physical existence. This is illustrated by Richard McCormick's "no potential for human relationships" group. (4) Personhood assessment: if there is only biological human life and no person who can generate rights, hence possess value, then the obligation to preserve life would be removed.

Our definitions of life and protectable human life affect the subsequent discussions in this book about euthanasia, physician-assisted suicide, withdrawal of treatment, and so forth. However, we need to begin with the metaquestions — what does it mean to be a person? and what is the meaning of health? — because these definitions influence our understanding not only of life, but also of death.

Doctrine of Human Nature and Understanding of Health

In contrast to contemporary medicine, the Judeo-Christian perspective of human nature starts with individuals and how their nature determines the meaning of health and sickness, healing and healers. The biblical definitions of health and sickness derive from the view that man/woman is a whole — body, mind, and spirit. This wholeness means that both physical and spiritual healing are important. Humans are created by God to live in community, not in isolation. This is why the vision of dying alone, abandoned by the medical profession as well as family and friends, may be our greatest fear. We share in the brokenness of our fallen human nature, even though we are created a little lower than the angels. We are all equal as children of God, made in God's image; but each person, though precious and unique, is not perfect.

If health is the integration of all aspects of our being, then being healthy reflects all that we were meant to be. There is a restlessness about our lives, a struggle to move toward completion, a yearning for something better. In these terms, total health is never reached and only briefly enjoyed. From a theological perspective, health is an eschatological idea, that is, it is what God promises and offers in the end. No one knows completely what health is because he/she has not totally enjoyed it. Health is a value, a process, not a goal — a journey, not a state. We experience brokenness in

7. See Paul Ramsey, *The Patient as Person* (New Haven: Yale University Press, 1970).

our lives — whether physical, spiritual, emotional, or mental — because we are not perfect beings. A wholistic view includes viewing us with respect to our environment — man/woman as a social being. We are not only defined by our internal workings but by our social relationships.[8]

Psychologically, this understanding of man/woman has important implications. People are made to be in relationships, to experience acceptance by others, and to find meaning and purpose in life outside of themselves. This orientation toward others is an important part of what it means to be healthy. This understanding of what it means to be human and healthy forms a prelude to the discussion about the sacredness of persons. This means that love, not autonomy, is the most prized virtue.

The Sacredness of Persons

Ethicists often make distinctions between being human and being a person. Engelhardt's social person and Fletcher's twenty criteria of humanhood, as well as Singer's criteria for nontreatment, all rely on certain criteria for what it means to be a human and what qualifies as protectable human life. The debates about abortion and euthanasia also involve perspectives on humanhood, personhood, and value of life. Both legal and ethical arguments are mounted on both sides of the issue. God has declared special protection of humans because they are sacred. This sacredness toward people "inspires *reverence*. Sacredness is a holy specialness that signals people to stand off." Karl Barth described it as follows: "Respect is man's astonishment, humility, and awe . . . at majesty, dignity, holiness, a mystery which compels him to withdraw, and keep his distance, to handle it modestly, circumspectly, and carefully."[9]

When we feel this reverence-like respect toward another, we have found his or her sacred personhood, the quality that makes him or her unkillable. The question here is whether to follow Albert Schweitzer's "reverence for life" in general or the sanctity of human life. Lewis Smedes says that it is "better, for believers anyway, to remember that while God breathes the breath of life into all things living, it is persons whom he loves

8. Abigail Rian Evans, *Redeeming Marketplace Medicine* (Cleveland: Pilgrim Press, 1999), pp. 67-116.

9. Karl Barth, *Church Dogmatics*, vol. III, pt. 4, trans. A. T. Mackay et al. (Edinburgh: T. & T. Clark, 1961), p. 339.

as his children."[10] However, if one returns to the creation story in Genesis, God's response to everything God created was that it was very good. For the purposes of our discussion, we are focusing on *human* life, though its glory may be enhanced by other life around it. Focusing on the sacredness of persons may protect us from an absolutist perspective of life where physical life would be extended even when the person is gone or would suffer unduly because of its continuation.

The sacredness of persons is also related to the concept of the dignity of persons. Autonomy should not be the principal virtue; nor do personhood, freedom, and reason equal dignity. This has been a much-neglected idea until the President's Council on Bioethics (2001-2009) reintroduced it into its deliberations. This concept of dignity is meant to protect the weak as we support human flourishing. The proof of who lacks dignity rests on the shoulders of the accuser, so to speak. True dignity is rooted in the divine; it is not a question of the potential for dignity but it is full-blown. Our concern should be for "life around the edges," as Leon Kass expresses it.[11]

Philosophical perspectives such as those of Immanuel Kant may value the individual, when he argues that a person is to be treated as an end rather than a means, based on his or her moral agency.[12] However, the problem with Kant's perspective is that he created a totally artificial separation between a person's intellectual and emotional life. Furthermore, since we could only know the phenomena (things as they appear), not the noumena (things in themselves), he opened the door to postmodernism and ultimately skepticism.

The Sanctity of Human Life

As we reflect on life as an ethical value, it is not reduced solely to sanctity of life but has many facets: value, respect, continuity, sanctity, and protec-

---

10. Lewis B. Smedes, "Respect for Human Life: Thou Shalt Not Kill," in *On Moral Medicine*, ed. Stephen Lammers and Allen Verhey (Grand Rapids: Eerdmans, 1987), p. 146.

11. Leon Kass lecture, "Defending Human Dignity: What it is and Why it Matters," as part of the Tocqueville Forum, School of Government, Georgetown University. Kass is professor at the John U. Neff Committee on Social Thought, University of Chicago, and Hertog Fellow at the American Enterprise Institute for Public Policy Research.

12. Immanuel Kant, *Groundwork of the Metaphysic of Morals*, trans. H. J. Paton (New York: Harper Torchbooks, 1956).

tion. The sacredness of persons gives rise to the sanctity of human life, but it raises the question whether we are referring to individual or collective human life. Life is a gift from God to be cherished. The sanctity of individual human life is grounded in the Judeo-Christian perspective that each one of us is made in God's image as an inviolate, unique person. Respect for persons is not tied to physical abilities, intellectual prowess, or societal contributions, but to the fact that we are all children of God.

> Life is a gift from God of which we are stewards. We have a vocation to nourish, protect, defend, and improve it. This view provides a matrix for the uniqueness of each person, because sanctity is not founded on the quality of life as judged either by self or others. According to this perspective, sanctity of life is founded on our love for each person as he/she is — with all the imperfections and unfulfillments — because God loves him/her. Hence, an individual's value is tied to his/her relationship to God. God's love for us as creatures is not the only grounding but, as Herbert Butterfield puts it, is "cross-referenced to eternity." Since life continues forever, albeit in a changed form, we should consider it holy.[13]

Societies that treated foreigners as less than human — as slaves or as possessions — have flourished. Greek popular morality tended to understand the individual not as a moral agent, but in terms of function or purpose. Thus were they the first utilitarians! Even Aristotle held that individuals should be loved on the basis of their virtue rather than simply on the basis of their existence. Human life was to be deemed sacred, but collectively rather than individually. As Basil Mitchell clearly points out, our ideas of human nature provide the basis for the sanctity of human life.[14] It is difficult to find a grounding for the sanctity of life in the individual sense outside of a religious framework. The sanctity of life is grounded in the Judeo-Christian perspective that each of us is made in God's image as an inviolate, unique person. Human life is sacred from conception to death. There are no gradations of value at different points of the spectrum. However, some would argue that one can concede its sacredness without arguing that all human life is protectable.

13. Abigail Rian Evans, "Is Abortion Fraying the Seamless Garement? Theology and Ethics at the Edge of Life," in *The Sanctity of Life,* ed. David Fraser (Princeton, N.J.: Princeton University Press, 1988), p. 65.

14. Basil Mitchell, *Morality Religious and Secular: The Dilemma of the Traditional Conscience* (Oxford: Clarendon Press, 1970), p. 131.

Protection of Human Life as Tied to Its Value

It is important to distinguish between value, respect, sanctity, and *protection* of human life. In Reformed theology, human life is a first-order value and the focal point of God's creation and redemption. God cherishes us and is committed to the good of all humans. God's concern for human life anchors respect for life. "Explicit scriptural expression of this respect for life is found in the commandment to do no unjustifiable killing. The Reformed tradition has discerned several elements in this command. The first is the obligation to avoid doing harm. A second is the obligation to protect and preserve life by doing what sustains it. Yet a third is the recognition that these first two obligations can come into conflict in specific situations so that both cannot be fulfilled. . . . It is conceivable in such a case that taking life may be justified as more consistent with respect for life."[15]

Protection of life for some is tied to a series of arguments about the beginning and the ending of human life. When human life begins — or more precisely, when an individual human life begins — is a matter of some debate. Three stages where it is reasonable to assume human life begins are: conception, when the unique genotype originates; segmentation, when it is irreversibly settled whether there will be one, two, or more individuals; and the early development of the fetus, when the "outline" of the cells contained is actualized in all essential respects, with only growth to come.[16]

Joseph Cardinal Bernardin's arguments about life as a seamless garment are based on our understanding that life is a continuum and of equal value at any given point. Genetics, abortion, capital punishment, modern warfare, care for the terminally ill — all are pieces of a larger pattern. Concern for life in any one of these areas requires a concern for the broader attitude in society about respect for life. The viability and credibility of the "seamless garment" principle depend on the consistency of its application.[17] The right to life and the quality of life are of equal concern; the problem is that these may come into conflict.

15. Stated Clerk of the Presbyterian Church in the United States, "The Nature and Value of Human Life," p. 4.

16. William Werpehowski and Stephen D. Crocco, eds., *The Essential Paul Ramsey: A Collection* (New Haven: Yale University Press, 1994), p. 165.

17. Joseph Cardinal Bernardin, "A Consistent Ethic of Life: Continuing the Dialogue," the William Wade Lecture Series, St. Louis University, March 11, 1984, Priest for Life, Teachings of the Catholic Church on Abortion: http://www.priestforlife.org/magisterium/bernardinwade.html (accessed May 28, 2009).

Abortion and active euthanasia for some may be the same act, morally speaking, just at opposite ends of the spectrum. The choice is simply the time at which we will destroy life. Paul Ramsey says: "Fundamental to ethical reasoning is the requirement that cases be treated similarly if they are similar in all relevant and important moral features, that is, Morison's appeal to the structure of the current arguments in favor of benign liberalized euthanasia."[18] In ethical terms, this is the proverbial "slippery slope." In other words, once humans at the edges of life are no longer valued, the value of everyone is threatened. Others would argue that, in the case of abortion, we are not talking about a person; but they would not disagree that the fetus is human.

There are guidelines for avoiding harm to and the protection of human life based on our finitude.[19] The finite and moral characteristics of human life also help us understand death in a way that influences how we fulfill the obligations to do no harm and to protect from harm. Finally, the relational and finite characteristics of human life help us with difficult decisions regarding who will be protected in certain circumstances. These implications will be examined more fully and specifically as we turn to the issues identified at the outset. Because humans are sacred and have dignity, we are called on to protect human life. The protection of human life — especially of the most defenseless, powerless, voiceless — warrants our special justice, that is, compensation for one's disadvantaged position by virtue of genetic, economic, social, or other factors, or lack of being an autonomous human being. It also stems from charity as it is interpreted in the Sermon on the Mount.

My arguments for the protection of human life are tied to cherishing the most defenseless and the most needy, who generate overriding moral claims on us. Hence, protection is not related to the individuals' gradations of development, ability for relationships, contribution to society, or intellectual or physical vitality; rather, it turns all these arguments on their head. It is precisely when most of these qualities are absent that we have the greatest moral obligation to protect the person: when the edges of life are most frayed, our theology and ethics must mend the garment of life.

From the perspective of the Old and New Testaments, the most de-

18. Paul Ramsey, "Three on Abortion: Protecting the Unborn, Abortion: A Review Article, Feticide/Infanticide Upon Request," *Child and Family Reprint Booklet Series* (1978), p. 14.

19. Stated Clerk of the Presbyterian Church in the United States, "The Nature and Value of Human Life."

fenseless are objects of special protection and concern. The nation of Israel was chosen because it was "one of the least of nations." David, a young shepherd, was called to slay the giant Goliath. Moses, timid and slow of speech, was appointed to lead his people to freedom. "But God chose what is foolish in the world to shame the wise" (1 Cor. 1:27).

In the New Testament there are three parables that especially capture this perspective. First is the scene in the Lukan account of the messianic banquet, where those persons who are disabled or less than whole, from society's perspective, that is, the lame, blind, poor, are the very ones who will replace the rich and powerful in the kingdom of heaven. Second is the description of the last judgment (Matt. 25) in which "the least of these" are, in a sense, representatives of Christ. Serving them is what constitutes the fulfillment of the Christian ideal. Third, the story of the Good Samaritan, where the person to be served or helped is the neighbor, that is, the person in need who presents himself to us.

This particular perspective may turn a utilitarian ethic on its head, that is, what is good for the individual is good for the whole, because a society that values each person above and beyond all else will be a just society where all participate. The problem with John Stuart Mill's (1806-1873) utilitarianism is that individuals become swallowed up in the group and lose their own distinct value. His philosophy of the greatest good for the greatest number often sacrificed the one.

Smedes discusses the protection of human life in terms of its sanctity, hence respect for human life that is grounded in the sixth commandment. "Most people still believe what the commandment tells them, 'Thou shalt not kill,' that every person is a gift of God, to himself and for his neighbor, a gift not to be abused by murdering hands. But there is a deep irony about our assent to the Sixth Commandment. For we are members of a race that habitually slaughters its own children. We honor those who kill, as long as they kill our enemies. We allow children far away to die of hunger while our own children gorge themselves."[20]

There are many interpretations of this commandment based on whether the translation is "kill" or "murder." The word *kill* in Exodus 20:13 and Deuteronomy 5:17 means "to murder, crush, or slay." The proper translation is, "You shall not murder." It is interesting that the King James Version of the Bible correctly translates the sixth commandment (in Matthew 19:18): "Thou shalt do no murder." The Hebrew word *ratsach* and the

20. Smedes, "Respect for Human Life," p. 143.

Greek word *phonenō* ("to murder, to kill"), which are used in the sixth commandment, both clearly mean "murder." Mark and Luke have the same Greek verb form: "Do not kill." Matthew inherits Mark's text and changes the verb form to agree with Exodus 20:13 and Deuteronomy 5:17. The meaning in Matthew is: "You shall not commit murder." The exact same verb form and command appears earlier, in Matthew 5:21: the passive form of this verb means "to die a violent death."[21]

It is interesting to note that the Hebrew language has a general word for killing, the verb *muwth* ("to cause to die"); the Greek language also has a general word for killing, the verb *apokteinō* ("to kill" — expressing a violent ending of someone else's life). That word is used 150 times in the Septuagint for the Hebrew *harag* (meaning "kill") and *mut* ("to cause to die"). Another Greek word is *teleutaō,* from the root *telos* (which means "goal" or "end"): the sense of this word is "to bring to an end," and it can also mean "to die." The Septuagint occasionally uses *thanatoō,* which means "to put to death or kill." However, these general terms for killing are not used in the sixth commandment; instead, the commandment uses very specific words that forbid murder.[22]

The thrust of the sixth commandment is the value of all people, whatever their status or role in society. It cannot be reduced merely to a command to refrain from murdering others. But can it be interpreted in any way to prohibit active euthanasia? Can we ever preside over the death of another person? The value of life cannot be reduced to physical life, since killing the spirit of another can be a more horrible death.

"The letter of this commandment asks us only to 'live and let live,' hardly a summons to heroic moral sacrifice. True, if everyone merely kept his hands off his neighbor's throat, life in our ravaged world would at least have a chance. But fulfilled in love this commandment requires much more."[23] What is behind this commandment seems to be the desire not only to protect humans but also to help them flourish, for example, providing free medical care for the elderly, prenatal care for indigent mothers, and health care insurance for all.

Although the case seems strong for the protection of *all* human life,

21. Information provided by James H. Charlesworth, George L. Collord Professor of New Testament Language and Literature, Director and Editor of the Princeton Theological Seminary Dead Sea Scrolls Project, Princeton, NJ.

22. Colin Brown, ed., *Dictionary of New Testament Theology,* vol. I (Grand Rapids: Zondervan, 1975), pp. 429-30.

23. Smedes, "Respect for Human Life," p. 145.

there are serious philosophers who argue for "developmental" protection. For example, Canon G. R. Dunstan, a leading British moral theologian, argues that Christian morality, Jewish morality, and English law do not grant absolute protection at every stage. He claims that absolute protection of the *conceptus* is the creation of a Roman Catholic moral tradition of the late nineteenth century. He supports gradations of protection of human life rooted in Hammurabi's Code, Hittite religion, the Septuagint, and one of the early church fathers, Tertullian. "Even Aquinas followed a developmental view of human life where the degree of punishments for abortion were tied to the stage of development, described in terms such as *attamati* and *mo exeik ouismenon* (not yet formed); however, all abortion was wrong."[24] We should note, however, that even Aquinas allowed abortion based on the principle of double effect: if the fetus would be the eventual murderer of the mother, then the fetus could be sacrificed to save the life of the mother.

Images of Life

In addition to these philosophical discussions of preserving and ending life are images or metaphors of life's meaning, a more poetic understanding of life. During my years of teaching a course on the subject of death and dying at Princeton Theological Seminary, I have used metaphors of life as a gift, a journey, a race, a dream, or a pilgrimage. For example, we generally understand life as a gift, though at other times it is a gift we may want to return. When we experience happiness and health, we are glad to be alive; we feel joy and gratitude, and we see life as a gift. This is different from the right to life. When we sense life as a gift, we do not so much feel a right to protection against assault as we feel a gratitude for what is given. In other words, we have not earned life — we have received it.

"There are paradoxes in the notion of life as a gift. Life is a gift we had to accept; none of us was in a position to choose not to be born. And it is strange even to think of our own lives as a gift to ourselves. But anyone who has deeply felt dependence on God knows that, while paradoxical, it is not nonsense: every person's life is God's gift to himself or herself."[25] If it

---

24. G. R. Dunstan, "The Moral Status of the Human Embryo: A Tradition Recalled," *Journal of Medical Ethics* 10, no. 1 (1984): 38-44.

25. Lewis B. Smedes, *Mere Morality* (Grand Rapids: Eerdmans, 1989), p. 109.

is true that it is a gift, then we should cherish it, not destroy it for ourselves or others. It is to be graciously shared and sustained. As we explore the understanding of life as a gift, we need to understand it with respect to the sovereignty of God. What is the relationship between the authority of God and the responsibility of humans vis à vis the sacredness of human life and its protection?

Our lives rest in the creative hands of a sovereign Lord. God knits together our inward parts in our mother's womb (Ps. 139:13). God keeps us alive moment by moment, breathing life into us, so that when God holds his breath, we die (Ps. 104:29), as Lewis Smedes exegetes this passage. Is it God alone who can take away life? Is it only God who decides the right time for a life to end? Does God's creative authority extend to this point?[26] This, of course, goes to the heart of the refusal of treatment, euthanasia, and physician-assisted suicide debates.

However, there is a paradox in this. When we are in the midst of sickness and suffering, life can become an almost unbearable burden. We may want to give this gift back to God. "But when we sense that life is a terrible burden, do others have the duty to force us to bear it beyond the span that nature itself dictates?"[27] Should we, in fact, be able to choose when we will die?

Life as a gift is a powerful image. However, it is interesting that my students' top choice every year in my Princeton course on death and dying was life as a journey. There is something in the way our world is designed that is fascinating — seasons, passages, stages of life — where we pass from one phase to another. Life seems good when our journey goes smoothly and is uninterrupted. Life is precious, and when serious illness interrupts our journey, we feel cheated no matter what our age is. Getting in touch with the meaning of life at all stages can be important to our preparation for dying.

Life as a journey, or pilgrimage, reminds us first of the biological rhythms of our life: moving from life to death. Much has been written about the seasons of life, that we pass from one season of life to another, with different experiences, goals, and so on. The upside of this approach is that we can rejoice at each stage or passage of life.[28] The downside is that,

---

26. Smedes, "Respect for Human Life," p. 147.
27. Smedes, "Respect for Human Life," p. 148.
28. See Abigail Rian Evans, *Healing Liturgies for the Seasons of Life* (Louisville: Westminster John Knox Press, 2004).

for some, life is upward and worthwhile up to a certain age — say, sixty-five — and then it is downward, drawing us inevitably toward death. This view can lead us to undervalue the frail elderly as candidates for death, thinking it not so bad when they do die. However, life should be good at any age. The preciousness, sacredness, godliness, and equality of all human life should form the foundation for our end-of-life decisions. We need to place our understanding of life within the context of the transcendent. After all, the end of life is the beginning of eternal life.

2. Contemporary Attitudes toward Death

When I Have Fears That I May Cease to Be

When I have fears that I may cease to be
   Before my pen has glean'd my teeming brain,
Before high-piled books, in charactery,
   Hold like rich garners the full ripen'd grain;
When I behold, upon the night's starr'd face,
   Huge cloudy symbols of a high romance,
And think that I may never live to trace
   Their shadows, with the magic hand of chance;
And when I feel, fair creature of an hour,
   That I shall never look upon thee more,
Never have relish in the faery power
   Of unreflecting love; — then on the shore
Of the wide world I stand alone, and think
Till love and fame to nothingness do sink.

John Keats (1795-1821)

Introduction

Death is considered un-American because we cannot control it. Most people in America today have tried to remove death from their minds; we are a death-denying society. Since half of the patients today die in hospitals, with transfusions and among strangers, rather than — as it was forty or fifty years ago — at home, with chicken soup and among family members,

17

it has become easier for us to wipe death from our minds. However, we are now discovering that the enemy is not death; rather, it is our unwillingness to incorporate it into our consciousness.[1] We remove the dying to the fortress that is the hospital, out of our sight. The dying need to feel that we care for them; they remind us, in turn, of eternal questions.[2] Americans' fear of death flies in the face of an understanding of death as a journey — the last great journey. Death is a process rather than an event, although when one considers drive-by murders or car accidents, one is reluctant to describe all deaths this way. However, poets and mystics write that dying is a process of transformation, transcendence, and finality. "The last is tragic, however happy the rest of the play is: at the last a little earth is thrown upon our head, and that is the end forever."[3] The specter of death can galvanize us like nothing else to look at the deeper issues of life, to see things in bold relief, and perhaps to recover new joy in life. As one dying person put it, "the ineffability of life," of seeing beauty all around, gives us an acceptance and peace.

In teaching courses over the years on death and dying, I have developed a questionnaire for students to use in interviewing people on their views about these issues, an instrument that provides a window into some views on death and dying (see Appendix D). One hundred fifty-seven individuals participated in the survey conducted by Princeton Theological Seminary students in my "Death and Dying" class in 2004. The profile of the participants was as follows: they were aged twenty-one to sixty (65 percent), and they represented a wide range of religious affiliations in the community from agnostic (3.2 percent, the low) to Presbyterian (57 percent, the high). The remainder simply identified themselves as "Christian" (16.6 percent), while 3.2 percent identified as Jewish. Eighty-eight percent described their current health as either "average" or "excellent"; 62 percent had reported that they had no role in the care of the dying, but 38 percent identified themselves as either chaplain, pastor, health care professional, patient, or family member involved with the dying. Certain responses to the survey were particularly interesting. When asked whether health care decisions were medical or moral, 79.4 percent said that they were *both*, though 20 percent held that they were only medical. But when they were

---

1. Sandol Stoddard, *The Hospice Movement: A Better Way of Caring for the Dying*, updated and expanded ed. (New York: Vintage Books, 1992), p. 6.

2. Stoddard, *The Hospice Movement*, p. 14.

3. Blaise Pascal, *Pascal's Pensées*, no. 210 (New York: E. P. Dutton, 1958), p. 61.

asked, "How do you evaluate health care treatment options?" the responses were widespread: 17.7 percent opted for "reading information"; 27.5 percent chose "consult a doctor"; 17.7 percent "talk with family"; 12.3 percent "talk with friends"; 15.6 percent "pray"; and 9.2 percent "other." When asked, "Does your belief in God affect your decisions?" 60.3 percent responded that belief affected their decisions "highly," while 28 percent reported that it affected their decisions "moderately." Only 10.9 percent felt that their belief had no effect at all.

The choice for a health care representative was revealing when they answered this question: "If you were incapacitated, who would you choose to make health care decisions for you?" Eighty-four percent chose "family member" as their first choice over the other options given: doctor (9.9 percent), clergy (1.9 percent), lawyer (1.9 percent), and friend (2.5 percent). *No* participant indicated that the "religious community" would be his or her first choice. This preference for the family is reflected in responses to other questions, such as, "Who would you consult before making a major health decision?" Fifty-six percent indicated that it would be the "family," followed by "friends" (16.5 percent), "pastor" (11.3 percent), and "religious community" (5.2 percent). When asked where clergy ranked in consultation concerning serious illness, 28 percent relegated clergy to fifth, and 50 percent ranked clergy as either third or fourth. In further questions concerning the impact that moral and religious beliefs had on health care decisions, when participants were asked about the ranking of religious *tradition* (as opposed to religious *community*), they ranked the tradition higher than either clergy or community: the religious tradition ranked first at 42.7 percent, while 46.3 percent ranked "family" as primary in influencing their moral system. When the same question was posed in a slightly differently form, 83.5 percent ranked "religious tradition" either first or second in the influence it has on their moral values.

As to beliefs concerning life after death, 66 percent said that they "strongly believe in it"; 12.8 percent indicated that they "tend to believe in it." As to what happens after death, 32.2 percent responded that they believed they would immediately be with God; 13.7 percent chose "When I die, all of me dies, but when Christ returns, I will be resurrected"; 17.6 percent chose "I cannot explain it; it is just a mystery that my body will die but my soul will be at peace somehow and somewhere. . . ." Only 8.2 percent chose "All I know for sure is that I will be judged; the rest depends on the judgment."

When asked about their *attitude* toward death, 53.8 percent saw it as "prelude to eternal life," while 19 percent indicated that they "feared" it. "Welcomed" was the response of 16.8 percent, and 10.3 percent indicated that it was the "end of existence." Likewise, when asked, "What does death *mean* to you?" 30.6 percent said, "It is the beginning of a new life"; 18.8 percent held that "it is the final stage (or process) of life." When asked, "Do these answers [concerning death] depend on your health status?" 66.7 percent answered that they did not, while 33.3 percent answered that they did. In light of this, it is perhaps significant that when they were asked, "Do you consider life itself or the quality of life more important?" 72.1 percent answered "quality of life," with 23.4 percent responding "life itself."

The answers to the question "What efforts do you believe ought to be made to keep a seriously ill person alive?" the responses were rather evenly divided: 11.3 percent chose "all possible efforts"; 30.5 percent chose "efforts that are reasonable for that person's age, physical condition, mental condition and pain"; 33.1 percent chose "after reasonable care is given, a person should be permitted to die a natural death"; and 25.2 percent responded, "Any and all care is completely up to the ill person, provided he or she is capable of making a decision; also, medically assisted suicide should be an option."

It is obvious from these responses that family trumps professionals in addressing end-of-life issues. This was even the case with this overwhelmingly religious sample. As a society, when we wrestle with the many quandaries that I will discuss in subsequent chapters, educating families should be our top priority. Even in the complexities of modern medicine, legal precedents, and moral dilemmas, in the final analysis people turn to loved ones for guidance and comfort.

In addition to surveys, there are a variety of ways that we attempt to understand death, but trying to describe it is daunting at best. Hence, I will investigate various images or similes of death: as inevitable, welcomed, feared, as a punishment, or as a gateway to eternal life. However, before we look at these images, there are two points on which to comment: the medicalization of death and death by inhuman institutions.

Medicalization of Death

We are living at a time when death has become medicalized. With the improvements in modern technology and medical expertise, people are dying more slowly than ever. However, we can also rejoice in the feats and gifts of modern medicine, which has enabled us to move from the concept of illness as a result of sin to a disease model of illness; we can rejoice at being released from a theology that equated sickness and guilt/judgment. Of course, this theology was already refuted in Scripture in the stories of Job (Hebrew Scripture) and the man born blind (John 9).[4]

However, one has to be careful in the critique of the medicalization of death. Doctors, nurses, hospitals, and medicines are also gifts from God. We should not lose sight of the miracles of modern medicine and how they have improved and enhanced — and yes, prolonged — life, often to our advantage. Think, for example, of the change in life expectancy in the United States: in 1950 it was 68.2 years, and in 2006 it was 77.7 years.[5]

- The preliminary age-adjusted death rate in the United States reached an all-time low in 2003 of 831.2 deaths per 100,000 population.
- Age-adjusted death rates declined for eight of the fifteen leading causes of death. Declines were seen for heart disease (down 3.6 percent) and cancer (down 2.2 percent), the two leading causes of death that account for more than half of all deaths in the United States each year. Declines were also documented for stroke (4.6 percent), suicide (3.7 percent), flu/pneumonia (3.1 percent), chronic liver disease (2.1 percent), and accidents/unintentional injuries (2.2 percent).
- Mortality increased for the following leading causes of death: Alzheimer's disease, kidney disease, hypertension, and Parkinson's disease.[6]

We are also living longer due to diet and social factors, which contribute as much as medicine does to this reality. It is interesting to compare the leading causes of death over the last century. In 1900 they were: pneumonia and influenza, tuberculosis, diarrhea and enteritis, heart disease, stroke, liver disease, injuries, cancer, senility, and diphtheria.[7] In 2005 the major

4. For an extensive discussion of this subject, see Abigail Rian Evans, *Redeeming Marketplace Medicine* (Cleveland: Pilgrim Press, 1999).

5. Melonie Heron, "Deaths: Final Data for 2006," *National Vital Statistics Reports* 57, no. 14 (April 17, 2009): 1 (last updated May 15, 2009): http://www.cdc.gov/nchs/data/nvsr/nvsr57/nvsr57_14.pdf (accessed Sept. 8, 2009).

6. "Life Expectancy Hits Record High," National Center for Health Statistics, February 28, 2005: http://www.cdc.gov/nchs/pressroom/05facts/lifeexpectancy.htm (accessed July 24, 2009).

7. "Leading Causes of Death 1900-1998," Centers for Disease Control, p. 67: http://www.cdc.gov/nchs/data/dvs/lead1900_98.pdf (accessed July 24, 2009).

causes were: heart disease, cancer, stroke (cerebrovascular diseases), lower respiratory diseases, accidents (unintentional injuries), diabetes, Alzheimer's disease, influenza/pneumonia, nephristis/nephrontic syndrome/ nephrosis, and septicemia.[8]

In the 1970s, Ivan Illich set forth his critique of the medicalization of society. In addition to a scathing critique of the medical profession, he declared that people are robbed of their power of observing the rituals of death because it has become medicalized. The church, on the other hand, has abandoned its rituals of dying, according to Illich, so people have no way to chart these passages.[9] Peter Sedgwick reflected this same thesis with his charge that we practice "the annexation of not-illness into illness."[10] In other words, criminal behavior, alcoholism, unhappiness, selfishness, and poverty were given medical explanations. Though physiology plays a role, it is not the only factor, as the medical model seems to suggest.

Today we rely on institutions to remove the so-called "misfits" of society, including those who are seriously ill and dying. This echoes Erving Goffman's description of "asylums" (his word for institutions), where we isolate society's misfits, including in hospitals.[11] We strip patients of their identity: we take away their clothes, personal effects, place them in unfamiliar surroundings, and rob them of their dignity. "Just at the moment that disease rips him out of his usual place in the community and makes him feel least secure in his dealings with fellows, the procedures of the hospital remind him acutely of this loss, by placing him in the hands of professionals — the nurse and the doctor — precisely those who seem unassailably secure in their own identities."[12]

In addition, there are the political and sociological aspects of death. "Insofar as death is a lifelong anticipation, the anthropologist or the literary critic can describe the death image of a society, the sociologist can

8. Hsiang-Ching Kung et al., "Deaths: Final Data for 2005, *National Vital Statistics Reports* 56, no. 10 (24 April 2008): 1: http://www.cdc.gov/nchs/data/nvsr56/nvsr56_10 .pdf (accessed July 24, 2009).

9. Ivan Illich, *Medical Nemesis: The Expropriation of Health* (Toronto: Bantam Books, 1976).

10. Peter Sedgwick, "Illness: Mental and Otherwise," *The Hastings Center Studies* 1, no. 3 (1973): 37.

11. Erving Goffman, *Asylums: Essays on the Social Situation of Mental Patients and Other Inmates* (New York: Anchor Books, 1961; reprint, Doubleday, 1990).

12. William H. May, "Institutions as Symbols of Death," *Journal of the American Academy of Religion* 44, n. 2 (1976): 215.

study the different forms under which it spreads in age-groups and classes, the psychologist can investigate the personal progress of each member through this pre-existing cultural reality."[13] During each period of history, society has developed rituals and practices to hasten or ease dying and death itself.

"While the 'Art of Dying' taught those of the Reformation era to face bitter death, to make ready and hope for a speedy end, compulsory treatments now eliminate all final agonies which might be easy but are labeled unnecessary in order to preserve us today for chronic disability or for cancer and decrepitude."[14] This rather dismal view of medical treatment may have a limited place as we see many of the fruits of medicine that have created longer, healthier lives.

Death does not seem as inevitable as it once was with the new ways we have of prolonging life — or, we might say, prolonging dying. One of the questions is: Which one of those are we doing? Should death be defined by doctors, or should the definition of death simply be acceptable to doctors? The difference is between when a person is dead and when he or she should be allowed to die. (I will discuss these issues further in the chapter on legal issues.) Some philosophers, such as Robert Veatch, have even suggested that we should be allowed to define our own death.

> Some end-of-life cases are so unclear, Veatch thinks, that people should be able to choose in advance the definition of death they want to be used to declare them deceased. "Most ordinary people, including most physicians, assume whether you're dead or alive is a science question," he says. Thanks to medical progress, terminally ill patients or victims of severe accidents can be kept on life support far beyond the point where they would have died naturally. Veatch asks whether being permanently unconscious and dependent on feeding and hydration tubes is still really life. If not, then people taken off that support are not killed, he argues, but are "made dead" or they "become dead." Veatch suggests that the law set a default definition, most likely whole-brain death, and let individuals opt out and sign a statement saying they want to be declared deceased either by cardiorespiratory death or higher brain death.
>
> Only two places on earth allow anything near this. The state of New

13. Ivan Illich, "The Political Uses of Natural Death," *Hastings Center Studies* 2, no. 1 (Jan. 1974): 6; see also Illich, *Medical Nemesis.*

14. Illich, "The Political Uses of Natural Death," p. 18.

Jersey allows orthodox Jews to opt out of the whole brain-death idea and use cardiorespiratory death because they traditionally see breath as the key to life. Japan uses the heart-and-lung criterion as a default, but lets people opt for whole-brain death so that they can donate organs.[15]

With its medicalization, death has moved from the home to the hospital. Allen Verhey says: "The homogenizing forces of technical rationality are not irresistible. Even so, Western medicine continues to expand both its technological powers and its sphere of influence, asserting its hegemony among the traditions of healing."[16] Medicine may explain death and give a language for it. However, that medical language may not be the language of patients, and they may feel unable to communicate their feelings.[17]

In *Sacral Power of Death,* William F. May argues that technological feats have not produced a "corresponding inner confidence in our relationships to death. We arrange for the marvels of modern medical care, because, to be sure, we desire the recovery of the sick but also because these devices offer us a means of avoiding sickness, aging, and dying. In the language of the sociologists, the *manifest* function of our cadre of experts in the helping professions is to provide the critically ill with better cure and care, but a *latent* social function of this specialization is the avoidance of an event with which we cannot cope."[18] It seems that the very doctors who preside over our deaths are the ones who help to remove the dying from sight. In addition, since physicians are trained to cure not care, families feel abandoned when nothing more can be done medically to cure them. One must, however, have compassion for the doctors who suffer as well from their finitude.

May describes the sacral power of death and how it confounds our ability to master it. It inspires both awe and fear and may leave us speechless in its presence.[19] This medicalization of death creates institutionalized

15. Tom Heneghan, "Should You Define Your Own Death?" *Reuters UK online,* July 18, 2007: http://uk.reuters.com/article/idUKL3067777420070717?pageNumber=2&virtualBrand Channel=0 (accessed May 20, 2009).

16. Allen Verhey, "The Spirit of God and the Spirit of Medicine: The Church, Globalization, and a Mission of Health Care," in *God and Globalization,* vol. 2: *The Spirit and the Modern Authorities,* ed. Max Stackhouse and Don Browning (Harrisburg: Continuum International Publishing Group, 2001), p. 108.

17. Verhey, "The Spirit of God," p. 112.

18. William F. May, "The Sacral Power of Death in Contemporary Experience," *Social Research* 39, no. 3 (Autumn 1972): 468.

19. May, "The Sacral Power," p. 469.

death. Institutions such as the hospital devour us. Philippe Aries proposes that the attempt to bring "wild death" into the hospital was an effort to domesticate it.[20] Caring for the dying is no longer an art but is reduced to a science. Part of this stems from our own desire to hide death from view. May traces this back to early Greek myths.

> The name of the nymph "Calypso," who encounters Odysseus as the embodiment of death, means literally the one who hides. The death-demon in Indo-Germanic and even pre-Indo-Germanic times, according to Herman Güntert, is a Hider-Goddess. A "mysterious hiding and shrouding" has been experienced as the first essential character-trait of the numinous, hidden power of death in early times. According to belief in traditional societies, the soul of the dead man journeyed to a hidden realm. In Ganda to this day, the deceased king is referred to as "going away" or "disappearing."[21]

It seems as if we still hide death because we really do not know what to do with it. We are all too familiar with the pain that the medical model of death and dying can impose. The medical profession often vacillates between overtreating — by removing us from our loved ones — or undertreating the accompanying pain and suffering. Communication between doctor, patient, and family may be very poor. Jane Brody wrote an article in 2003 about her mother's death when she was sixteen years old.

> The year was 1958, I was 16 and my mother was lying in a hospital bed connected to all sorts of tubes and was dying of cancer. As her life slipped away, a nurse slapped an oxygen mask on her face and asked me to hold it. There was no chance for either of us to say goodbye or "I love you." I carry this medicalized memory of my mother's death with me to this day. . . .

Brody goes on to cite another case of 22-year-old Dave Fulkerson, who was hit by a car while he was jogging with his girlfriend. When he first arrived in the intensive care unit, his family was not allowed to see him for three hours. By then, he could no longer talk. Further, only one person was allowed in for five minutes every two hours. Finally his parents fell asleep in

20. Philippe Aries, *Western Attitudes toward Death from the Middle Ages to the Present,* trans. Patricia M. Ranum (Baltimore: Johns Hopkins University Press, 1974).

21. William F. May, "Institutions as Symbols of Death," *The Journal of the American Academy of Religion* 44, no. 2 (1976): 211.

the waiting room, only to be awakened by the nurse, who told them that their son had died.[22]

Unfortunately, the medicalization of death also includes the influence of economics. An article published in *The Boston Globe* discusses how such costs are assessed and the concept of the so-called RVU. "What it really stands for is Relative Value Unit, a bloodless term to measure the productivity of a physician every hour of his or her day. The more RVUs you accumulate, the more money you make." RVUs were introduced when a "reform bill years ago embedded them into the Medicare structure in hopes of reining in the spectacular rise in costs. They have since spread beyond Medicare to hospital management and even to doctors' group practices." An oncologist, Dr. Jerome Groopman, points out RVU's problems: "'It's like a runaway train,' says Groopman, who compares RVUs to the odious billable hours in law firms. The analogy is not strictly perfect, because one is strictly about time, but the larger truth is they are both about money. Groopman has been on the warpath against RVUs for ages. 'There are no RVUs for spending an hour with a grieving family, or sitting with a confused third year medical student. There are no RVUs for the humanistic core of medicine that drew me into this profession in the first place.'"[23]

Death by Inhuman Institutions

Another reality of modern society is not only physical death, but spiritual death, that is, what is caused by inhuman institutions. This is what I would label, in Pauline language, the powers and principalities against which we rage.[24] This is a type of living death, a slow death, a death that eats away at the marrow of our bones. It is caused by repression of and prejudice toward certain people. William Stringfellow described this as "institutional death" in Harlem: "I could recognize that the death which so persistently threatened me, the death so aggressive in my body, the death signified in unremitting pain, the death which took the appearance of sickness — that death was familiar to me. I had elsewhere encountered that same death.

22. Jane E. Brody, "Facing Up to the Inevitable, in Search of a Good Death," *New York Times,* December 30, 2003: http://query.nytimes.com/gst/fullpage.html?res=9501E1DD133 EF933A05751C1A9659C8B63&sec=&spon=&pagewanted=1 (accessed Jan. 24, 2008).

23. Sam Allis, "Relative Value Unseen," *The Boston Globe,* March 1, 2009, p. A2.

24. Walter Wink, *Naming the Powers: The Language of Power in the New Testament* (Philadelphia: Fortress Press, 1984).

(Actually, I had *everywhere* encountered that same death). There I contended in daily practice with death institutionalized in authorities and agencies and bureaucracies and multifarious principalities and powers. Relentless, ruthless dehumanization which they work. Death theologically as a militant moral reality."[25]

Some teenagers in Washington, D.C., called this "the inevitability of death," because their daily life included drugs, guns, jail, and poverty. They did not expect to see adulthood. They suffered to a large extent from an unjust and prejudiced society where death might seem welcome. I saw this same institutionalized death in parts of Brazil, where people were eating from garbage cans and many were living in *favelas* with eighteen people to a six-foot room. The same injustices plague people of color in the United States, where death rates of treatable diseases are higher among African-Americans than their Anglo counterparts. Generally, this reality is described as health disparities. The infant mortality rate in 2003 was: 5.7 infant deaths per 1,000 live births for whites, compared to 13.5 for blacks.[26] According to the 2000 U.S. census, African-Americans account for 13 percent of the U.S. population, or 36.4 million individuals. Major health disparities for African-Americans are:

- HIV/AIDS: in 2005, African-Americans accounted for 47 percent of all HIV/AIDS cases. Non-Hispanic whites accounted for only 30 percent.[27]
- Heart Disease and Stroke: in 2004, the African-American male age-adjusted death rate for heart disease (342.1 per 100,000) was 27.3 percent higher than for white American males (268.7),[28] and 55.4 percent higher than for white American males for stroke (74.9 per 100,000 vs. 48.2).[29]

25. William Stringfellow, "On Living Biblically Now," *The Witness* (Ambler, PA: The Episcopal Church Publishing Company, 1976), unnumbered pages.

26. Center for Disease Control, "Table 19: Infant, neonatal, and postneonatal mortality rates, by detailed race and Hispanic origin of mother: United States, selected years 1983-2003": http://www.cdc.gov/nchs/data/hus/hus06.pdf#019 (accessed Jan. 24, 2008).

27. U.S. Department of Health and Human Services, Office of Minority Health, "HIV/AIDS and African Americans": http://www.omhrc.gov/templates/content.aspx?ID=3019 (accessed Jan. 24, 2008).

28. U.S. Department of Health and Human Services, Office of Minority Health, "Heart Disease and African Americans": http://www.omhrc.gov/templates/content.aspx?ID =3018 (accessed Jan. 24, 2008).

29. U.S. Department of Health and Human Services, Office of Minority Health,

- Cancer: the death rate for cancer was 38.4 percent higher for African-American males (331 per 100,000) than for white American males (239.2) in 2003.[30]
- Adult immunization: influenza vaccination coverage among adults sixty-five years of age and older are 63 percent for whites and 40 percent for African-Americans in 2005. The gap for pneumococcal vaccination coverage among older adults reflects a similar disparity, with 61 percent for whites and 41 percent for African-Americans.[31]
- Diabetes: the age-adjusted death rate for African-Americans in 2004 was more than twice that for white Americans (48.0 per 100,000 vs. 21.5).[32]

Death As Inevitable

As I have mentioned, Americans appear to live in a death-denying culture even though death is inevitable and certain. An ancient tale from India dramatically illustrates the sense of the inevitability of death.

> A Baghdad merchant once sent his servant out to buy provisions. The servant came back pale with fear, saying "Master, just now in the bazaar I was jostled by a man in the crowd. I turned about and I saw Death. He stared at me and made a threatening gesture. Therefore, lend me your horse and I will ride to Samarra where Death cannot find me." The merchant lent him his horse, and the servant mounted it and rode off as fast as he could gallop. And then the merchant himself went to the bazaar, and as he strolled around, he, too, saw Death standing in the throng. He approached him and said, "Why did you make a threatening gesture to my servant when you saw him earlier this day?" But

---

"Stroke and African Americans": http://www.omhrc.gov/templates/content.aspx?ID=3022 (accessed Jan. 24, 2008).

30. U.S. Department of Health and Human Services, Office of Minority Health, "Cancer and African Americans": http://www.omhrc.gov/templates/content.aspx?ID=2826 (accessed Jan. 24, 2008).

31. U.S. Department of Health and Human Services, Office of Minority Health, "Immunizations and African Americans": http://www.omhrc.gov/templates/content.aspx?ID=3020 (accessed Jan. 24, 2008).

32. U.S. Department of Health and Human Services, Office of Minority Health, "Diabetes and African Americans": http://www.omhrc.gov/templates/content.aspx?ID=3017 (accessed Jan. 24, 2008).

Death replied, "That was not a threatening gesture — merely a start of surprise. You see, I was astonished to find your servant in Baghdad, for tonight I have an appointment with him in Samarra."[33]

The same idea of inevitability is found in Hebrew Scripture. Ecclesiastes 3:2, 4: "A time for birth, a time for dying . . . a time for tears, a time for laughter." Death is seen as part of the rhythm of life. Likewise, we read in Ecclesiastes 8:8: "No one has power over the wind to restrain the wind, or power over the day of death; there is no discharge from the battle, nor does wickedness deliver those who practice it."

Death As Welcome

In light of the fear and pain of dying, there are circumstances where death is welcome. Socrates first immortalized the perspective of death as a friend: "Come, O friend death." With the advent of technological advances, many people beg to be allowed to die. Some even believe that with the on-set of so many frailties of old age, death would be welcome. In *Gulliver Travels,* Jonathan Swift writes about the Struldbrugs, who never die but continuously age. At first Gulliver thought this would be a marvelous state of affairs; but his descriptions turn vivid and terrifying.

Upon hearing about the immortals but before meeting any of them, Gulliver was very excited about the possibilities of immortality and gave a great speech. In it he stated the possibilities of living forever, of not dying as ordinary mortals do. He could choose a dozen of them, from the most ancient to contemporaries. His choice would be of those whose remembrance, experience, and observation was astute and who had led lives of useful virtue both publicly and privately. He listed the advantages of such a long-range point of view, of being able to re-experience history, of great discoveries which could be made through such interaction. He enlarged on many topics "which the natural Desire of endless Life and . . . Happiness could easily furnish me with."

However, when he encountered the Struldbrugs he changed his mind considerably because they continued to age with all the worst infirmities of old age. "They were not only opinionative, peevish, covetous, morose, vain,

---

33. Bruce G. Epperly, *At the Edges of Life: A Holistic Vision of the Human Adventure* (St. Louis: Chalice Press, 1992), p. 1.

talkative, but incapable of Friendship, and dead to all natural Affection, which never descended below their Grandchildren." At 80, their marriages were dissolved. They were declared dead legally so their heirs could inherit. They were put on a small allowance, which they supplemented through asking for a token of remembrance called a SLUMSKUDASK as a way of getting around the laws forbidding begging. They were unemployable, not able to purchase land or take leases nor be witnesses in court. At 90, along with losing their teeth and hair, they have lost their memories. When they talk, they forget names of things. They can't read because their memories fail between the beginning and end of the sentence.[34]

It is not only Gulliver who recognizes that death can be welcome, but those in unremitting pain or those who feel they have fulfilled their lives and are ready for eternity.

Death As Feared

Death brings sorrow, and death is not a friend, as Socrates or the Stoics may have viewed it. Death is tragic because of the uniqueness of each human being. There is only one person like Jane or Scott or Rachel. God has made each one of us a special and singular human being. Nor is death natural. It was not in the order of things, but it entered the world through sin.

What may be true, however, is that we may think more about death as we age. The American Association of Retired Persons (AARP) conducted a survey of their constituents, which reflects some interesting findings. To varying degrees, those surveyed say they believe in:

- God (94 percent)
- Life after death (73 percent)
- The existence of spirits or ghosts (53 percent)
- Heaven (86 percent) and hell (70 percent)

While 66 percent say their confidence in life after death has increased as they have gotten older, 20 percent report being frightened when they consider what will happen to them when they die. In examining the

34. Jonathan Swift, *Gulliver's Travels*, pt. 3, chap. 10, ed. Robert A. Greenberg, rev. ed. (New York: Norton Critical Editions, 1970), pp. 177-84.

possible influences of afterlife beliefs and demographic variables, three factors emerge as most strongly related to the fear of death:

- Being somewhat religious (compared to "very religious" and "not at all religious")
- Believing that death is the end
- Belief in the existence of hell

When gender, employment, age, education, and marital status are all taken into account, "level of income" emerges as the only demographic factor significantly related to fear of death and as a strong predictor of being afraid to think about it. One possible explanation is that, for those whose financial status is less secure, thinking of death may be a stressful reminder of the uncertainties in their lives and the potential strain their deaths would place on family members.[35]

There is no doubt that many people fear death both because of the unknown of what lies beyond and the punishment they anticipate for sins committed. Rollo May sees a relationship between an obsession with sex and the fear of death. Sex can demonstrate that we are still young, attractive, and virile and are not yet dead. Fear of death permeates all our experiences, which at its heart reflects our vulnerability. Many will do anything to keep death at bay and are willing to go through months of painful treatment to add a few weeks to their lives.

Fear of death also stems from the terror of ceasing to be, hence the loss of all meaning. Ernest Becker, influenced by Thomas Szasz and his study of psychiatric patients, wrote his books *Birth and Death of Meaning* and *The Denial of Death* to explore these questions. His aim was to reconcile the fundamental human contradiction between mind and body and the answer to the perennial question, Who am I? He believes that we need to recognize both our animal bodies and our spiritual search for meaning.[36]

---

35. Jean Koppen and Gretchen Anderson, *Thoughts on the Afterlife Among U.S. Adults 50+* (Washington, DC: AARP, 2007). This national random telephone survey of 1,011 Americans aged fifty and over was conducted for AARP and *AARP The Magazine* by International Communications Research (ICR), from June 29 to July 10, 2006.

36. "Ernest Becker," *EMuseum@Minnesota State University, Mankato online:* http://www.mnsu.edu/emuseum/information/biography/abcde/becker_ernest.html (accessed Sept. 3, 2004). "Ernest Becker was the son of Eastern European Jews who immigrated to the U.S. at the turn of the century. When he was eighteen he joined the army and served in a second-line infantry battalion that liberated a Nazi concentration camp. After the war, he

We fear the death of meaning more than the death of the body itself. True self-knowledge, Becker believed, springs from our understanding of how self and society are woven out of the structures of meaning. Becker believed that the most worthwhile intellectual questions were of human nature, human destiny, and the meaning of life. They are the identity questions of adolescents: Who am I, and what is my relationship to the cosmos? What is the meaning and purpose of my life, and how should I live it?[37] Becker describes our basic terror in the face of death, and he describes how religion and culture are used to lessen or repress the fear of our mortality. Hence, when we face the reality of death, we are left with a choice between heroism and fear (or mental illness).[38]

Our fear of death causes us to hide its reality. Heretofore, in children's stories such as the Grimm and Anderson fairy tales, death was frequently mentioned. It also appeared in classics such as Charles Dickens's *The Old Curiosity Shop* (which famously included the death of the character Little Nell) and Louisa May Alcott's *Little Women* (the character Beth's death). Nowadays death is portrayed in the media as violent, coming as it does by guns or car accidents, and thus it is wrapped in fear and far from most people's everyday experience. As cartoon (and "realistic" cartoonish) characters are shot and come back to life, there is a sense of unreality about death: it seems to be short-lived.

We mask real death because we are afraid that we are not immortal — that this could be the end — and we do not want to admit it. As a matter of fact, death may have replaced sex as a taboo in drawing-room conversations. When it does push into our lives, we are told not to mourn, which could be a release and catharsis for our sorrow, but instead our emotions shut down. We are never ready for death; life's concerns are too absorbing,

---

lived in Paris working as an intelligence attaché for the State Department, but he got bored of it quickly. After a long period of reflection, he decided he wanted to devote his life to understanding himself, the human condition and the meaning of life. He chose anthropology, because the term means 'the study of man.' Ernest's passion for knowledge was his dominant quality. He asked everyone whose intellect he respected for a list of the books which had most influenced their thinking. When he heard of an author he had not read, he headed immediately for the library, checked out a pile of books and retired to his office for a marathon of reading and note-taking which did not end until he had digested the ideas of the newly discovered author."

37. Ibid.

38. Commented on by Epperly, *At the Edges of Life*, pp. 16-17, based on Ernest Becker, *Denial of Death* (New York: The Free Press, 1973).

and we cannot bear to leave those we love. If we already have a serious ill-ness, then we may bargain with death: "Just let me live till my son is mar-ried, or my daughter finishes college, or I can visit my home once more." Or, when we think about death in the future, we dicker with death: "Just let it be fast when my time comes. Spare me a lingering, painful illness."

One thing is clear: we have to face this mystery alone. No one can die for us. Death may come today, tomorrow, in a decade, or several decades; it can be a long, drawn-out process or can result from a sudden tragedy. The thread between life and death is fragile. In caring for the dying, physicians are challenged in each dimension of their personhood. William James called death "the worm at the core of man's pretensions to happiness," while La Rochefoucauld observed: "Death and the sun are not to be looked at steadily." What do we do with our accumulated losses as caregivers? How do we establish a new balance in our emotional economy when an important investment is lost? At what cost? And to whom?[39]

Despite the fear of death, many people in both the medical and psy-chiatric professions believe that dying people really want very much to talk about their impending death but are rarely given an opportunity to do it. In the 1960s, Elisabeth Kübler-Ross wrote of the five stages through which the dying patient passes: denial, anger, bargaining, depression, and accep-tance.[40] As people experience these emotions, of course, not always in pro-gressive stages, they need health care professionals, family, and friends to assist in giving voice to their experience and to find meaning in the midst of their dying.

The Funeral Industry in the United States

No book on death and dying would be complete without a reference to the funeral industry. The funeral homes reflect the American desire to hide death by cosmetic wonders performed on cadavers, to the point that they look better than they did in life. Flowers and saccharine music complete the picture, and an elaborate vocabulary of euphemisms has been developed to circumvent the fact that a death has even taken place. The way funeral homes conduct their business is partially fed by Americans' fear of death.

39. Balfour Mount, "Care of Dying Patients and Their Families," in James B. Wyn-gaarden, Lloyd H. Smith, and J. Claude Bennett, eds., *Cecil Textbook of Medicine,* vol. I, 19th ed. (Philadelphia: Saunders, 1992), p. 31.
40. Elisabeth Kübler-Ross, *On Death and Dying* (New York: Macmillan, 1969).

However, funerals and funeral homes respond to changing numbers, and customs are changing a great deal in the United States. In 2005, a total of 2,448,017 resident deaths were registered in the United States; by the year 2030, the annual death rate will have increased by about 30 percent. However, the "baby boomers," as one article put it, are "under-ritualized. . . . Religious observance is on a downswing, families are scattered around the country, and thus attendance at funerals has dropped significantly."[41] And they do not want to spend a lot on funerals.[42] One wonders if funerals are more cultural than religious. (Obtaining statistics on the number of funerals done in each year is not possible because the funeral industry reports the number of contacts, not services conducted, annually.)

There is no doubt, however, that funerals are still big business: the funeral directors' object is often to charge as much as possible and mask the fact that the person is really dead, what some call the "Sleeping Beauty syndrome" (airbrushing is the latest technique for making people look better than they did in life). "Americans spend between $11 billion and $15 billion on funerals each year. The 2007 average funeral cost about $6,580 — not including the expense of the cemetery or mausoleum, which could add thousands more."[43] For many families, it is one of the most expensive purchases they will make.[44] Poorer families in the inner city spend a proportionately higher percentage of their income on funerals, exemplifying what some call "the Nike syndrome," in which the urban poor often wish to reflect in their funerals a higher status than they could achieve in life.

The funeral industry has a 300 to 800 percent average markup on its merchandise and services.[45] And funeral directors often show the most expensive merchandise first. Families often make up for what they did not do in a person's life by the way they treat that person in death. The best way to avoid these traps is to visit the funeral home when a loved one first be-

41. "Deaths: Final Data for 2005," National Vital Statistics Reports 56, no. 10 (April 24, 2008): http://www.cdc.gov/nchs/data/nvsr/nvsr56/nvsr56_10.pdf (accessed Mar. 5, 2009).

42. Judith Newman, "At Your Disposal: The Funeral Industry Prepares for Boom Times," in Dying, Death and Bereavement, ed. George Dickinson, Michael Leming, and Alan Mermann, 5th ed. (Guilford, CT: Dushkin/McGraw Hill, 2000/2001), p. 28.

43. Kimberly Palmer, "How to Plan an Affordable Funeral," U.S. News and World Report, October 17, 2007: http://www.usnews.com/blogs/alpha-consumer/2007/10/17/how-to-plan-an-affordable-funeral.html (accessed Dec. 17, 2008).

44. Judith Newman, "At Your Disposal," pp. 28ff.

45. Steven Dale Soderlind, Consumer Economics (Armonk, NY: M. E. Sharpe, 2001), p. 381.

comes terminally ill, that is, before grief clouds one's decisions on coffins and other matters. If churches conduct courses on death and dying, they can invite a funeral director for a session, which goes a long way toward helping prepare people for the decisions they will need to make.

How to assess the funeral industry is a complex matter. In many ways, we have made them what they are because of our unwillingness to handle the deceased in our lives. Whether it is grief, avoidance, fear, or feeling uncomfortable, we want someone else to do our work. Some of the parents of my Princeton Seminary students were funeral directors who had a strong sense of ministry. In addition, in *The Undertaking,* Thomas Lynch, funeral director, poet, and essayist, tells his own story of being a funeral director in a small Michigan town. His excellent insights into the positive role of a funeral director and his work with church colleagues provide a contrast to the negativity toward the funeral industry. He recounts how he prepared the body and did the funeral for his own father as an act of love.[46]

There is both a commercial and compassionate side to the funeral industry, as noted by Emory professor Thomas Long, who went "undercover" several years ago at the National Funeral Directors Association annual meeting. His negative reaction to the commercialism — for example, the push to sell the most expensive caskets — was balanced by his meetings with funeral directors who saw their work as a calling.

> Mainly, what struck me favorably was the way that many funeral directors see themselves as "called," involved in a vocation of human compassion and that the best of these funeral professionals, like the most alert among the clergy, are keenly aware that they perform their ministries of mercy in a swiftly changing social context. Funeral directors swim in the same boiling and fermenting cultural soup as do ministers, and the same trends that have so shaken the confidence of the mainline churches in recent decades have also profoundly affected funeral homes. Like many ministers, funeral directors are often unsure about the nature of the forces at work producing these changes, but they are eager to discern, in the face of perplexing and shifting patterns in regard to death and ritual, the proper role and character of the funeral service.[47]

46. Thomas Lynch, *The Undertaking: Life Stories from the Dismal Trade,* 3rd ed. (New York: Norton, 1997).

47. Thomas Long, "The Funeral: Changing Patterns and Teachable Moments," *Journal for Preachers* 19, no. 3 (1996): 5.

What concerns Long, however, is how funeral professionals treat death as a business, with all the attendant marketing ploys and tolerance of merchandising gimmicks. For example, a symposium on cremation preferences in America referred to how to sell more merchandise to the cremation consumer. Another more unusual cremation product, offered by the LifeGem company, converts cremated remains into diamonds.[48] The business angle is also evident simply when a funeral director complains that "the clergy have taken the funeral away from us." Of course, it is a fact that funeral directors collect fees from grief-stricken people, so it is a fine line between business and ministry.[49]

Cremation Becomes More Common

In 2006, nearly thirty-four percent of the deceased were cremated in the United States.[50] Cremation began in 1876 when Dr. Julius LeMoyne built the first crematorium in Washington, Pennsylvania. Crematoria began for a number of reasons, among them a desire to reform burial practices and the medical profession's concern with health conditions in early cemeteries. Since 1975, the Cremation Association of North America has become more regularized: that year it had more than 425 crematoria performing nearly 150,000 cremations annually; in 2003 there were 1,858 crematoria performing 695,637 cremations, accounting for 29 percent of all death disposals in the United States.[51] Seventy percent of disposals of the deceased in Britain are cremations rather than burials. Families are developing their own rituals, some keeping the ashes in their homes for many years before scattering them. Other older people have wished to preserve the old family cemeteries; some have kept their spouses' gravesites and -stones as a way of honoring them.[52]

48. Allison Lind, "Forever Diamonds," *The Peninsula Gateway,* November 24, 2009, p. 10D.

49. Long, "The Funeral," p. 4.

50. "Economic woes increasing cremation numbers," *United Press International, UPI.com,* December 15, 2008: http://www.upi.com/Top_News/2008/12/15/Economic_woes_increasing_cremation_numbers/UPI-76251229360151/ (accessed Jan. 6, 2009).

51. "History of Cremation," *Cremation Options:* http://www.cremationoptionsinc.com/history/ (accessed Mar. 5, 2009).

52. Leonie A. Kellaher, "Grave Practice — Using Disposal to Make Good," in *A Good Death,* ed. Alison and Colin Johnson, Leveson Papers #4 (Solihull, UK: Foundation of Lady Katherine Leveson, 2003), p. 44.

An emerging challenge for funeral homes is how to transform cremation from an event that they dub, "You call, we haul, that's all," to a full-blown ritual, that is, something that can be profitable for the funeral industry. The vessels for holding the ashes have become quite diverse, from urns shaped like cowboy boots to golf bags to jewelry, and so forth. Before the latter part of the twentieth century, cremation was the exception rather than the rule, and for many conservative Christian groups that is still true.[53]

In addition, there are new practices emerging surrounding burial and cremation. Now people want to be buried or cremated with their cell phones. The trend, which began in South Africa, has now spread to a number of countries, including Ireland, Australia, Ghana, and the United States. The idea of people being buried with their cell phones originated in Cape Town, where some people's belief in witchcraft meant that they feared they could fall under a spell, be put to sleep, and actually be buried. The phones were to be put into the coffins with them in case they woke up. In Australia people wanted to be buried with the totems that they felt represented their lifestyle, which might include their mobile phone or their Blackberry.[54] There is no way to know whether this is some eccentricity or a growing trend.

Changes in Funeral Customs

In addition, there are dramatic changes in American culture concerning funerals.

> Increasingly there seems to be the trend that, rather than the leaders of the church orchestrating how the services are to be conducted, the family (including non-Christians) are planning the funeral. The result is a strange mixture of the sacred and the secular. At one moment the congregation is singing "Rock of Ages, Cleft For Me," and then, presently, over the public address system, George Jones is lamenting, "He Stopped Lovin' Her Today." Instrumental selections are alternated with

53. Stephen Prothero, *Purified by Fire: A History of Cremation in America* (Berkeley: University of California Press, 2001), pp. 10, 40.

54. "Handsets get taken to the grave," *BBC News online,* March 29, 2006, quoting The Future Laboratory, a London-based think tank: http://news.bbc.co.uk/2/hi/technology/4853548.stm (accessed Apr. 8, 2009).

a cappella singing. Too, women are being encouraged to mount the pulpit to read poetry or the Scriptures. Family members are invited to make comments regarding the deceased — which may be inappropriate, leaving the impression that the person, who perhaps was not even a Christian, is spiritually secure.[55]

A funeral can take on a wholly secular aura with no mention of God, no reading of Scripture, sacred reflections, or hymns. Popular music is played, and the dress is casual. Wayne Jackson says: "It is as if there is no thought at all of eternity. Too, more and more, folks are simply 'too busy' to attend funerals. I have conducted services on occasion when scarcely a dozen would be in attendance — sometimes fewer!"[56]

Another shift in funerals and burials is a return to more family involvement, though this is still a modest number. "A movement toward home after-death care has convinced thousands of Americans to deal with their own dead. A nonprofit organization called Crossings maintains that, besides saving lots of money, home after-death care is greener than traditional burials — bodies pumped full of carcinogenic chemicals, laid in metal coffins in concrete vaults under chemically fertilized lawns — which mock the biblical concept of 'dust to dust.'[57] Cremating an unembalmed body (or burying it in real dirt) would seem obviously less costly and more eco-friendly. But more significant, according to advocates, home after-death care is also more meaningful for the living."[58]

Families are taking a more active role in burying their dead. The executive director of Funeral Consumers Alliance has written about the "surprising resurgence of interest in private, family-directed funerals. Formerly confined to a few hippies (I mean that affectionately) in Northern California, or in the pages of Lisa Carlson's *Caring for the Dead, Your Final Act of Love,* home funerals are finding new life in volunteer groups and in the mainstream media. In 2004, Public Television aired an hour-long doc-

55. Wayne Jackson, "Funeral Customs — Past and Present," *Christian Courier online,* 23 June 2004: http://www.christiancourier.com/articles/825-funeral-customs-past-and-present (accessed Mar. 4, 2009).

56. Jackson, "Funeral Customs — Past and Present."

57. *Crossings: Caring for Our Own at Death, A Home Funeral and Green Burial Resource Center:* http://www.crossings.net/ (accessed Apr. 8, 2009).

58. Max Alexander, "The Surprising Satisfactions of a Home Funeral," *Smithsonian.com,* March 2009: http://www.smithsonianmag.com/arts-culture/Presence-of-Mind-Which-Way-Out.html (accessed Mar. 16, 2009).

umentary on the topic."[59] However, some states have laws concerning burial that require a funeral director to handle the remains.[60] Articles about family burials are frequently appearing in the press; one such item concerns the burial of a ninety-two-year-old farmer:

> When Nathaniel Roe, 92, died at his 18th century farmhouse in New Hampshire the morning of June 6, his family did not call a funeral home to handle the arrangements.
>
> Instead, Roe's children, like a growing number of people nation-wide, decided to care for their father in death as they had in the last months of his life. They washed Roe's body, dressed him in his favorite Harrods tweed jacket and red Brooks Brothers tie and laid him on a bed so family members could privately say their last good-byes.
>
> The next day, Roe was placed in a pine coffin made by his son, along with a tuft of wool from the sheep he once kept. He was buried on his farm in a grove off a walking path he traversed each day. "It seemed like the natural, loving way to do things," said Jennifer Roe-Ward, Roe's granddaughter. "Let him have his dignity."[61]

The article goes on to say:

> The cost savings can be substantial, all the more important in an economic downturn. The average American funeral costs about $6,000 for the services of a funeral home, in addition to the costs of cremation or burial. A home funeral can be as inexpensive as the cost of pine for a coffin (for a backyard burial) or a few hundred dollars for cremation or several hundred for cemetery costs.[62]

Funerals in the United Kingdom

It is instructive to view the changes of funeral practices in England, since the Anglican Church has always been known for its rituals. The movement

59. Joshua Slocum, FCA Executive Director, "Caring for Your Own Dead: Myths and Facts," Funeral Consumers Alliance, January 30, 2009: http://www.funerals.org/newsandalerts/consumer-alerts/471-caringownlynchresponse (accessed Mar. 5, 2009).

60. Katie Zezima, "Is Backyard Burial the Next Big D.I.Y. Trend?" *The Virginian-Pilot,* July 22, 2009, p. 3.

61. Zezima, "Backyard Burial," p. 3.

62. Zezima, "Backyard Burial," p. 3.

is away from the church to the crematorium. Further, the use of the funeral home without using the church, as well as people devising their own rites and rituals, has become more common. The language of sin is gone, and so are references to the decaying body and soul.[63] Others speak of the English as "believing without belonging": that is, they don't go to church but still believe in the resurrection (p. 6).

In the United Kingdom — with the shift from church dogma to individual taste — it is not the church or the Bible that shapes the funeral, but the preferences of the chief mourner (p. 7). Furthermore, changes in the funeral litany to a more personalized one means that in the funeral service the pastoral dimensions are more pronounced (p. 19). These are what Tony Walter calls "mix and match" funerals, largely secular with a bit of Scripture thrown in. To buttress his argument, he says that in the 1662 Prayer Book there were eight pages for the funeral that declared, "You *shall* do." In the *Common Worship* book there are 180 pages full of choices. "The coffin *may* . . . ; a hymn *may* be sung" (p. 9). Authority has shifted from God, faith, and church to the mourners. Here we may raise the question about how far we go from revealed religion to personalized spirituality.

A dramatic case in point was the funeral of Princess Diana, in which "Candle in the Wind" was the focal piece of music, and the eulogy was a diatribe against the press and the royal family, a ceremony where the Anglican clergy seemed like extras in a Hollywood production. That may seem harsh, but it certainly was a far cry from the stately Church of England funeral of yesterday.[64]

There is now a term in England, "second funerals," which refers to later memorial services, the scattering of ashes months later, the planting of a tree, the unveiling of a monument or bench, a birdbath, a building, or the instituting of a scholarship (p. 24).

Death As Punishment

Moving from the image of death as feared and this image's influence on funeral practices, we will examine a related one: death as punishment.

63. Tony Walter, Richard Bragg, Mark Pryce, and Janet Eldred, "A Good Funeral," in *A Good Death*, Leveson Papers #14, p. 4. Hereafter, page references to "A Good Funeral" will appear in parentheses in the text.

64. Fleming Rutledge, "The Gospel According to Elton John," *The Living Church* 215, no. 15 (Oct. 12, 1997): 15.

This is based on the Genesis passages of Hebrew Scripture as well as the Pauline view of death as the last enemy to be conquered. Bonnie Miller-McLemore describes the modern angst that death is a kind of punishment, even though many have thought that we left behind God and sin. However, McLemore believes that this remains a residual feeling: "Our inability to prevent, control or cure major causes of death has forced us to question the 'one-bug' model. Even though scientists have found cures for some diseases, Dubos and others suspect that the mere discovery of specific bacteria did not itself cause their decline. Rather, other factors — pure food, pure water and pure air — also played a part. . . . Some theorists directly link cancer, for example, to a breakdown in close personal relationships or to feelings of loss, anxiety, depression, hostility or hopelessness. For example, when someone we know suffers a heart attack unexpectedly, we find ourselves saying with surprise that the person never struck us as 'the kind of person' who would experience heart problems. We have a certain personality type in mind when we make this judgment. Robert Morison goes so far as to argue that Wesleyan or middle-class virtues of cleanliness, prudence and moderation are the significant factors behind high health standards."[65]

However, in *Redeeming Marketplace Medicine,* I have made the point that a person can be responsible for maintaining as good a state of health as possible without being morally culpable when he or she falls ill.[66]

A deeper problem, however, is that mainstream culture does not provide ill people with resources to help them face these questions. They no longer have language with which to express the condemnation that they feel. The liver-cancer patient does not know how fully to account for the possibility of having failed to meet responsibilities or of being guilty for the onset of illness. People lack what Frederick Hoffman calls the "compensatory forces of remorse and penance" necessary to comprehend commission and atonement. Moral responsibility for death is thrust upon them. Yet they are directed away from confessional and willed levels of moral development and understanding and are left with a poorly balanced, distorted moral economy: they cannot calculate their proper responsibilities for death as a predictable result of understandable causes. . . . [Hoffman argues that] without a devel-

65. Bonnie J. Miller-McLemore, "Doing Wrong, Getting Sick, and Dying," *The Christian Century,* February 24, 1988, pp. 186-90, quoting from p. 187.
66. Evans, *Redeeming Marketplace Medicine,* pp. 119-31.

oped ethical sense and a way to account for moral deficiencies, people can no longer prepare for death. Personal anguish about culpability before illness and death was better managed within the modern medical model, which was developed at the turn of the century. The medical establishment at that time exhaustively explained illness and death in rational, scientific, "morally neutral" terms. Doctors certified that the causes of disease resided in micro-organisms, not in personal, moral or religious factors.[67]

However, medicine now has begun to recognize the importance of lifestyle-related factors to good health. Lifestyle diseases are defined as "a disease associated with the way a person or group of people lives." Such diseases include "atherosclerosis, heart disease and stroke, obesity and type two diabetes; and diseases associated with smoking and alcohol and drug abuse."[68] These diseases are some of the top killers of Americans. "Conversely, 'good' patients who have purposely not smoked, for example, expect 'rewards' for their good behavior, such as being spared heart disease or lung cancer. People who contract one of these diseases become deeply troubled when doctors cannot determine its natural cause; they may develop a vague, haunting sense of moral failure. Furthermore, their sense of justice is upset when, as happens all too often, those who compliantly avoid behavior that might aggravate their illness recover no more quickly — or in some cases even more slowly — than others who are less 'well behaved.' Such an experience is very disillusioning."[69] So friends who are health nuts but die of heart attacks anyway suggest something singularly unfair about the supposed moral nature of the universe, which represents one aspect of the Christian theodicy questions. Why would God allow a good person to die a premature death? "Veatch claims that death is 'our last quest for responsibility.'"[70] Is this quest — for what I call "negotiated death" — a holy one or not? In our search for autonomy, have we ended up with physician-assisted suicide and the Dignitas Society as the only options?[71]

67. Cf. Miller-McLemore, "Doing Wrong, Getting Sick, and Dying," pp. 188-89.

68. Medicine.Net.com: http://www.medicinenet.com/script/main/hp.asp (accessed Aug. 20, 2009).

69. Miller-McLemore, "Doing Wrong, Getting Sick, and Dying," p. 189.

70. Miller-McLemore, "Doing Wrong, Getting Sick, and Dying," p. 190.

71. "How to Contact Dignitas in Switzerland," Weblog of Derek Humphry, Founder of Hemlock Society, February 6, 2006: http://assistedsuicide.org/blog/2006/02/06/how-to-contact-dignitas-in-switzerland/ (accessed Aug. 12, 2009).

Death As a Gateway to Life

Near-Death Experiences (NDE)

Since the 1970s, notions of the nature of death have been challenged and chronicled by scientific studies of death-related phenomena. Such "life after death" studies were taken up in the United States by Raymond Moody, Elisabeth Kübler-Ross, and others, and they are controversial at best. Can we claim that they are telling us what it is like to die? The jury is still out, but it is notable that all recorded cases seem to have the same experiences. People who were clinically dead and came back to life describe moving into a bright light with an overwhelming presence of love, experiencing God's presence, and then returning to life changed and reborn. Their stories include out-of-body experiences, travels down tunnels, and encounters with angels or deceased loved ones. This phenomenon has been labeled near-death experience (NDE).[72]

> Raymond Moody, a young psychiatrist, pieced together reports by 150 people that he describes in his book *Life After Life.* These people had either been resuscitated after being pronounced dead, had come close to dying through injury or illness, or had been with people who told them of their experiences as they died. The account does not represent any one person's experience, but contains the points that recur again and again, despite the variety of people reporting and despite the range of events that brought them to the brink of death.
>
> Others, notably psychiatrist Elisabeth Kübler-Ross, believe that the end of the body is not the end of life. Kübler-Ross has collected hundreds of similar stories from people who have been declared dead and then recovered. Although her research is independent of Moody's and of Osis and Haraldsson's, the reports of her patients are similar; they become detached from their bodies; they feel a sense of elation and wholeness; they are drawn toward a light; and they meet a being — often a deceased loved one — who helps them move from life to death. From her research Kübler-Ross concludes that upon death, we leave the body and go on to another kind of existence.[73]

72. Anita Bartholomew, "After Life: The Scientific Case for the Human Soul," *Reader's Digest,* August 2003, p. 124.

73. Jonathan Rosen, "Rewriting the End: Elisabeth Kübler-Ross," *The New York Times Magazine,* January 22, 1995, p. 24.

Kübler-Ross's assertion raised many eyebrows, as is indicated in Jonathan Rosen's 1995 article in *The New York Times Magazine*: "[Kübler-Ross's previous work on death and dying] . . . made it more shocking to pick up a copy of her book *On Life After Death,* and read: 'My *real* job is, and this is why I need your help, to tell people that death does not exist.' Finding that passage, and others like it (for example, the one describing how she was visited by a dead patient in a hallway at the University of Chicago), is like turning on the television and hearing Billy Graham declare that there is no God."

Rosen goes on to reflect: "[Kübler-Ross's] appeal to an impatient and uncertain age has won her a wide following as the millennial clock ticks down. The shift in her work is emblematic of a transformation in the culture at large, and Kübler-Ross has clearly helped to bring about that change. She bought her farm from Raymond Moody, the man many consider the father of near-death experiences and the major promoter of books testifying to encounters with the beyond. His book, *Life After Life,* has sold more than 11 million copies since it was published in 1975 — with a foreword by Elisabeth Kübler-Ross."[74] Rosen continues:

> Betty J. Eadie, whose account of her own near-death experience, *Embraced by the Light,* made history by appearing simultaneously on the hardcover and paperback best-seller lists of the *New York Times,* helped Kübler-Ross present illustrations at a 1993 lecture she gave in New York. "She is a heroine," Eadie told me, "an idol of mine."
>
> Melvin Morse, a pediatrician who wrote the introduction to *Embraced by the Light* and whose 1990 book about near death experiences of children, *Closer to the Light,* was a national best seller, began his research into the paranormal as a way to disprove claims he heard Kübler-Ross make on a Seattle television show in the 80's about the spiritual nature of dying. "I thought we could have some fun with her," he told me, though he has since become her greatest champion and is writing a book that begins with a tribute to Kübler-Ross' contributions not only to the field of death and dying, but to the "next stage" as well.
>
> "Mankind has finally learned to look at death and when you look, you find," Kübler-Ross told me. "The time is right now." Whether these books represent the further evolution of our understanding of life and death, or a terrible betrayal depends upon whom you ask.[75]

74. Raymond Moody, *Life After Life* (Boerne, TX: Mockingbird Books, 1975).
75. Rosen, "Rewriting the End," p. 24.

Kübler-Ross's earlier insights on death and dying emphasized how death can bring us self-awareness and self-acceptance, as she wrote in *Death: The Final Stage of Growth.*[76] Death is the final stage of growth as the self (spirit) is eternal. Kübler-Ross also discussed this in *Wheel of Life,* where she had conversations with the dead through channeling a Native American man. Kübler-Ross has left herself open to considerable critique from her medical colleagues, who question her scientific research. They point out that death is not a single happening, a sharply defined end in a moment, but is actually a drawn-out sequence of biological events. The "deaths" of the organs and cells that form the human body occur at their own rates; the death of the whole person is a fleeting moment tied to no single isolated organic event. As of now, there is simply no sure way to know when death occurs.[77]

How to interpret these phenomena is problematic. Is it because some brains are wired in a particular way, or because we do travel to another world, or perhaps these visions are drug induced or glimpses of eternity? The question is: Can any of this be proven scientifically by the gold standard of research replicability. Some researchers, such as Susan Blackmore, declare that they can be indexed by physiological events; others say that they are proof that consciousness may not reside totally in the brain.[78]

Under local anesthesia during brain surgery, for instance, patients sometimes report seeing things from an "out-of-body" perspective.[79] However, there are others who do not think this is a sufficient explanation. "Six percent of those resuscitated after cardiac arrest reported NDEs. Both van Lommel and the British researchers believe that these findings suggest consciousness could exist in the absence of a functioning brain. 'You can compare the brain to a TV set,' says van Lommel. 'The TV program is not in your TV set.' So where is consciousness? Is it in every cell of the body? 'I think so,' says van Lommel."[80]

One dramatic story recounted by Pam Reynolds defies rational explanation:

76. Elisabeth Kübler-Ross, ed., *Death: The Final Stage of Growth* (Englewood Cliffs, NJ: Prentice Hall, 1975), pp. 164, 166. I am indebted to Bruce Epperly for this interpretation of Kübler-Ross, in his *At the Edges of Life: A Holistic Vision of the Human Adventure* (St. Louis: Chalice Press, 1992).

77. Moody, *Life After Life,* pp. 30-31.

78. Susan Blackmore, *Dying to Live: Near-Death Experiences* (Amherst, NY: Prometheus Books, 1993), p. 127.

79. Bartholomew, "After Life," p. 126.

80. Bartholomew, "After Life," p. 128.

45

In the summer of 1991, Pam Reynolds learned she had a life-threatening bulge in an artery in her brain. Neurosurgeon Robert Spetzler, director of the Barrow Neurological Institute in Phoenix, told the 35-year-old Atlanta mother of three that in order to operate he would have to stop her heart. During that time her brain function would cease. By all clinical measures, she would be dead for up to an hour. While Reynolds was under anesthesia, leads from a machine that emitted a clicking sound were plugged into her ears to gauge her brainstem function (the brainstem plays a part in controlling hearing as well as other involuntary activities). Additional instruments tracked heartbeat, breathing, temperature and other vital signs. Her limbs were restrained; her eyes were lubricated and then taped shut. As Spetzler powered up the surgical saw to open the patient's skull, something occurred that never registered on any of the sophisticated monitoring devices. Reynolds felt herself "pop" out of her body. From a vantage point just above Spetzler's shoulders, she looked down on the operation. She "saw" Spetzler holding something that resembled an electric toothbrush. A female voice complained that the patient's blood vessels were too small. It appeared to Reynolds that they were about to operate on her groin. *That couldn't be right,* she thought. *This is brain surgery.* Reynolds then assumed that whatever they were doing inside her skull had triggered a hallucination. But even though her eyes and ears were effectively sealed shut, what she perceived was actually happening. The surgical saw did resemble an electric toothbrush. Surgeons were, indeed, working on her groin. Catheters had to be threaded up to her heart to connect to a heart-lung machine. Spetzler gave the order to bring Reynolds to "standstill" — draining the blood from her body. By every reading of every instrument, life left Reynolds' body. And she found herself traveling down a tunnel toward a light. At its end, she saw her long-dead grandmother, relatives and friends. Time seemed to stop. Then an uncle led her back to her body and instructed her to return. It felt like plunging into a pool of ice water. After she came to, Reynolds told Spetzler all that she'd seen and experienced. "You are way out of my area of expertise," Spetzler said. And twelve years later, he still doesn't know what to make of it.[81]

"Two other researchers, Karlis Osis and Erlunder Haraldsson of the American Society of Parapsychological Research, gathered similar evi-

81. Bartholomew, "After Life," p. 124.

dence of life after death. They interviewed doctors and nurses in America and India who had been at the bedside of patients who described such experiences. Some patients had visions of a religious figure or of deceased loved ones who had taken the dying person away to another realm. Most of the patients consented to this invitation to die with serenity. But those under the influence of medical [interventions] . . . that can lead to hallucinations — drugs, fever, etc., were more likely to be frightened and even scream for help."[82]

Arthur Koestler (1905-1983) argues for similar perspectives based on physics research and parapsychology. From historiography and polemical writings, such as his bestseller *Darkness at Noon,* and his later critically reviled work *The Roots of Coincidence,* he became interested in parapsychology.

> In the late 1970s, Koestler postulated that death does not signify total extinction. "It means merging into the cosmic consciousness," he wrote in an essay on life after death, comparing the process of dying to "the flow of a river into the ocean." Summoning the rhetorical powers of his youth, the elderly writer foresaw the end. The river, he wrote, "has been freed of the mud that clung to it, and regained its transparency. It has become identified with the sea, spread over it, omnipresent, every drop catching a spark of the sun. The curtain has not fallen; it has been raised." Ironically, after a lifetime of earthly visions, it was that glowing picture of an afterlife that gave Arthur Koestler the courage to face death by his own hand.[83]

Near-death experiences reflected by the subjects studied have certain common visions that differ from ordinary hallucinations and that vary according to culture. However, whether people actually survive death is not necessarily proven. Part of the argument is that it cannot be proven scientifically because it involves nonmaterial phenomena. P. M. H. Atwater offers the perspective that "the Sylvan Fissure, temporal lobes, limbic system, and other unique sections of the brain are highly charged during near-death states." However, scientific explanations of near-death states do not exist. These experiences defy intellectual or rational expla-

---

82. Moody, *Life After Life,* pp. 30-31.

83. Patricia Blake, "Rootless Cosmopolitan of the Age," *Time magazine online,* March 14, 1983: http://www.time.com/time/magazine/article/0,9171,951992-1,00.html (accessed Aug. 20, 2009).

nation.[84] Medical researchers would never use the word "soul," but some find the idea that NDEs are triggered by the failing brain to be inadequate. They speculate that NDEs may be evidence, not of an afterlife, but of the fact that consciousness does not reside solely in the brain.[85] What is interesting about these stories is that in earlier times they would be called miracles.

There is a great deal of debate about how to interpret these NDEs. Ken Ring summarizes the NDE literature in his book *Lessons from the Light*. He concludes that if religious people believe that the soul is separate and distinct from the physical body, then out-of-body experiences are part of a spiritual experience not verified by scientific explanation, since it cannot be measured scientifically. He speculates that one day perhaps science will be able to measure the soul departing from the body.[86]

In Germany, Lutheran pastor Johann Hampe, in his book *Sterben ist doch ganz anders,* describes these phenomena in theological terms.[87] It is interesting that some would say that these phenomena are similar to what is described in the Tibetan *Book of the Dead.*[88] Principal among these phenomena are numerous accounts of people who experience "out-of-body" visions in which they are looking down at their corpse stretched out. In most of these accounts the self looks at the body but is unable to enter it. The body is described as waxen and inert, sometimes terribly disfigured by an accident, and then after CPR or an injection or another procedure, the "soul" reenters the body and the person becomes alive again. This is not to be confused with a dream, because there is a closeness to reality that dreams never have.

Hampe makes a leap from these phenomena to the question of where the "dead" Christ was during the three days in the tomb. He refers to 1 Peter 3:19-20; 4:6, where the apostle says that Jesus descended to the dead in

84. Near-Death Experiences and the Afterlife, "The NDE should be able to be demonstrated empirically," www.neardeath.com/experiences/skeptic01.html (December 14, 2005).

85. Bartholomew, "After Life," p. 127.

86. Kenneth Ring, Evelyn Elsaesser Valarino, and Caroline Myss, *Lessons from the Light: What We Can Learn from the Near-Death Experience* (Needham: MA: Moment Point Press, 2006), chap. 2.

87. Johann Hampe, *To Die Is Gain* (Atlanta: John Knox Press, 1979).

88. W. Y. Evans-Wentz, ed., *The Tibetan Book of the Dead: Or, the After-Death Experiences on the Bardo Plane, according to Lama Kazi Dawa-Samdup's English Rendering,* 3rd ed. (New York: Oxford University Press, 1960).

order to preach to them. Hampe qualifies this discussion by saying that it is not the most important tenet of his faith, but it does provide insight into the destiny of the person.[89] His perspective is not embraced by most thinkers who discuss NDE.

Some theologians, such as Hans Küng, are very skeptical about these phenomena and rather forcibly come out against the life-after-death research. Küng declares that it is based on a total misunderstanding of the nature of death, the death of the whole organism, biological death, which is different from clinical death. "Even those who have researched into death do not dispute that someone who has had experiences of dying and can subsequently report them has not gone through the phase of death but through a particular phase of life." On these points he holds that when people chronicled in the research say their experience is "coming back from the dead," it is in fact a misnomer. However, the reason behind his refutation is taking issue with the argument that these after-death experiences somehow prove the existence of heaven or eternity. Küng does not lean toward Ernst Bloch's *"peut-être,"* but neither does he rely on reason or experience to bring us to this point, but rather "a reasonable trust."[90]

Immortality of the Soul

The NDE phenomena raise the question of the immortality of the soul. Many believe this doctrine is Christian, but it is actually Greek and Egyptian. Nowadays immortality is discussed in somewhat general terms — not of the soul per se. Robert Jay Lifton describes five modes of immortality that we need for historical continuity, which death threatens; in other words, it helps to cushion the impact of death and give it some significance.

The first mode is that of the biological, or the biosocial: that is, we live on in our children — in a sense, a biological continuity. In the second there is the creative mode: that we live through our works, whether the works of talent, art, or science, or simply the impact we have on the people around us. This is tied to what we do, the feelings that we express that have life beyond the moment as they affect others. A third mode is the religious one of symbolic immortality. This is life after death, "but more universally,

---

89. Hampe, *To Die Is Gain,* pp. 34, 39, 51, 111-12.

90. Hans Küng and Walter Jens, *A Dignified Dying* (London: SCM Press, 1995), pp. 8, 9, 12.

it's the idea of some degree of spiritual attainment that helps one to transcend death and accept it." A fourth mode is that we are one with the earth: "ashes to ashes, dust to dust." We return to the earth from which we sprang, because life is a continuous cycle. The fifth mode is that of experiential transcendence: it is similar to the state induced by meditation.[91] Of course, the main intellectual roots of immortality are from Greek philosophy, where the Platonic ideal necessitates a body/soul dualism in which the soul is the ideal form that lives forever.

One wonders what comfort we can find from these contemporary attitudes toward death. Ultimately they are lacking. Ray Anderson, in his book *Towards a Theology of Human Death,* captures the tension between a yearning for immortality and Christ's different answer to that hunger:

> Socrates could have escaped death, and Jesus could have eased Pilate out of his predicament. Yet Socrates and Jesus would not accept Crito's advice to leave town, and Jesus looked Pilate squarely in the eye and said, "You could have no power over me unless it had been given you from above" (John 19:11). . . . Both Jesus and Socrates had a theology of death which was the logical outcome of their theology of life. . . . Socrates, as Plato tells us the story, scoffed at the suggestion of his friends that he pay a small bribe and thereby escape death. "You are mistaken," he told them, "if you think that a man who is worth anything ought to spend his time weighing up the prospects of life and death. He has only one thing to consider in performing any action; that is, whether he is acting rightly or wrongly. . . . True philosophers," Socrates continued, "make dying their profession." The "rehearsal of death" which characterizes the philosophy of Socrates is the process of perfecting the soul in its true knowledge of the eternal. Life and death were viewed as opposites, and because death had no power to extinguish the soul, but rather liberated it so that it might return whence it came, the life of the soul is eternal and rooted in the life of the divine. Hence, Socrates' theology of death is the logical outcome of his theology of the immortal soul. . . . Jesus, on the other hand, did not face his death with the equanimity of soul that characterizes the death of Socrates. "Now is my soul troubled," cried out Jesus. "And what shall I say? 'Father, save me from this hour'? No, for this purpose I have come to this hour. Father, glorify thy name" (John 12:27-28).

91. Robert Jay Lifton, "The Politics of Immortality," *Psychology Today* (November 1970): 70ff.

For Jesus, life and death are not logical opposites as they are for Socrates. Life and death both belong to that existence that issues from God. Therefore both life and death are subject to divine authority. "Do not fear those who kill the body but cannot kill the soul," Jesus had already taught. "Rather fear him who can destroy both body and soul in Gehenna [hell]" (Matt. 10:28).[92]

Like Anderson, we yearn for a deeper look into this mystery and into the Christian doctrine of the resurrection, concerning how the Christian faith informs our views of death, which I will address in the final chapter of this book.

---

92. Ray S. Anderson, *Theology, Death and Dying* (Oxford: Basil Blackwell, 1986), pp. 37-38.

II. NEGOTIATED DEATH

3. End-of-Life Choices: Distinctions and Debate

Death Be Not Proud

Death be not proud, though some have called thee
Mighty and dreadfull, for, thou art not so,
For, those, whom thou think'st, thou dost overthrow,
Die not, poore death, nor yet canst thou kill me.
From rest and sleepe, which but thy pictures bee,
Much pleasure, then from thee, much more must flow,
And soonest our best men with thee doe goe,
Rest of their bones, and soules deliverie.
Thou art slave to Fate, Chance, kings, and desperate men,
And dost with poyson, warre, and sicknesse dwell,
And poppie, or charmes can make us sleepe as well,
And better then thy stroake; why swell'st thou then;
One short sleepe past, wee wake eternally,
And death shall be no more; death, thou shalt die.

John Donne (1572-1631)

Introduction

In Part II of this book I will examine the phenomenon of "negotiated death" with respect to aid-in-dying, euthanasia, suicide, and treatment choices from ethical, medical, legal, and religious perspectives. With the advent of technological medicine, negotiated death is a new reality that gives us more choices about how and when we die. In the past, when we were gravely ill, "nature took its course" in one sense, or, more precisely, a disease or illness ran its course and death came more quickly. Modern medicine, with its miracle drugs, complicated surgeries, organ transplants (with ever-increasing types), and substitute body parts has been a gift. Alongside these medical feats, better diet, clean water, and better living conditions have led to increased longevity. Unfortunately, this "gift" also has a price: many people feel as though they are prisoners of the very technology that prolongs their lives, since it can lengthen their dying as well as enhancing their living.

"The ubiquitousness of technology has forced us to bear a new responsibility, that is, to defend our end-of-life instead of just experiencing it. We must consider the degree of resentment towards these unwelcome tasks. Although we wish to control the end of our life, we generally do not want to consider it in advance."[1] The opponents to the 2009 health care reform bills falsely declared that so-called "death panels" would be instituted to force people to choose euthanasia. (The emotionalism in these debates is hard to understand.[2]) Other concerns are that economics may create pressure for euthanasia because of health care costs associated with the last year of life. "The 2008 Dartmouth Atlas of Health Care found that billions of dollars are spent each year in the United States on aging patients in the last six months of life."[3] This study found that an average of $25,358 was spent on each Medicare patient in his or her last six months of life.[4] Furthermore, more services per patient did not necessarily provide a higher quality of care. "A *Forbes* article, 'Obamacare Dives Into End-of-Life Debate,' has a sub-title of 'Medicare Spends $100 Billion Annually on Patients' Final Year of Life. What the New Bill Says — and Doesn't Say — About Treatment of the Dying.'"[5]

The irony of modern times is that, as we find better and better tech-

1. Jeffrey T. Berger, "The Call for Physician-Assisted Suicide: What Can Be Learned?" *Trends in Health Care, Law and Ethics* 9, no. 4 (Fall 1994): 14.

2. David Gibson, "Obama's Altar Call for Health Care Reform: Conscience Protections and No Federally Funded Abortion," *Politics Daily*, August 19, 2009: http://www.politicsdaily.com/2009/08/19/obamas-altar-call-for-health-care-reform/ (accessed Aug. 26, 2009).

3. Kay Lazar, "Who Decides When You Die?" *The Boston Globe*, February 16, 2009, p. A12: http://www.boston.com/news/health/articles/2009/02/16/who_decides_when_you_die/ (accessed July 20, 2009).

4. Lazar, "Who Decides When You Die?"

5. "Article Examines Responses to End-of-Life Care in House Healthcare Reform Bill," *Hospice News Network* 13, no. 28 (July 28, 2009).

nologies to sustain and prolong life, we have less regard for the very persons whom our technologies support. "Patients are therefore left to believe that their only choices are acquiescence to unrestrained life-sustaining technology or abandonment by their physician. With this kind of a choice, it is not surprising that people facing terminal illness might want some control over the time and manner of their demise."[6]

The context of the current debates is an aging population: a growing number will be affected by these debates in the foreseeable future. Americans are living longer than ever before. In 2006, there were an estimated thirty-seven million people aged sixty-five and older living in the United States, accounting for just over 12 percent of the total population. There were 50,364 persons aged 100 or more in 2002 (0.02 percent of the total population). This is a thirty-five percent increase from the 1990 figure of 37,306.[7] In 2050 there will be an estimated 33 million in the sixty-five to seventy-four-year-old age group, 30 million in the seventy-five to eighty-four-year-old age group, 18 million in the eighty-five to ninety-nine-year-old age group, and 2.5 million in the 100-years-and-older age group.[8] Projections indicate that by 2050 the composition of the older population will be 61 percent non-Hispanic white, 18 percent Hispanic, 12 percent black, and 8 percent Asian.[9]

In light of this exponential explosion of older adults in the United States, as we enter this rather murky ethical terrain concerning end-of-life decision-making, we need to draw on all the resources at our command to enhance the last season of life, not end it. Technology overshadows our final years, and thus, instead of dying well, we are separated from our loved ones by machines. (In later chapters I will present alternatives to this, such as hospice and the support of faith communities.)

6. Christine K. Cassel, "The Popular Movement for Physician-Assisted Suicide — What the Public Is Saying, What Physicians Are Hearing," *The Western Journal of Medicine* 157, no. 2 (Aug. 1992): 192.

7. "A Profile of Older Americans: 2003," Department of Health and Human Services, Administration on Aging: http://www.aoa.gov/AoAroot/Aging_Statistics/Profile/2003/index.aspx (accessed Apr. 21, 2009).

8. "U.S. population aged 65 years and older: 1990 to 2050 (in millions)," last updated August 6, 2009, National Institute on Aging, U.S. National Institutes of Health: http://www.nia.nih.gov/ResearchInformation/ConferencesAndMeetings/WorkshopReport/Figure4.htm (accessed Aug. 25, 2009).

9. "Older Americans 2008: Key Indicators of Well-Being," Federal Interagency Forum on Aging-Related Statistics, March 2008, p. 4: http://www.agingstats.gov/agingstatsdotnet/main_site/default.aspx (accessed Apr. 21, 2009).

Americans Divided on End-of-Life Decisions

The American public is divided about aid-in-dying, which is reflected in a variety of polls over the last few years. A 2005 Pew poll found that 46 percent of U.S. citizens were in favor and 45 percent were opposed to legalizing doctor-assisted suicide. The findings suggest that Americans want to be allowed to die, that is, allowed to refuse life-sustaining treatment; but they are evenly split concerning actively bringing about death, and further split into camps sharply defined by religion. We are becoming more sophisticated in making distinctions about these complex issues.

In other polls, 60 percent acknowledged "a moral right" to take one's own life when "suffering great pain" and having no hope of improvement. "The three-way split in opinions about legalizing physician-assisted suicide in general became a virtual 50-50 split when the respondents were asked about how they felt about the possibility for themselves. Could they 'imagine any situation where you, yourself, might want a doctor to end your own life intentionally by some painless means if you requested it?' 'Yes,' said 50%; 'no' said 47%, with 3% declining to answer." Religious affiliation also influences these practices. "'By two to one (61 percent to 30 percent), white evangelical Protestants opposed physician-assisted suicide laws; by nearly identical margins, white mainline Protestants and seculars approve of such laws,' the Pew researchers reported. 'Catholics, on balance, oppose such laws (by 50 percent to 40 percent).'" "A national poll of 1,005 adults issued by Religious News Service in September 2003 showed that Americans find physician-assisted suicide more acceptable morally than suicide. As to physician-assisted suicide, 45% said it was morally acceptable and 49% that it was morally wrong. As to suicide, 14% said it was morally acceptable and 81% that it was morally wrong." Also, when a person has made these decisions for a family member, he or she is more likely to accept suicide and physician-assisted suicide as moral.[10]

Most surveys of North American health care professionals reflect their opposition to physician-assisted suicide. Nurses in intensive care units strongly support good pain management for dying patients and

---

10. Information in this paragraph and the preceding one from Peter Steinfels, "Supreme Court Decision in Right-to-Die Debate May Signal Time Out," *The New York Times,* Death with Dignity National Center online, February 11, 2006: http://www.deathwithdignity .org/news/news/nytimes.02.11.06.asp (accessed Mar. 13, 2006).

withholding or withdrawing life-sustaining therapies when death is inevitable. The vast majority oppose assisted suicide and euthanasia. Edmund Pellegrino and Daniel Sulmasy argue that physician-assisted suicide runs counter to the Hippocratic Oath. Sulmasy points out that its injunction to apply dietetic measures for the benefit of the sick "does not imply that futile treatment is required but rather therapy which is hopeless can be withdrawn."[11]

Other polls provide information on people's fears about dying. Eighty-three percent of those questioned said they did not want to be a burden to loved ones at the end of their lives. However, only 53 to 57 percent had spoken with their spouses, partners, or families about their wishes for end-of-life care, and only 10 percent had discussed these issues with their primary-care physicians.[12]

In its cartoons, popular culture — over a fifteen-year period — has come to portray medical technology as progressively more threatening. The cartoon patient has changed from robust to skeletalized, and technology has changed from simple to dominant and ominous — if not evil.

> In the first cartoon (by Nelson), a man and woman are sitting in a living room. He, reading the *Gazette,* turns to her and says, "There have been so many medical breakthroughs lately, that if you aren't dead already, you probably never will be." The setting is a comfortable home environment, the most prominent features of the cartoon being the overstuffed chairs, the characters themselves, two lamps and an end table. In another cartoon (Stayskal) two rather robust male patients are in hospital beds. One turns to the other and says, "I'm going to take a nap, watch my plugs, will you?" The characters themselves, the beds, the overhead lamps and the furniture dominate the cartoon. In the background there is some vaguely outlined equipment, IVs on a standard, an oxygen mask in the bed and a tiny heart monitor. The environment is "low-tech."
>
> Then there is a change in the depictions of the cartoons. In the next two-panel cartoon, a family member is ushered by the physician through a door that says "Technology R Us." The first panel says, as they progress, "The good news is your father is still alive . . ." In the second panel the caption continues: ". . . the bad news is that apart

11. Daniel Sulmasy, "Killing and Allowing to Die," PhD diss., Georgetown University, 1996, pp. 20-21.

12. Lazar, "Who Decides When You Die?"

from the readouts, you can't tell." The family member hangs his head. The patient is barely discernible in the dark, nondescript, dripping, and ominous looking "technology" that covers half of the frame. In the next cartoon (Wright), a policeman is standing over a bedfast patient saying, "Trying to die, eh, Mr. Smith! You could get the [electric] chair for this." The patient is cachexic, contractured, and diminished by the ominous, if not evil looking, dark technology that now takes up three-quarters of the frame. In the final cartoon (Oliphant), a moribund patient, whose head alone shows above the bed sheets, is surrounded by a morass of life-sustaining technology, dripping wires, and lines. The caption reads, "Condemned to life."[13]

The Debate

In many ways, technology has created or at least exacerbated the debates concerning death and dying. One of the reasons is that medicine's advances and patient autonomy may clash. Medicine says, "We will do everything to keep you alive," while many patients say, "No, I want to choose when and how I will die." These debates have accelerated in the United States because people suffer from chronic conditions, which have longer periods of gradually going downhill and dying, and they do not want to continue these prolonged dying experiences.[14] Barry Clark refers to us as "living longer and dying slower."[15] The essence of the debates, to some degree, concerns the question, When is the right time to die? Who decides — the patient, family, doctor, or the law?

The danger is that the right to die can become a duty to die. For instance, while John Cobb claims that he is referring only to the individual's freedom to choose death and not to the right to determine that others should die, he does admit that because of limited resources we may eventually have to choose to withhold treatment from someone in a vegetative state even if that person had earlier expressed wishes to be kept alive.

13. Marsha D. M. Fowler, "Suffering," in *Dignity and Dying: A Christian Appraisal,* ed. John F. Kilner, Edmund D. Pellegrino, and Arlene B. Miller (Grand Rapids: Eerdmans, 1996), pp. 45-46.

14. Margaret Pabst Battin, *Ending Life: Ethics and the Way We Die* (New York: Oxford University Press, 2005), p. 18.

15. Barry Clark, "Killing with Kindness or Curing with Care," in *A Good Death,* Leveson Paper #4 (Solihull, UK: Foundation of Lady Katherine Leveson, 2003), p. 37.

Cobb states clearly that he does not want the right-to-die to become the right-to-kill; this is, however, always a potential danger of the right-to-die position.[16]

"Negotiated death" reflects a certain presumption that an individual wants total control over his life, including choosing when he will die. The civil rights, feminist, and liberation movements have fed Americans' thirst for autonomy and freedom. Actually, the issue we now see being raised is not choosing death but reviewing a range of medical options of how we live while dying. How do we connect autonomy and responsibility? Where do we stand in the spectrum of available choices? The moral tensions are between the right to choose versus the sanctity of life, our autonomy versus physician responsibility, and physician-assisted suicide versus refusal of treatment. Where is our moral compass? Rather than using the word "euthanasia" (good death), we might talk instead about *euapothenesto* ("good dying") to help clarify the situation.

The use of language is very important as we attempt to define the various ways that death can occur. The earlier distinctions between a "natural death" and a medically orchestrated one are not as clear as they once were: the concept of choosing the time you die with medical assistance is before us. In contemporary debates these possibilities were first highlighted by the practices of Timothy Quill and Jack Kevorkian, though their approach, certainly legally if not morally, was substantially different. Kevorkian, by direct intervention — that is, administering lethal doses of medicine — ended terminal patients' lives at their request, though not exclusively so. On the other hand, Quill gave patients the means to do it, but did not commit the act himself. In fact, the latter was the one who invented the term "physician-assisted suicide," which he used to distinguish it from euthanasia, though "aid-in-dying" is a more accurate description.[17]

One of the pertinent questions is: *would* a terminally ill patient's collecting enough barbiturates and taking them on her own be considered a suicide? What additional element is added if the physician writes the prescription, as opposed to the person's collecting the drugs on her own? Does it morally sanction or encourage the choice? The answer for many

---

16. See John Cobb, "The Right to Die," in *Matters of Life and Death* (Louisville: Westminster John Knox Press, 1991), p. 66.

17. Press Kit, Caring and Compassion Society, p. 2. "Aid-in-dying" is the accurate, unbiased term to describe terminally ill patients' end-of-life choices.

seems to be yes. But why? Is it because doctors are traditionally under-stood to preserve life, not end it? And yet this approach to ending one's suffering and pain seems to overlook the fact that, with the expansion of hospice and palliative care, there are other ways of controlling pain, in-cluding palliative sedation. When people have their pain controlled, they are usually not asking for lethal doses of medicine.

A further complication is the timing. Should humans be able to choose the exact moment of their deaths? Perhaps the difference is be-tween recognizing that we are in the irretrievable process of dying versus choosing death, which is different from refusal of treatment. In a sense, it ends up labeling a lethal dose of medicine as treatment, that is, treatment for the pain. There are those, such as Ray Frey, who argue that these dis-tinctions cannot be retained because they are not always logical, and be-cause the outcome is the patient's death.

> Nor is anything achieved by trying to carve out another difference in intention. It might be claimed, for example, that in supplying the pill, the doctor must intend the patient's death, whereas in the withdrawal case he may well not intend this. But in the pill case he may well not in-tend death; he may take himself only to supplying a means of death to someone who will not take the pill or who wants it only for reassur-ance, if he continues to deteriorate. And in the withdrawal case, he may well intend death and withdrawal of feeding tubes as the way of achieving this. In both cases, the doctor remains a part cause of a death. Moreover, what those who opposed physician-assisted suicide and active voluntary euthanasia have insisted upon is that doctors may not kill, not that they may not intend death. In the pill case, even if the doctor intends death, the pill can only kill the patient if the patient de-cided to swallow it. The doctor does not kill the patient whatever the intention of the doctor.
>
> To those who oppose physician-assisted suicide and active volun-tary euthanasia, withdrawal is seen as an alternative, one that is sup-posed to be grounded in differences in causal structure between with-drawal and, say, pill cases. I do not think there is any difference in causal structure. . . .
>
> Interestingly, consent does not separate the withdrawal and the pill cases. In the withdrawal case, the patient consents to what the doctor does to him. In the pill case, the patient asks for the pill the doctor pre-scribes, chooses then to swallow the pill, and dies as a result. It is not as

if the pill is foisted on the patient; and it is certainly not true that the pill is crammed into the patient's mouth.

Thus, I do not see withdrawal as an alternative to physician assisted suicide and active voluntary euthanasia because I think the cases are alike, causally, without there being any other significant moral differences between them. I do not think anything is gained, therefore, by trying to make out passive death as something quite different from active death, in the context of the withdrawal and pill cases. . . .

The reason treatment is so important in his case is because he can end a life that illness and disease has led him to think he no longer wants to live. There does not appear to be any absence of intention on his part, when it comes to ending his life.[18]

Both sides in the debate over "aid-in-dying" versus prohibiting assistance in dying are guilty of using inflammatory language, such as "allowing people to suffer and robbing them of their choice" versus "killing helpless people." Although we may acknowledge the logic of some of Frey's argument, it fails by collapsing motive, act, and outcome. E. D. Pellegrino also raises important questions concerning the complicity of the doctor who writes the prescription for a lethal drug dose, even if the patient is the one who actually takes it — because of the intent of the doctor to aid the patient to bring about his own death.[19]

Clarifying Definitions

Since controversy over definitions of terms forms such an important part of the current debates, at the outset we will offer some clarifying definitions. *Euthanasia* literally means "good death," but the modern practice means ending a terminally ill patient's life where an agent other than the patient is involved. *Direct euthanasia* is defined as bringing about another person's death in one of three ways: against the patient's desire, which is active, involuntary euthanasia; without the patient's consent; or at the request of a rational and self-conscious patient, which is voluntary euthanasia. "In active euthanasia, the physician administers a lethal dose of medication, such as potassium chloride. The physician both supplies the

18. Ray Frey, "Passive Death," in *Philosophical Reflections on Medical Ethics,* ed. Nafsika Athanassoulis (New York: Palgrave/Macmillan 2005), pp. 205-07.
19. A note from E. D. Pellegrino to the author, Jan. 19, 2010, concerning this subject.

means of death and is the final human agent in the events leading to the patient's death."[20]

Active euthanasia is killing: it is an act of commission, that is, the active intervention to bring about another person's death. Hence, "active" and "direct" are synonymous. *Passive euthanasia* is allowing a person to die or refraining from actions that might prolong life. Thus, indirect and passive euthanasia are the same, because *indirect euthanasia* is the failure to prevent death; it is omission, the failure to perform certain acts. *Suicide* is death by one's own hand, in which the primary intent is to end one's physical life or suffering. *Heroic self-sacrifice* is giving up one's life for a cause, principle, or another person: it is other-regarding. *Physician-assisted suicide* is arranging death by mutual agreement between the patient and physician. It is not directly caused by the doctor, so it might be more accurately labeled "aid-in-dying," since patients must take the lethal dosage themselves. "In assisted suicide, the patient swallows a lethal dose of drugs or activates a device to administer the drugs. Physicians might assist in a variety of ways. They might provide the means for suicide, provide information about it, or refer the patient to the Hemlock Society for information."[21]

The clearest way to distinguish between these acts may be in terms of who acts last. In physician-assisted suicide, the patient is the last causal actor; in euthanasia, the doctor is. Suppose a competent patient voluntarily requests assistance in dying and his doctor supplies him with a pill that produces death. If the patient voluntarily swallows it, the death is physician-assisted, since the doctor has supplied the means of death; but the doctor has not forced the patient to swallow the pill or otherwise coerced the death that ensues.[22]

Treatment options for the gravely ill person include the refusal of treatment by the patient, the withdrawal of treatment, the withholding of treatment, palliative sedation, ordinary versus extraordinary treatment, reasonable or unreasonable interventions as defined by the illness or the individual patient. "Active euthanasia and assisted suicide are usually distinguished from withholding or withdrawing interventions, which are also termed 'allowing to die' or 'passive euthanasia.' Ethically and legally, medical interventions may be withheld or withdrawn if a competent patient or

20. Bernard Lo, *Resolving Ethical Dilemmas: A Guide for Clinicians*, 2nd ed. (New York: Lippincott, Williams and Wilkins, 2000), p. 156.

21. Lo, *Resolving Ethical Dilemmas*, p. 156.

22. Frey, "Passive Death," p. 200.

an appropriate surrogate refuses them. A patient's refusal of life-sustaining treatment is honored because patients have a right to be free of unwanted bodily invasions. Under such circumstances, the underlying *illness,* not the action or inaction of the *physician,* is considered the cause of death. Therefore concern that assisted suicide or active euthanasia is improper should not lead physicians to impose interventions that are not wanted by the patient or surrogate."[23]

The Metaquestions

In analyzing the ethical questions concerning discontinuing life-support technologies, physician-assisted suicide, and the withdrawal of food and water, we observe that they need to be within a framework of the underlying questions. Theology deals with ultimate meaning and purpose and can assist us in placing these deep questions of life into perspective. These metaquestions concern our views of life; who is dying; views of death; the distinction between the process of dying and the state of death; how death occurs; and the patient-physician relationship.

Views of Life   The different views of life that I discussed in chapter 1 vary, from an absolutist perspective (vitalism: life is good at any cost with no qualifiers); a prima facie value (life is good but can be laid aside for higher values); or a relative value (life is good only if a certain level of existence is possible). All serious moral theories place a high value on life, so that the burden of proof is on those who want to disregard or override this value. However, there is a great diversity of perspectives that influence one's position on end-of-life choices.

A backdrop to our view of life is the question of the degree of recovery possible for the seriously ill person. Is it restoration to a fully autonomous, rational life, or is it life where relationships are still possible and care can be received? As Roman Catholic moral theologian Richard McCormick has pointed out, what we mean by recovery is a problem. It can mean at least three things: (1) return to a full state of health; (2) return to a lesser state perhaps with severe physical or mental disturbance; (3) return to vital functions without consciousness. Those who hold an absolute value for life would advocate treatment of the patient if any of these three levels were

23. Lo, *Resolving Ethical Dilemmas,* p. 157.

possible, whereas those who want a very high quality of life would not accept treatment if it only meant the third category.[24] Related to this point is the concept of futile treatment, which I discuss in greater detail later in this chapter.

Who Is Dying?

Our view of who is dying can influence our position on these issues. For those who use a criterion of personhood, some deaths are more acceptable than others. Should it make any difference — morally speaking — whether it is an eight-cell embryo in a Petri dish, a fetus at three months of gestation, a newly born spina bifida baby, a comatose patient, a severely mentally challenged adult, a twenty-year-old Rhodes scholar, or a forty-year-old mother of four children who is dying? Of course, if we hold a theological position of the dignity and worth of each person as a child of God, these distinctions are not meaningful and none would be candidates for euthanasia. If we contrast several ethicists' positions on human life, we can see how those positions affect their positions on euthanasia.

Tristram Engelhardt makes a distinction between human biological life and human personal life. Fetuses, infants, and the comatose are not persons because they are not rational and self-conscious. Children have a higher value because of their social role. Hence, if a handicapped newborn is dying, surrogate refusal — or withdrawal of treatment — is permissible as long as the parent decides it in light of a cost-benefit analysis and as long as such an act does not threaten the value of the "child" per se.[25] This is different from stopping futile treatment, since Engelhardt's criterion is based on a concept of the social person.

Richard McCormick believes that all human life has value, but that physical life may not be the best place to realize that value if there is no longer any potential for human relationships. Since the essence of being human is living in relationship, if the person can no longer experience re-

24. Richard McCormick, "To Save or Let Die: The Dilemma of Modern Medicine," in *Contemporary Issues in Bioethics*, ed. Tom L. Beauchamp and LeRoy Walters (Belmont, CA: Wadsworth, 1978), pp. 331-37.

25. Tristram Engelhardt, Jr., "Ethical Issues in Aiding the Death of Young Children," in *Beneficent Euthanasia*, ed. Marvin Kohl (Buffalo, NY: Prometheus Books, 1975), pp. 180-92; see also Engelhardt, *The Foundations of Bioethics* (New York: Oxford University Press, 1986).

lationships, a choice of no treatment is morally permissible, and it is a necessary evil.[26]

Paul Ramsey holds that all human life is of equal value and worth and thus is not dependent on any criteria of personhood or humanity. Life and death are gifts of God, and we deny our humanity if we make death decisions for ourselves or others. Passive euthanasia is only justified (though Ramsey would use the term "cessation of treatment" instead) if the person is in the process of dying. This would not be considered a decision for death based on the quality of life, but would be a choice of how to die based on medical indications.[27] Ramsey makes a good point that the question is not *who* is dying, but rather the fact *that* they are dying, that determines our view of refusal of treatment. Every human life is of infinite worth. Therefore, decisions for treatment should not be based on an assessment of personhood, but on medical considerations of diagnosis and benefits and burdens for the good of the patient.

Views of Death   In chapter 2, I discussed perspectives on death that influence our stance on these issues. Is death good, evil, or morally neutral? Is it a friend or an enemy, the end of all existence or a gateway to eternal life? First, death is a mystery that we can never totally comprehend; it is beyond our ability to encompass it completely within our rational explanations. For those who believe in immortality or future resurrection, death is a good, because both of these states are better than our physical one: the sooner we get from the physical realm to the immortal, the better. Others view death as freeing our souls from the prison of the body (the Greek view), or freeing them to unite with God (some parts of Pauline theology), but they differ from Paul's concept of the resurrection. For others, viewing death as good is to see it as a natural part of the process of life, not something to be feared. Like Heidegger, those see the specter of death as providing an urgency and purposefulness to life.[28]

However, many people view death as evil. It is the cessation of all that we could be, an end to human existence and to all we hold dear. Death as an enemy has also been part of the Christian perspective: that is,

26. McCormick, "To Save or Let Die."

27. Paul Ramsey, *The Patient as Person* (New Haven: Yale University Press, 2002), pp. 124-44.

28. Martin Heidegger, *Being and Time: A Translation of Sein und Zeit* (Albany: State University of New York Press, 1996).

it is the last enemy that Christ had to conquer (1 Cor. 15). Thus does the Christian see death as both friend and foe: because Christ has conquered it, we can look forward to eternal life (see chapter 12 for a further discussion of these concepts). On the other hand, if life is a primary good, then physical death is an evil, though physical pain and suffering can make death seem welcome. In such a case, the irony is not that we want to cease to be but that we want the suffering to stop. "But the creative tension of death also precludes active euthanasia or assisted suicide. Euthanasia advocates have embraced death as friend but have lost sight of death as enemy. They have too readily embraced death as being merely the natural end of life. Euthanasia proponents not only usurp God's sovereign control over life and death, but fail to recognize that death is a powerful, mysterious enemy that is not welcomed without qualification. It fails not only to affirm the biblical teaching regarding the 'last great enemy' which will one day be destroyed, but to acknowledge the experience of people in the face of death."[29]

Still a third position is that death is morally neutral. It is a state of nonbeing, which includes the absence of pain and pleasure, and it is a natural event that takes place when it should. If life is absurd, as some existentialists hold, then death removes that absurdity and meaninglessness.

Death is an undesired state, and it is to be held at bay as long as suffering does not overwhelm us. If life is of primary value, we should beware of rushing into the arms of euthanasia as some sort of savior. However, we should remove pain and suffering whenever possible and accept the fact that physical mortality is our destiny — but that it is overcome by Jesus Christ's resurrection.

The Distinction Between the Process of Dying and the State of Death

The neurological standard for the determination of death was under fire shortly after the Brain Death Criteria by Harvard were put into place in 1968. (I discuss the legal aspects of brain death in the chapter on legal issues.) "There is controversy as well about the use of the traditional cardiopulmonary standard in the organ procurement practice known as 'controlled donation after cardiac death' (controlled DCD). Here, too, there is debate about whether, at the time that organs are taken, the donor is truly dead. But, with controlled DCD, there is also a more acute danger

---

29. Dennis Hollinger, "Theological Foundations for Death and Dying Issues," *Ethics and Medicine* 12, no. 3 (1996): 62.

that the quality of end-of-life care for the patient-donor will be compromised."[30] These concerns arise to some degree because of the lack of clarity between the process of dying and the state of death. In December 2008, the President's Council on Bioethics upheld brain death criteria but provided a better philosophical rationale than its 1981 forerunner commission did. The problems of defining life and death are both clinical and philosophical, and as Hans Jonas has argued, the intrinsic connection between the empirical realities of biological death and the conceptual framework is too weak to provide the moral grounds for the removal of organs.

Edmund Pellegrino proceeds to critique the philosophical definitions of death, which all lack empirical precision, that is, the verification of the loss of integrative functions, inability to engage with the environment through spontaneous breathing, total loss of conscious mental capacity (here death of the organism is tied to the death of one organ, that is, the brain), and the separation of soul and body. Determination of death should not be tied to decisions about donation of organs, and Pellegrino warns of the dangers of Veatch and Truog's position that we abandon death criteria as necessary for decisions about taking organs and instead use the expressed preferences of the patient to donate. Questions of treatment and nontreatment have become part of the debates about determining death, but the recognition of medical futility is not abandonment of the patient; clinical futile treatment can, in fact, "convert beneficence into maleficence." The value of a treatment should always be weighed, and the subject's family should be part of the decision whenever possible.

> The consensus position (of the President's Council on Bioethics in 2008) for using a neurological standard to determine death in the United States may be stated in this way: "Whole brain death" — but no other sort of injury that leaves circulation and respiration intact — is an appropriate standard for determining the death of a human being.
>
> A question addressed by the Council is, "Does a diagnosis of 'whole brain death' mean that the human being is dead?" That is to say, the central question is not, "Does a diagnosis of 'whole brain death' mean that the human being is eligible to be a heart-beating organ donor?"

30. Information in this and the following three paragraphs from "Controversies in the Determination of Death: A White Paper by the President's Council on Bioethics," The President's Council on Bioethics, Washington, DC, December 2008, p. 1: www.bioethics.gov.

However, a few Council members argued that there was sufficient uncertainty about the neurological standard to warrant an alternative approach to the care of the "brain dead" human being, and the question of organ procurement or an alternative was the cessation of a heartbeat and brain death.[31]

Besides determining the time of death, a distinction is needed between the process of dying and the state of death. The conflating of death and dying has led to misunderstanding about euthanasia. There are also differences between prolonging dying and extending life. First, extending life is concerned with using life-support measures for a patient who would otherwise shortly die. So at this point the patient is not in the process of dying and there is hope for recovery. Thus the cessation of treatment is not indicated. As Hans Jonas has pointed out, the new technologies have given us a way of sustaining life but no new ways of determining death.

> We do not know with certainty the borderline between life and death, and a definition cannot substitute for knowledge. Moreover, we have sufficient grounds for suspecting that the artificially supported condition of the comatose patient may still be one of life, however reduced — i.e., for doubting that, even with the brain function gone, he is completely dead. . . . I see lurking behind the proposed definition of death, apart from its obvious pragmatic motivation, a curious remnant of the old soul-body dualism. Its new apparition is the dualism of brain and body. . . . The body is as uniquely the body of this brain and no other, as the brain is uniquely the brain of this body and no other.[32]

Another important concern is the prolonging of dying. Paul Ramsey distinguished between those who are already in an irretrievable process of dying and those whose lives are being extended. His emphasis is that we should be about dying well, which entails choosing the way we live until we die, not choosing the means or end of death. It is from this perspective that he wants to outlaw the use of the word "euthanasia," either passive or active, because etymologically it means a good death, while our concern is dying well *(euapothnēskō)*.[33] Stopping treatment for comatose patients

31. Edmund D. Pellegrino, Chairman, President's Council on Bioethics, Letter of Transmittal to the President.

32. Hans Jonas, "Against the Stream: Comments on the Definition and Redefinition of Death," in *Contemporary Issues in Bioethics*, ed. Beauchamp and Walters, pp. 265-66.

33. Paul Ramsey, *Ethics at the Edges of Life* (New Haven: Yale University Press, 1978).

does not mean that we are practicing passive euthanasia, because we are not choosing the means or ends of death; instead, we are merely moving from curative to caring treatment. What this really boils down to is that, if dying well is a possibility, as in a hospice (free of most pain, etc.), euthanasia is never a question — because that would be an admission of defeat.

How Death Occurs   I will discuss the determination and means of death extensively in the chapter on legal issues and in another section of this present chapter. Death can be by natural causes, caused by someone else (a range of categories), or suicide (self-killing). How death occurs is of special interest to the law and those who use the principle of double effect. (For example, the intent of large doses of morphine is to ease pain, not to cause death.)

Patient-Physician Relationship   In addition, questions concerning death and dying should be viewed within the patient-physician relationship. The covenant relationship of patient and physician entails certain duties arising from this special relationship. These duties are concerned with both medical and ethical areas. Medically, the best procedures and resources and knowledge that a physician has at his or her disposal should be used. Ethically, these duties involve truth-telling, confidentiality, procuring informed consent, and respect for persons; it is marked by trust, fidelity, and honesty. Growing out of this relationship, acts of beneficence as well as nonmaleficence *(primum non nocere)* are to be practiced. Decisions on the care for the dying are within this context. It seems that the doctor should work toward improving the quality of life, not hastening its end. Furthermore, one of the central principles governing this covenant is at least the prima facie — if not the primary — value of preserving life. If the maintenance of life is laid aside for other values, the burden of proof and justification rests on the one who does this.

If in the care of patients it is true that life is a primary good, then death — that is, the end of life — can never be good. In the dying process, we need to look for the best ways to die: with grace and dignity, as free from pain as possible, surrounded by those who love us, and receiving the best medical care available. It is not good death but good dying that should be our goal. Of course, for people of faith there are also the possibilities of remissions, cures, and miracles.

The rights of the patient and the duties of the physician must be held in a creative tension. The doctor is not simply the instrument of the patient, à la Aristotle, where doctors are animated tools. If the patient is com-

71

petent, rational, and autonomous, based on the principle of respect for persons, it is morally permissible for him or her to refuse any treatment, even if it is life-sustaining. Furthermore, the physician must provide information that leads to informed consent, which logically entails the right of refusal. However, this decision needs to be made with respect to the principle of the value of life, which is always invoked in the midst of the decision process concerning treatment; in fact, a tension constantly exists between these two principles.

We have a right to choose the way we live while dying, but do we have the right to choose death itself? This perspective, in a way, raises the moral status of patient autonomy. It is on this point that ethicists strongly disagree. For example, Beauchamp, Veatch, Singer, and others would label this an overarching principle, whereas Ramsey, Pellegrino, and others argue that the patient's autonomy should be limited if she demands treatment the doctor deems harmful or violates the doctor's values. In one sense a patient's autonomy does not override that of the physician's. Furthermore, as a partner in the covenant relationship, the physician has a duty of beneficence and nonmaleficence that generally falls on the side of preserving life. The physician on her side must also be assured that the patient is giving a valid and informed consent to either refuse or cease curative treatment while knowing all the consequences.

Bowen Hosford and others have pointed out that often patients are not given full information.

> Under the ethical principle of autonomy and the legal maxim that people can control treatment for their own bodies, the resolution of many ethical dilemmas should be easy. Health care providers need merely ask the patients. But some of them shrink from revealing to people that they might die. I attended a discussion concerning a respirator-dependent, 61-year-old man, who was affected by drugs and depression and was only intermittently lucid. Was he competent during the lucid periods to make his own decision on whether a DNR order should be entered, and if so could such a decision remain effective when he was not lucid?
>
> But the suggestion to a patient that it is time to die is not necessarily repugnant. Dr. Eric J. Cassell, a New York internist and frequent writer on ethical aspects of medicine, described that in *The Healer's Art.* "It is possible to suggest to the patient that the time has come to leave, but at the same time it is necessary to reassure him that it is all right to leave

and that it is not going to hurt. We are all afraid of unknown pain, but things rarely hurt as much as we thought they were going to. When this is explained to a patient, the doctor is amazed to discover that the patient becomes more peaceful; that pain, if present, becomes less severe and more bearable; and that within a relatively short time, the patient dies."[34]

Patients may not have perfect mental faculties, but they can still make rational decisions. For example, at Dartmouth-Hitchcock Medical Center, a 67-year-old farmer with malignant melanoma refused additional surgery and chemotherapy after earlier treatment had been unsuccessful. His competence was in question, because he had had two strokes that left him unable to do mental calculations as well as before, and he had trouble remembering recent events.[35] The question is, should his choices still be honored?

Together the patient and physician, when the irreversible process of dying has begun, have a duty to seek the care that will ensure the least pain and the greatest dignity and respect for the patient. If the competent patient refuses lifesaving treatment and dies, those cases may fall within the category of refusal of treatment, not passive euthanasia, since it is an act of the patient himself. This is distinguished from suicide, where the patient is the agent of his own death. A physician who accedes to the patient's request to cease treatment is not involved in euthanasia, but is simply allowing the patient to die, which is both legally and morally accepted by the American Medical Association. However, if the patient requests the physician or another person to kill him by a direct act, for example, by air in the veins, this is active euthanasia and not morally or legally justifiable within the patient-physician relationship. (I will discuss physician-assisted suicide further in the next chapter.)

On the other hand, if a patient is incompetent or of diminished autonomy, she should be protected at all costs. Only when a living will has previously been written by the patient when competent, or a physician or relative or friend can bring corroborated oral testimony that she did not want extraordinary treatment if she was in the irreversible process of dying, can life-sustaining treatment be withheld or stopped.

However, if the wishes of the incompetent or never-competent patient are unknown, the need to protect the defenseless — based on the sanc-

34. Bowen Hosford, *Bioethics Committees: The Health Care Provider's Guide* (Rockville, MD: Aspen Publications, 1986), p. 246.
35. Hosford, *Bioethics Committees*, p. 247.

tity of life — and the difficulty of applying the reasonable person standard make it neither morally nor legally justifiable to withhold lifesaving treatment from him unless he meets the brain-death criteria. (But the Saikewicz case, discussed in the legal chapter, did allow no treatment absent the brain-death criteria.) In cases of the competent or incompetent patient, it is not permissible to withdraw palliative care, even if treatment is problematic.

Distinctions in the Debate

Having reflected on the metaquestions that frame the debate concerning end-of-life choices, we will now return to their distinctions. Since controversy surrounds these terms — especially "euthanasia," as Ramsey suggests — it may be impossible to use them any longer in moral analysis. However, it is worth exploring if there is any meaningful distinction between them and how these differences affect our assessment of the morality of various acts. (The next chapter will analyze suicide and physician-assisted suicide in more depth.)

Types of Euthanasia

Direct/Indirect = Active/Passive   We will begin by analyzing the acts involved. A person's death in this analysis of euthanasia can happen in these ways: against his desire; without his consent; or at his request. Bringing about another's death against his desire would be active, involuntary euthanasia. Withdrawal of treatment without a person's consent would be passive, involuntary euthanasia.

Some people support passive euthanasia, based on respect for persons. The rationale is that it allows the patient dignity in the process of dying, and does not prolong it. The intent is not to bring about the patient's death but to change the circumstances in which the process of dying takes place: the presence of loved ones, not machines, and allowing the patient as much autonomy as possible. When treatment is stopped, the physician has not chosen death for the patient but the termination of treatment. However, passive euthanasia is different from termination of treatment, since this practice can be without the patient's request. The term "euthanasia" should not be used for refusal or withdrawal of treatment, since that obscures the difference between these acts.

In euthanasia, the intention is to directly terminate the life of the patient. Death would not take place "at that moment" without someone directly causing it. However, administering high levels of morphine in cases of extreme pain in the final hours of life in order to hasten a patient's death is not euthanasia. In Roman Catholic theology, the agent's motivation is the crucial point when applying the principle of double effect.[36] This principle is complex, as Daniel Sulmasy has eloquently argued. Although intentions are morally relevant, if the specific intention of an action is that another should die, then it is morally reprehensible, except in cases of direct self-defense or rescue. This is a distinction with a difference. Ectopic pregnancy termination is not the application of the principle of double effect but of self-defense or rescue, that is, rescuing the mother.[37] Physician-assisted suicide and euthanasia are, therefore, never justified under the principle of double effect.

Commission/Omission = Killing/Allowing to Die The moral difference between these acts is between acts of omission and commission. Omission is the failure to perform a certain act: in this situation, not connecting life-support systems or other medical treatment. (It is debatable whether supplying food and water is considered treatment, as I have noted in the disagreements in the Cruzan case in the legal chapter.) Acts of omission are labeled passive euthanasia, or letting die. Commission is a positive action: that is, it is an active intervention to bring about another person's death, and acts of commission are labeled killing, or active euthanasia.

Philosopher Peter Singer and others suggest that there is no great moral difference between the act and the omission because: (1) we must take responsibility for what we do, and a decision to do something or the decision not to do something are both decisions; (2) our intuition that there is a difference between allowing to die and killing is not reliable; (3) the avoidance of suffering must take precedence over the prohibition

36. "Nature and Content of the Rule of Double Effect. Although variously formulated, the traditional rule of double effect specifies that an action with 2 possible effects, one good and one bad, is morally permitted if the action: (1) is not in itself immoral, (2) is undertaken only with the intention of achieving the possible good effect, without intending the possible bad effect even though it may be foreseen, (3) does not bring about the possible good effect by means of the possible bad effect, and (4) is undertaken for a proportionally grave reason." Daniel Sulmasy, "The Rule of Double Effect," American Medical Association, *Archives of Internal Medicine* 159 (Mar. 22, 1999): 545.

37. Sulmasy, "Killing and Allowing to Die," pp. 8-9, 11, 418-19.

against killing.[38] One can question this position because of the different moral intents of the agent. The passive/active distinction in euthanasia may not be morally irrefutable, as Singer, Rachels, and others have suggested. However, it can be crucial — psychologically and socially — to a good patient/physician relationship. Furthermore, simply wanting someone dead is not the only morally relevant point: our reason for wanting them dead may be what is morally objectionable as well as legally relevant.

James Rachels agrees with Singer that there is no significant moral difference between killing and allowing to die. He offers three reasons for this position: (1) it leads to less humane decisions than might otherwise be the case (cruel and prolonged death); (2) it leads to a decision on morally irrelevant grounds; (3) the "bare difference," that is, the motive is of no moral importance. The form of this argument involves considering two imaginary cases in which there are no morally relevant differences present, save the "bare difference": that is, one is a case of killing and the other of letting die. Rachels uses the now famous illustration of Smith and his cousin. Smith stands to inherit money from a six-year-old cousin, who drowns in a bathtub. In the one scenario Smith pushes his cousin's head under the water and the cousin dies. In the other scenario, Smith stands by and watches his cousin drown. Rachels argues that the intent of the agent is identical in both cases, that is, for the cousin to be dead.[39]

Tom Beauchamp responds to Rachels's position, saying that the latter has not proved that the distinction is not relevant. First, Beauchamp points out, the active-versus-passive difference may not always be morally relevant; but sometimes it is, and thus society should continue to use this distinction. Second, Rachels's analysis only applies to relevantly similar cases, such as the drowning or letting drown of the cousin in the bathtub, whose death produces a gain for the agent involved. Beauchamp questions whether most cases of active/passive euthanasia really involve gain for the agent. Using a utilitarian calculus, we can show that passive euthanasia is preferable because, in view of medical fallibility, we would lose fewer patients. (A case in point is that of Karen Ann Quinlan: if air had been injected into her veins instead of taking her off the respirator, she would have died instead of lingering on for a decade.) In other words, medical fallibility supports the passive or let-die approach as being morally better.

---

38. Peter Singer, *Writings on the Ethical Life* (New York: Ecco Press, 2000), pp. 105-235.

39. James Rachels, "Active and Passive Euthanasia," in *Contemporary Issues in Bioethics*, ed. Beauchamp and Walters, pp. 291-94.

Beauchamp concedes that Rachels's third point, the "bare difference," does not matter because it is the justifying reasons and not the active/passive distinction that determine the morality of the act.[40]

Beauchamp's argument seems persuasive because the justifying reasons are what are crucial, especially within the physician-patient relationship. If a doctor's patient is dying and the former prefers to play bridge, hence not responding to a call to go to the hospital, and hence the patient dies, then she has done a wrong act — even if it is not killing but letting die. On the other hand, if the doctor passes an accident victim along the highway, she is not liable. It is morally permissible for her to do it, but it is not morally praiseworthy. This is the same distinction I made earlier between causing and permitting harm. Others enter this debate by saying that this distinction is crucial, but allowing someone to die, so to speak, is only justifiable if it is the result of withholding futile treatment. (I will discuss futile treatment later in this chapter.)

The justifying reasons for committing an act are crucial, especially within the physician-patient relationship. To a lesser degree, doctors who refuse to accept HIV patients and nurses who ignore the hospital room buzzer of a difficult patient have also done something morally wrong. These acts are not strictly immoral, but they are ethically suspect and are certainly not conducive to engendering trust in the health care provider–patient relationship. On the other hand, if a doctor injects a lethal dose of morphine into his patient, as in the "It's Over, Debbie" case reported in *The Journal of the American Medical Association,* then the doctor may be morally and legally culpable of murder.[41]

Arguments in Support of Active Euthanasia

As we examine the distinctions between types of euthanasia, we find some classic arguments for the moral legitimacy of active euthanasia:

40. Tom Beauchamp and James Childress, *Principles of Biomedical Ethics* (New York: Oxford University Press, 1979), pp. 107-9. The 4th edition of this book (1994) explores both the differences and similarities to killing and allowing to die and concludes about the difference between the two: "Rightness and wrongness depend on the merit of the justification underlying the action, not on the type of action it is" (p. 225).

41. Anonymous, "It's Over, Debbie," *Journal of the American Medical Association* 259, no. 2 (Jan. 8, 1988): 272. "It's Over, Debbie" is a brief first-person narrative in which a gynecology resident, called to the emergency room for a patient painfully dying of ovarian cancer, administers a dose of morphine that brings about her death.

Individual liberty: the right of free choice, that is, autonomy; the right to die; the right to act as though it does not harm anyone else, including the right to choose the time I die — even if it is by someone else's hand.

The loss of human dignity: If one's quality of life is so diminished due to pain, deterioration of bodily processes, or becoming an extreme burden to others, then ending one's life is the right course of action. Baroness Warnock's proposal in this regard caused a firestorm of criticism.

> The influential medical ethics expert Baroness Warnock has caused a furor by suggesting in an interview in the Church of Scotland's magazine *Life and Work* that elderly people suffering from dementia should consider ending their lives because they are a burden on the NHS and their families. She said that people in mental decline are wasting people's lives because of the care they require and should be allowed to opt for euthanasia even if they are not in pain and that there is nothing wrong with people being helped to die for the sake of their loved ones or society. Her comments were criticized by MPs, charities and campaigners. Neil Hunt, the chief executive of the Alzheimer's Society, said: "I am shocked and amazed that Baroness Warnock could disregard the value of the lives of people with dementia so callously. With the right care, a person can have good quality of life very late into dementia. To suggest that people with dementia shouldn't be entitled to that quality of life or that they should feel that they have some sort of duty to kill themselves is nothing short of barbaric."[42]

Prevention of cruelty. If the patient's suffering is protracted and unendurable, with no hope of recovery, then euthanasia is a duty. The purpose is to end the pain. This argument is related to the one made from mercy, that if someone is in excruciating pain and hopelessly injured, we should put her out of her pain. Sarah Bachelard, among others, believes that this is a spurious argument because it overlooks the power of human community, which is very different from empirical capacities that can be shared by humans.[43]

Peaceful death. A person should be able to choose the time of his dying, that is, negotiated death, so he can have a death to his liking if he is suf-

---

42. "Dementia sufferers may have a 'duty to die,'" News Update, November 2008, email from Leveson Link: leveson-link-bounces@gn.apc.org (accessed Dec. 1, 2008).

43. Sarah Bachelard, "On Euthanasia: Blindspots in the Argument from Mercy," *Journal of Applied Philosophy* 19, no. 2 (Aug. 2002): 131.

fering through a painful and terminal illness. The recent case of Sir Downes described in the legal chapter is an illustration of this moral argument.[44]

Proponents of active euthanasia point to the success of the Netherlands policy of active euthanasia, with its side constraints, both legal and self-regulated by health professionals, which has protected against possible abuses. (Of course, in the last few years more data has emerged that attests to the growing abuses of this policy; I will discuss this in greater depth in the legal chapter.)

The pro and con arguments concerning euthanasia are supplemented by several additional options that are currently being discussed: voluntarily stopping eating and drinking (VSED), terminal sedation (TS), physician-assisted suicide (PAS), and voluntary active euthanasia (VAE). The question is whether there are any moral differences between these practices. Some believe that the distinctions are crucial, others that they are inconsequential. In other words, if the person wants to be dead, should we not make this possible as swiftly and painlessly as possible? The medical profession, on the whole, thinks that there is a difference both legally and morally, since "it is generally legally impermissible for physicians to participate in physician-assisted suicide (PAS) or voluntary active euthanasia (VAE) in response to such patient requests. The recent Supreme Court decisions that determined that there is no constitutional right to PAS placed great emphasis on the importance of relieving pain and suffering near the end of life but gave states rights in this arena (hence three states' approval of PAS). The Court acknowledged the legal acceptability of providing pain relief, even to the point of hastening death if necessary, and left open the possibility that states might choose to legalize PAS under some circumstances."[45] However, VSED, TS, PAS, and VAE are considered interventions of last resort for competent, terminally ill patients who are suffering intolerably in spite of intensive efforts to palliate and who desire a hastened death.[46]

As one explores these alternatives, they appear less and less desirable. Why are we in this situation of needing to decide among a series of options, each one worse than the last? British philosopher Luke Gormally ar-

44. John F. Burns, "With Help, Conductor and Wife Ended Lives," *The New York Times online*, July 15, 2009, p. A4: http://www.nytimes.com/2009/07/15/world/europe/15britain.html (accessed July 21, 2009).

45. Timothy E. Quill, Bernard Lo, and Dan W. Brock, "Palliative Options of Last Resort," *Journal of the American Medical Association* 278, no. 23 (Dec. 17, 1997): 2099-2100.

46. Quill, Lo, and Brock, "Palliative Options of Last Resort."

gues that "acceptance of the practice of voluntary euthanasia in our society would be a significant further step in the direction of barbarism: voluntary euthanasia = intentional killing of a patient in the course of medical care."[47] Words such as "euthanasia is killing and barbarism" have more or less set the terms of the debate.

Theologians as distinguished as Hans Küng argue against the position that "[p]eople must endure to their 'ordained end.' What end is ordained? Does God really control the reduction of human life to purely biological life?"[48] In *Dying with Dignity* (1995), Küng recommended the Swiss position on active euthanasia to relieve suffering. This is not an argument such as Peter Singer's — that somehow persons become nonpersons or less human — but rather that they have the right to a dignified dying: what some people call killing, others call compassion. In the United States, three states — Oregon, Montana, and Washington — that allow physician-assisted suicide have called their legislation "Death with Dignity Act."

The Nature of Medical Treatment for the Seriously Ill

The second category in end-of-life issues is the nature of treatment. Is it extraordinary or ordinary, unreasonable or reasonable? Also, there are now distinctions made between palliative and terminal sedation, and how both of them differ from euthanasia. Are these differences morally justifiable?[49] Here we are not equating refusal or withdrawal of treatment with passive euthanasia. In addition, there are distinctions among the withholding, the withdrawing, and the refusal of treatment. In 1988, the British Medical Association report against euthanasia did not condone intentional killing by omission as morally wrong, such as that of severely handicapped infants being deprived of hydration so that they would not be a "lingering survivor."[50] In Britain there is confusion about the definition of terms, which downplays advance directives and misunderstands them as

47. Nigel Cameron, ed., *Death Without Dignity* (Edinburgh: Rutherford House, 1990), pp. 48-49.

48. Hans Küng and Walter Jens, *A Dignified Dying*, trans. John Bowden (London: SCM Press, 1995), p. 26.

49. Simon Woods, *Death's Dominion: Ethics at the End of Life*, in the series *Translations in End of Life: Hospice*, ed. David Clark (Berkshire, UK: Open University Press, 2007), p. xiv.

50. Cameron, *Death Without Dignity*, p. 64.

tools of euthanasia rather than as statements of treatment options. Britain has failed to pass an aid-in-dying bill, partly due to the problematic nature of the British definitions. Some prefer the term *kalothasia* ("beautiful death," from *kalos,* meaning beautiful), which is referred to as "collateral euthanasia," or collateral *kalothanasia*.[51]

Treatment Options

Treatment vs. Nontreatment   Ethicists have outlined criteria for the treatment and nontreatment of patients. Joseph Fletcher emphasized a loving act for the patient, the quality of life, as well as the degree of suffering. Richard McCormick justified withdrawal or refusal of treatment when the potential for human relationships is gone. Paul Ramsey's criteria for the cessation of treatment was when the patient was in the irretrievable process of dying, but he insisted on equality of life rather than quality of life as grounds for stopping treatment.

Refusal or Withdrawal of Treatment   Our discussion so far has focused on the act, but the agent is equally important. Many people believe that the wishes of the patient are the only morally relevant point in the distinction between euthanasia and refusal of treatment. The refusal of treatment has several facets: the patient's right of self-determination, a proxy decision where consent is not possible, or presumed consent (infants or mentally incompetent). Refusal of treatment refers to the patient's decision for herself, whereas euthanasia is an act performed on behalf of the patient, even if asked by her. Of course, one of the recently debated issues is that of executive decision-making: for example, where patients may be competent to choose what food they want but are not judged competent to choose whether they want lifesaving surgery. This seems to be a slippery slope that can take away the patient's right to make medical decisions. Since suicide is also a personal decision, is it morally the same as refusal of treatment? Refusal of lifesaving treatment is not the moral equivalent of suicide, because the result is not certain, that is, death.

The other category of refusal is proxy refusal of treatment, for instance, for a child by his parents, or by a health-durable power of attorney for an incompetent person. There are legal precedents for proxy consent

---

51. Barry Clark, "Killing with Kindness," p. 40.

for cessation of treatment. Proxy refusal of treatment is only morally justifiable in limited circumstances that are in the patient's best interests or wishes. These circumstances include: those who are beyond the reach of care; those who previously expressed a desire not to receive extraordinary treatment; those who are in the irretrievable and certain process of dying.

"Refusal of treatment" is an unhappy phrase, because what it really means is having control over our dying process. Terminal patients may accept pain medication and food and water, but not a respirator or the twentieth surgery, which they view as prolonging their dying. Hence, refusal of treatment is concerned with the process of dying, while suicide is an act of death itself. Even the Roman Catholic Church affirmed the right to refuse treatment, while it did not, of course, endorse euthanasia.[52]

It is interesting to note that the Patient's Bill of Rights (1972) does not refer to a right to die, but to the right to refuse lifesaving therapy. Judge Cardozo, in *Schloendorff v. the Society of New York Hospital*, referred to the right to determine what will be done to one's body. The Natural Death Act of California (1976) specifically denies that it establishes any precedent for mercy killing, but establishes only the right to refuse certain lifesaving therapies when a person has a terminal disease. The advance directives legislation in other states is similar. These legal documents and cases do not establish the right to die, but the right to choose the process of dying.

The refusal of treatment is a relative right, that is, relative to one's condition. The right to refuse treatment is grounded in respect for persons' informed consent, autonomy, and religious beliefs. These grounds can be applied to oneself but not a third party. For example, children of Jehovah's Witnesses in recent cases have been given blood transfusions over their parents' objections.

Another aspect of the treatment question is whether it should be initiated in the first place or withdrawn without a person's consent. These latter cases arise when consent is not possible, as with newborns, young children, the comatose, persons with severe mental disabilities, and those in severe and relentless pain. The example of Dax Cowart illustrates the complexity of issues such as autonomy, paternalism, and quality of life. As the result of a freak accident in the summer of 1973, twenty-five-year-old Dax

---

52. Pope John Paul II, "Teaching on Suicide and Euthanasia," excerpted from Gospel on Life, no. 65, *Catholics for the Common Good:* http://www.ccgaction.com/index.php?q=life/euthanasia/teaching/encyclical/suicideandeuthanasia (accessed July 20, 2009).

Cowart was badly burned over 65 percent of his body. Both eyes, both ears, and both hands were damaged beyond repair. Large doses of narcotics were required for minimal pain relief. He pleaded with his caregivers to be allowed to die, and also stated several times that he wanted to kill himself. The physicians at Parkland Hospital in Texas turned to his mother to obtain consent for all his treatments, even though she was not appointed his legal guardian, and even though Dax was determined by psychiatric evaluation to have full decision-making capacity. There was a constant struggle of will between Dax and his mother. Ultimately, he recovered from the burns, albeit severely disfigured. He successfully sued the oil company responsible for his burns, which left him financially secure. Later, he attended law school at Baylor University. He attempted suicide twice after his rehabilitation period. He eventually finished law school and married. He is now apparently happy, but he still believes the doctors were wrong to follow his mother's wishes over his. However, the case advanced respect for patient autonomy all around the country.[53]

Refusal of treatment and heroic self-sacrifice are sometimes confused with suicide. Refusing treatment can be choosing a way of dying; committing suicide is choosing death. Put another way, in refusing treatment the agent is not the primary actor. The refusal of treatment may be an expression of concern on the part of the patient for the health of his or her family. Suicide, on the other hand, is often a hostile act in which a person feels that he has lost control of his life. Heroic self-sacrifice is other-regarding, involving a principle or another person, for example, dying while saving a person from a fire or from drowning in a lake.

Is suicide wrong in and of itself, or does it depend on the circumstances, that is, the intent and condition of the agent — the consequences, means, and motive? Is it justified or unjustified, rational or irrational? To some extent, our answers are influenced by what we include under the concept of suicide. Bioethicist Tom Beauchamp of Georgetown University suggests that the concept may be so bent out of shape that it is no longer usable.[54] At a minimum, we should separate it from other related concepts. The primary distinction among euthanasia, refusal of treatment, and suicide is that the last is solely at one's own hand: it is a direct act in which the primary intent is to end one's physical life.

---

53. For more on the "Dax Cowart Case," see William F. May, *The Patient's Ordeal* (Bloomington: Indiana University Press, 1991), pp. 15-35.

54. Beauchamp and Childress, *Principles of Biomedical Ethics,* p. 188.

Physician-assisted suicide is different from the above, and I will discuss it in the next chapter.

Ordinary/Extraordinary Treatment = Reasonable/Unreasonable   It is helpful to make distinctions between ordinary and extraordinary treatment. The withholding of "extraordinary" treatment should not be considered active euthanasia; but the difficulty is in how we define "extraordinary."

The distinctions between these are constantly shifting, as related to the individual patient. Even nasal-gastric feedings in some instances are considered extraordinary, as the Conroy and Barber cases (*Barber v. Superior Court of California* [1983], concerning Clarence Herbert) have established. Some refer to these as "futile treatment."[55]

Robert Veatch has suggested substituting the terms "reasonable/unreasonable" for "ordinary/extraordinary" with regard to treatment. However, this distinction may be just as arbitrary and subjective as the "ordinary/extraordinary" terms. How can we extrapolate based on the perspective of a rational adult about what would be reasonable for a newborn or person with severe mental disabilities?

Futile Treatment   In discussing different categories of treatment, Pellegrino and others remind us of the long-standing category of futile treatment.[56] Whether initiating or sustaining interventions for dying patients will serve their good is the criterion for treatment. However, when cure is no longer possible, care, comfort, and relief of pain and suffering are still a moral obligation.[57] The public's dual fear of under- or overtreatment has caused us to neglect this category of futile treatment. Assessment of futility depends on answering these questions: "Will the proposed inter-

55. Pat Milmoe McCarrick, "Withholding or Withdrawing Nutrition or Hydration," *Barber/Nejdl v. Superior Court of Los Angeles County,* 147 Cal. App. 3d 1006,195 Cal. Rptr. 484 (1983), "III. Court Cases," Scope Note 7 (first published Nov. 1986, last revised 1988), National Reference Center for Bioethics Literature, Kennedy Institute, Georgetown University, p. 5: http://bioethics.georgetown.edu/publications/scopenotes/sn7.pdf (accessed July 21, 2009).

56. For a discussion of the history of the concept, see Edmund D. Pellegrino, "Decisions at the End of Life: The Use and Abuse of the Concept of Futility," in *The Dignity of the Dying Person,* Proceedings of the Fifth Assembly of the Pontifical Academy for Life (Feb. 24-27, 1999), ed. Juan De Dios Vial Correa and Elio Sgreccia (Vatican City: Libreria Editrice Vaticano, 2000), pp. 219-41.

57. E. D. Pellegrino, "Futility in Medical Decisions: The Word and the Concept," *HEC Forum* 17, no. 4 (2005): 308.

vention be effective? Will it be beneficial, and will the burdens imposed by the intervention be justified if the desired end is attained?"[58] The partnership of physician, patient, and family should make this assessment. As Pellegrino has pointed out, Pope Pius XII anticipated these problems by declaring that treatments that were extraordinary and excessively burdensome could be withdrawn under certain circumstances. Pellegrino uses this term not as a moral principle but as a prudential clinical judgment, that is, the inability of a treatment to achieve its purpose. Pellegrino advocates a balance between the three criteria of effectiveness, benefit, and burden.[59]

There are, however, certain dangers of the abuse and misuse of futility, which include: abandonment by doctors; vulnerability of patients to political and economic agendas that co-opt the futility principles; misuse of the concept to justify physician-assisted suicide and euthanasia; the application of this diagnosis too quickly, that is, without time for the family to adjust to the reality of what is happening.[60] This is a question of determining when attempts to continue treatment are no longer indicated. The inability to make these determinations created tragedies like the Nancy Cruzan case (see the legal issues chapter). A more recent question about treatment concerns palliative and terminal sedation. Is this treatment or passive euthanasia?

Palliative/Terminal Sedation   Terminal sedation (TS) is controversial because doctors are unsure if it is painless or whether the patient in his unconscious state is unable to communicate about his pain.[61] In terminal sedation, patients are put into a deep coma with the continuous infusion of phenobarbital. They may be awakened or not after it has been initiated. Palliative sedation actually means the sedating of the patient to the point of unconsciousness. However, "the average survival in terminal sedation cases is just 1.5 to 3.1 days."[62] Some call this "total sedation" or "sedation of the imminently dying." Palliative sedation has been termed a procedure of last resort, to be implemented only when all other procedures for the dying, such as symptom control of dyspnea, nausea, agitated delirium, have

58. Pellegrino, "Futility in Medical Decisions," pp. 311-12.
59. Pellegrino, "Decisions at the End of Life," pp. 241, 220, 227.
60. Pellegrino, "Futility in Medical Decisions," pp. 314-15.
61. Quill, Lo, and Brock, "Palliative Options of Last Resort," p. 2100.
62. Margaret P. Battin, "Terminal Sedation: Pulling the Sheet Over Our Eyes," *Hastings Center Report* 38, no. 5 (2008): 30.

failed.[63] The Veterans Administration has developed a protocol for its use when a DNR order exists and a person is in the final stages of dying. There is a signed statement of informed consent authorizing general anesthesia by the patient or surrogate (if the patient is incompetent). It is also assumed that a variety of safeguards are in place ensuring the best care for the patient. This especially requires the participation of a health care professional with expertise in this kind of care.

Philosopher Margaret Battin points out the dangers of believing that this solves the problems in end-of-life decisions:

> The principle of mercy requires that pain and suffering be relieved to the extent possible. These two principles operate in tandem to underwrite physician-assisted dying: physician assistance in bringing about death is to be provided just when the person voluntarily seeks it and just when it serves to avoid pain and suffering or the prospect of them. *Both* requirements must be met.
>
> Opponents base their objections to physician-assisted dying on two other concerns. One is the sanctity of life, a religious or secular absolute respect for life that is held to entail the wrongness of killing, suicide, and murder. This principled objection holds regardless of whether a patient seeks assistance in dying in the face of pain and suffering. The second objection is that physician-assisted dying might lead to abuse. This concern is often spelled out in two ways: physician-assisted dying risks undercutting the integrity of the medical profession, and institutional or social pressures might make people victims of assisted dying they did not want. . . . Terminal sedation is often proffered as an alternative last resort measure that can overcome these practical and ideological disputes.

Battin argues that terminal sedation is an inadequate solution on these grounds:

> [1] Consent is not possible.
> [2] Thus, the rationale for the use of terminal sedation in effect *requires* that the patient suffer.
> [3] *The sanctity of life.* The dispute over the principle of the wrongness of killing, or the sanctity of life, has focused mainly on ending a

---

63. For the following discussion, see "Ethics of Palliative Sedation," A Report by the National Ethics Committee of the Veterans' Health Administration (March 2006), pp. 1-4.

person's life before it would "naturally" end. Terminal sedation does not honor this principle. Rather, it unarguably causes death, and it does so in a way that is not "natural."

[4] Yet there is nothing in the practice of terminal sedation that offers greater protection against the possibility of abuse in either of these forms than does direct physician-assisted dying.

The implausible effort to draw a completely bright line between continuous terminal sedation and euthanasia makes the practice of terminal sedation both more dangerous and more dishonest than it should be — and makes what can be a decent and humane practice morally problematic. . . . There is no reason that terminal sedation should not be recognized as an option, but there are excellent reasons why it should not be seen as the *only* option — or even the best option — for easing a bad death.[64]

Is terminal sedation different from euthanasia or physician-assisted suicide? Most people would disagree with Battin, concluding that it is different based on intention and proportionality: the death is due to the disease, *not* the sedation. Therefore, it can be seen as the equivalent of forgoing life-sustaining treatment. However, artificial feeding and hydration could be concurrently administered with the sedation, though this would prolong the dying process. It is important to note that terminal sedation is for the "imminently dying," not simply the terminally ill. The Veterans Administration policy restricts it to the former group as well as to those who have a DNR order and are suffering from physical pain and not simply existential suffering. If the patient improves, terminal sedation will be discontinued.[65]

The Role of the Agent

Our discussion so far has focused on the various acts, but equally important are the agents and their intentions. The principal agents are the patient, the doctor, and the family members. Some who support voluntary euthanasia argue that it is mercy killing; others assert that the act of euthanasia is not an act of mercy, no matter what the intention is. Ethicist Arthur Dyck speaks of *benemortasia* (good dying), the obligation to act

64. Battin, "Terminal Sedation," pp. 27-28, 30.
65. "Ethics of Palliative Sedation," pp. 1-4.

kindly. By contrast, Marvin Kohl proposes that the act of euthanasia can be the kindest thing we do.[66]

Many people believe that the wishes of the patient are the only morally relevant point. But what happens when the patient's wishes are ambiguous or the patient is unable to give consent because she is uninformed, mentally incompetent, incoherent, or lacks executive medical decision-making capacity? The doctor is also one of the agents because, generally speaking, he or she is the one to oversee the treatment.

The moral distinctions between euthanasia and the refusal of treatment are related to the agent, as Quill, Lo, and Brock argue in their illuminating essay entitled "Palliative Options of Last Resort."

> I suggest that the patient's wishes and competent consent are more ethically important than whether the acts are categorized as active or passive or whether death is intended or unintended by the physician. With competent patients, none of these acts would be morally permissible without the patient's voluntary and informed consent. Any of these actions would violate a competent patient's autonomy and would be both immoral and illegal if the patient did not understand that death was the inevitable consequence of the action or if the decision was coerced or contrary to the patient's wishes. The ethical principle of autonomy focuses on patient's rights to make important decisions about their lives, including what happens to their bodies, and may support genuine autonomous forms of these acts.
>
> I believe that clinical, ethical, and policy differences and similarities among these 4 practices need to be debated openly, both publicly and within the medical profession. Some may worry that a discussion of the similarities between VSED and TS on the one hand and PAS and VAE on the other may undermine the desired goal of optimal relief of suffering at the end of life. Others may worry that a critical analysis of the principle of double effect or the active/passive distinction as applied to VSED and TS may undermine efforts to improve pain relief or to ensure that patient's or surrogate's decisions to forgo unwanted life-sustaining therapy are respected. However, hidden, ambiguous practices, inconsistent justifications, and failure to acknowledge the risks of accepted practices may also undermine the quality of terminal care and put patients at unwarranted risk.

66. Arthur Dyck, "Beneficent Euthanasia and Benemortasia," in *The Morality of Killing*, ed. Marvin Kohl (London: Peter Owen Press, 1974), pp. 71-89.

Allowing a hastened death only in the context of access to good palliative care puts it in its proper perspective as a small but important facet of comprehensive care for all dying patients.[67]

Ethicists Join the Conversation

We now turn to ethicists to shed light on this thorny subject. I have selected philosophers espousing different positions in order to show a range of perspectives on end-of-life issues.

Joseph Fletcher (1905-1991)

As a situationalist (the context determines what is right or wrong) and consequentialist (the results of the act are more important than the act itself) writing in the 1950s through 1970s, Joseph Fletcher suggests that the treatment of compromised patients is to be weighed in the balance with other goods. He uses a formula of proportionate good from which to decide about treatment or nontreatment. Life itself is not an absolute value or right, but there is a "qualified respect for human life." He questions who qualifies as a person: embryos, fetuses, or even genetically compromised newborns may not qualify as persons, hence may be allowed to go untreated. The overriding value is whatever promotes well-being and reduces suffering. The central ethical question posed by Fletcher is: "When should we end a life?" — out of love, or *agapism,* as William Frankena characterizes Fletcher's position.

On the grounds of both proportionate good and personhood criteria, Fletcher leaves little ethical basis for the defense and protection of the weak and the helpless. Ramsey sees such criteria as leading to moral Armageddon, because people become expendable.

For Fletcher, the degree of suffering is the criterion for decisions on treatment/nontreatment. Suffering is evil when we cannot expect anything but suffering, that is, death is better than life when the degree of suffering is unreasonable: "It is harder morally to justify letting somebody die a slow

67. Timothy E. Quill, Bernard Lo, and Dan W. Brock, "Palliative Options of Last Resort," in *Terminal Sedation: Euthanasia in Disguise?* ed. Torbjörn Tännsjö (Dordrecht, Netherlands: Kluwer Academic Publishers, 2004), pp. 8, 11.

and ugly death, dehumanized, than it is to justify helping him to avoid it. . . . If the end sought is the patient's death as a release from pointless misery and dehumanization, then the requisite or appropriate means is justified."[68] Reflecting on Fletcher's position, we might pose these questions: Are we to use psychological or physical measurements of suffering? Can suffering ever be good? For Fletcher, suffering seems to include the absence of a reasonable degree of independence and mental capacity. Suffering, though, is both relative and subjective (as I discuss below in chapter 7).

Richard McCormick (1922-2000)

McCormick, a Roman Catholic moral theologian, believes that physical life is a relative good, and the duty to preserve it is a limited one. The fundamental principle for him is the preeminence of human relationships because they are at the core of how we manifest love of God and neighbor. Hence, whenever a newborn or comatose elderly person, for example, no longer has any potential for human experience or relationships, nontreatment is morally permissible. To put it another way, when life's potentiality for other values is gone, then the quality of life is too low to justify treatment. This is described as the life that is submerged in the struggle to survive.[69] However, one must be careful in interpreting "quality of life," according to McCormick, because it embraces many more limitations to living than do the narrow definitions of quality of life of Engelhardt, John Fletcher, and Joseph Fletcher. McCormick would not include any personhood criteria, as Joseph Fletcher and Engelhardt do in determining the quality of life. Neither does a person's ability to generate rights as an autonomous person affect how we value him as an individual. McCormick would probably limit John Fletcher's unjustifiable suffering as grounds for nontreatment only to include those who could not experience human relationships and not relate it to pain or severe disability.

In understanding McCormick, we may find it helpful to examine the traditional Roman Catholic position as expressed by Pope Pius XII. Pius focused on the patient by affirming the right to refuse treatment, but not

68. Joseph Fletcher, *Humanhood: Essays in Biomedical Ethics* (Buffalo, NY: Prometheus Books, 1979), pp. 147, 154-55.
69. Richard McCormick, "Save or Let Die: The Dilemma of Modern Medicine," *The Journal of the American Medical Association* 229 (1974): 172-76.

affirming euthanasia, in the face of suffering.[70] In 1980, the Roman Catholic Church issued its most comprehensive pronouncement on euthanasia in nearly thirty years. It maintained its traditional ban on suicide, abortion, and mercy killing, but it issued new guidelines on using "extraordinary" means to prolong life.

> The declaration said that doctors may "judge that the investment in instruments and personnel is disproportionate to the results" that can be expected. It added that doctors may also decide that "the techniques applied impose on the patient strain or suffering out of proportion with the benefits" he may receive. "When inevitable death is imminent in spite of the means used," the statement said, "it is permitted in conscience to take the decision to refuse forms of treatment that would only secure a precarious and burdensome prolongation of life, so long as the normal care due to the sick person in similar cases is not interrupted. . . . In such circumstances the doctor has no reason to reproach himself with failing to help the person in danger," said the declaration, which was issued by the Vatican's Sacred Congregation for the Doctrine of the Faith. The patient also may ask that his life not be prolonged through extraordinary means, the document said. "Such a refusal is not the equivalent of suicide; on the contrary, it should be considered as an acceptance of the human condition, or a wish to avoid the application of a medical procedure disproportionate to the results that can be expected or a desire not to impose excessive expense on the family or the community." . . . These advances, McCormick said, make yesterday's statement an important one. It "walks the middle course between killing and overtreatment — the two extremes we are confronted with today. It should be a helpful document."[71]

For example, a doctor's concern may be to relieve suffering; if the secondary effect is the death of the patient, the doctor is thus not culpable. Theologians and philosophers argue that the killing of an innocent is against God's will. Therefore, acts of beneficent euthanasia are never directly permissible, as Byron Sherwin and Joseph Sullivan maintain. Daniel Maguire shows that in certain cases direct positive intervention to bring

70. Pope John Paul II, "Teaching on Suicide and Euthanasia."
71. Marjorie Ilyer, "Vatican Eases Its Position on Prolonging of Life," *The Washington Post,* June 27, 1980, p. A1.

death is compatible with Roman Catholic ethical theory.[72] Glanville Williams criticizes this double-effect principle, because, he says, it means keeping your mind off one of the consequences, that is, the death of the patient. He believes that this is hypocritical. "When a result is foreseen as certain, it is the same as if it were desired or intended."[73] But Sulmasy argues that this is an erroneous application of the principle of double effect.[74]

McCormick's positions become clearer as we note his criticism of other ethicists' perspectives, such as those of James Rachels, who denies the moral distinctions between commission/omission, between killing and letting die. There is first the question of suffering, which McCormick sees as having more to do with the way it is removed than its existence itself. Medicine may be able to do more about suffering than Rachels allows, to which the hospice movement is a testimony. As McCormick points out, if one could or should save someone and does not, he has committed a moral wrong, and that difference is lost when we discard the killing/letting die distinction. From McCormick's perspective, Rachels is wrong when he says that the doctor decides that death is no greater evil than the patient's continued existence. The doctor has not decided for death, but for the termination of certain treatment, which is not euthanasia.

McCormick believes that the distinction between killing and letting die, or the distinction between commission and omission, is important to maintain because of the profound social and psychological effects on patients were these distinctions to disappear. Passive versus active euthanasia may not be a morally irrefutable distinction metaphysically, but it may be crucial, psychologically and socially, in the patient-physician relationship to assure the continual primacy of *primum non nocere* and benefits to the patient. It may help in distinguishing between an agent who wants someone dead and another agent who does not. However, these terms should not carry all the ethical freight for decisions concerning end of life. In fact, in the situations that McCormick argues, they should not be labeled euthanasia at all.

McCormick's major positions on these issues are found in his now classic article "Save or Let Die."[75] He analyzes the case of the baby boy

72. Marvin Kohl, *Beneficent Euthanasia* (Buffalo: Prometheus Books, 1975), p. xiii.

73. Glanville Williams, *The Sanctity of Life and the Criminal Law,* Carpentier Lectures at Columbia 1956 (1958), p. 286.

74. Sulmasy, "The Rule of Double Effect," p. 545.

75. McCormick, "Save or Let Die," p. 172. Hereafter, page references to this essay will appear in parentheses in the text.

Houle, who died in February 1974 following court-ordered emergency surgery. He had genetic abnormalities, and death was predicted in a very short time, so his parents did not consent to surgery. But the Maine judge ruled: "At the moment of live birth there does exist a human being entitled to the fullest protection of the law. The most basic right enjoyed by every human being is the right to life itself." (Note his use of *live* birth.)

The other case McCormick discusses is the now famous Johns Hopkins case in which a child was born with Down syndrome and duodenal atresia. The parents did not consent to an operation to correct the problem, and the child was allowed to die of starvation after fifteen days (p. 172). McCormick embraces a middle course between sheer concretism and dogmatism, where substantive standards and broad community guidelines are possible: "[B]ut I believe we must never cease trying, in fear and trembling to be sure" (p. 173). We need to develop criteria for quality of life. If only some compromised infants receive surgery and others do not, there is a line to be drawn, and McCormick argues that we cannot draw back from this task. In this particular case, James Gustafson disagreed with the physicians who did not operate. He argues that there was a need for a better assessment of the child's intelligence and broader perspectives on the meaning of suffering. However, Gustafson only says what he would not do, not why.

McCormick argues that the Christian tradition is a middle path between medical vitalism (which preserves life at any cost) and medical pessimism (which kills when life seems frustrating, burdensome, "useless"). Life is a basic and precious good, "but a good to be preserved precisely as the condition of other values." Here quality of life enters. "The very Judeo-Christian meaning of life is seriously jeopardized when undue and unending effort must go into its maintenance" (p. 174). The means to the necessity to preserve life can be extraordinary if that kind of life (painful, poverty-stricken, deprived, oppressive) would be excessively hard for the individual. Life is not a value in itself that is to be maintained at all costs, but only as other values can be attained through it (p. 175). Guidelines and potential for human relationships are associated with an infant's condition: for example, do we allow an anencephalic infant to die, but not one with Down syndrome?

The caveats about treatment are: (1) human judgment of the doctor; (2) mistakes will be made, but they should not paralyze us into inaction; (3) allowing some infants to die does not mean that they are not worthwhile, but that the value of their life cannot be realized in physical existence; (4) an individual makes a decision whenever possible, otherwise parents decide with a physician (p. 175). Christianity is on the side of the defenseless, powerless, and unwanted; it cherishes them as our neighbors in greatest need. Thus children are spared when they can experience our caring and love (p. 176).

Paul Ramsey (1913-1988)

Paul Ramsey, a Methodist ethicist and bioethics pioneer, launched the field of bioethics in his classic book *Patient as Person* (1970); his views on death and dying are principally reflected in that book and *Ethics at the Edges of Life* (1980). His is an ethic of caring for the dying. He questions the use of the word "euthanasia," arguing that it is an incorrect term since its use is applied to the way we die. Ramsey suggests a word such as "pre-mortem care" to convey the ethics and practice of caring for the dying.[76] He stakes out the preeminence of the protection of human life and eschews the term "euthanasia" as unusable. Nor does he find distinctions between "active and passive" and "direct and indirect" euthanasia particularly helpful.

Life is a gift from God. To choose death is to throw the gift back to the giver, that is, God. Ramsey's medical ethics are based on a "*canon of loyalty* between the man who is the patient/subject and the man who performs the medical investigational procedures." (*Canon* can also be applied to physician-patient relationships.) The patient has entered into a covenant with the physician for his complete *care,* not for continuing useless efforts to *cure.* As Ramsey later states, "The right medical practice will provide those who may get well with the assistance they need, and for those who are dying with the care and assistance they need in their final passage."[77]

His position on treatment/nontreatment is based on the principle of equality of persons. All human lives have equal and independent value. This view is grounded in the belief of the inherent dignity and worth of every human being and God's love for each life. Therefore, decisions for treatment or nontreatment are not based on quality of life but broad categories of types of cases not to be saved. It is interesting that McCormick

76. Ramsey, *The Patient as Person.*
77. William Werpehowski and Stephen D. Crocco, eds., *The Essential Paul Ramsey: A Collection* (New Haven: Yale University Press, 1994), pp. 177, 208.

(Roman Catholic) and Ramsey (Methodist), both grounded in the Judeo-Christian tradition, come to slightly different conclusions.

Ramsey moves from an equality-of-life principle to a medical-indications policy that develops guidelines for treatment/nontreatment on medical grounds. The heart of Ramsey's medical-indications policy is that decisions to treat or not to treat should be the same for the normal and the "abnormal." However, treatment no longer need be conveyed if it prolongs the dying rather than enhances the living, that is, of the person who is in the irretrievable process of dying. When in doubt, err on the side of treatment, unless there is a medical reason for saying that treatment might make the person worse or would, in any case, not help. In *Ethics at the Edges of Life,* Ramsey says that there are really only four standards for making decisions to withhold or withdraw treatment: the ordinary-vs.-extraordinary means distinction, standard medical-care policy, a patient's right to refuse treatment, and a medical-indications policy.[78]

Ramsey's criteria still apply decades later, because decisions are based on the efficiency of the treatment. What treatment should be administered includes whatever will benefit the patient and alleviate harm; it should never be related to criterion of personhood or quality of life. Therefore, the decision is between beneficial and nonbeneficial treatment. Medically indicated treatment, therefore, is any procedure that will cure or improve the illness or impairment of the person. Ramsey's standard definitions of ordinary and extraordinary treatment are noteworthy. "*Ordinary* means of preserving life are all medicines, treatments, and operations which offer a reasonable hope of benefit for the patient and which can be obtained and used without excessive expense, pain or other inconvenience. *Extraordinary* . . . means all medicines, treatments, and operations which cannot be obtained without excessive expense, pain, or other inconvenience, or which, if used, would not offer a reasonable hope of benefit."[79]

Ramsey is adamant that almost any policy of selection is better than one based on selecting one specific patient over another on grounds other than illness and need. In fact, treating every fourth neonate would be more just than allowing for special interest and quality-of-life judgments. Triage is never a justifiable approach in the neonatal nursery or the intensive care unit. When terminating treatment, one has to take the cost to the family

78. Quoted in Glenn C. Graber and David C. Thomasma, *Theory and Practice in Medical Ethics* (New York: Continuum, 1989), pp. 115-18.

79. Werpehowski and Crocco, *The Essential Paul Ramsey,* p. 199.

into consideration, as well as the interests of the nondying patient. Ramsey refers to the ethics of caring for the dying. However, it is interesting that, when he gave the Bampton lectures at Columbia University during the controversy surrounding the Quinlan case, he said that she should be disconnected from her life support and allowed to die in her parents' arms.[80]

Edmund Pellegrino (1920-)

Pellegrino is truly a Renaissance man, being conversant with and published in theology, philosophy, classical literature, medicine, pharmacology, nursing, and virtually every subset of topics within the health care field. As a Roman Catholic physician-philosopher, Pellegrino provides an important amplification to Ramsey's medical-indications policy. Much of what Pellegrino says about death and dying should be viewed in the context of his understanding of the patient-physician relationship. The physician should never be an instrument of death, only of giving life. "The physician has a moral obligation to conduct the decision-making process so that the patient's capacity to make his own decisions is enhanced to the degree that the illness permits."

Pellegrino also insists on the importance of the patient's moral right to make his or her own decision, which should be grounded in informed consent, not autonomy.[81] He also makes the distinction between treatment and care: even if treatment should be withheld in the extreme circumstances of irreversible or the final stages of dying, care should always be extended. He agrees with the Vatican's position that food and hydration come under the category of care.[82]

Pellegrino's bioethical principles are shaped by his inclination toward Greek philosophy, especially an Aristotelian view of virtue. He is the quintessential Roman Catholic moral philosopher who not only uses Aquinas well but draws on the rich tradition of Greek classical literature, including material from the Hippocratic corpus, which is especially evident when he discusses the physician as a virtuous person.[83] The virtue

---

80. Ramsey, *Ethics at the Edges of Life*, p. 156.

81. Edmund D. Pellegrino and David C. Thomasma, *For the Patient's Good: The Restoration of Beneficence in Health Care* (New York: Oxford University Press, 1988), p. 166.

82. E. D. Pellegrino, "Ethics," *Journal of the American Medical Association* 256, no. 15 (Oct. 17, 1986): 2122-24.

83. Pellegrino and Thomasma, *For the Patient's Good*, p. 116.

of beneficence applies both to the patient and physician. Pellegrino places this relationship in what he calls the "architectonics of the healing relationship."

Both Ramsey and Pellegrino comment on the Karen Quinlan case, which established the groundwork for the right-to-die arguments on the basis of patient autonomy. "As far as could be determined, she interpreted her good as discontinuance of life-support measures. Quinlan's physician defined her good in another way: as preservation of her life by carrying out medical indication — respiratory assistance. In our view, the physician reduced the patient's good to one dimension — medical good — while ignoring the other levels of patient good as we have defined and reversing the priority of good."[84] This harks back to the distinction that Pellegrino made directly and Ramsey made indirectly between what is morally good and what is morally right: something may be morally right, objectively speaking, but not good for a particular patient or person in that situation. As Ramsey observes, since the Quinlan case, discontinuance of certain life-support ventures in permanently comatose patients has received legal and ethical sanction.[85]

Intensive debate has centered on whether artificial intrusion and hydration are to be classified as medical treatment and also discontinued if futile or burdensome to the patient. The American Medical Association asserts that physicians must never cause death, and they distinguish clearly between treatments that can be withdrawn and care that may not. For Pellegrino, feeding and hydration are specifically mandated as care and must be given to comatose patients. Of course, some would argue that the nasal-gastric tube is a medical procedure and considered invasive. Pellegrino argues: "In my view, human life has enormous intrinsic value and, therefore, we cannot dispose of it at will when it loses instrumental value. But in view of our inevitable human condition under certain specific conditions, when there is a disproportionate relationship between the burdens and the effectiveness of benefits, life support may be withdrawn."[86]

He goes on to say that there are four practical ethical questions that must be answered in any clinical decision to withhold or withdraw life-sustaining treatment: Who decides? By what criteria? How are conflicts

84. Pellegrino and Thomasma, *For the Patient's Good*, p. 191.
85. Pellegrino, "Ethics," pp. 2122-24.
86. E. D. Pellegrino, "Decisions to Withdraw Life-Sustaining Treatment: A Moral Algorithm," *Journal of the American Medical Association* 283, no. 8 (Feb. 23, 2000): 1065-67.

among decision-makers resolved? How are conflicts prevented? In defining the terms in the euthanasia debate, Pellegrino has this to say: "I will use the term 'euthanasia' in its loose contemporary sense as the act of direct, deliberate and intentional killing of a human being for a generally commendable end such as the relief of pain or suffering. I will use assisted suicide to mean providing the means whereby suffering persons may kill themselves."[87]

It comes as no surprise that Pellegrino is opposed to both active euthanasia and physician-assisted suicide. He has mounted ten powerful nonreligious arguments against euthanasia as clinically unsupportable:

- Euthanasia and physician-assisted suicide are not necessary acts of beneficence.
- Autonomy is illusory.
- The view of "compassion" is distorted.
- Euthanasia and physician-assisted suicide are not dignified deaths.
- Euthanasia and physician-assisted suicide are not "private" decisions.
- The ethics of physician-patient relationship are undermined.
- Effects on health-care professionals are ignored.
- There is a deleterious impact on society.
- It collapses the distinction between killing and letting die, which is still valid.
- It leads to the slippery slope, which is a stark reality.[88]

One of the arguments Pellegrino addresses head-on is the concern for suffering as grounds for terminating a life. He claims that "for the secularist extinction of the suffering person is a rational act of compassion. For the Christian believer suffering is to be relieved to the extent possible under the constraints imposed by Biblical teaching and Christian ethics." He goes on to say: "Christians and secularists differ however in the moral status they assign to compassion. For the humanist the emotion of compassion becomes the principal justification, for Christians compassion has a different meaning. Compassion should accompany moral acts but does not justify them. Compassion cannot justify intrinsically immoral acts

87. E. D. Pellegrino, "Euthanasia and Assisted Suicide," in *Dignity and Dying: A Christian Appraisal,* ed. Kilner, Miller, and Pellegrino, pp. 105-19.

88. Edmund D. Pellegrino, "Outline: The Case *Against* Euthanasia and Physician-Assisted Suicide," unpublished essay. Used with permission.

such as usurping God's sovereignty over human life." He posits his argument on the parable of the Good Samaritan: " . . . and he was moved by compassion" (Luke 12:33). All of the acts of the Samaritan were moved by compassion toward the man who fell among thieves. Pellegrino continues: "Like their secular counterparts Christians are called upon to relieve pain and suffering, but because suffering has meaning even though a mysterious one, Christians can offer something more than extinction to the suffering person. . . . To deny dignity to those whose sensorial states are impaired is to deny their respect of them as persons. In the Christian view, a dignified death is one in which the suffering person takes advantage of all the measures available to relieve pain and ameliorate the things that caused the loss of imputed dignity but also recognizes that his innate dignity remains."[89]

Peter Singer (1946-)

Peter Singer, a bioethicist at Princeton University, is the polar opposite of Ramsey and Pellegrino. He has caused a firestorm of criticism for his positions on nontreatment of severely disabled persons or the seriously ill elderly. However, I believe that some of his positions have been misunderstood or taken out of context, which he has indicated in his loving care of his own frail mother.

"The notion that human life is sacred just because it's human life is medieval," [Singer says] talking about the treatment of the hopelessly ill. "The person that used to be there is gone. It doesn't matter how sad it makes us. All I am saying is that it's time to stop pretending that the world is not the way we know it to be." When the death of a disabled infant will lead to the birth of another infant with better prospects of a happy life, the total amount of happiness will be greater if the disabled infant is killed. The loss of happy life for the first infant is outweighed by the gain of a happier life for the second. Therefore, if killing the hemophiliac infant has no adverse effect on others, it would, according to the total view, be right to kill him.[90]

89. Pellegrino, "Euthanasia and Assisted Suicide," p. 113.
90. Michael Specter, "The Dangerous Philosopher," *The New Yorker,* September 6, 1999, pp. 46, 48.

However, charges that Singer's views smack of the Nazi policy of euthanasia — considering that he had relatives who died in the Holocaust — are at best unhelpful and at worst simply not true. It is important to examine the whole of his ethics, not simply extract controversial quotes.

Singer's position is predicated on his belief, like Joseph Fletcher's, that personhood requires more characteristics than simply being a member of homo sapiens. Fletcher names twenty criteria for being human, while Singer highlights "rationality and self-consciousness."[91] The latter also criticizes the inconsistencies of the traditional "sanctity of life" ethic, which leads to outcomes we do not want.[92]

Singer denies that he is opposed to people with disabilities. "I believe that society should give more support to people with disabilities," Professor Singer said in an interview with Beth Abernathy for the Public Broadcasting System's *Religion and Ethics Newsweekly*. His perspective on euthanasia is that when a rational person who has, for example, terminal cancer, repeatedly asks to be killed, he should be. Of course, his use of the words "be killed" is where the controversy rests; it would be much less controversial if that patient simply refused treatment. Regarding the nontreatment of severely disabled newborns or infants, Singer says that, with the support of the parents and advice of doctors, "[i]t would be justifiable to take active steps to end that infant's life swiftly and more humanely than by allowing death to come through dehydration, starvation or untreated infection."[93]

Religious Views of End-of-Life Choices

Moving from moral to religious positions on end-of-life choices, our research showed that every religion that took a position on euthanasia opposed it, except the Unitarian Universalists. However, the United Church of Christ indicated that people have a right to their own choices, and some Methodist conferences supported euthanasia. The chart on the following pages provides specific information on the different religions' positions, though not all the religions chose to comment on this issue.

91. Joseph Fletcher, "Indications of Humanhood: A Tentative Profile of Man," *Hastings Center Report* 2, no. 5 (1972); Singer, *Writings on the Ethical Life*, p. 128.

92. Singer, *Writings on the Ethical Life*, pp. 165-69.

93. Jeff Milgram, "A Man of Reason Stands Up for His Ethics in a New Book," *Greater Princeton Extra*, December 5, 2000.

	Treatment Termination	Removal of Feeding Tubes	Assisted Suicide/ Active Euthanasia
ADVENTIST (Seventh-Day Adventist)	Approved formal consensus in favor of passive euthanasia (allowing to die) in some cases (Oct. 9, 1992).		Approved formal consensus opposing active euthanasia (Oct. 9, 1992).
BAPTIST (American Baptist Churches)	The individual's right to make his/ her own decisions regarding life-sustaining treatment or measures should be enhanced through relevant advance directive legislation (approved Dec. 1990).		
BAPTIST (Southern Baptist Convention)	Resolution to "reject as appropriate any action which, of itself or by intention, causes a person's death" (June 1992).	Resolution supports efforts to discourage designation of food and/or water as "extraordinary" medical care for some patients (June 1992).	Resolution to "vigorously denounce assisted suicide as an appropriate means of treating suffering" (July 1996).
CHRISTIAN CHURCH (Disciples of Christ)	As member of the Religious Coalition for Reproductive Choice, shares in the strong affirmation of liberty of conscience and freedom of individual choice on moral-ethical questions related to personal behavior (2007).	Resolution 7724 further encourages congregations to study issues of dying with dignity (1977).	The customary reasons for euthanasia — patient suffering and irreversible condition — are nullified by the biblical witness to meaningful suffering and to possible healing.

	Treatment Termination	Removal of Feeding Tubes	Assisted Suicide/ Active Euthanasia
CHURCH OF CHRIST, SCIENTIST (Christian Scientist)	"The restoration of health and well-being comes best through spiritual re-generation rather than through mate-rial methods. A choice for medical treatment is a free choice of con-science." Mary Baker Eddy, *Science and Healing*		No official position on euthanasia or any other social or personal issues, but Christian Science teachings regarding life, death, and ill-ness entail that eu-thanasia and as-sisted suicide are not a genuine ex-pression of the faith.
CHURCH OF JESUS CHRIST OF LATTER-DAY SAINTS (Mormon)	Public Issues state-ment suggests that when dying be-comes inevitable, it should be seen as a blessing and pur-poseful part of eter-nal existence. No obligation exists to extend mortal life by unreasonable means.	Allowing a person to die from natural causes by removing a patient from arti-ficial means of life support, as in the case of a long-term illness, does not fall within the definition of euthanasia.	Public Issues state-ment declares that a person who par-ticipates in eutha-nasia — deliber-ately putting to death a person suf-fering from incur-able conditions or diseases — violates the command-ments of God.
EASTERN ORTHODOX CHURCHES (Greek Orthodox)	The Church distin-guishes between eu-thanasia and the withholding of ex-traordinary means to prolong life. It af-firms the sanctity of human life and man's God-given re-sponsibility to pre-serve life. But it rejects an attitude that disregards the inevitability of physical death. "Stand of the Church on Controversial Is-sues" (2006)		Euthanasia consti-tutes the deliberate taking of human life and as such is to be condemned as suicide on the part of the individ-ual, and a form of murder on the part of others who as-sist in this practice. "Stand of the Church on Contro-versial Issues" (2006)

	Treatment Termination	Removal of Feeding Tubes	Assisted Suicide/ Active Euthanasia
EPISCOPAL CHURCH	No moral obligation to prolong dying by extraordinary means and at all costs if the dying person is hopelessly ill and has no hope of recovery. Such decisions should ultimately rest with the patient or proxy, as expressed in advance directives. Resolution 1991-A093	When the means of artificial nutrition become painful or burdensome to a dying patient, it is morally acceptable to remove these means. *Faithful Living, Faithful Dying: Anglican Reflections on End of Life Care* (Morehouse Publishing, 2000)	It is morally wrong to intentionally take a human life in order to relieve the suffering caused by incurable illness, including a lethal dose of medication or poison, use of lethal weapons, homicidal acts, and other forms of active euthanasia. Resolution 1991-A093
JEHOVAH'S WITNESSES	When there is clear evidence that death is imminent and unavoidable, the Scriptures do not require that extraordinary (and perhaps costly) means be employed to stretch out the dying process.		Active euthanasia is murder and violates the sanctity of life, Christian conscience, and obedience to governmental laws. Assisted Suicide is condemned alongside all forms of suicide. "Life is Worth Living" (2006)
JUDAISM (Reform)	Removing the cause of delay of death or refraining from doing what will prevent dying, when death is otherwise imminent, is permitted. CCAR Responsum, 1994	Maintaining feeding tubes is preferable to avoid ethical concerns about death by starvation, but removal of tubes is not forbidden. It remains the choice of the patients and their families. CCAR Responsum 1994	The sanctity of human life means life may not be shortened or terminated because of considerations of patient convenience or usefulness, or sympathy with the patient's suffering. Positive steps that hasten death are prohibited. CCAR Responsum 1994

	Treatment Termination	Removal of Feeding Tubes	Assisted Suicide/ Active Euthanasia
JUDAISM (Conservative)	Disagreement among rabbis over withholding treatment. *USCJ Review,* 2001	Some rabbis permit withholding or withdrawing medication, including artificial nutrition and hydration, from an incurably ill patient, including patients in persistent vegetative state. *USCJ Review,* 2001	Euthanasia/Assisted Suicide must be distinguished from appropriate withholding of treatment. *USCJ Review,* 2001
JUDAISM (Orthodox)	Patient may choose to decline medical treatment that is not in itself life-sustaining. Rabbi Yitzchok Breitowitz, "The Right to Die: A Halachic Approach"	All life-prolonging measures (i.e., nutrition and water) are required, unless a person cannot be kept alive for more than three days (*goses* — refers to a patient who is estimated to have less than three days to live and is therefore unclean). Daniel Eisenberg, "End of Life Choices in Halacha"	Active in efforts to restrict physician-assisted suicide. UO Institute for Public Affairs, 2000
LUTHERAN CHURCH (Missouri Synod)	Discontinuing extraordinary or heroic means for prolonging life belongs to proper medical care. Administering pain-killing medications, even at the risk of hastening death, is permissible. Advance directives are encouraged. "Christian Care at Life's End" (Feb. 1993)	In some circumstances, feeding tubes may constitute "extraordinary" means of prolonging life and could then be removed. "Christian Care at Life's End" (Feb. 1993)	Euthanasia is a synonym for mercy killing, which involves suicide and/ or murder, and is contrary to God's law. Synodical resolution 6-02 (1995)

	Treatment Termination	**Removal of Feeding Tubes**	**Assisted Suicide/ Active Euthanasia**
Evangelical Lutheran Church	Treatment may be withdrawn, withheld, or refused if the patient is irreversibly dying or the treatment imposes disproportionate burdens. Message on End of Life Decisions, adopted by ELCA Church Council (Nov. 1992)	It is permissible to withdraw food and hydration when they no longer improve a patient's condition or prevent death from that condition. Message on End of Life Decisions, adopted by ELCA Church Council (Nov. 1992)	Active euthanasia deliberately destroys life created in the image of God and is contrary to Christian conscience and stewardship of life. While doctors of terminal patients in great pain often face difficult ambiguities, deliberate injection of drugs or other means of terminating life are considered acts of intentional homicide. Message on End of Life Decisions, adopted by ELCA Church Council (Nov. 1992)
MENNONITE CHURCH	Informal approval of removing obstacles that impede a natural death and advocacy against medical attitudes that assume death must be put off at all costs.		*As human life is a sacred trust from God, participation in hastening the death process would not be approved. Resolution on Health Care (1992)

	Treatment Termination	Removal of Feeding Tubes	Assisted Suicide/ Active Euthanasia
UNITED METHODIST CHURCH	Every person has a right to die with dignity, with loving personal care and without efforts to prolong terminal illnesses merely because the technology is available to do so. Decisions about cessation of treatment are left to the patient and their family, although medical and pastoral advice is encouraged. Book of Discipline of the United Methodist Church (2004)	*Support for withdrawing artificial nutrition in the *Cruzan* case (1990) as consistent with the tradition of conscience.	Washington Initiative 119 to legalize physician-assisted suicide and voluntary euthanasia was endorsed by the Pacific Northwest Conference of the United Methodist Church in 1991, but the United Methodist Book of Discipline (2004) officially opposes euthanasia and assisted suicide.
CHURCH OF THE NAZARENE	Decisions about termination of treatment should consider quality of life and prospects for recovery. Personal dignity can be served by allowing a patient to die. Church of the Nazarene Manual, 2005, pp. 56-57	Allowing a terminally ill patient to die by withdrawing artificial feeding and hydration can be a Christian decision in some instances. Church of the Nazarene Manual, 2005, pp. 56-57	Euthanasia — the intentional and overt merciful termination of life of a patient for whom death is imminent — is categorically rejected. Church of the Nazarene Manual, 2005, p. 56
PENTECOSTAL (United Pentecostal)	*Some informal acknowledgment that life-sustaining treatment can appropriately be terminated for patients with incurable terminal illness or in a persistent vegetative state.	*No consensus about disconnecting artificially supplied food and water.	*Strong (informal) opposition to assisted suicide and active euthanasia.

	Treatment Termination	Removal of Feeding Tubes	Assisted Suicide/ Active Euthanasia
Presbyterian Church U.S.A.	It is unnecessary to prolong the life or the dying process for a person who is gravely ill with little or no hope for remission.		Several study documents examine "all sides" of the euthanasia debate and offer resources for discussion, but there is no denominational position.
Reformed Church in America	Permits withholding or withdrawing life support systems for patients whose life is "not autonomically viable." Resolution R-9, adopted by RCA General Synod 1976		No one can claim a "right" to take his or her own life, even in extreme suffering, because humans are only stewards of the life that God has given. Statement approved by RCA General Synod, 1994
ROMAN CATHOLICISM	"Extraordinary" measures that provide little or no benefit to the patient or result in disproportionate burdens can be discontinued. The rule of double effect permits the use of medication with the intent to relieve pain, even if death may be hastened. Catechism 3.2.2.5, para. 2278-79	For some theologians and ecclesiastical leaders, "extraordinary" measures can include medical nutrition and hydration.	Euthanasia is an act or omission with the intent to cause death, in order to eliminate suffering. The killing of an innocent human being violates divine law, offends the dignity of the human person, is a crime against life, and an assault on humanity. Catechism 3.2.2.5, para. 2277
UNITARIAN UNIVERSALIST ASSOCIATION	Each person has an inviolable right to determine in advance the course of action if there is no reasonable expectation of recovery from extreme physical or mental disability. 1988 Resolution "The Right to Die with Dignity"		Advocacy of the right to self-determination in dying and the release from legal penalties of those who, under proper safeguards, honor the rights of terminally ill patients. 1988 Resolution "The Right to Die with Dignity"

	Treatment Termination	Removal of Feeding Tubes	Assisted Suicide/ Active Euthanasia
UNITED CHURCH OF CHRIST	Affirms individuals' right not to have life unnecessarily lengthened by extraordinary measures. Resolution 91-GS-44, Eighteenth General Synod, 1991		Favors individuals' right to make decisions regarding death and encourages legal protection of these rights. Resolution 91-GS-44, Eighteenth General Synod, 1991
ISLAM	All life-sustaining measures are to be employed to prevent premature death, but if life cannot be restored, it is futile to maintain a person in a vegetative state by heroic means of animation.		Suicide is forbidden in Islamic law. Physicians must not take positive measures to terminate a patient's life.
BUDDHISM	Emphasis is placed on clarity of mind at the time of death, so some treatments may be rejected if thought to cloud the mind.		Involuntary euthanasia generally disapproved, but there are varying positions on voluntary euthanasia.
HINDUISM	Treatment that is seen as unnaturally prolonging death may be refused on the principle that it disrupts the cycle of death and rebirth.		Although suicide as an ascetic spiritual practice may be affirmed, assisted suicide and euthanasia on account of pain or suffering would generally be seen as leading to bad karma.
SIKHISM	Maintaining a patient in a vegetative state for extended periods is generally not encouraged.		The timing of life and death is placed in God's hands, thus assisted suicide and euthanasia are generally not seen as acceptable.[94]

94. This chart has been adapted from Courtney S. Campbell, "Religious Ethics and Active Euthanasia in a Pluralistic Society," *Kennedy Institute of Ethics Journal* 2, no. 3 (Sept. 1992):

Conclusion

Now that we have analyzed the various facets of distinctions and debates concerning end-of-life choices, we conclude that the vast majority of health care professionals, ethicists, religious bodies, and the general public oppose active euthanasia. Euthanasia, as previously defined, is death of a terminal patient by someone else. The conflicting values in the euthanasia debates are: the autonomy of an individual to choose when to die versus the inherent wrongness of killing. This dilemma often can be resolved by the relief of the patient's pain and suffering, which reduces the desire to arbitrarily end one's life.[95] Deciding the morality of an act is also tied to the intent of the agent as well as the long-term consequences of the decision. Since we live in an imperfect world, every choice we make may create some harm, unhappiness, or even wrong. Ramsey and McCormick explored this decades ago in their book *Doing Evil to Achieve Good*.[96] We always need to act in humility, love, forgiveness, and restitution. It is not our responsibility to judge others for the positions they hold, or stoop to sloganism or emotionalism, but rather lay out the case and argue for our position compassionately and clearly. We live under God's grace, and it is only by God's strength that we can make the hard choices realizing sometimes we may make the wrong ones.

A great deal of this book addresses material that flies in the face of the morality of active euthanasia (AE). It is important to emphasize again that this is not the same as cessation or refusal of treatment, palliative sedation, or necessarily aid-in-dying. The one thing that seems to emerge from our analysis is that AE is not only unacceptable legally but also morally. We ground our objections on the following reasons:

God's sovereignty. Only God has dominion over life and death; therefore, euthanasia is usurping God's place. We are God's: "For you were bought with a price; therefore glorify God in your body" (1 Cor. 6:20). We should turn our lives over to God. Those who argue from this premise are vulnerable to the criticism that we already "interfere with God" when we care for the world by farming, practicing medicine, and so forth, but this is morally different from the ending of another person's life.

The sanctity of human life. Life is inviolable and should not be taken

---

253-77, with thorough review and updates by Miriam Diephouse McMillan, Feb. 2009. Any material for which updated information could not be found is marked with an asterisk.

95. Battin, *Ending Life*, p. 18.

96. Richard A. McCormick and Paul Ramsey, *Doing Evil to Achieve Good: Moral Choice in Conflict Situations* (Lanham, MD: University Press of America, 1985).

under any conditions: the sixth commandment is added to buttress this argument, as we discussed in chapter one. Not only is life sacred, but so are persons, especially those who are vulnerable by virtue of their illness and condition.

Defenselessness of the patient. This argument is related to the previous one. It is precisely the defenseless, powerless, and the unwanted who are to be cherished as our neighbor in greatest need. A powerless patient may be too vulnerable to freely choose to have her life terminated. In addition, her motivation may often be to stop the pain (which could be controlled) rather than end her life.

The wedge argument. Euthanasia erodes the strictures against taking life. If this practice becomes too easy, it will be used not only on the incurably ill, but also the socially "deviant." This act, if raised to a general line of conduct, would injure humanity, thus making it wrong in individual cases (Kant's universability principle). The wedge argument is related to the slippery-slope concern, which says that once we allow euthanasia in some cases, incompetent patients or persons with disabilities may also be at risk.

Possible abuse. A uniform policy of euthanasia would give too wide a discretion to the medical profession. Furthermore, real informed consent would be too difficult to obtain in terminal cases if euthanasia were a general policy because the presupposition would be in favor of euthanasia. Physicians need to be saving lives, not ending them, and the matter of deciding who are candidates for AE is difficult, and the timing of it even more problematic. People change their minds, as we can see by the fact that a large percentage of patients in Oregon who receive doctors' prescriptions for lethal doses of medicine never take them.

Wrong diagnoses and new treatments. There are the "hopelessly" incurable patients who do recover, as well as the false positives and inexplicable remissions. These cases argue against applying general criteria for euthanasia in similar cases because of the exceptions. In fact, there are rare cases of people coming out of deep comas.

Undermines the goal of medicine, which should be life, not death. This could lead to loss of trust between patients and their physicians, as we have discussed earlier, about the canon of loyalty between doctors and their patients based on the Hippocratic Oath.

I hope that these discussions on end-of-life decisions will continue as we seek clarity and compassion in the choices we make, while we respect those with whom we disagree, as we work together for just and humane decisions that will help those who are dying.

4. The Right to Die:
Suicide and Physician-Assisted Suicide

The Suicide's Argument

Ere the birth of my life, if I wish'd it or no,
No question was asked me — it could not be so!
If the life was the question, a thing sent to try,
And to live on be Yes; what can No be? To die.

NATURE'S ANSWER

Is't returned, as 'twas sent? Is't no worse for the wear?
Think first, what you are! Call to mind what you were!
I gave you innocence, I gave you hope,
Gave health, and genius, and an ample scope.
Return you me guilt, lethargy, despair?
Make out the invent'ry; inspect, compare!
Then die — if die you dare!

Samuel Taylor Coleridge (1772-1834)

French existentialist Albert Camus wrote: "There is but one truly serious philosophical problem and that is suicide — judging whether life is worth living amounts to answering the fundamental question of philosophy."[1] Suicide has also been the subject of some of the greatest novels.

1. Albert Camus, *The Myth of Sisyphus and Other Essays,* trans. Justin O'Brien (New York: Knopf, 1964), pp. 3-4.

For example, Dostoevsky's hero Kirillov in *The Possessed* plans to kill himself to become God, in order to prove his independence and terrible new freedom.[2]

Definitions of Suicide

The preceding chapter has provided an overview of various distinctions in the euthanasia debate. This chapter will be an in-depth investigation of suicide and physician-assisted suicide (PAS) — and whether they are different from each other. To define suicide, we must distinguish it from other death-inducing acts. Suicide has been defined as self-killing, self-homicide, self-murder, or self-death. Until recently the definition of suicide as an active ending of one's own life seemed straightforward. Tom Beauchamp has offered this definition of suicide: a person's own death is intentionally self-caused, and that person's action is noncoerced.[3] This definition suggests that suicide is self-killing, though some people refer to it as *compelled* self-killing, where severe depression makes the person feel that it is the only viable exit.

Voluntary self-killing in the sense of heroic self-sacrifice, where the intention is directed toward the benefit of others or to serve others, is considered praiseworthy. There is a gradation of blame or praiseworthiness with respect to self-killing, rather than an absolute prohibition. In other words, certain grounds are allowed for justifying self-killing. So when is self-killing justified? The answer depends on the intention of the agent rather than the act itself. The stories of suicide in the Bible are viewed in a variety of ways, but they generally relate to remorse and guilt for wrongdoing: Samson pulled the pillars of the temple down on himself and the Philistines to atone for his sin against God (Judg. 16:30); Saul fell on his sword to prevent being killed by the enemy (1 Sam. 31:4); Ahithophel hanged himself because his counsel was not followed (2 Sam. 17:23); Zimri was defeated in battle and burned himself to death in a house (1 Kings 16:18); and Judas, filled with remorse for betraying Jesus, went out and hanged himself (Matt. 27:5).

2. Fyodor Dostoevsky, *The Devils* or *The Possessed,* trans. David Magarshack (New York: Penguin Books, 1971), p. 615.

3. Tom L. Beauchamp and Robert M. Veatch, *Ethical Issues in Death and Dying* (Upper Saddle River, NJ: Prentice Hall, 1996), p. 98.

From the nineteenth to the twentieth century, suicide moved from being a sin to a crime to a sign of a mental illness (though Thomas Szasz is one who criticizes the cataloging of suicide as a mental illness).[4] In the twentieth century the suicide of the aging and infirm was often regarded as an expression of freedom and autonomy; in the twenty-first century, some would argue, it is a right that generates an obligation on the part of doctors to make it possible if one is unable to do the act.

At its heart, suicide generally concerns issues of physical, psychological, or spiritual pain and suffering, where life has lost its purpose and meaning. The person prefers death to his "living death." How one regards suicide can be described in a series of opposites. Suicide is irrational/rational; courageous/cowardly; intrinsically wrong/situationally justified; harmful to others/beneficial to others; harmful to self/beneficial to self. Depending on which of these categories a person chooses, she or he is seen as supporting or opposing suicide.

One of these categories, "rational suicide," has recently come to the forefront.

> Rational suicide, a coinage dating back nearly a century, has also been called balance-sheet suicide, suggesting that sane individuals can objectively weigh the pros and cons of continued life, and then decide in favor of death. . . .
>
> Margaret P. Battin, professor of philosophy at the University of Utah, is a defender of the idea — one she calls, given the aging of the population, "an issue for the coming century." Rational suicide, says Battin, "represents one of the fullest forms of expression of one's autonomy. It is the right of people to shape the ends of their lives." . . .
>
> Daniel P. Sulmasy . . . couldn't disagree more. . . .
>
> Nor do those two positions represent the whole spectrum of opinion. There are also those who view any rational suicide as a failure of a medical system that should have identified a patient calling for help. "Most suicidal persons desperately want to live," states the Web site of the American Association of Suicidology, a group devoted to the understanding and prevention of suicide.[5]

4. Thomas Szasz, *The Myth of Mental Illness,* rev. ed. (New York: Harper Perennial, 1984).

5. Barron H. Lerner, "A Calculated Departure: For Someone in Good Health, Can Suicide Ever Be a Rational Choice?" *Washington Post,* March 2, 2004: http://www.biopsychiatry.com/misc/suicide.html (accessed Sept. 13, 2009).

Can old people convincingly argue that they have completed their lives and want to check out before experiencing a stroke or other debilitating illness? Is this kind of rational suicide, often called "elder suicide," ever justified? Rational suicide was given visibility in 2003 by the suicide of feminist Carolyn Heilbrun. Over a period of several years, she publicly discussed her desire to commit suicide. Her book *The Last Gift of Time* (1997) described life after age seventy as "dangerous, lest we live past both the right point and our chance to die." She took her own life at age 77.[6] More recently, the assisted suicide of British conductor Sir Edward Downes at Dignitas Center in Zurich, Switzerland, has raised questions that I will go into in the legal and euthanasia chapters.

By using neutral categories rather than terms such as "right" or "wrong," or "good" or "evil," we avoid labeling suicide as either a sin or a praiseworthy act. In fact, one can conclude that it is the lesser of two evils: a life of unrelenting pain and suffering for oneself and family versus a quick death (though studies of surviving family members have shown that their guilt and pain is intense in the wake of a suicide).

The distinction between suicide and heroic self-sacrifice is an important one. Christ's death is the quintessential illustration of heroic self-sacrifice. In self-sacrifice, the focus is on the good for others that can be achieved by one's death — that is, other-regarding, not self-regarding. Beauchamp uses the example of the Vietnamese monk who poured gasoline on himself to protest the war, or a father who killed himself in the midst of famine to provide food for his children, or the story of Mother Maria, who chose to die in the gas chamber of Beken in the place of an ex-Jewish communist girl (who survived and later became a Christian). Joseph Fletcher calls Mother Maria's act suicide, a form of euthanasia, and he justifies both. Paul Ramsey, on the other hand, describes this as courageous self-sacrifice, not suicide.[7] "[The] condition causing death is not brought about by the agent for the purpose of ending his life."[8]

The case of Socrates is more difficult to determine whether we consider it suicide or heroic self-sacrifice. As we read the *Crito* and *Phaedo* in the *Dialogues of Plato*, when Socrates was accused by the state of introducing new gods and of corrupting the youth, he refused his friends' offer to

---

6. Vanessa Grigoriadis, "A Death of One's Own," *New York Magazine*, Dec. 1, 2003: http://nymag.com/nymetro/news/people/n_9589/ (accessed Mar. 3, 2009).

7. Paul Ramsey, *Deeds and Rules of Christian Ethics* (New York: Scribner, 1967), p. 205.

8. Beauchamp and Veatch, *Ethical Issues*, p. 98.

help him escape from prison, instead drinking the poison given to him (as the method of his execution). He declared that death was the better part, where his soul would be freed from his body, and he would be in the presence of greater men than on earth.[9]

Statistics on Suicide

With a definition of suicide, it is helpful for us to learn whether it is on the increase, because some argue that suicide reflects a failure of our health care system — that is, it is a major preventable public-health problem. There are an estimated 8 to 25 failed suicide attempts for every suicide death. Men and the elderly are more likely to have fatal attempts than are women and youth. A surprising fact is that older Americans are disproportionately more likely to die by suicide; that is, as a group they have the highest rates of suicide. Of every 100,000 people aged sixty-five and older, 14.3 died by suicide in 2004, compared to the national average of 10.9 suicides per 100,000 people in the general population. Non-Hispanic white men aged eighty-five or older had an even higher proportionate rate: 17.8 suicide deaths per 100,000.[10]

Suicide in the elderly is partly connected with lack of adequate end-of-life care. The risk of depression in the elderly increases as their risk of vulnerability and other illnesses increases, when ability to function becomes limited. Estimates of major depression in older people still living in the community range from less than 1 percent to about 5 percent, but rises to 13.5 percent in those who require home health care and to 11.5 percent in elderly hospital patients.[11] Among adults aged sixty-five years and older, there is one suicide for every four suicide attempts. Among males, adults aged seventy-five years and older have the highest rate of suicide (37.97 per 100,000 population). Among non-Hispanic white males 85 and older, the rate of suicide is 53.17 per 100,000, while the total population of 85 and older had a rate of 18.8 per 100,000. The rate for all males over 75 is 35.7 per

9. *The Dialogues of Plato,* Harvard Classics (New York: Collier, 1909), pp. 31-113.

10. "Suicide in the U.S.: Statistics and Prevention," *National Institute of Mental Health,* February 5, 2009: http://www.nimh.nih.gov/health/publications/suicide-in-the-us-statistics-and-prevention/index.shtml (accessed Apr. 13, 2009).

11. "Older Adults: Depression and Suicide Facts," *National Institute of Mental Health,* January 27, 2009: http://www.nimh.nih.gov/health/publications/older-adults-depression-and-suicide-facts-fact-sheet/index.shtml (accessed Apr. 13, 2009).

100,000, while for the total population of 75 and over the rate is 15.9 per 100,000.[12] If suicide rates are already high among the elderly, what would legal physician-assisted suicide do to exacerbate suicide level — either by direct or indirect means?

According to the World Health Organization (WHO) in 1968, a half million people in the world per year died of suicide. In 1974, the WHO reported that 1,000 persons per day committed suicide.[13] With an average of fifty-three countries, the age-standardized suicide rate was 15.1 per 100,000 in 1996.[14] In the year 2000, approximately one million people died from suicide: a "global" mortality rate of sixteen per 100,000, or one death every forty seconds. In the last forty-five years, suicide rates have increased by sixty percent worldwide. Suicide is now among the three leading causes of death among those aged fifteen to forty-four years (both sexes); these figures do not include failed suicide attempts, which are up to twenty times more frequent than successful suicides.[15] It is not always clear, however, what qualifies as suicide.

Reasons for Suicide

Perspectives on suicides have been addressed by a wide variety of philosophers, from Aquinas and Kant to Hume and Engelhardt. Justifications for suicide include the principle of autonomy, loss of dignity, the degree of pain and suffering, loss of value to the community, sparing of one's family, and low quality of life. On the other hand, philosophers and theologians argue that we have a duty to prevent suicide because of obligations to God, obligations to other people, obligations to ourselves, ambiguity toward death, and temporary mental illness. Besides these more analytical analyses of suicide, it is important to recognize the struggles of living that people face.

12. "Suicide Facts at a Glance," Centers for Disease Control and Prevention, National Center for Injury Prevention and Control, Summer 2008: http://www.cdc.gov/Violence Prevention/pdf/Suicide-DataSheet-a.pdf (accessed Mar. 3, 2009).

13. Margaret Pabst Battin, "Suicide," *Encyclopedia of Bioethics,* ed. Warren Thomas Reich, vol. 5, rev. ed. (New York: Simon and Schuster/Macmillan, 1995), pp. 2444-50.

14. "The World Health Report 2001 — Mental Health: New Understanding, New Hope," chapter 2, "Suicide": http://www.who.int/whr/2001/en/index.html (accessed Apr. 13, 2009).

15. "Suicide Prevention," World Health Organization, 2009: http://www.who.int/ mental_health/prevention/suicide/suicideprevent/en/ (accessed Apr. 13, 2009).

A Closer Look at Completed Suicides in the United States in 2004

- Suicide was the 11th leading cause of death in the United States.
- The total number of suicide deaths was 32,439.
- The overall rate was 10.9 suicide deaths per 100,000 people.

Suicide was the eighth leading cause of death for males and the sixteenth leading cause of death for females.

- Almost four times as many males as females die by suicide.
- Of every 100,000 young people in each of the following age groups, the following number died by suicide. Suicide was the third leading cause of death in each of these age groups.
  - Children ages 10 to 14: 1.3 per 100,000
  - Adolescents ages 15 to 19: 8.2 per 100,000
  - Young adults ages 20 to 24: 12.5 per 100,000
- Almost four times as many males as females in the 15-to-19 age group died by suicide.
- More than six times as many males as females in the 20-to-24 age group died by suicide.
- Of every 100,000 people in each of the following ethnic/racial groups, the following number died by suicide:

  Highest rates:

  - Non-Hispanic Whites: 12.9 per 100,000
  - American Indian and Alaska Natives: 12.4 per 100,000

  Lowest rates:

  - Non-Hispanic Blacks: 5.3 per 100,000
  - Asian and Pacific Islanders: 5.8 per 100,000
  - Hispanics: 5.9 per 100,000

Source: "Older Adults: Suicide and Depression Fact Sheet," *National Institute of Mental Health,* January 27, 2009: http://www.nimh.nih.gov/health/publications/older-adults-depression-and-suicide-facts-fact-sheet/index.shtml (accessed Mar. 3, 2009).

In the strictest sense, suicide is the deliberate taking of one's own life. It is possible to imagine circumstances in which such an action would reflect a perception of a conflict of fundamental obligations, as well as circumstances in which no such perception is reflected. The first kind of situation is possible where individuals find themselves experiencing intense, unrelieved pain. The choice might be the paradoxical one of protecting oneself from harm by ending one's life. Fortunately, the availability of medical treatment to control pain probably leads us to question the likelihood of such an irreducible conflict in most situations.

Another conflict might be perceived as irreducible when emotional suffering is especially excruciating. For example, the death of a spouse with whom one has lived for many years can leave one with a sense of radical loneliness. However, this person may need to be helped to see that such loneliness is part and parcel of human finitude and that other ways of overcoming its harm are possible. The role of third-party, supportive assistance in this circumstance would obviously be crucial.[16]

Reasons for suicide can be categorized as *sociological, psychological, physical,* and *spiritual/moral.*

Sociological

French sociologist Émile Durkheim (1858-1917) referred to several types of suicide: *egoistic* suicide, which results from personal isolation; *anomic* suicide, which is a lack of participation in the social structure; and *altruistic* suicide, which is considered good under certain societal circumstances, such as hara-kiri.[17]

Psychological

The psychological reason for suicide was described by Freud as a breakdown of ego defenses and release of destructive energy, resulting in a sense

16. "The Nature and Value of Human Life: A Paper Adopted by the 121st General Assembly and Commended to the Church for Study," PC(USA), 1981.

17. Émile Durkheim, *Suicide: A Study in Sociology,* trans. John A. Spalding (New York: Free Press, 1951). Some have called Durkheim's model sociogenic. See Battin, "Suicide," in Reich, ed., *Encyclopedia of Bioethics,* 5: 2446-50.

of helplessness, hopelessness, and negative self-image.[18] Analyzing the psychological intentionality of suicide is not easy. Is it voluntary or is there a compulsive behavior that leads to it? Is suicide an act of mental health or mental illness? Some people on psychotropic drugs commit suicide due to the effects of their medication.

Physiological

The physiological reasons for suicide are extreme pain, a terminal condition with no hope of recovery, and treatment that is extremely prolonged with no possible recovery. This is the category most often cited for physician-assisted suicide.

Spiritual/Moral

The fourth reason for suicide is moral or spiritual. With regard to the moral character of the suicide agent, for some, such as the ancient Stoics and Epicureans, suicide is considered an act of human self-control and thus noble. However, Aristotle, Augustine, and Aquinas considered suicide cowardly and thus spiritually destructive.[19] Some claim that "Christianity invites acts of suicide," but Darrel Amundsen challenges that view: instead, persecution/martyrdom are of an altogether different moral category. The current legal opinions that are based on a historical acceptability of suicide, he says, are simply wrong.[20] Karl Barth makes general statements about the ending of one's life that can be misunderstood: "Self-destruction does not have to be taking of one's own life. Its meaning and contention might well be a definite, if extreme form of the self-offering required of man."[21] Barth affirmed that life is a gift to be cherished. His statement above seems to collapse the terms suicide and heroic self-sacrifice. However, the main spiritual reason for committing suicide may be a loss of

18. Thomas Ellis, "Psychotherapy with Suicidal Patients," in *Suicide Prevention: Resources for the Millennium,* ed. David Lester (Philadelphia: Routledge, 2001), p. 131.

19. Battin, "Suicide," p. 2446.

20. Robert F. Weir, ed., *Physician-Assisted Suicide* (Indianapolis: Indiana University Press, 1997).

21. Karl Barth, *Church Dogmatics,* trans. Thomas Torrance and Geoffrey Bromiley, vol. III, pt. 4 (London: T. & T. Clark, 1960), p. 410.

hope, a sense that a person is up against a wall and has no exit from her problems. When lethal doses of medicine are prescribed but not used, it is perhaps because people feel that there is this alternative. Simply knowing that is freeing.

Arguments Supporting Suicide

The reasons people have for committing suicide are different from the morality or immorality of the act itself. American philosopher Richard Brandt (1910-1997) concludes that the state, intent, and motive of a person determines whether that person committing suicide is morally blameworthy. Here the distinction is between the act, which may be considered wrong, and the agent's motive, which can be assessed as positive. (This, of course, is the old debate whether the ends can ever justify the means.) There are several arguments concerning the acceptability of suicide. Is there a right? Is it moral? Should assisted suicide be allowed? What are the reasons for committing suicide?

The Right to Suicide

The first set of arguments in favor of suicide relate to the right to suicide; this stems from the argument that, if we have the right to live, we have the right to die. (This argument is tautologous, since everyone will die.) The right to suicide can be both positive and negative: a negative right of noninterference and a positive obligation. These positive rights include the right to die, the right to end one's life, the right to be allowed to end one's life, the right to be assisted, and the acceptance by the state of its legality. (In other words, insurance companies would pay insurance benefits to beneficiaries of a suicide victim.) Suicide has been legal since 1961. Since rights generate duties, some argue that others have a duty to assist one who wants to — but cannot — commit suicide. There are those who reason that we should be able to choose our own time of death and that no one should impose on us the need to live out a life of suffering: that is, that we have a right to a painless, clean, and neat death.

Glanville Williams summarized the reasons for the right to suicide: we have no duty to society to stay alive; not all would-be suicides are mentally disturbed; personal liberty requires the freedom to commit suicide.

Even those who argue that we have a right to suicide agree that there should be limitations to that right. For example, the act must be based on a realistic assessment of one's life situation, so-called rational suicide, perhaps in the face of a terminal illness. The degree of ambivalence about the act must be minimal. One must also be aware of possible misdiagnosis and fleeting suicidal thoughts.[22] Others, such as E. D. Pellegrino, argue that rights language is a legal, not a moral or theological, argument concerning suicide.

Moral Justifications of Suicide

There are a number of reasons offered for justifying suicide as morally acceptable. Some arguments are based on Hume's refutation of Aquinas's opposition to it, and others refute religious prohibitions against suicide.

To End Life Is Not God's Providence   Peter Singer, a secular Jew, eschews any religious arguments that oppose suicide or physician-assisted suicide. "No patient should be made to die in ways that, while meeting the moral or religious precepts of some, are anathema to their own."[23] Since God has given us free will and responsibility for our actions, so that, if someone chooses to end her life, we cannot judge people as wrong on the basis of God's prohibitions.

David Hume, the eighteenth-century Scottish philosopher (1711-1776), examines Aquinas's major objections to suicide one by one, and he takes a tack that is different from Singer's antitheological argument.[24] He says that suicide is not against God's will and does not encroach on God's established order for the universe. Since God created and set in motion the laws of nature — and human nature — we are free to act in relationship to them. For example, as a house will fall because it is subject to the laws of gravity, so a person will die if he kills himself. God does not alter these general laws, so we are free to dispose of our own lives. The ending of life is no more in the providence of God than the preservation of life. Since people die of natural causes, it is gratuitous to refer to nonnatural divine

---

22. Tom L. Beauchamp and James Childress, *Principles of Biomedical Ethics* (New York: Oxford University Press, 1979), p. 91.

23. Peter Singer, "Changing Ethics in Life and Death Decision Making," *Society* (July/Aug. 2001): 15.

24. David Hume, "Of Suicide," in *David Hume: Dialogues Concerning Natural Religion*, ed. Richard H. Popkin (Indianapolis: Hackett Publishing Company, 1998), pp. 97-105.

causes and be afraid to end our lives for fear of God's punishment. Furthermore, if we can interfere with the course of nature by diverting rivers or inoculating against smallpox, then the same reasoning should hold for ending a painful life. We are not passive in the face of the natural laws that God has set in motion.

Overwhelming Pain and Suffering   The second argument for supporting suicide is that we should not impose on others the need to live out a life of suffering. Engelhardt supports this in terms of a person experiencing a wrongful life. This he defines as a quality of life that is too low and causes someone to "go away from life." Love of self can lead to self-destruction to end the pain, the frailties of old age, or a lingering terminal illness. Put another way, Hume says that if I am tired of life or in too much pain, I am recalled from my station. Therefore, it is not possible to prove that God's will is for me to remain alive.

To Fulfill One's Duty   One of the examples of this is a duty to one's family to end one's life. A man I knew in Brazil in the 1960s was ill, and he committed suicide so that his children would have money for food. He was the father of eight children, and his medical expenses were putting his family into permanent debt. As Kant declared, it is better to sacrifice one's life than one's morality, though Kant himself opposed suicide.[25] However, some would argue that this is heroic self-sacrifice, not suicide, in which sacrifice to save another's life, not death, is the goal.

To Achieve the Greatest Good for the Greatest Number   One individual life may bring untold suffering on others, such as that of a hardened sex offender who had harmed many people; so it is better to end that life than to harm other people. Prisoners of war who take a cyanide pill in order not to reveal secrets that could cause others' deaths are sometimes cited in this argument, but this act is also probably heroic self-sacrifice.

To Exercise Autonomy   As Thomas Szasz argues, we must respect the freedom of others;[26] or as Camus says, the last act of courage is suicide.

---

25. H. J. Patton, *The Categorical Imperative: A Study in Kant's Moral Philosophy* (London: Hutchinson, 1958), pp. 117-19.

26. Thomas Szasz, *Myth of Mental Illness*; see also Szasz, *The Theology of Medicine* (Baton Rouge: Louisiana State University Press, 1977).

Many argue that we should be able to die in any way that we choose, and no one should be able to legislate that. A person should not be forced to carry disproportionate burdens by living; so if she desires to do so, she should be able to end her life. Suicide does not harm society but rather ceases to do a small good. Furthermore, if we are no longer able to promote the interest of society, it would be more laudable to remove ourselves from being a burden to society. Thus there is no social obligation to continue one's existence; obligations to others are not limitless.

Arguments Against Suicide

Those who argue that suicide is wrong do not accept any of the reasons for suicide — that is, rage, passion, pain and suffering, insanity, and loss of pleasure — as adequate justifications for ending one's life. We have an obligation for the welfare of others, and that means that prevention is imperative. This obligation is due to: (1) ambivalence: the wish may be to stop the pain rather than end one's life; (2) the impulsive nature of suicide; (3) the negative effects on survivors and the general community. These arguments are both ethical and theological in nature. The language to describe the unacceptability of suicide is often in terms of obligations. This line of reasoning was used by Saint Thomas Aquinas.

Obligations to Other People

Aquinas argues that suicide is unjust to others in that it deprives the community of our contribution. Also, suicide offends those others who view it as immoral. In Aquinas the good of society takes precedence over the freedom of an individual. Suicide is also contrary to the inclination of nature, which is love of self; therefore, it is a mortal sin.

If we are children of God who have received life as a gift and are stewards of our body, suicide would undermine our stewardship. If our membership in the human community is part of what it means to be a person, then certain obligations may flow from that fact. Aquinas argued that since every part belongs to a whole and we belong to a community, the community is injured if we kill ourselves. On the other hand, if the principal focus is our autonomous nature as free agents, then liberty prevails and it would be considered paternalistic to intervene. In this view, autonomy trumps solidarity; but for those who oppose suicide, being human involves being a social creature. Hence, it is not based on obligations to the community as much as it is being true to our communal nature.[27] Furthermore, we have all seen the devastating impact suicide has on a family and the suffering it brings.

Immanuel Kant (1724-1804) grounded his objections to suicide on the moral principle of duty to the community (as in Aquinas) as well as to self, referring to the duties to one's rational self. Hence, self-interested self-destruction is contradictory because love for self is not a consistent reason for destruction of self. In destroying our bodies we are destroying our selves. Life is an end in itself, so we may not have the power to dispose of our life. A dead person cannot fulfill his duty, for he has gone beyond the limits of free will. However, there is a distinction between suicide and risking one's life against an enemy as a supererogatory act of self-sacrifice — which would not be considered suicide. In fact, Kant says that sometimes it may be necessary to sacrifice one's life in order to fulfill one's duty.[28]

Obligations to Oneself

Aquinas believed that life is naturally good, and thus we have an obligation to preserve it. Passion or insanity may cause us to contemplate suicide, but then we realize the horrible nature of the contemplated act. Self-destruction is a violation of charity to God. The desire to commit suicide may stem from a temporary ambivalence toward life. For example, a person seeks treatment from a physician, and the latter fails to give it; so in frustration she contemplates suicide. If we do not intervene, it is a form of cooperation in the patient's hopelessness, because her attitude toward life may change.

Suicide is wrong because every part belongs to the whole: each human belongs to the community and thus injures the community by killing herself. Suicide is wrong because we cannot use our freedom against ourselves. Suicide degrades human nature below the animal level because humanity is something inviolable. It is not justified on grounds of unhappi-

27. Thomas Aquinas, *Summa Theologica*, III, q. 64, a. 5, trans. Fathers of the English Dominican Province (Westminster, MD: Christian Classics, 1981), pp. 1462-64.

28. Immanuel Kant, *Ethical Philosophy: The Complete Texts of the Grounding for a Metaphysics of Morals*, trans. James W. Ellington (Indianapolis: Hackett, 1983).

ness, because that would make pleasure the aim of our life, whereas it should be duty. Suicide eliminates the opportunity for future moral growth. In addition, there is no such thing as a life free of suffering; therefore, we may not use suffering as grounds for suicide. Furthermore, there is a duty for others to help relieve our suffering.

Obligations to God

God has given us the gift of life, and to end our life would be an act of ingratitude for the life that God has given us. We did not call ourselves into existence; we may not call ourselves out of it. God has power over life and death, as reflected in the passage from Job: "The Lord gives, the Lord takes away, blessed be the name of the Lord" (Job 1:21). Suicide is a sin against God and against God's purpose for us because we belong to God, and God alone has the power over life and death and wants us to preserve it. "We enter into God's presence unsummoned," says Aquinas, and others (e.g., Blackstone) have echoed this view. Suicide is wrong on the grounds that "it is a sin against God because one rushes precipitously into the Lord's presence without being summoned."[29] Although Kant opposes suicide, he starts from a premise that is different from that of Aquinas. Kant's argument is *not* that God opposes suicide, hence we should not do it; rather, suicide is an abomination, hence God opposes it.

The Nature of Physician-Assisted Suicide: Is it Suicide, Euthanasia, or Aid-in-Dying?

One of the initial problems we have in discussing physician-assisted suicide is whether to classify it as suicide, aid-in-dying, rational suicide, or some other designation. Most surveys of North American health care professionals reflect the respondents' opposition to physician-assisted suicide. Nurses in intensive care units strongly support good pain management for dying patients and the withholding or withdrawing of life-sustaining therapies to allow unavoidable death. Others point out the need for patient-physician discussions.

---

29. Paul Ramsey, *Ethics at the Edges of Life* (New Haven: Yale University Press, 1978), p. 147.

The insights that the issue of physician-assisted death provides include difficulties with medical decision-making, inadequacies in the physician-patient interaction, the need to develop some kind of consensus regarding acceptable medical options of the patient and the need to improve the quality of patient autonomy. We must look past the immediate debate and identify the underlying problems. Attention ought to focus on helping health professionals fill their current roles more effectively and on developing a healthcare system that can better identify and respond to concerns of patients.[30]

The vast majority of nurses oppose physician-assisted suicide and euthanasia. But wider professional and public dialogue on end-of-life care in intensive care units is warranted.[31] The public dialogue can actually take us back to the Hippocratic Oath: Edmund Pellegrino and others argue that physician-assisted suicide runs counter to it. The latter even argues that compassion is insufficient grounds for physician-assisted suicide:

> But regardless of whether patients use Kevorkian's machine or Quill's compassionate prescription for sedatives, they are dead by premeditated intention. In either case, physicians, who are the necessary instruments of the patient's death, are as much a moral accomplice as if they administered the dose themselves.[32]

Peter Steinfels puts it this way: "For example, the public responded differently to the query about legalizing doctor-assisted suicide than to a question about 'a moral right' to end one's life under various conditions. Neither those in favor of legal doctor-assisted suicide nor those against it constitute a majority, but a full 60 percent acknowledged 'a moral right' to take one's own life when 'suffering great pain' and having 'no hope of improvement.' Smaller percentages recognized such a moral right under less extreme circumstances."[33]

30. Jeffrey T. Berger, "The Call for Physician-Assisted Death: What Can Be Learned?" *Trends in Health Care, Law and Ethics* 9, no. 4 (Fall 1994): 15.

31. Kathleen A. Puntillo et al., "End-of-Life Issues in Intensive Care Units: A National Random Survey of Nurses' Knowledge and Beliefs," *American Journal of Critical Care* 10 (2001): 216-29.

32. Edmund D. Pellegrino, "Compassion Needs Reason Too," *Journal of the American Medical Association* 270, no. 7: 874.

33. Peter Steinfels, "Supreme Court Decision in Right-to-Die Debate May Signal Time Out," *The New York Times on the web*, February 11, 2006: http://www.deathwithdignity .org/news/news/nytimes.02.11.06.asp (accessed Mar. 13, 2006).

And Valerie Vollmar says: "A national poll of 1,005 adults issued by Religious News Service in September 2003 showed that Americans find physician-assisted suicide more acceptable morally than suicide. As to physician-assisted suicide, 45% said it was morally acceptable and 49% that it was morally wrong. As to suicide, 14% said it was morally acceptable and 81% that it was morally wrong."[34]

If one is opposed to suicide, then opposition to physician-assisted suicide would seem to logically follow. However, this is not necessarily true, due in part to the involvement of another person, which shifts the moral ground. Many prefer to position the argument concerning the acceptability or unacceptability of physician-assisted suicide on a continuum of palliative care. However, defining physician-assisted suicide as care seems a stretch.

At the core of the debate is whether physician-assisted suicide should be uniformly or categorically prohibited, or whether it should be offered as one of several options as long as there are sufficient guidelines in place. It appears that, for logical consistency, those who oppose physician-assisted suicide would need to oppose active voluntary euthanasia, but not necessarily passive euthanasia or the refusal of treatment, where the motive is different and the outcome uncertain. However, the three states that have legalized aid-in-dying — Washington, Oregon, and Montana — have made a clear distinction legally between *physician-assisted suicide,* which requires the patient to administer to him- or herself the lethal dose of medicine, and *euthanasia,* death by the direct act of the doctor. (As an aside, in September 2009, Montana was considering whether to make aid-in-dying a constitutional right.) This reminds us of James Rachels's point quoted in chapter 3: If the intent is for someone to die, it does not matter how it happens.

Some of the recent interest in physician-assisted suicide may result from overtreatment or an attempt to gain some control over the inadequacies of end-of-life care. We feel that technology has overpowered us. If a physician is willing to help us, it seems more acceptable. In a nutshell, the frustration in the patient-physician relationship — where patients feel as though they have lost their autonomy — has become clear.[35] This focus on

34. Valerie J. Vollmar, website on physician-assisted death, Willamette University College of Law: "Recent Developments in Physician-Assisted Suicide, March 2004": http://www.willamette.edu/wucl/pdf/pas/2004-03.pdf (accessed Apr. 8, 2009).

35. Berger, "The Call for Physician-Assisted Death," pp. 13, 15.

patient autonomy may undermine the patient-physician relationship; instead, the doctor, on the basis of futile treatment, may terminate treatment. "How should physicians respond when competent, terminally ill patients whose suffering is not relieved by palliative care request help in hastening death? If the patient is receiving life-prolonging interventions, the physician should discontinue them in accordance with the patient's wishes. Some patients may voluntarily stop eating and drinking. If the patient has unrelieved pain or other symptoms and accepts sedation, the physician may legally administer terminal sedation."[36]

There are some in the physician-assisted suicide debate who raise the fact of an increasingly older population, which increases health care expenditures: thus they claim that physician-assisted suicide would save money. In a thorough analysis of that question, however, economist Merrill Matthews, vice president of domestic policy and policy advisor for the National Center for Policy Analysis, concludes that a general estimate of $251 million (based on figures used in a 1998 publication, which makes them twelve years old) could be saved on health care costs for the last year of life, or about $35,000 per person. Given this pattern, the savings would be modest. For example, in a survey of Dutch physicians, 69 percent said that they had shortened a patient's life by less than twenty-four hours, and in 16 percent of the cases it was shortened less than a week. Hence the savings, given this pattern, would be miniscule.[37] A disproportionate share of medical costs occur at the end of life. Almost one-third of Medicare expenditures are attributable to the five percent of beneficiaries who die each year, and about one-third of expenses in the last year of life are spent in the final month. Previous studies suggest that most of these costs result from life-sustaining care, including resuscitation and mechanical ventilation.[38]

In debating the pros and cons of physician-assisted suicide, some are concerned that it will increase the overall number of suicides, especially among the elderly. But according to the experience of Oregon, the first state in which physician-assisted suicide was legal, that was not the case. Oregon has seen only a modest increase in the number of intentional sui-

36. Timothy E. Quill, Bernard Lo, and Dan W. Brock, "Palliative Options of Last Resort," *Journal of the American Medical Association* 278, no. 23 (Dec. 17, 1997): 2099.

37. Margaret P. Battin, Rosamond Rhodes, and Anita Silvers, eds., *Physician Assisted Suicide: Expanding the Debate* (New York: Routledge, 1998), pp. 315, 320.

38. "Studies investigate health care at the end of life," *Medical News Today, Archives of Internal Medicine* 169, no. 5 (Mar. 9, 2009): 480-88, 493-501: http://www.medicalnewstoday.com/articles/141558.php (accessed May 11, 2009).

cides since physician-assisted suicide was approved by a 51 percent majority of the electorate in 1994, a law requiring that a physician wait fifteen days before assisting a suicide. (In November 1997, voters overwhelmingly rejected a ballot measure that would have repealed the law.) There were 525 suicides in Oregon in 1994, 526 in 1995, and 533 in 1996.[39] Since 1997, more than 340 people — mostly ailing with cancer — have used Oregon's measure to end their lives.[40]

> The legalization of assisted death has been associated with substantial improvements in palliative care in Oregon, in areas including the appropriate training of physicians, the communication of a patient's wishes regarding life-sustaining treatment, pain management, rates of referral to hospice programs, and the percentage of deaths occurring at home. Effective palliative care and hospice services may address many of the key reasons why patients request assistance in dying, such as loss of autonomy, dignity, and the ability to care for themselves in a home environment — and that may lead some to change their minds.
>
> Because of the nature of their medical practices or personal objections to involvement, most physicians in Oregon have never written a prescription for a lethal dose of medication; in 2007, 45 physicians wrote 85 prescriptions issued (with a range of 1 to 10 prescriptions per doctor). If the experience in Washington is similar, however, there will eventually be more prescriptions and deaths because Washington has more people (6.5 million, as compared with 3.7 million in Oregon).[41]

Since the longest history of physician-assisted suicide is in the Netherlands, that country's figures on suicides are also informative. In 2004, there were a total of 1,514 suicides per 100,000 for all ages and genders.[42]

In terms of the practice of physician-assisted suicide in the Netherlands, their policies are regulated and their guidelines are as follows: the patient must repeatedly and explicitly express the desire to die; the patient's decision must be well informed, free and enduring; the patient must be suf-

39. Oregon Center for Health Statistics, State Dept. of Health; see http://oregon.gov/DHS/ph/pas/index.shtml for up-to-date information.
40. Associated Press, "Washington state to allow 'dignity' deaths," *msnbc online,* March 1, 2009 www.msnbc.msn.com/id/29454171 (accessed Mar. 2, 2009).
41. Robert Steinbrook, MD, "Physician-Assisted Death — From Oregon to Washington State," *New England Journal of Medicine* 359, no. 24 (2008).
42. "Suicide rates (per 100,000) by gender, Netherlands, 1950-2004," World Health Organization: http://www.who.int/mental_health/media/neth.pdf (accessed Apr. 24, 2009).

fering from severe physical or mental pain with no prospect for relief; all other options for care must have been exhausted or refused by the patient; euthanasia must be carried out by a qualified physician; the physician must consult at least one other physician; and the physician must inform the local coroner that euthanasia has occurred.[43] There is some question, though, whether these guidelines are always followed. Theo Boer, who sits on the Regional Review Committee on Euthanasia in the Netherlands and has analyzed 1,200 reports submitted between the years 2005 and 2009, says that there has been very little abuse of the guidelines set forth. He describes the practice of euthanasia as morally solid.[44] However, there are those in the Netherlands who have indicated that more palliative treatment options should have been given to those patients requesting euthanasia from the beginning of the institution of the policy. Now there is more extensive training for physicians in palliative care options. "Since about 1995, Dutch hospitals and physicians have gradually updated the quality of palliative care so as to match standards found in the U.K. and the Scandinavian countries. This had the following effect: according to a nationwide survey published in 2007, there was a dramatic decrease in the numbers of euthanasia: from 3,500 in 2001 to 2,300 in 2005, a decrease of 34%."[45]

Some people believe that the term itself is suspect, that physician-assisted suicide is really active euthanasia and not suicide at all, because another agent is involved. Actually, this is not strictly true, because the patient is still the agent of his own death. Special interest groups raise public policy issues that certain categories of people will become prime candidates for physician-assisted suicide, such as persons with physical and mental challenges, those of certain classes or races or age, or those without health insurance. Some have even argued that the United States should not even consider physician-assisted suicide unless there is universal health care.[46]

The push for physician-assisted suicide is rooted in the same desire for autonomy that I noted in chapter 3 above. Interestingly enough, however, feminists such as Susan Wolf support abortion but argue against

43. John Horgan, "Death with Dignity: Science and the Citizen," *Scientific American* (Mar. 1991): 17.

44. Theo A. Boer, "Euthanasia in a Welfare State: Experiences from the Review Procedure in The Netherlands," paper presented at Society of Christian Ethics meeting, January 12, 2010, p. 1.

45. Boer, "Euthanasia in a Welfare State," p. 2.

46. Horgan, "Death with Dignity," p. 20.

physician-assisted suicide because abortion represents liberty to be free of bodily invasion, whereas physician-assisted suicide invites bodily invasion.[47] This line of argument was the theme of a lead article in *Trends in Health Care, Law and Ethics,* which was devoted to the legacy of Karen Ann Quinlan: it declared that there are no parallels between physician-assisted suicide and these other practices.[48]

> That definition clearly embraces the right to be free of unwanted bodily invasion. But it is not at all clear that it covers a right to be free to obtain bodily invasion for the purpose of ending your own life. This is not an artificial distinction. Removing an unwanted fetus from the body restores the status quo ante (not being pregnant) and allows a woman to continue her life plan before it was interrupted by unwanted pregnancy. Removing unwanted life-sustaining treatment also restores the status quo ante (life with a disability or illness) and allows a person to continue what may be a dying process. But assisted suicide removes nothing from the body and restores no status quo. It intervenes to change the life course radically.[49]

Is Physician-Assisted Suicide Different from Euthanasia?

Dan Brock argues that voluntary active euthanasia and physician-assisted suicide are morally the same and both should be allowed based on self-determination and autonomy.[50] Frances Kamm has also applied distinctions between active and passive euthanasia — and killing versus letting die — to physician-assisted suicide in her closely reasoned essay "Physician Assisted Suicide, Euthanasia, and Intending Death."[51] While many of these practices seem to blend together and the practices are more and

47. Susan Wolf, "Physician Assisted Suicide, Abortion, and Refusal of Treatment," in Weir, *Physician-Assisted Suicide,* pp. 167-201.

48. Russell L. McIntyre, "The Significance of the Legacy of Karen Ann Quinlan," *Trends in Health Care, Law and Ethics* 8, no. 1 (Winter 1993): 7-16.

49. McIntyre, "The Significance of Quinlan," pp. 7-16. This argument, for many, is very offensive in terms of its description of the unborn as "unwanted bodily invasion."

50. Dan W. Brock, "Physician-Assisted Suicide Is Sometimes Morally Justified," in Weir, *Physician-Assisted Suicide,* pp. 86-103.

51. Frances Kamm, "Physician Assisted Suicide, Euthanasia, and Intending Death," in Battin, Rhodes, and Silvers, *Physician Assisted Suicide: Expanding the Debate,* pp. 28-62.

more difficult to distinguish, the ultimate fact determining their morality is not whether someone is dead but how they got that way.

A number of subissues have surfaced of late under "Palliative Options of Last Resort," the title of an interesting article by Quill, Lo, and Brock, which asks whether physicians should, if palliative options fail, provide the means to end the patient's life.[52]

The more one analyzes physician-assisted suicide vis-à-vis related practices, the more it becomes clear that the language itself is very confusing. In other words, if suicide is self-killing, then if a physician helps a person die, can that still be considered suicide — or is it voluntary euthanasia at the person's request? Active euthanasia also has several subsets — at someone's request or without his consent. If someone asks to die but does not have the physical ability to execute the act, do we call this assisted suicide? This misuse of language masks the real moral issue. However, if the physician leaves a lethal dose of medicine and the patient takes it, or if the physician administers the lethal injection herself, even at a patient's request — these two acts are morally different.

The Morality of Physician-Assisted Suicide

One could apply the six basic ethical principles most often used by ethicists to physician-assisted suicide to see how many doctors, if any, could support this practice. If we agree with Robert Veatch that ethical principles are like traffic lights at which drivers must stop before proceeding — or as Beauchamp and Childress declare, that fundamental principles are at the heart of their bioethics — then it might be helpful for us to see whether any of these classic principles are applicable to physician-assisted suicide: beneficence and nonmaleficence, justice, respect for persons, fidelity and loyalty, promise-keeping, and truth-telling.[53]

Many who support physician-assisted suicide use beneficence and respect for persons to ground their position. In other words, if the pain and suffering is too great, it is a kindness to provide a quick and easy end. The same is true for respect for persons, which many interpret as autonomy:

52. Timothy E. Quill, Bernard Lo, and Dan W. Brock, "Palliative Options of Last Resort," in *Terminal Sedation: Euthanasia in Disguise?* ed. Torbjorn Tannsjo (New York: Springer, 2004), pp. 1-14.

53. Beauchamp and Childress, *Principles of Biomedical Ethics* (1979 and subsequent editions).

that is, people should be allowed to die the way they want to die. The other principles — respect for persons, fidelity, promise-keeping — apply most directly to the patient-physician relationship and generally apply to trust in this relationship that is premised on sustaining, not terminating, life.

Independent of how we feel about the morality or immorality of physician-assisted suicide, it is clear that it is an act of great sadness. This was powerfully dramatized by a documentary film entitled *Death on Request,* directed by Maarten Nederhorst (Fanlight Productions). This is a Dutch-language film (with English subtitles) portraying the final day in the life of a man, accompanied by his wife, who dies by physician-assisted suicide. The entire film is extremely sad and sobering.[54]

Physician-Assisted Suicide Is Wrong (Unacceptable) Generally speaking, those who oppose physician-assisted suicide (PAS) use religious arguments most frequently. In fact, the doctor's religious convictions do influence whether she or he practices physician-assisted suicide. Religiously committed doctors are more likely to oppose physician-assisted suicide and less likely to practice it, while doctors claiming to be agnostic or atheist are more likely to favor euthanasia.[55] Edmund Pellegrino argues strongly against PAS on religious grounds:

> Many societies today are moving rapidly toward social acceptance and legal permission in the acceleration of death by euthanasia and assisted suicide. Few things are more antithetical to Christian tradition and the biblical teaching about the sovereignty of God over human life. All Christians have a duty of evangelization, of responding in authentic fashion as Christians to the direction our society is moving and the forces driving it in that direction.[56]

On the other side of the equation, religious patients are less likely to request it. "Studies indicate that religious people can better cope with pain, are less depressed, have stronger family ties, and report greater satisfaction with life in general. This means they are less likely to request physician-

54. *Death by Request,* film directed and produced by Maarten Nederhorst, first aired on October 20, 1994, in Amsterdam.
55. "Religion Is a Factor," *Connection* 1, no. 4 (Summer 1997).
56. Edmund D. Pellegrino, "Euthanasia and Assisted Suicide," in *Dignity and Dying: A Christian Appraisal,* ed. John F. Kilner, Arlene Miller, and Edmund D. Pellegrino (Grand Rapids: Eerdmans, 1996), pp. 105-99.

assisted suicide?"[57] Pellegrino addresses head-on the Christian argument from mercy, acknowledging that there is some support for physician-assisted suicide for the purpose of relieving suffering; but he argues that this is a false justification because of the improvements in pain control. Compassion in itself does not trump every decision, because it can be "usurping God's sovereignty over human life." Furthermore, relieving suffering can be applied to all kinds of acts that are based on an unacceptable quality of life, which is a slippery slope at best. Pellegrino challenges us to examine the deeper theological issues.[58]

A slightly different religious perspective in opposition to PAS is argued by Dennis Prager, author of *The Nine Questions People Ask about Judaism.* His position is based on Judaism's opposition to taking one's own life or the life of someone else, whether that person is approaching death or is a healthy person with decades of life ahead. Both cases, he says, are murder. Furthermore, the first priority of a Jewish physician is to save his or her patient's life while being sympathetic to pain and suffering.[59]

The reasons for opposing PAS are often parallel to the anti-suicide arguments. Susan Wolf says that gender makes a difference in analyzing PAS, arguing that women may be more prone to request PAS.[60] However, based on significantly higher rates of male suicide, that seems unlikely. One of the most problematic categories of people who would request PAS are those with mental illness. (Should they automatically be excluded if PAS were legalized? Is hopelessness or depression adequate grounds for PAS?) Legal cases have involved this issue, but it remains unresolved. Euthanasia advocate Pieter Admiraal "doubts whether assisting the suicides of mental patients will, or should, become accepted. 'I think we will hesitate forever,' he says, 'because there is always hope that we can cure these patients.'"[61]

Some of the reasons to oppose physician-assisted suicide are: (1) the implication that certain lives are not worth living; (2) the premise that some have a duty to die; (3) the existence of better medical alleviations as well as responses to this cry for help; and (4) the granting of too much

57. "Religion Is a Factor."

58. Pellegrino, "Euthanasia and Assisted Suicide," pp. 108, 110, 111-12.

59. Dennis Prager, "Physician-Assisted Suicide: A Jewish Perspective," Center for Christian Bioethics, Loma Linda University, *Update* 21, no. 2 (Oct. 2006): 1-8.

60. Wolf, "Physician Assisted Suicide, Abortion, and Refusal of Treatment," pp. 167-201.

61. Horgan, "Death with Dignity," p. 17.

power to physicians and the destruction of the trust relationship between physician and patient.

Physician-Assisted Suicide Is Right (Acceptable)   Howard Brody concludes that PAS is "a compassionate response to a medical failure" as long as necessary safeguards against abuse can be instituted.[62] Doctors should both relieve suffering and preserve it, so physician-assisted suicide may achieve the former. Some fear that people with disabilities may want PAS if society does not provide better support systems. Therefore, if some people experience undue suffering with no medical recourse, they may view PAS as their only option. Others argue that PAS should be available in carefully prescribed situations. This is, according to William Winslade, "the least undesirable choice" (despite his ambivalence toward the policy), so it is the lesser evil for some people. He does not believe PAS violates a physician's basic duty to sustain a patient, and it may lessen the suffering.[63] However, Daniel Callahan challenges the pro-PAS arguments by suggesting alternative medical approaches that would eliminate its necessity.[64]

Conclusion

As humans live longer, the arguments for and against PAS will increase. Many believe that if pain is controlled, psychological support is provided, and loved ones remain present, the requests for aid-in-dying may fade. The answer to our original question about whether suicide and PAS are different acts, the answer is yes and no: yes — because there is another agent involved in facilitating the act; no — because the motive is the same: death by one's own hand. However, both are different from euthanasia, which is death directly by someone else's hand. If PAS becomes legalized throughout the United States, it could change the landscape of the doctor-patient relationship and lead us down a dangerous road, a road that we may be better off not traveling. The availability of PAS could mean its inevitability.

62. Howard Brody, "Physician-Assisted Suicide *Is* an Acceptable Practice for Physicians," in Weir, *Physician-Assisted Suicide,* pp. 136-51.

63. William Winslade, "Physician-Assisted Suicide: Evolving Public Policies," in Weir, *Physician-Assisted Suicide,* pp. 224-39.

64. Daniel Callahan, "Self-Extinction: The Morality of the Helping Hand," in Weir, *Physician-Assisted Suicide,* pp. 83-85.

5. Organ Donation: The Last Gift of Life

To Remember Me

Give my sight to the man who has never seen a sunrise, a baby's
   face or love in the eyes of a woman.
Give my heart to a person whose own heart has caused nothing but
   endless days of pain.
Give my blood to the teenager who was pulled from the wreckage of
   his car, so that he might live to see his grandchildren play.
Give my kidneys to one who depends on a machine to exist from
   week to week.
Take my bones, every muscle, every fiber and nerve in my body and
   find a way to make a crippled child walk.
Explore every corner of my brain. Take my cells, if necessary, and let
   them grow so that, someday, a speechless boy will shout at the
   crack of a bat and deaf girl will hear the sound of rain against
   her window.
Burn what is left of me and scatter the ashes to the winds to help
   the flowers grow.
If you must bury something, let it be my faults, my weaknesses and
   all prejudice against my fellow man.
Give my sins to the devil.
Give my soul to God.
If, by chance, you wish to remember me, do it with a kind deed or
   word to someone who needs you.
If you do all I have asked, I will live forever.

Robert N. Test

Introduction

As we consider questions of death and dying, organ donation and transplantation is another way of extending our lives. The moral, theological, medical, and economic issues surrounding donation and transplantation impinge on end-of-life issues. For the dying person, receiving an organ may be lifesaving. For the family of a deceased loved one, donating that person's organs (if previously indicated by the dying person) may provide solace in the face of their loss, that death brought life to another person. However, there is a great deal of misinformation and misunderstanding about this subject, which causes many people to decide against donation. This is unfortunate because the majority of doctors and agencies involved in this field are highly moral and medically competent professionals. However, some doctors are also hesitant to become involved in this field. Therefore, the American Medical Association passed a policy in 2006 to help guide doctors through these difficult situations.[1] This chapter will deal principally with the donation of major organs, rather than tissue, bone marrow, or blood donation — since those can regenerate themselves.

Organ donation is a question of altering our bodies for survival: the survival of the recipient of an artificial, animal, or human organ, and the survival of the donor without his or her body part. Jesse Barber, deceased chairman of social medicine at Howard University, called organ donation the last gift of life. William F. May refers to it as Christian self-sacrifice based on Jesus Christ's offering of his body and blood. First-person stories or our own personal experiences may change our perspective on this subject.

Having been involved with organ donation through my ministry, I have seen the gifts and challenges at first hand. The health ministries that I directed in Washington, D.C., in the 1980s had, as one of their affiliated projects, the Kidney Foundation of D.C., which provided educational events in collaboration with Howard University Medical School Transplant Program. I served as an ethicist on the Southeast Organ Procurement Foundation (SEOPF) Committee, which sets policies for donation and transplantation. Perhaps my most interesting involvement, though, came when I was a pastor, and parish members were struggling with whether to

---

1. "Organ Donation: Medical Ethics and Public Appeals," *American Medical News on the web,* August 14, 2006: http://www.ama-assn.org/amednews/2006/08/14/edsa0814.htm (accessed Apr. 14, 2009).

donate the organs of a brain-dead relative or needed assistance in finding an organ for a family member. There was the case of a twelve-year-old boy who had only a few weeks left to live with his diseased liver, and whose parents asked for my help because of their lack of funds for a liver transplant. Another couple had a two-week-old baby who needed a liver transplant within a month or he would die from a very rare disease. He did receive the transplant. These stories illustrated to me the serious problem we face in this country in supplying a sufficient number of organs for those needing a transplant, for whom these are often matters of life and death.[2]

When organ donation becomes personal in one's life, it takes on a whole new dimension. One of the social-medical questions that arises is whether celebrities, the well-connected, or the wealthy should be able to jump the queue.

A celebrity like Apple CEO Steve Jobs scores a rare organ transplant and the world wonders: Did he game the system? The rich have plenty of advantages that others don't. But winning the "transplant lottery" involves more than the size of your wallet — and true medical need.

A Tennessee hospital has confirmed that it performed a liver transplant for Jobs, putting him among the 6,500 or so Americans each year who get these operations. Nearly 16,000 others are waiting for such a chance. No one can buy a liver transplant — that's against federal law. And no one is suggesting that Jobs or the doctors who treated him bent any rules to show him favor. The hospital said he was the sickest person waiting for a liver when one came available. However, people who understand how the transplant system works, and who have the money to make the most of what they learn, have a leg up on getting the body part they need. A Jobs who lives in Palo Alto, California, was able to get on a shorter waiting list in Tennessee. Here's where money comes in.

To get on a transplant center's list, a prospective patient must go there, be evaluated by the staff and have tests to confirm medical need.

2. Emanuel D. Thorne, "The Dilemma of the Body's Growing Value," *The Public Interest* (Spring 1990). Jeremy Bentham, in an 1831 essay entitled "Of What Use is a Dead Man to the Living?" argued that autopsies should be allowed because of the usefulness of human bodies to research. Indeed, Bentham invited his friends to observe the dissection of his own body upon his death. Bentham thought, moreover, that donors of exceptional quality could, once dead, inspire future generations of thinkers by their physical presence. In that spirit, each year since his death in 1832, the trustees of University College, London, bring out Bentham's preserved body during their annual deliberations.

If accepted, the patient must be able to get to that center within seven or eight hours if an organ becomes available. That means renting or buying a place nearby or being able to afford a private jet, or $3,000 to $5,000 for a chartered plane to fly on short notice. People can get on the wait lists as long as they meet the terms.[3]

Stories both fictional and real abound on this topic. The account of the father who wanted to donate his heart to his dying son and the woman who asked to hear her husband's heartbeat in the recipient raise questions: Should either of these requests be granted?[4] Organs, of course, have a personal meaning and significance to people, and Christians wonder if one organ has more significance than another. Since our bodies, according to Christian Scriptures, will be transformed after death (1 Cor. 15: "The perishable will be raised imperishable"), the answer seems to be no. However, we do place special symbolic value, for example, on the heart or the brain or perhaps even the blood. But there is no biblical warrant for claiming that God has consecrated one part of our body over another.

My thesis is that organ donation is a supererogatory act of charity grounded in self-giving love. It is based on the principles of beneficence, stewardship of the body and respect for persons, mutuality of relationships, justice, fidelity (the binding nature of special relationships), and the primacy of saving life. Organized giving, not routine taking, is morally preferable because it affirms the autonomy of the person over the use of her body. It respects the whole person, viewing the body as well as the mind and spirit as an integral part of what constitutes a person. It allows a person to perform an act of charity, that is, donating organs rather than violating her responsibility for the future use of her body. However, based on the insufficient number of organs compared to the staggering need, a person has a moral imperative to consider donating her organs after death. This imperative is grounded in charity, not autonomy.

In addition to the medical and ethical grounding for organ donation, there are certain side constraints that must be applied: (1) fully informed and valid consent of both parties; (2) spiritual or psychological benefit to the donor; (3) recipient selection based on need, not socioeconomic fac-

3. Marilynn Marchione, "Money Can Increase Chances on Transplant Lists," *The Virginia-Pilot,* June 25, 2009, p. 9.

4. Allen D. Verhey, "Organ Transplants: Death, Dis-organization, and the Need for Religious Ritual," in *Caring Well,* ed. David H. Smith (Louisville: Westminster John Knox Press, 2000), pp. 147-50.

tors; (4) no element of commercial exchange; (5) use of cadaver or artificial organs wherever possible; and (6) a practice of systematic giving, not indiscriminate harvesting of organs.

James Childress, the foremost ethicist in the area of organ donation and transplantation, has outlined the major themes that should form future dialogue on this subject.

> First, it will not be possible, I believe, to reverse the conception of the ownership of donated organs that has shaped many organ allocation policies over the last decade. Barring major changes in the methods of organ procurement, the community will continue to be viewed as the owner of donated organs, with the implication that transplant professionals serve as trustees and stewards of those organs and those organ allocation policies must be formulated with public as well as professional input.
>
> Second, I affirm the moral relevance of several moral principles or values in organ allocation, as well as the common metaphor of balancing. Even though it is not always possible to give each principle or value "equal weight" at every point in time, an allocation system based upon any one factor would result in injustice.
>
> Third, the process of balancing principles and values over time in organ donation policies rightly involves public participation, justification, and accountability, which need to be extended to admission to the waiting list. There are important "moral connections" between organ procurement and organ allocation. Organs are donated by and for the public, and the public, as the owner of the donated organs, should play an important role in setting the criteria for their allocation and distribution. Furthermore, confidence in the justice of policies of organ allocation and distribution appears to be an important condition for the public's willingness to donate cadaveric organs.
>
> Fourth, balancing principles and values occurs over time so that UNOS [United Network for Organ Sharing] can, quite legitimately, change the weights or points it assigns to different factors in allocation, in light of significant public principles and values and empirical evidence about the effects of existing allocation policies.[5]

The principal questions we will consider in this chapter are:

5. James F. Childress, "Ethics and the Allocation of Organs for Transplantation," *Kennedy Institute of Ethics Journal* 6, no. 4 (1996): 397-401.

(1) Is organ donation legally permissible?
(2) On what moral grounds can we justify giving organs?
(3) Is organ donation obligatory or supererogatory?
(4) What elements are necessary to assure an organ donation that is ethically permissible?
(5) What factors are morally relevant in the selection of a donor class?
(6) What are the views of religious communities?

Facts about Supply and Demand of Organs

Number of Organs Needed

The supply of organs is short. As of February 2009, 100,820 persons were waiting for organs in the United States.[6] Those awaiting kidney transplants constitute by far the highest percentage of organ recipient need. There are more than 78,000 Americans waiting for a kidney transplant, according to the United Network for Organ Sharing.[7] Worse, the gap between the number of patients waiting and the number of kidney transplants performed has grown by 110 percent in the last decade. Patients needing a kidney transplant wait about five years for a donated organ.[8] There were 16,406 kidney transplants from July 1, 2007, to June 30, 2008, of which 5,862 were from living donors.[9] The number of people waiting for a liver versus the number of liver transplants in a given year was as follows:

1995: waiting — 5,700; transplants — 3,900
1997: waiting — 9,500; transplants — 4,000
1999: waiting — 14,100; transplants — 4,500
2001: waiting 18,300; transplants — 5,000

6. See the website www.unos.org, the United Network for Organ Sharing, for a daily update of most statistics in this chapter.

7. "U.S. Transplantation Data," April 10, 2009: http://www.unos.org/data/default.asp?displayType=usData (accessed Apr. 14, 2009).

8. Kevin B. O'Reilly, "Kidney Foundation Plan Targets Financial Barriers to Donation," *American Medical News on the web,* February 23, 2009: http://www.ama-assn.org/amednews/2009/02/23/prsb0223.htm (accessed Apr. 14, 2009).

9. Scientific Registry of Transplant Recipients, Arbor Research Collaborative for Health with the University of Michigan: www.ustransplant.org (accessed Feb. 24, 2009).

Liver transplants are the second most needed: 15,723 are currently on the waiting list.[10] Other organ transplantation needs are much rarer; no other organ has more than three thousand persons who are currently on its waiting list.[11]

In Europe, there is a "chronic shortage of transplant donors. There are currently 56,000 patients waiting for a suitable organ donor in the EU, while it is estimated that twelve people die every day while waiting for transplants. Massive differences exist among the EU member states in organ donation: Spain, a country often cited as Europe's leading light for progressive organ donor legislation, performs 34.6 organ donations per million people, while in Romania the figure is 0.5 per million."[12]

Number of Transplants

In 2008, 27,958 human organ transplants were performed in the United States, continuing the trend in the upper twenty-thousands for the latter half of the decade of 2000.[13] The states where the most organ donations have been performed to date are California, Pennsylvania, Texas, and New York, with Florida coming in a close fifth.[14] (The number of conditions and types of organs is found in Appendix G at the end of this book.)

Cost of Transplants

Transplants are very expensive, with costs varying depending on the type of organ, the particular hospital, and the possibility of complications after surgery. Average costs, not including pre-transplant or follow-up treatments, are estimated as follows:

---

10. From the UNOS website (www.unos.org), as of March 12, 2009.

11. "U.S. Transplantation Data": http://www.unos.org/data/default.asp?displayType =usData (accessed Mar. 12, 2009).

12. "Commission Unveils Plans to Improve Organ Donation," *EurActiv.com,* December 10, 2008: http://www.euractiv.com/en/health/commission-unveils-plans-improve-organ -donation/article-177949 (accessed Feb. 24, 2009).

13. "Transplants in the U.S. by State," The Organ Procurement and Transplantation Network: http://www.optn.org (accessed Mar. 12, 2009).

14. "Transplants in the U.S. by State."

- Heart: $650,000
- Lung: $400,000
- Double Lung: $550,000
- Heart/Lung: $875,000
- Liver: $520,000
- Kidney: $250,000
- Pancreas: $300,000
- Kidney/Pancreas: $370,000
- Kidney/Heart: $760,000
- Liver/Kidney: $660,000
- Intestine: $900,000
- Bone Marrow (autologous): $270,000
- Bone Marrow (allogeneic related): $480,000
- Bone Marrow (allogeneic unrelated): $600,000
- Cornea: $23,300[15]

Organs from nonhuman donors, known as xenotransplants, can be even more expensive. The cost of the Baby Fae baboon heart transplant in 1984 was an estimated $1 million. This amount could pay for 30,000 office visits to an inner city clinic.[16]

Types of Organs

The list of organs or body parts that are being transplanted is increasing, to include faces, arms, and so forth. Whether we can technically do whole brain transplants remains to be seen, but we already transplant brain tissue for Parkinson's patients, which has raised the question of using fetal tissue. Types of transplants are constantly changing. For example, there have been two face transplants: one in Boston at Brigham Women's Hospital in April 2009, and another at the Cleveland Clinic in December 2008.[17]

---

15. "How much does an organ transplant cost?" © 2007 National Foundation for Transplants: www.transplants.org (accessed Mar. 12, 2009).

16. "Financing a Transplant," *Transplant Living:* http://www.transplantliving.org/ (accessed Apr. 14, 2009).

17. Associated Press, "Boston Hospital Performs Face Transplant," *msnbc.com,* April 10, 2009: http://www.msnbc.msn.com/id/30152143/ (accessed Apr. 13, 2009).

In 2004, a bullet ripped away Connie Culp's nose, cheeks and upper jaw. Metal fragments sprayed into her skull and stripped her face away, leaving nothing except for her eyes, her chin and forehead. . . .

In 2005, Culp came to the Cleveland Clinic for treatment. After 30 surgical procedures, none had restored her basic functions.

"The last resort and the last option were to consider face transplantation," said [Dr. Maria] Siemionow. Transplant recipients have to take immunosuppressing anti-rejection drugs for the rest of their life.

Doctors involved in Culp's treatment said the surgery was not about aesthetics, but to restore Culp's basic abilities.[18]

William F. May suggests two broad kinds of organ transplants:

(1) *heteroplastic* and (2) *homoplastic*. The first refers to transplanting organs from a lower species of animal to a human person; the second, to transplanting organs from one human being to another. Homoplastic transplants are subdivided into those (a) from the bodies of dead persons to living persons and (b) from one living person to another, or transplants *inter vivios*.[19]

Animal parts have been in use for several decades as a bridge to permanent human organ transplants, but there is now discussion of permanent transplantation of animal organs. This also raises the question of artificial parts and xenografts and transplants of animal organs. The *FDA Consumer Magazine* describes the current status of such xenotransplants: "Of all animals, baboons and pigs are the favored xenotransplant donors. Baboons are genetically close to humans, so they are most often used for initial experiments. Six baboon kidneys were transplanted into humans in 1964, a baboon heart into a baby in 1984, and two baboon livers into patients in 1992."[20] This introduces the question of identity: How many alien or artificial parts can I have and still be me?

With the huge shortage of organs, science is developing more and

---

18. "First U.S. Face Transplant Photos Reveal Before and After Pics," http://www.healthcheckr.com/first-u-s-face-transplant-photos-reveal-before-after-pics-3 (accessed July 20, 2010).

19. William F. May, "The Ethics of Organ Transplants," *Ethics and Medics* 21, no. 7 (July 1996).

20. Rebecca D. Williams, "Organ Transplants from Animals: Examining the Possibilities," *FDA Consumer Magazine*, U.S. Food and Drug Administration, June 1996: http://www.fda.gov/fdac/features/596_xeno.html (accessed July 21, 2008).

more artificial organs, for example, the totally mechanical heart. The CardioWest temporary Total Artificial Heart (TAH-t) is the world's first and only FDA-approved totally artificial heart (it received FDA approval on October 15, 2004, following a ten-year pivotal clinical study). Originally designed as a permanent replacement heart, it is currently approved as a bridge to a human-heart transplant for patients who are dying because both chambers of their hearts are failing (irreversible end-stage biventricular failure). There have been more than 780 implants of the CardioWest artificial heart, accounting for more than 150 patient years of life on this device. In the ten-year pivotal clinical study of the CardioWest artificial heart, 79 percent of patients receiving the artificial heart survived to transplant.[21] This is the highest bridge-to-transplant rate for any heart device in the world. The AbioCor Replacement Heart received FDA approval under a Humanitarian Device Exemption (HDE) on September 5, 2006. The AbioCor is approved for use in severe biventricular end-stage heart-disease patients who are not eligible for heart transplants and have no other viable treatment options.[22]

Ethicist Kenneth Vaux is disturbed by the human discontent with mortality and the ambition we have for infinitely interchangeable parts and pieces. So if we move to more and more plastic and animal parts, do we continue to be human?[23]

Recipients of Transplants

Matching the ethnicity of the donor with that of the recipient increases the success rate, so a lack of organs donated by multicultural populations can limit the number of recipients from those populations. Transplant recipients in 2006 by ethnicity: Caucasian 21,175; African American 4,547; Hispanic 4,455; Asian 679; other 338.[24]

21. *New England Journal of Medicine* 351 (2004): 859-67, cited in "Artificial Heart," *CardioWest website:* http://www.syncardia.com/ (accessed June 4, 2009).

22. "FDA Approves First Totally Implanted Permanent Artificial Heart for Humanitarian Uses," U.S. Food and Drug Administration, *MedSun: Newsletter #8*, October 2006: http://www.accessdata.fda.gov/scripts/cdrh/cfdocs/medsun/news/printer.cfm?id=625 (accessed June 4, 2009).

23. Otto Friedrich, "One Miracle, Many Doubts," *Time*, December 10, 1984, pp. 70-73, 77.

24. "Multicultural Perspectives," based on the Organ Procurement and Transplantation Network (OPTN) data as of October 6, 2007: www.donatelife.net (accessed Apr. 14, 2009).

There is also tension regarding whether organs should be shared on a local or national basis. "In April of 1998, Donna Shalala, the Secretary of Health and Human Services, issued a regulation requiring that organs must be allocated according to uniform medical criteria and that organ sharing must take place over broad enough areas to ensure that organs can reach the patients who need them most. In effect, she sought to overturn the strict local priority in favor of a more uniform national list based on medical need. . . . UNOS has put up great resistance, expressing a strong preference for retaining local priority."[25] No further policy updates have been implemented since then.

History of Organ Transplantation

The history of transplantation — that is, some part or product of another person implanted into someone else — can be traced to blood transfusions in the 1920s. The first successful transplant of a major human organ, a kidney, was in 1954. Advances in transplant technology, including improved surgical techniques and immunosuppressive therapy, now permit routine transplantation of the kidney, liver, heart, heart-lung, pancreas, eyes, and other tissue — with rapidly rising success rates. However, despite all the success in improving organ donation rates, organ transplantation continues to raise difficult moral and policy problems: How should organs be obtained and distributed? Who should perform transplants? Who should pay?

In terms of the number of donors, the Uniform Anatomical Gift Act, passed in 1968 in all fifty states and the District of Columbia, reflected individuals' rights to determine the use of their organs while encouraging voluntary donation. This Act allows individuals to donate their organs after death via an organ donor card or (in many states) their driver's license. If no card was signed, families could donate organs unless the individual clearly objected to donation. The act was revised in 1987, but at that time it was adopted by just twenty-six states. It was again revised in 2006. This revision retains the basic policy of the 1968 and 1987 anatomical gift acts by retaining and strengthening the "opt-in" system that honors the free choice of an individual to donate his or her organs (a process known in the organ-transplant community as "first-person consent" or "donor designation").

25. Robert M. Veatch, "A New Basis for Allocating Livers for Transplant," *Kennedy Institute of Ethics Journal* 10, no. 1 (March 2000): 75-80.

This revision also preserves the right of other persons to make an anatomical gift of a decedent's organs if the decedent had not made a gift during his lifetime. It also strengthens the right of an individual not to donate organs by signing a refusal that also bars others from making a gift of a person's organs after the individual's death.[26]

In response to the shortage of organs, the 1984 National Organ Transplant Act (PL 98-507) expanded and centralized the nationwide network for procuring organs and matching donors and recipients. In addition, forty-two states and the District of Columbia have passed "required request" or "routine inquiry" legislation that requires hospital personnel to ask family members of suitable donors about donation. The way in which family members are asked to donate makes a huge difference in the outcome. The Minnesota statute, for example, requires hospitals to establish a procedure to identify potential organ donors to (1) assure that families are made aware of the option of organ and tissue donation and the option to decline; (2) require that the organ procurement agency be notified; and (3) establish medical criteria and practical considerations regarding the suitability and feasibility of organ donation for transplantation. Preliminary evidence indicates that these laws serve to increase the number of organs donated.

Medical Issues in Transplantation

Paul Ramsey, when resolving bioethical quandaries, always turned to a medical indications policy as part of their resolution. The following criteria for transplantation are fairly standard: There should be a *life-threatening need* on the part of the patient. This might seem straightforward, but weighing the need of a particular patient and the degree to which a procedure is not life-threatening to the donor may not be that straightforward. There should be a *known benefit to the patient*. The organ recipient should benefit medically from the organ. *Tested medical procedures* should be used. Transplants need to have been practiced and refined so that it is not simply experimentation. Of course, in the early years of Christian Barnard's groundbreaking heart transplantations, they were certainly experimental. Without experimental transplants, how can medical professionals deter-

26. "Revised Uniform Anatomical Gift Act 2006 (Last Revised and Amended in 2007)," National Conference of Commissioners on Uniform State Laws: www.anatomicalgiftact.org (accessed Apr. 14, 2009).

mine their efficiency?[27] *The procedure should not be life threatening to the donor.* There are certain organs that obviously cannot be donated, such as the heart from a live person or a kidney if the donor only has one. The *type of organ* may make a difference if it will benefit the patient, and it may determine the effect of the organ on the recipient as well. Does one feel guilty about having someone else's parts, especially if it is the heart?

If you accept Descartes's idea that the person is a soul inside a body, you can say that the soul is there even if the brain has been transplanted. How do different recipients truly feel? How does a 250-pound male construction worker feel about having the heart of an eighteen-year-old female? How does a black man feel about having a white man's heart? As Joseph Fletcher pointed out, if the entire brain were transplanted, it would be a body transplant. From this perspective, the "person" being saved would be the donor.

Legal Issues

Ownership

In order to determine the question of ownership, we need to analyze the substances that make up a human. According to Margaret Swain and Randy Marusyk, there are three levels to classifying substances that constitute a whole human being: (1) person and persona; (2) functional body unit: blood, an organ, a cell (each of which can carry out its function in another person's body); and (3) something produced from human material, such as a cell line or cloned genetic material. It is the third type that may generate issues of property rights.

The first level deals with the uniqueness of a person in her entirety. The second level is a *res nullius* categorization. Ownership would be acquired by the first person who took possession of the tissue. However, if the tissue or blood were to be returned to the person, it would continue to be hers, but held in trust by the doctor or other agents. So this classification pertains to temporarily removed tissue.

Tissue that is permanently removed from a body would fall under a

27. Claudia Wallis and Steven Holmes, "Baby Fae Stuns the World," *Time*, November 12, 1984: http://www.time.com/time/magazine/article/0,9171,926947,00.html (accessed Apr. 16, 2009).

third level of classification, *res communes omnium,* "things that by natural law are the common property of all humans." Only after products were created from the human material would property rights be created. This is linked to John Locke's view of human labor, which creates rights in the product produced by one's labor. The laborer would own everything produced except the original genetic material, which would continue to belong to the body. "If a human gene is cloned into a million copies of that gene, the laborer would own only the million copies but not the original gene."[28]

How would this analysis apply to the John Moore case, in which his cancerous spleen cells were used to develop lucrative pharmaceutical products without his consent? A California state court ruled that a person may retain property rights to tissues and cells removed during surgery and subsequently used in scientific research.[29]

Categories of Donors

In addition to general questions regarding the legal aspects of organ donation are specific ones concerning organ donors. First, in the case of autonomous donors, organ donation is legal if there is fully informed consent. The problem is determining whether a person has been fully informed. Is it really possible to project what life without a particular organ would be like? The limits to donation are as follows: (1) it cannot inflict death, for example, liver donation, and (2) it cannot severely incapacitate, for example, donation of an eye.

Legally, in the second class of donors, such as those with diminished autonomy as children and the mentally disabled, the following stipulations are made: (1) parental consent is necessary, and (2) a review of such consent is needed by a committee or court. Cases such as *Strunk v. Strunk* (incompetent brother a kidney donor to brother with renal failure) were based on the benefits argument to the donor because of his close attachment to his brother. Hence, those with diminished autonomy may legally be donors.[30]

28. Margaret S. Swain and Randy W. Marusyk, "An Alternative to Property Rights in Human Tissue," *Hastings Center Report* 20, no. 5 (1990): 12-13.

29. "Private parts = private property? — John Moore Case," *Science News,* July 30, 1988.

30. *Strunk v. Strunk* 445 S.W.2d 145 (Ky 1969). The mother of a mentally disabled 27-year-old man petitioned the court for authority to allow a kidney from that son to be transplanted into his 28-year-old brother, her other son, who was suffering from a fatal kidney dis-

The 1956 Masden case seemed to establish a legal ground for donation that was called identical twin "solidarity."[31]

The third class of "donors," cadavers, is legally encompassed within the Uniform Anatomical Gift Act, which makes cadaver donation legal in all fifty states.[32] The flaw for some is that it does not prohibit the sale of cadaver organs. In terms of routinely salvaging organs from cadavers, the only legal barrier may be the First Amendment to the U.S. Constitution, in which freedom of religion is guaranteed since some religions oppose violating the body after death (see discussion of this below in this chapter). The law allows fairly wide latitude concerning the question of organ donation; hence ethical guidelines are needed for decision-making.[33] One way to avoid problems with choosing appropriate classes of donors is to use artificial organs or alternative therapies, such as medication.

Ethical Considerations

There are six major ethical considerations: (1) informed consent; (2) selection of donor; (3) selection of recipient based on need and benefit; (4) no commercial exchange; (5) giving, not harvesting; and (6) wise allocation of scarce resources.

Informed Consent

Informed consent is based on giving people the right to choose and assuring minimal risk. The quality of informed consent is influenced by numerous factors, such as: the economic and social status of the person, that is,

---

ease. The state circuit court adopted the findings of the county court, which held that the operation was necessary and that the disabled brother's well-being would be more severely jeopardized by the death of his brother than by surgery. On appeal, the Kentucky Court of Appeals affirmed the lower court's decision, holding that a court of equity had the power to authorize the surgery when the findings of the lower court were based on substantial evidence.

31. Paul Ramsey, *The Patient as Person* (New Haven: Yale University Press, 1970), p. 165.

32. National Conference of Commissioners on Uniform State Laws, "Revised Uniform Anatomical Gift Act (2006) (Last Revised or Amended in 2007)," October 24, 2007: http://www.Anatomicalgiftact.Org/Desktopdefault.Aspx?Tabindex-1&Tabid=63 (accessed Apr. 14, 2009).

33. Jeneen Interlandi, "Not Just Urban Legend," *Newsweek on the web,* 10 January 2009: http://www.newsweek.com/id/178873 (Apr. 14, 2009).

the more desperate he is, the less likely is informed consent; the use of nontechnical words; the provision of consent forms with clear explanations; the separation of the doctor-patient and subject-researcher relationship; and providing as much information as possible even at the risk of losing a potential participant.

Some doubt whether, in certain circumstances, consent can really be informed. More important, from the ethicist's viewpoint, is the fact of consent itself. It is here that Paul Ramsey's analysis focuses on the importance of consent and its relationship to proxy consent. The principle of consent for Ramsey is the cardinal canon of loyalty drawing persons together in medical practice and investigation. Fidelity is the bond between consenting persons where both are recognized as having value. Consent is possible because of our potential to be co-adventurers; consent is necessary because of the tendency to overreach the relationship. This should be a partnership where mutuality between persons exists. In other words, consent once given must be continually renegotiated.[34]

The only exception to informed consent is when persons are in extreme danger and cannot give consent. We then turn to assumed or implied consent, which could be in effect to save a person's life. However, when in doubt, we should always lean against the excess of the defect, à la Aristotle: we strive for the mean — consent — because the goal of research is always trying to draw us away. Determining whether consent is truly informed is very difficult. However, consent is essential for respect of persons.

Deciding on full disclosure vis-à-vis informed consent is not always straightforward. Some patients will suffer undue anxiety as a result of full disclosure. However, this assessment can often lead to paternalism on the part of the researcher or even one's personal physician. The scientific method has a public character, and it should be open to criticism. This is part of the testing of its hypothesis: errors are systematically criticized as part of the process.[35]

Selection of Donor Class

If we move from the criteria for ethically permissible organ donation to donors, what classes of donors are morally acceptable and unacceptable? What factors are morally relevant in the selection of a donor class? Can we

34. Ramsey, *The Patient as Person*, pp. 9-11.
35. Ramsey, *The Patient as Person*, pp. 1-58.

even use the word "donor" if organs are taken from those who *do not have* — or never *did have* — competence to give permission. The word "donor" already suggests those who can give consent. The four classes generally under consideration are autonomous persons, persons with diminished autonomy, newborns and fetuses, and cadavers.

Autonomous Persons   Autonomous individuals are those who are free, responsible, mentally competent adults; they may be related or unrelated living donors. Special problems do exist with relatives, who are medically preferable but are more susceptible to emotional turmoil. Some people have even referred, for example, to moral blackmail or competing obligations to a spouse or other children that may surface. The issue is whether they can ever give free and informed consent with so many emotional factors at work?

Unrelated donors present a problem because of mixed motivations, whether altruistic, pecuniary, or psychological; hence, they are rarely used. However, if they are both fully informed and do experience spiritual or psychological benefits, they should be acceptable donors. Questions arise about religiously motivated donors, those whom some surgeons consider unstable, who come forward saying, for example, "Jesus told me to give my arm to someone else," and so forth. Are they donating from religious altruism, or is their motivation inappropriately pathologized? In making the case for a distinction between religious faith and pathological "religiosity," we must see the challenge of assessing the religiously motivated potential donor. There are some researchers who question whether unrelated donors can be altruistic. Since most donors are motivated by relationships, genetic kinship, or emotional connection, religious convictions require clinicians to create new assessment tools for donors. "This may be difficult for some clinicians who lose their bearings, but this does not mean that donors must also lose theirs."[36]

Persons with Diminished Autonomy   This category includes children, prisoners, the mentally disabled, and the comatose or the terminally ill. The two categories most often under consideration are twins and siblings. Both groups may include minors, adult siblings, or parents who may or

36. David J. Dixon and Susan E. Abbey, "Religious altruism and the living organ donor," *Progress in Transplantation,* September 2003: http://findarticles.com/p/articles/mi_qa4117/is_200309/ai_n9294849/?tag=content;col1 (accessed Apr. 16, 2009).

may not be mentally competent. These groups all have in common their inability to give informed consent. Since informed consent is a necessary criterion — not to be substituted by proxy consent — and since they cannot choose to donate their organs, their organs are actually being taken from them, not donated by them. In view of that, should people from these groups donate organs? Benefits to either donor or recipient are not relevant, because the first condition of informed consent cannot be met. In other words, if we define organ donation as an act of charity, and acts of charity can only be performed by autonomous persons, then those of diminished autonomy are unable to donate organs.

A tension exists here, however, if one believes that special relationships create obligations that override autonomy. Hence, obligations from special relationships may necessitate donation, for example, a kidney between brothers. But is the covenant relationship, as well as bodily integrity, destroyed when we take an organ? Richard McCormick develops a slightly different line of reasoning for human experimentation that could also be applied in this situation. The case of *Strunk v. Strunk* is an illustration of this: an incompetent brother was allowed to donate his kidney to his brother with renal failure because of his close attachment to his brother. The logic here is that, if those with diminished autonomy were able to decide, they would want to perform this act of charity.[37]

Newborns and Fetuses   The controversy surrounding fetal body parts includes the debate about the conception or abortion of a fetus for the sole purpose of taking its organs, tissue, or bone marrow. There have been a number of recent cases of desperate parents needing bone marrow or tissue for their dying child who have pursued this path. If we rigorously follow informed consent, this would be morally unacceptable. Furthermore, there is the special case of the anencephalic newborns (born without a brain): some consider them a primary source of organs.

Cadavers   With increasing moral dilemmas surrounding live donors, cadavers are now being considered. McCormick, Ramsey, and others support the option. At first, cadavers seem ideal from an ethical standpoint because they are morally neutral. However, complications are involved. First, there are the medical problems of removing the organs in time (for

---

37. Richard A. McCormick, S.J., "Public Policy and Fetal Research," *How Brave a New World?* (New York: Doubleday, 1981), p. 84.

the kidney, thirty minutes to one hour), of communication between the donor's physician, who is caring for her patient in the process of dying, and the transplant surgeon, who is watching over the body for the organs he wishes to harvest (the legal requirement is that these be two separate individuals). The biggest problem with cadaver donations is the pressure to broaden the definition of death, that is, cessation of neocortical functions rather than the mechanical functions of the heart.

> The Pittsburgh protocol proposed a two-minute waiting period to assure that the patient would not auto-resuscitate. Once the patient was declared dead, the heart would be restarted and the corpse ventilated to support the continued profusion of organs. . . . Since the University of Pittsburgh was a leading transplant center, the proposal occasioned widespread comment and analysis. How, it was asked, could you declare death by irreversible cessation of heart and respiration when, in fact, you could medically restart the heart and ventilate the lungs? How is the patient dead if the heart is once again beating? What is the meaning of irreversible cessation?[38]

"In September 2001 the ethics committee of the American College of Critical Care Medicine and the Society of Critical Care Medicine (S.C.C.M.) issued a position paper entitled 'Recommendations for Nonheartbeating Organ Donation.' The S.C.C.M. committee supported the proposition that it is ethically and medically acceptable to participate in the procurement of organs from non-heartbeating cadaver donors. . . . The S.C.C.M. committee estimates that as many as 20 percent of potential donors are now in this category."[39] In most states the legal definition of death requires "irreversible cessation of all functions of the entire brain, including the brain stem."[40] (I discuss these issues further in the legal chapter.)

An added problem of cadaver organs is the lower survival rate for these transplants. The following shows the one-year patient and organ graft survival rates:[41]

---

38. John J. Paris, "Harvesting Organs from Cadavers: An Ethical Challenge," *America* (April 29, 2002): http://www.americamagazine.org/content/article.cfm?article_id=1806 (accessed Aug. 14, 2008).

39. Paris, "Harvesting Organs from Cadavers."

40. Kirsti A. Dyer MD, MS, FT, "Legal Definition of Death," *About.com,* August 24, 2006: http://dying.about.com/od/glossary/g/legaldeath.htm (accessed Apr. 14, 2009).

41. Congressional Kidney Caucus: 25 Facts About Organ Donation and Transplanta-

	Patient Survival Rate	*Graft Survival Rate*
Kidney (cadaveric)	94.8%	87.5%
Kidney (live donor)	97.7%	93.5%

According to the United Network for Organ Sharing (UNOS), kidneys transplanted from living donors typically survive about eleven years; kidneys transplanted from deceased donors typically survive about eight years.[42]

The ethical problems of the stewardship and integrity of the body and caring for the dying while benefiting from them are difficult dilemmas. Informed consent to donate is through the Uniform Anatomical Gift Act, which explains that there will be mutilation of a donor's body after death. Psychological benefits to the donor are also presented, that is, helping someone else to live by donating one's body for good purposes, whereas the nondonating alternative would be simple anatomical decay.

What is important, according to Ramsey and McCormick, is organized giving, not the routine taking of cadaver organs. Society is better when giving and receiving is the rule. Respect for humans includes the integrity of the person, which extends to the human body, and that should continue after death. In other words, cadaver organs may be used if donated by a stated intention of the future donor before his or her death. This is in contrast to some recent proposals that cadaver organs should be routinely taken unless there are instructions to the contrary. One interesting suggestion is for the military to have a uniform policy of organ harvesting of war casualties; but this would fail to meet the moral grounds that organs should be given rather than taken.

Criteria for Selection of Recipient

Selection of a recipient is both a medical and moral issue. Procedures for selecting transplant recipients vary among transplant centers. Typically, an interdisciplinary team does an initial evaluation of the patient based on

---

tion, February 2002: http://www.house.gov/mcdermott/kidneycaucus/25facts.html (accessed Sept. 3, 2009).

42. "Talking About Transplantation," United Network for Organ Sharing, January 2009, p. 8: http://www.unos.org/SharedContentDocuments/Living_Donation_Booklet_Final.pdf (accessed Apr. 16, 2009).

objective medical criteria: diagnosis, extent of disease, probability of success, and (sometimes) financial and social factors. Transplant candidates are then placed on the center's waiting list. Regional organ procurement agencies and hospitals that perform transplants belong to UNOS, based in Richmond, Virginia. This network obtains and matches organ donors with recipients. When an organ becomes available, the patient highest on the waiting list with suitable tissue and blood type receives the transplant. This procedure raises complex questions: Who should decide? Using what process? Based on what additional criteria? Suggested decision-makers include patients, physicians, and appropriately constituted committees, which in turn raises other concerns: Can physicians be asked to make these rationing choices without undermining the patient-physician relationship? Can committees overcome the biases of their membership? No agreement has been reached on who the decision-makers should be, but there is consensus that they must be held accountable for a fair selection process.

The main criterion for the selection of a donor-organ recipient is benefit, and that is usually defined medically. In the 1980s the University of Pittsburgh Transplant Center developed a set of possible criteria for recipient selection and conducted a survey to determine evaluation of them. They provide us with an opportunity to reflect on various factors that can be taken into account; but not all of them are equally applicable to individual cases.

> *Ability to pay:* whether or not the prospective recipient has enough money or insurance to pay for the required services.
> *Addiction:* whether or not the prospective recipient has a physical dependence on alcohol or other drugs that may have contributed to liver disease.
> *Age:* how many years the prospective recipient has lived.
> *Favored group:* whether or not the prospective recipient is a member of a particular group, identified by geographical location, veteran status, income, profession, and so forth.
> *Length of benefit:* the length of the recipient's expected survival with treatment.
> *Likelihood of benefit:* How likely is it that the desired medical outcome will in fact occur?
> *Longevity:* whether or not the prospective recipient will live longer because of the treatment.

Progress of science: How much scientific knowledge may be gained from treating the prospective recipient?

Psychological ability: the ability of a prospective recipient to cope emotionally and intellectually with the treatment regimen.

Quality of benefit: the quality of life the prospective recipient may expect if accepted for treatment.

Resources required: whether or not the prospective recipient will be likely to require particularly long and expensive treatment.

Gender: whether the prospective recipient is male or female.

Social value: how much society, including people individually, will benefit if the prospective recipient is treated.

Special responsibilities: whether or not the physical life of at least one other person, or something equally important, depends on whether or not the prospective recipient lives.

Supportive environment: how supportive (financially, emotionally, etc.) the prospective recipient's family, friends, and community are likely to be over the course of treatment.

Willingness: the expressed or implicit desire of the prospective recipient to undergo treatment.[43]

Although these are helpful criteria, they should not all be applied in every case. Their ranking could vary from one case to another. One person has recommended that the selection of organ recipients should be correlated with those who are willing to donate their organs.[44]

In a recent request for an update on these criteria, I received the following response from Dr. Michael DeVera, Thomas E. Starzl Transplantation Institute, University of Pittsburgh Medical Center: "We don't have a formal written protocol outlining these criteria. As you know, liver transplant is widely accepted now as the definitive treatment for end-stage liver disease. In general, medically 'suitable' patients who have end-stage liver disease and have good social support are deemed as good candidates and are placed on the list."[45]

43. Selection criteria sent for evaluation by the author in the 1980s by the University of Pittsburgh Medical Center Transplant Center.

44. John Powers, chairman and founder, FirTH Alliance, LLC, Alexandria, Virginia, in a conversation with the author in February 2009.

45. "Even if patients have enough money to qualify for a transplant, the transplant center must also deem them good candidates psychologically and socially. The criteria vary widely. In a survey he conducted in the late 1980's, Dr. James L. Levenson, a professor of psy-

Some suggest that patients should be ranked based on the expected gain in years-of-life compared to continuing dialysis. "However, such a system comes with a number of significant trade-offs, with some ethnic and age groups being more likely to benefit from transplants, and therefore ranking higher than others. The challenge for policy makers is to create a ranking system that takes into account those who do not meet maximum benefit requirements."[46] Caplan and Coelho note that "our desire to rescue the sick conflicts with our desire to do the greatest good for the greatest number of persons with scarce resources."[47]

The selection of recipients is primarily grounded in the principle of justice. Access to organs — human, animal, or artificial — should only be based on life-threatening need. When competing claims exist, survival is the criterion for selection unless a donor designates the recipients, such as a parent to her child. When competing survival claims are at stake, the first person to present the need is the one to whom we are obligated. The lack of sufficient numbers of organs for those in need is reaching staggering pro-

---

chiatry, medicine and surgery at the Medical College of Virginia in Richmond, found that the criteria used vary according to organs. Heart-transplant programs are the strictest, he said, kidney programs the most lenient, and liver programs are in between. Among the factors that transplant centers said they weighed as contraindications are not having a spouse or relative or close friend for support, having suffered a recent death or loss of someone close to you, being a felon, having a history of criminal behavior, having a family history of mental illness, having schizophrenia, suffering from depression, having attempted suicide, being demented, having a personality disorder and being mentally retarded. But a patient rejected by one program might be accepted by another. For example, 54 percent of liver programs said they always exclude demented patients, 23 percent said that dementia weighed against a patient, but nearly 20 percent said it was irrelevant. Dr. Levenson also found variations in the listing of alcoholics and drug addicts. For liver transplants, most centers require that the person demonstrate abstinence for some period of time, usually from six months to a year, before the transplant. But insurance programs often impose their own criteria, with some refusing to pay altogether for a person with alcoholic liver disease and others imposing longer periods of abstinence than the medical center requires. Dr. Levenson said that 'justice would seem to call for the same criteria everywhere' in excluding patients from transplant lists. But, he added, 'the countervailing argument is that we don't have enough experience and enough data to know exactly what the right answer is.'" Gina Kolata, "Getting on a Transplant List Is the First of Many Hurdles," *The New York Times on the web,* June 10, 1995: http://query.nytimes.com/gst/fullpage.html?res=990CE7DC113 -AF933A25755C0A96395 8260&sec=health&spon=&pagewanted=all (accessed Mar. 4, 2009).

46. "Transforming Kidney Transplant Policy," *Medical News Today,* May 24, 2007: http://www.medicalnewstoday.com/articles/71409.php (accessed Apr. 14, 2009).

47. Quoted in Barbara J. Russell, "Fair Distribution and Patients Who Receive More than One Organ Transplant," *Journal of Clinical Ethics* 1, no. 13 (Spring 2002): 41.

portions in the United States, and this raises the question whether those who are not citizens of the United States should be recipients. The need for organs in itself becomes a kind of moral imperative to consider donating one's organs after death. Surprisingly, multiple types of organ (MTO) transplantation are viewed in basically the same way as single-organ and first-time transplants, except for the additional survivability criteria. What effect does this have on our interpretation of justice as fairness considering the extreme scarcity of organs?[48]

There is general agreement that candidate selection be primarily based on medical criteria: most importantly, the need for a transplant; and second, the probability of benefit from a transplant. Race, gender, and other demographic criteria are inappropriate unless they influence the medical outcome. It is also the case that some doctors may place their patients on a waiting list prior to an imminent need for an organ, which raises the problem of using length of time on the list as a criterion. Other suggested criteria, such as whether the patient has a social network of support, or whether the patient's lifestyle brought on the problem (alcoholism resulting in a liver disease) is more controversial. Moreover, even the agreed-on category of medical criteria is fuzzy. Do medical criteria, for example, include the existence of a family support network, which may increase the probability of a successful outcome? Finally, it has been suggested that, once a waiting list is established (based on medical and perhaps other criteria), the final selection from among equally eligible patients be on the basis of a lottery.

No Commercial Exchange

Financial Incentives The underlying theological question concerning selling organs is whether we own them in the first place. The fact that money can dictate and corrupt also comes into play: that is, there is a danger in connecting health care and business. While I served on the Southeast Organ Procurement Foundation (SEOPF) Ethics Committee, we received an offer from a German man wanting to sell his kidney. He first offered it for $40,000; when we did not respond, he lowered the price to $25,000. We did not accept his offer. Swain and Marusyk have presented an interesting proposal about a three-tiered legal structure of the sub-

---

48. Russell, "Fair Distribution," p. 42.

stances constitutive of human beings. "We propose instead a legal structure in which transplantable human tissue entails no property rights, but
in which such rights can be created in new forms of tissue through the investment of labor."[49]

In the previously mentioned case of John Moore, he donated his tissue
from a cancer operation to be used in medical research; he later sued when
he found out that doctors were trying to patent the unique, disease-fighting
abilities of his cells. The California court awarded him a share of any profits
from the tissue, and then the case went to the U.S. Supreme Court.[50]

Much has been made in the media of the black market in human organs. Selling organs has become a growing problem, as the poor are selling
their organs for the basic necessities of life.[51]

> Transplant tourism accounts for about 10% of global transplants. . . .
> Pakistan has always been a popular destination for the transplant tour-
> ist, and there are reports that in some villages in poor areas of Paki-
> stan, almost no one has both kidneys. Across the border in India
> where legislation banning the commercial sale of organs was intro-
> duced 10 years ago, it was recently reported that tsunami survivors in
> Chennai, whose livelihoods were destroyed, had to resort to selling
> one of their kidneys in order to survive. The typical asking price for a
> kidney is about US $15,000, but desperate donors usually receive a
> tenth of this at most. Much of the fee allegedly goes to middle-men or
> the hospitals where the transplant takes place.
>
> As long as the demand for organs outstrips supply, punitive mea-
> sures will be ineffective: organ trafficking will just go further under-
> ground. Initiatives to dramatically increase the legal supply of organ
> donation, such as the proposal for the EU-wide donor card, are ur-
> gently needed. Cultural and social barriers regarding deceased dona-
> tion should also be addressed. Otherwise, although ethically and mor-
> ally suspect, the case for legalizing and regulating the commercial sale
> of human organs may appear to have the upper hand.[52]

"Organ trafficking accounts for around 10 percent of the nearly
70,000 kidney transplants performed worldwide annually, although as

49. Swain and Marusyk, "An Alternative to Property Rights," p. 12.
50. "Private parts = private property? — John Moore Case."
51. Jeneen Interlandi, "Not Just Urban Legend."
52. "Legal and Illegal Organ Donation," *The Lancet* 369, no. 9577 (June 2007): 1901.

many as 15,000 kidneys could be trafficked each year. China, India, Pakistan, Egypt, Brazil, the Philippines, Moldova, and Romania are among the world's leading providers of trafficked organs. If China is known for harvesting and selling organs from executed prisoners, the other countries have been dealing essentially with living donors, becoming stakeholders in the fast-growing human trafficking web."[53] As of 2009 , the legal matter of trafficking in organs has moved to the United States with the case of Levy Rosenbaum (it existed before that, but Rosenbaum's was the first prosecuted case).

> The possibility that organ trafficking is going on in the United States — and that the surgery took place in this country — was raised last week with the arrest of Levy Izhak Rosenbaum in an FBI sting.
>
> The New York man was charged with plotting to buy a kidney from an Israeli and sell it to an American patient for $160,000. Prosecutors said Rosenbaum was secretly recorded boasting that he had brokered "quite a lot" of transplants over 10 years.
>
> If the allegations are true, it would be the first documented case of organ trafficking in the United States and would confirm something many medical insiders long suspected was going on, transplant experts said.
>
> Buying or selling organs is illegal in the United States and nearly everywhere else in the world. But there is a thriving black market because demand far outstrips supply. In the United States alone last year, 4,540 people died awaiting kidneys. . . .
>
> According to prosecutors, Rosenbaum was shockingly familiar with the U.S. system and how to beat it. Sellers and recipients would concoct stories about being relatives or friends to fool hospitals into thinking no money was changing hands. . . .[54]

The American Medical Association is calling for a change in current federal law so that pilot studies could be conducted on the possible benefits of offering financial compensation for organ donation. About 80 percent of families agree to donate the organs of a loved one on life support who is brain dead or suffering severe brain trauma if the process is done right. The study would help to determine how many of the remaining 20 percent would be con-

53. "Organ Trafficking: A Fast-Expanding Black Market," *Jane's on the web,* March 5, 2008: http://www.janes.com/news/publicsafety/jid/jid080305_1_n.shtml (Apr. 4, 2009).

54. *The Virginia Pilot,* July 7, 2009, p. 8.

vinced to help out if they were offered incentives — such as paying for their loved one's funeral service, college scholarships for the deceased donor's children, tax incentives, or even cash to the families for donating.[55]

Other advocates, such as Fern Schumer Chapman, believe that the only way to increase the supply is by putting a price tag on specific organs. Donors could contract with a firm to sell their usable body parts, with a fee going to their estate; or a health-insurance agency could pay the next of kin for a dead relative's organs. Society doesn't expect people to work for free. Why does it expect people to give organs for nothing?[56] Radcliffe-Richards further argues that the burden of proof rests on those who oppose selling organs because there is a known benefit to the seller (money) and to the buyer (life).[57] In fact, it has been argued that not to allow the selling of a kidney by a live donor, for example, is an infringement of the potential vendor's autonomy.

Still, many people are leery of the fallout from financial gain entering into the calculus. There is a widespread argument against selling organs, but what about the donation of umbilical cord blood or general blood? Others say that the arguments that organ sales cloud free choice and the need for money means being coerced by poverty are spurious because there are other ways to eliminate poverty, and prohibiting organ sales will not do it. Furthermore, there is much more danger in unregulated selling on the black market, which has a much higher risk of abuse.[58] The proposal for commercial gain from organ sales seems morally and theologically suspect. There are several reasons for opposing an ownership view of our bodies. Body parts should not be bought and sold as if our bodies were slaves to be auctioned to the highest bidder. The body is a sacred trust from birth to death to burial. As I will discuss below, a stewardship model is my aim.

55. Joyce Tsai, "AMA Wants to Evaluate Organ Donation Rewards," *Dallas Business Journal,* July 18, 2008: http://www.bizjournals.com/dallas/stories/2008/07/21/story11.html (accessed Apr. 14, 2009).

56. Editorial, "Debate: Don't Put a Price on Human Organs," *USA Today,* January 1, 1989, p. 8A.

57. Janet Radcliffe-Richards, Rainer W. G. Gruessner, and Enrico Benedetti, "Pro: The Philosopher's Perspective," in *Living Donor Organ Transplantation* (Dubuque, IA: McGraw-Hill Professional, 2007), pp. 88-90.

58. Janet Radcliffe-Richards et al., "The Case for Allowing Kidney Sales," in *Bioethics: An Anthology,* ed. Helga Kuhse and Peter Singer, 2nd ed. (Hoboken, NJ: John Wiley and Sons, 2006), pp. 487-90.

Giving, not Harvesting

Routine harvesting in the absence of permission is morally questionable, presumed consent aside. Organized giving of organs is morally preferable because it affirms the autonomy of the person over the use of his body. It respects the whole person because it views the body as well as mind and spirit as integral parts of what constitute a person. It allows a person to perform an act of charity, that is, donating organs rather than violating his responsibility for future use of his body. Of course, there is the reality that, even when a person has signed an organ donor card, his wishes can be trumped by the family's refusal.

Allen Verhey expresses how the Uniform Anatomical Gift Act (UAGA) positively influenced the shift toward giving rather than harvesting: "The language and the legislation recognized that although Dr. Barnard [or any other doctor] might want my heart, it was not his to take; it could only be given — and only by those with the authority to make such a gift, that is to say, by the person whose body it is while alive and/or by the family whose responsibility it is to dispose of the body appropriately when the person dies."[59] The societal values that influenced the UAGA include: saving lives and improving the quality of life; respecting individual autonomy; promoting a sense of community through acts of generosity; showing respect for the decedent; and showing respect for the wishes of the family.[60]

In the most recent development, European Union countries have called for an organ donor card and phone hotline to ensure that all donation is voluntary and altruistic.[61] "The level of organ donation does not come close to meeting the demand, and nearly 10 people die every day in Europe while waiting for an organ. There are wide variations between Member States in organ donation rates, ranging from 34.6 donations per million population in Spain to 6 per million population in Greece."[62]

---

59. Verhey, "Organ Transplants," in *Caring Well*, ed. Smith, p. 158.

60. "Organ Transplantation: Issues and Recommendations, 1986," the report of the Task Force on Organ Transplantation, in *Source Book in Bioethics: A Documentary History*, ed. Albert R. Jonsen, Robert M. Veatch, and LeRoy Walters (Washington, DC: Georgetown University Press, 1998), p. 424.

61. "MEPs Back Europe Organ Donor Card," *BBC News on the web*, April 22, 2008: http://news.bbc.co.uk/2/hi/europe/7358789.stm (accessed Apr. 14, 2009).

62. "Questions and Answers on Organ Donation and Transplantation in the EU," *Europa Press Releases RAPID*, June 27, 2006: http://europa.eu/rapid/pressReleasesAction.do ?reference=MEMO/06/251 (accessed Apr. 14, 2009).

Routine inquiry should be coupled with voluntary giving. The mother of a young child who suffered brain death describes how, though she had not previously considered organ donation, she found solace in the opportunity that was presented to her: "I can honestly admit that out of my personal tragedy something beautiful has blossomed, a living memorial to my daughter. And I truly believe that this was made possible because I was contacted by someone who epitomized my concept of what compassion is all about."[63]

Wise Allocation of Scarce Resources

A 2005 Gallup poll revealed that more than 50 percent of the population of the United States was willing to donate organs after death. However, inefficiencies in the current system mean that even willing donors may not donate because families raise objections or there is a question about consent.[64] We have raised the challenges in securing organs. The question remains how best to use those available organs, as well as weighing the cost of transplants against other urgent health care needs, in a society where forty-seven million have had no health care insurance at all to cover their basic health needs.

Moral Grounds for Donation

In light of the realities of need for and costs of organs, what are the moral guidelines that can be used in allocation of scarce medical resources — dollars or procedures? There are several ethical considerations: (1) the greatest good for the greatest number, or justice as fairness; (2) protection of the most defenseless; the most needy should receive priority, that is, compensatory justice; (3) the neighbor in need, a person who presents herself to us, as in the parable of the Good Samaritan (Luke 10:29-37); and (4) cost versus benefit.

Allocation is difficult because some celebrities, or people who go

---

63. "Organ Transplantation: Issues and Recommendations, 1986," p. 426.

64. Scott Carney, "The Case for Mandatory Organ Donation," *wired.com,* May 8, 2007: http://www.wired.com/medtech/health/news/2007/05/india_transplants_donorpolicy (accessed Apr. 2009).

public with heart-wrenching stories, or local people may jump the queue. It is not straightforward, and thus foundational moral principles are needed. These principles are well tested and are directly applicable.

Beneficence

Sacrificial love based on Jesus' example of the crucifixion may challenge us to forgo our best interests to save someone else's life. The application of other moral grounds for justifying organ donation is generally rooted in beneficence.

The primacy of saving life, or life as a primary good — doing whatever is reasonably necessary to save a person — is a justification for donation. This perspective may be applied to society as a whole rather than to one particular individual. However, the danger here is that those individuals who are considered of "more value" to society may be the organ recipients. At this point, beneficence and justice may clash; but if we take respect for persons seriously, we would not allow a category of "more valuable" individuals. Furthermore, quality of life is a consideration if the person needing an organ believes that the pain and suffering is not worth the procedure. The linking of the donating and receiving of organs is invoked in the application of this principle.

Autonomy and Stewardship of the Body

If we believe that, based on the Kantian respect for persons, we are to be treated as free, autonomous individuals responsible for our decisions, then we should be free to use our bodies as we wish. Both a Judeo-Christian stewardship notion and a philosophical autonomy view of the body support this perspective: "I alone am responsible for my own body and to what use I put it." "I have the right to make decisions that affect me, such as donating my organs." Justice Cardozo said, in *Schloendorff v. Society of New York Hospital,* that each person has control over his or her own body regardless of the risk or effect on other dependents.[65]

65. *Schloendorff v. Society of New York Hospital,* 211 N.Y. 125, 105 N.E. 92 (1914), was a decision issued by the New York Court of Appeals in 1914 that established principles of informed consent and *respondeat superior* in United States law. The plaintiff, Mary Schloen-

However, pure autonomy does not seem to be a sufficient moral principle if we regard the effect of our actions on others. In addition, our view of the body does influence our perspective vis-à-vis organ donation. Based on an ownership view of the body, one argues that I have absolute rights over my body, and if I choose to give away parts of it or mutilate it, the decision is mine entirely, à la Tristram Engelhardt's autonomy-based ethics. This means that the man I cited above who wanted to sell his kidney for $40,000 to the SEOPF should have been allowed to do it.

In contrast to the autonomy rule is a stewardship view of the body: that is, my body is a gift held in trust to be nourished and cared for. This view can be used to defend arguments either for or against organ donation. For some, such as Paul Ramsey or the traditional Roman Catholic moral theologians, stewardship of the body means that parts of the body may only be sacrificed for the whole. We have the power, not the right, to do anything we want with our body. Ramsey buttresses this leaning against mutilation with the Jewish perspective on the integrity of the flesh, what he calls body integrity, which should not be jeopardized. Self-mutilation is not a moral good in itself, but it is justifiable only on the grounds of a greater good: my spiritual benefit and the saving of another's life.[66]

The Mutuality of Persons in Relationship

The principle of autonomy can be in conflict with our covenantal relationship with others. Men and women are not in subordination, but in ordina-

---

dorff, was admitted to New York Hospital and consented to being examined under ether to determine if a diagnosed fibroid tumor was malignant, but withheld consent for removal of the tumor. The physician examined the tumor, found it malignant, and then disregarded Schloendorff's wishes and removed the tumor. The Court found that the operation to which the plaintiff did not consent constituted medical battery. Justice Benjamin Cardozo wrote in the Court's opinion: "Every human being of adult years and sound mind has a right to determine what shall be done with his own body; and a surgeon who performs an operation without his patient's consent commits an assault for which he is liable in damages. This is true except in cases of emergency where the patient is unconscious and where it is necessary to operate before consent can be obtained." Schloendorff, however, had sued the hospital itself, not the physicians. For this reason, the Court found that a nonprofit hospital could not be held liable for the actions of its employees — a principle that became known as the "Schloendorff rule." The Court would later reject the "Schloendorff rule" in the 1957 decision of *Bing v. Thunig*.

66. Ramsey, *The Patient as Person*, p. 165.

tion: the natural, moral bond to one's neighbor. Unlike the claims of totality, our connectedness to one another is not necessarily on a physical plane, but is on a spiritual, intellectual, psychological, and moral plane. Humans are not meant to live in isolation; rather, they are to find their fulfillment in relationship. Part of what constitutes being human and moral is to exist in community. What happens to one member of the community affects the others. If someone's life is threatened by the loss of an organ and another person can spare his organ, the whole community benefits by his donation. Michael Wilson, who describes health as a community responsibility, also reflects this position.[67] We are our brothers'/sisters' keepers; therefore, our organs are not simply created for us alone, and since we are part of a greater whole, they should be available to others. In a sense, they belong to others as well. This is similar to McCormick's expansion of the doctrine of totality: we are part of the community, and hence our bodies, so to speak, belong to others.

Justice

Coupled with this argument of mutuality is a Rawlsian application of the principle of justice.[68] Justice, as fairness, may require a sharing of organs so the least advantaged achieve a general community standard by receiving a paired organ from a healthy person. Access to organs — human, animal, or artificial — should only be based on need; no other criteria should answer the claims of justice. When competing claims exist, the possibility of survival should be the criterion for selection.

Covenant Fidelity

The principle applied here — covenant fidelity — is akin to mutuality in relationships. We not only live in a community but in special relationships. These relationships create responsibilities and promises based on covenant fidelity that bind people together. This canon of loyalty forms a basis for organ donation.[69] The relationship between parent and child is one such

---

67. Michael Wilson, *The Hospital — A Place of Truth: A Study of the Role of the Hospital Chaplain* (Birmingham, UK: University of Birmingham Press, 1971).

68. John Rawls, *A Theory of Justice* (Cambridge, MA: Belknap Press, 1971).

69. See Paul Ramsey's discussion on covenant relationship in *The Patient as Person*.

covenant, in which we care for our child's health: if the child's life is threatened by the loss of an organ, a parent may, based on this canon of loyalty,
donate a paired organ to the child. I say *may*, not *must*, because there are
side constraints to this obligation. It is still considered an act of charity.
One constraint to donation is the necessity of informed and valid consent.
Another one is honoring competing obligations, that is, to other children
or to a spouse.

Donation to a child usually deepens the bond in the relationship,
though one must be aware of the possible "tyranny of the gift." Renée Fox
describes this tyranny as the degree of responsibility and indebtedness a
recipient may feel toward a donor, a mutually indentured relationship.[70]
More problematic is the relationship between siblings: How binding is it,
for example, for a twin to donate a kidney to the other twin? This has been
considered in many cases because they represent a perfect match.

Social Utility

The last category is that of social utility. This principle is tied to
McCormick and Wilson's exposition of the community, our responsibility
to it, and what we will do to achieve social utility. In other words, if large
numbers of people are dying because they need liver or heart transplants,
this will adversely affect society. We need people to make their contribution to society, à la John Stuart Mill's utilitarian principles. Utility is also
tied to patient survival.

Is Organ Donation Obligatory or Supererogatory?

Once we establish strong moral grounds for organ donation, we become
open to the danger of making it obligatory. There is a difference between

70. "The "tyranny of the gift" is an artful term coined by sociologists Renee Fox and
Judith Swazey to capture the way in which immense gratitude at receiving a kidney can
morph into a sense of constricting obligation. In their book *Spare Parts: Organ Replacement
in American Society* (1992), Fox and Swazey write: "The giver, the receiver, and their families,
may find themselves locked in a creditor-debtor vise that binds them one to another in a
mutually fettering way." See also Sally Satel, "When Altruism Isn't Moral," *The American*,
January 30, 2009: http://american.com/archive/2009/when-altruism-isnt-moral (accessed
Feb. 25, 2009).

an act being permissible and its being mandatory. Asserting that an act is permissible implies that, if certain circumstances exist and certain criteria and conditions are satisfied, then an act is allowed and considered moral. If an act is judged mandatory, then there exists an overriding obligation to perform it, no matter what the conditions, circumstances, or other values at stake.

We have attempted to guard against making organ donation obligatory by using the side constraints of the principles of autonomy, stewardship of the body, and a medical indications policy. In other words, it is not morally imperative in every circumstance to donate one's organs. The problem arises especially in the case of relatives, where one is targeted as the most suitable donor, for example, to save a brother's life. Can one refuse in good moral conscience?

As Hans Jonas has expressed it, organ donation is a gift of life, a super-erogatory gift beyond duty and claim.[71] It stems from the highest sentiments of self-sacrifice and reflects, among other things, the Judeo-Christian tradition of giving of one's self. The intention, to save another's life, is morally akin to heroic self-sacrifice; thus the agent donor would be similar to James O. Urmson's description of a hero.[72]

Religious Communities' Attitudes toward Organ Donation and Transplantation

William F. May contrasts various religious perspectives on organ donation. He characterizes the Judeo-Christian tradition as seeing the body as real and good, in contrast to the Christian Scientist tradition, which thinks of it as unreal — a kind of Manichean view of the body as evil. The body and spirit are indivisible in this existence, so we should not regard the body lightly; but we can still donate our body parts.[73]

Religious tradition has shown great respect for the body, even as we believe that "the person" is no longer there after death. For this reason, burial rather than cremation was the tradition of the early church, and this

71. Hans Jonas, "Philosophical Reflections on Experimenting with Human Subjects," in *Philosophical Essays* (Upper Saddle River, NJ: Prentice-Hall, 1974), p. 131.

72. James O. Urmson, "Saints and Heroes," in *Essays in Moral Philosophy*, ed. A. Melden (Seattle: University of Washington Press, 1958).

73. William F. May, *The Patient's Ordeal* (Bloomington, IN: Indiana University Press, 1991), pp. 187-91.

still dominates in some churches. This powerful aversion to tampering with the body should cause us to have strong warrant against mutilating it.

Along with other church fathers, Augustine did not agree that burial was necessary for the resurrection of the body. In fact, there seems little basis for concluding that those who have been mutilated by accident, disease, or other forms of destructive death will have any less of a resurrected body than those with so-called perfect bodies. However, there is probably little agreement with the position that Christian burial is in itself an antimoral act.

It is this respect for the body and the desire to enter into God's presence intact, coupled with a fear of abuse by medical science, that has engendered opposition to organ donation and transplantation in the African-American community. In working with black churches to educate people about these issues, I have found that abstract presentations are of little value. Testimonials by donors and recipients within the context of a worship service were the most effective means of education.[74]

Traditionally, the Roman Catholic theology of the body was based on the doctrine of totality as promulgated by Popes Pius XI and XII, which allowed no destruction or mutilation of oneself except when the good of the whole body was at stake. This reflected Aquinas's position that a diseased member could be sacrificed for the good of the whole organism. As historically applied, this doctrine did not allow self-mutilation for the sake of one's neighbor. Therefore, being traditionally based on the doctrine of totality, organ donation was not justified.

More recently, however, this very doctrine of totality has been extended by some Roman Catholic theologians and philosophers to include not only permission, but also an incentive or imperative, to donate one's organs. Augustine Regan, and later Bernard Haring, argued that a logical extension of totality would include the unity between people based on our fullest nature being expressed in community.[75] Richard McCormick, as I

74. Jessee Barber and Clive Callendar, *The Last Gift of Life*, a video produced by Howard University Medical School and aired in many black churches in Washington, DC, which was very effective in recruiting donors and recipients.

75. Augustine Regan, "The Basic Morality of Organic Transplants Between Living Humans," *Studia Moralia* 3 (1965): 320-61, cited by Charles Curran in *Changes in Official Catholic Moral Teaching* (Mahwah, NJ: Paulist, 2003); Bernard Haring, *The Law of Christ*, p. 242, cited by Albert R. Jonsen, "From Mutilation to Donation: The Evolution of Catholic Moral Theology Regarding Organ Transplantation," Catholic Social Concerns Lecture Series, University of San Francisco, March 29, 2005: http://www.usfca.edu/lanecenter/pdf/Jonsen_OrganDonation.pdf (accessed Apr. 28, 2009).

have mentioned above, further advanced this argument to include the use of our organs in the service of others. Furthermore, we derive both spiritual and psychological benefit from such donation. Beneficence is a two-way street.[76]

As a Protestant, Ramsey disagrees with McCormick's extension or what he labels the misinterpretation of the doctrine of totality. Here follows an interesting exchange between them. His first objection is based on the "sticky benefits" theory. If we include self-love and benefits as resulting from organ donation, then we pervert its meaning as an act of charity. True Christian love seeks only the good of the neighbor, with no reward in view.

His second objection to this extension is its disregard of bodily integrity. Furthermore, he embraces the Jewish perspective of the integrity of the flesh, which should not be jeopardized.[77] Self-mutilation is not a moral good in itself, but is justifiable only on the grounds of a greater good, that is, my spiritual benefit and the saving of another's life. If our organs belong to others as well as ourselves, then we are no longer unique, inviolate persons: any mutilation may be justified. If the meaning of being a person in community includes organ donation, there are no limits to the number of organs we can be expected to donate. The presumption to donate could constantly accelerate — to the point of including the heart, liver, and eyes.

McCormick criticized Ramsey's analysis on several grounds. He first points out that acts of charity and self-love are not mutually exclusive. The Bible itself says: "Love your neighbor as yourself." It is possible that bodily integrity can only be grounded in self-love. According to McCormick, Ramsey overlooks the difference between self-love and *inordinate* self-love.[78]

Organ donation, which is motivated by desiring good for the recipient, is not cancelled as an act of charity just because the donor may receive some benefit. All acts of Christian love can be said to eventually benefit the giver; they provide a sense of satisfaction in obeying God's command, of fulfilling our raison d'être, of assuring eternal life. Furthermore, as Charles Curran observes, Ramsey's concern with bodily integrity may itself be a form of self-love.[79]

---

76. Richard McCormick, "Transplantation of Organs: A Comment on Paul Ramsey," *Theological Studies* 36 (1975): 508.

77. Ramsey, *The Patient as Person,* pp. 166, 181.

78. McCormick, "Transplantation of Organs," p. 508.

79. Charles E. Curran, *Politics, Medicine, and Christian Ethics: A Dialogue with Paul Ramsey* (Philadelphia: Fortress Press, 1973), p. 140.

McCormick's second point is that a risk-benefit formula can answer Ramsey's concern about wholesale transplantation. Organ donation based on the interrelatedness of reasons does not justify every individual case; it may be permissible, even praiseworthy, but it is not obligatory in every case, such as with people of diminished autonomy. The risk of psychological or physical damage to the donor must be weighed against the benefit to the recipient. Hence, McCormick does modulate his position.

Specific Positions of Religious Bodies

In addition to ethical insights, religious perspectives are valuable. Robert Boven's report for *International Organ and Tissue Retrieval Directory* surveyed Protestant, Catholic, Eastern Orthodox, and Jewish beliefs about organ donation.[80] Generally speaking, all major religious traditions support donation as a supererogatory but desirable act, and transplantation as acceptable. For the purposes of comparison, the following is a summary of some religious positions.

Sixty-nine of the ninety-six (72 percent) faith groups did not respond. Of the twenty-seven who replied, one-third had no position. Those who had a position varied widely. Eastern Orthodox had religious scruples against transplants because they had experienced disrespect for the remains of the deceased in their home countries. Orthodox Jewish law has conflicting views on organ donation. Ordinarily it does not permit mutilation of the body or even autopsies, but donation is allowed based on the higher good of saving an organ recipient's life. However, the death criterion used is the cessation of cardiac and circulating function; thus, organs such as the heart are eliminated because tissue degeneration may have already set in.

Since this 1980 survey was incomplete and is now over two decades old, I conducted a new survey as part of this book to produce up-to-date research. The results of my research covered the following groups: Adventist, American Baptist, Southern Baptist, Christian Church (Disciples of Christ), Church of Christ, Scientist (Christian Scientist), Church of Jesus Christ of Latter-Day Saints (Mormon), Greek Orthodox, Episcopal Church, Jehovah's Witnesses, Reformed Judaism, Conservative Judaism, Orthodox Judaism, Lutheran — Missouri Synod, Evangelical Lutheran

80. Robert W. Boven, *The International Organ and Tissue Retrieval Directory,* 5th ed. (Spring Lake, MI: Books of Value, 1980).

Church, Mennonite Church, United Methodist Church, Church of the Nazarene, Pentecostal (United Pentecostal), Presbyterian Church, Reformed Church in America, Roman Catholicism, Unitarian Universalist Association, United Church of Christ, Buddhism, Hinduism, Islam, Shinto, and Sikhism.

There is a range of expressed perspectives that reflect their overall theology. The vast majority of religions that take a position on organ donation support it. The exceptions are Christian Scientists, who do not use medical remedies but rely on God's continuous care. By deduction, one can conclude that they would not support organ donations. This is also true of Jehovah's Witnesses, since they oppose all blood transfusions.[81] In addition, the Shinto faith believes that interfering with the body after death brings bad luck, since the body is considered to be impure after death; thus they would allow neither donation nor transplantation.[82]

In 1998 the Southern Baptists published a resolution, "Resolution On Human Organ Donations," which encourages physicians to request organ donation in appropriate circumstances; encourages voluntarism regarding organ donations in the spirit of stewardship, compassion for the needs of others, and alleviating suffering; recognizes the validity of living wills and organ donor cards, along with the right of next of kin to make decisions regarding organ donations; and that nothing in the resolution be construed to condone euthanasia, infanticide, abortion, or harvesting of fetal tissue for the procurement of organs.[83] The Assemblies of God, in its support of organ donation, sets it in the context of Christian witness.

A fascinating possibility is to imagine the impact if Christian donors were to stipulate that their donated organs be accompanied by a handwritten letter telling of the donor's life, testimony, and relationship with Christ. . . .

The realization that organ donation saves lives and provides for a continuing witness of God's love and grace does not mean that failure to donate organs would be sinful. All of us should seek God's will for

81. Ramsey, *The Patient as Person*, p. 166.
82. "Organ Donation in Shinto," *BBC Religion and Ethics — Shinto:* http://www.bbc.co.uk/religion/religions/shinto/shintoethics/organs.shtml (accessed Feb. 12, 2009).
83. Southern Baptist Convention, 1998: http://www.sbc.net/resolutions/amResolution.asp?ID=791 (accessed Nov. 10, 2008).

our choices in this matter. It should be discussed fully with one's entire family.[84]

The Episcopal Church gives informal encouragement to donate.[85] The Mennonite Church has no stated position, but advocates stewardship of health resources.[86] Both the ELCA and Missouri-Synod Lutherans support donation as a precious gift of life, and they see no theological reason for people not to donate.[87] The United Methodist Church believes that organ donation is an act of charity and self-sacrifice and encourages its members to donate while following protocols that prevent abuse to donors and their families.[88] The Presbyterian Church (USA) issued this statement:

> Whereas, Almighty God in his infinite wisdom has permitted the modern day miracle of organ transplants; and whereas, an essential part of this miracle is the donation of organs, often at a time of great stress and trauma to family members; and whereas, we as followers of Christ are especially called to be good stewards of what God has provided; therefore, be it:
>
> *Resolved,* That the Presbytery of the Cascades overture the 207th General Assembly (1995) to encourage its members and friends to sign and carry Universal Donor Cards, and that
>
> 1. Those called to provide pastoral care receive training and materials to help families make informed decisions concerning organ donation
>
> 2. The Presbyterian Church (USA) incorporates, where appropriate, materials on organ donation in its curriculum and stewardship materials

---

84. General Council of the Assemblies of God: Organ Donation: http://www.ag.org/top/beliefs/contempissues_19_organ_donation.cfm (accessed Sept. 3, 2009).

85. *Faithful Living, Faithful Dying: Anglican Reflections on End of Life Care* (Harrisburg, PA: Morehouse Publishing, 2000), p. 138.

86. See "Resolution on Health Care, 1992": http://www.mcusa-archives.org/library/resolutions/healthcare-1992.html (accessed Nov. 10, 2008).

87. "To Encourage Donation of Kidneys and Other Organs (Resolution 8-05)," FAQ's "Life Issues": http://www.lcms.org/pages/internal.asp?NavID=2537 (accessed Jan. 29, 2009); "Organ Donation and Cremation," Evangelical Lutheran Church in America, 2009: http://www.elca.org/Growing-In-Faith/Worship/Learning-Center/FAQs/Organ-Donation-Cremation.aspx (accessed Jan. 29, 2009).

88. From *The Book of Discipline of The United Methodist Church — 2004*, The United Methodist Publishing House; "Social Principles — Organ Transplantation and Donation": http://archives.umc.org/interior.asp?mid=1766 (accessed Jan. 29, 2009).

3. The church at all levels be encouraged to evaluate and comment on the advances in organ transplantation in the light of Christian Scripture.[89]

The Church of the Nazarene allows members to donate unless they have personal scruples against the practice, and it urges fair distribution of organs among those who need them the most.[90] The Reformed Church in America encourages its members to take necessary steps to become qualified donors.[91] The United Church of Christ encourages its members to become informed donors, to register with organ procurement organizations, and to share their desires with family members.[92] The Unitarian Universalist Association has no official position, but is generally affirmative of self-determination in all aspects of dying.[93]

Roman Catholicism has several statements on organ donation and transplantation.

Roman Catholicism says that organ transplants are in conformity with the moral law if the physical and psychological dangers and risks to the donor are proportionate to the good sought for the recipient. Organ donation after death is a noble and meritorious act and is to be encouraged as an expression of generous solidarity. It is not morally acceptable if the donor or his proxy has not given explicit consent. Moreover, it is not morally admissible to bring about the disabling mutilation or death of a human being, even in order to delay the death of other persons.[94] The fundamental questions here were considered by Pope Pius XII, who noted that the crucial issue concerns the type of organ being transplanted. Pius condemned as immoral the transplantation of the generative organs (ovaries and testes) of a lower animal to

89. Presbyterian Church (USA), Minutes of the 207th General Assembly — 1995: Overture 95-47 On Organ Donations.

90. *Church of the Nazarene Manual, 2005*, p. 367: http://www.nazarene.org/files/docs/Manual2005_09.pdf (accessed Feb. 2, 2009).

91. "Report on Christian Action": http://images.rca.org/docs/mgs/2000MGS-Action.pdf (accessed Feb. 9, 2009).

92. UCC General Synod, 2003: http://www.ucc.org/assets/pdfs/synod/gs24minutes.pdf (accessed Feb. 9, 2009).

93. 1988 General Resolution, "The Right to Die with Dignity," *Unitarian Universalist Association of Congregations,* 2009: http://www.uua.org/socialjustice/socialjustice/statements/14486.shtml (accessed Feb. 9, 2009).

94. Catechism of the Catholic Church, 3.2.2.5.1, St. Charles Borromeo Catholic Church: http://www.scborromeo.org/ccc/p3s2c2a5.htm#2276 (accessed Feb. 5, 2009).

a human being — obviously because of the dignity and sanctity of human procreation. But he said that "the transplantation of a cornea from a non-human being to a human being would not raise any moral difficulty if it were biologically possible and were warranted."[95]

It can be concluded from his statement that transplanting organs other than the generative from lower species of animals to human beings is morally acceptable provided that one acts in accord with the usual norms for experimentation on human subjects: free and informed consent, reasonable expectation of success, etc.[96]

The Greek Orthodox views expressed by some theologians (without official sanction) are that "organ transplantation cannot be prohibited, but the chance of success should be high, taking the real need into account, evaluating carefully the impact on both donors and recipients. While no one is obligated to give an organ, such a donation should be encouraged as an expression of Christian love; on the other hand, organ transplants from the dead involve different problems — in particular, the hastening of the death of the potential giver for the sake of the potential recipient, which is considered wrong."[97]

Reform, Conservative, and Orthodox Judaism all affirm the need for participation in donation and transplantation with an encouragement to educate as many Jews as possible about the Halakic understanding of the issues.[98]

Hinduism, Islam, and Sikhism allow organ donation. Hinduism has no official position, although many would view it as a generous act that would bring good karma. Since the soul departs the body at death, there is no danger in removing organs.[99] Sikh teachings put great emphasis on self-

95. "Allocution to a Group of Eye Specialists," in *The Human Body: Papal Teaching,* selected and arranged by the Monks of Solesmes (Boston: St. Paul Editions, 1960), p. 645.

96. May, "The Ethics of Organ Transplants."

97. Stanley S. Harakas, "The Stand of the Orthodox Church on Controversial Issues, 6 August 2006," Greek Orthodox Church of America, 2008: http://www.goarch.org/ourfaith/ourfaith7101 (accessed June 5, 2009).

98. URJ Bio-Ethics Program Guide #9, "Organ Donation," 1997; "Reform Positions On . . . ," *Reform Judaism Magazine Online,* 2008: http://reformjudaismmag.org/Articles/index.cfm?id=1049 (accessed Nov. 24, 2008); "Life and Death Responsibilities in Jewish Biomedical Ethics," United Synagogue of Conservative Judaism, 2008: http://www.uscj.org/Biomedical_Ethics5550.html (accessed Nov. 24, 2008); Halachic Organ Donor Society: http://hods.org/index.shtml (accessed Apr. 14, 2009).

99. "Hinduism and Organ Donation," *BBC Religion and Ethics — Hinduism:* http://

less giving and sacrifice. Furthermore, the physical body is not needed in the continuous cycle of rebirth.[100] Islam has no law against organ donation.

Buddhism has no rules for or against organ donation, and it is up to the individual; but some beliefs about consciousness remaining in the body after death may make some Buddhists uneasy about the removal of organs.[101]

Conclusion

In closing, I return to our initial theme of organ donation as the last gift of life. Given the urgent need and lifesaving nature of receiving an organ, as a society we should do everything in our power to encourage medically needed and freely given organs. The poem "To Remember Me," which began this chapter, was framed within a perspective about organ donation from which all of us could benefit:

> The day will come when my body will lie upon a white sheet neatly tucked under four corners of a mattress located in a hospital busily occupied with the living and the dying. At a certain moment a doctor will determine that my brain has ceased to function and that, for all intents and purposes, my life has stopped. When that happens, do not attempt to instill artificial life into my body by the use of a machine. And don't call this my deathbed. Let it be called the Bed of Life, and let my body be taken from it to help others lead fuller lives.[102]

www.bbc.co.uk/religion/religions/hinduism/hinduethics/organdonation.shtml (accessed Feb. 12, 2009).

100. "Sikhism and Organ Donation," *BBC Religion and Ethics — Sikhism:* http://www .bbc.co.uk/religion/religions/sikhism/sikhethics/organdonation.shtml (accessed Feb. 9, 2009); "Sikh Patient's Protocol for Health Care Providers," *SikhWomen.com:* http://www .sikhwomen.com/health/care/protocol.htm (accessed Feb. 9, 2009).

101. "Buddhism and Organ Donation," *BBC Religion and Ethics — Buddhism:* http:// www.bbc.co.uk/religion/religions/buddhism/buddhistethics/organdonation.shtml (accessed Feb. 12, 2009).

102. Robert Noel Test, "To Remember Me."

6. Legal Questions: Cases and Laws Addressing End-of-Life Issues

On the Laws: Book II.4

MARCUS: Let us, then, once more examine, before we come to the consideration of particular laws, what is the power and nature of law in general; lest, when we come to refer everything to it, we occasionally make mistakes from the employment of incorrect language, and show ourselves ignorant of the force of those terms which we ought to employ in the definition of laws.

QUINTUS: This is a very necessary caution, and the proper method of seeking truth.

MARCUS: This, then, as it appears to me, has been the decision of the wisest philosophers — that law was neither a thing to be contrived by the genius of man, nor established by any decree of the people, but a certain eternal principle, which governs the entire universe, wisely commanding what is right and prohibiting what is wrong. Therefore, they called that aboriginal and supreme law the mind of God, enjoining or forbidding each separate thing in accordance with reason. On which account it is that this law, which the gods have bestowed upon the human race, is so justly applauded. For it is the reason and mind of a wise Being equally able to urge us to good or to deter us from evil.

Marcus Tullius Cicero (106-43 BC)

Although I do not purport to address all the legal questions surrounding death and dying in this book, many of them are germane to the current debates about physician-assisted suicide, euthanasia, and organ donation and transplantation that I have discussed in the preceding chapters. Since the late 1970s, legal issues have become intertwined with bioethical and medical ones; therefore, it is necessary to review legal rulings and cases to understand the status of negotiated death. What we need to guard against is jumping too quickly to resolve ethical dilemmas by legal means. Because of the lack of shared values in the United States, we depend on the law to settle our differences. In bioethics much of the debate has shifted to the courts: as novelist Saul Bellow (1915-2005) put it, we live in a world of moral interregnum, where we have used up all our old values without replacing them with new ones.[1] Some states have brought suits against physicians practicing euthanasia, such as the case of *State of Michigan v. Jack Kevorkian;* in other states, such as Oregon and Washington, the law allows aid-in-dying but not euthanasia.

Legal Questions Concerning Death

The law is interested in several questions with regard to death: *cause:* a diagnosis of the cause of death is important for the definition of death; *circumstances:* what the factors were surrounding the death; *time:* the time when a person died (this is determined by the opinion of a doctor); *pronouncement of death:* performed by a doctor and affecting how the law uses the determination of death.

Ethicists ask whether a person is alive, dead, or dying. No such distinctions exist in the eyes of the law. Since *Roe vs. Wade* (1973), a fetus is considered protectable human life only if capable of independent life, even if that is by artificial means. The law looks for a clear separation between life and death; however, the law is ambiguous on this issue, since fetuses can inherit property. In addition, the Scott Peterson case in California (his killing of his pregnant wife) brought charges that two murders were committed (mother and unborn child). In 2005, Peterson was sentenced to death by lethal injection (he remains on death row in San Quentin State Prison while his case is on appeal to the Supreme Court of California).[2]

---

1. Sukhbir Singh, ed., *Conversations with Saul Bellow: A Collection of Selected Interviews* (New Delhi: Academic Foundation, 1993), pp. 79-80.
2. "Peterson sentenced to death for wife's slaying," *CNN.com online,* March 17, 2005: http://www.cnn.com/2005/LAW/03/16/peterson.case/index.html (accessed Apr. 15, 2009).

All jurisdictions require that the victim of a murder be a natural person: that is, a human being who was alive at the time of being killed. Most jurisdictions distinguish between legally killing a fetus and an unborn child as different crimes: the distinction between the *illegal abortion of a fetus* and the *unlawful killing of an unborn child* is that what is defined as "an unborn child" in these jurisdictions is an infant who could survive if it had been born, while certain fetuses could not. The law appears contradictory on the question of protectable human life: on the one hand, the fetus is only protectable if it is viable on its own *(Roe vs. Wade)*, whereas a person such as Karen Ann Quinlan can be kept on a life-support system even when there is no hope of conscious life. The two fundamental legal outcomes for others when someone is declared dead are: (1) they can inherit property, and (2) they can receive insurance benefits. However, insurance benefits cannot be paid out until ninety days after death. Questions remain. In the case of a car accident, for example, is a person in a coma legally dead or in the process of dying? When are his heirs eligible for benefits? When can an accident victim's organs be used if the person has previously agreed to donate? (Most jurisdictions use brain-death criteria for organ retrieval.) These are important questions, but treatment decisions do not lend themselves to legal rulings.

How Death Occurs

The range of illegal causes of death according to the law are: homicide, murder, manslaughter, suicide, cannibalism, war, feticide, infanticide, child sacrifice. These may be classified with regard to "inevitable" death versus "adventitious" death. The question of how a death occurs is perhaps the pivotal issue in deciding if a certain death is, in fact, a good death. Is the process by which death occurs morally acceptable or morally unacceptable? Our answer, using different examples, will change as a function of the moral criteria we use.

Within the medical context, death may occur by natural causes; by a person bringing about his or her own death through suicide; or by someone causing another's death at the request of the decedent or against his desire and without his consent. It is how death happens that is both a moral and a legal issue. As we discuss the legality of euthanasia and physician-assisted suicide, the question of whether it is murder or manslaughter arises. The law makes clear distinctions among different types of murder: intent to kill, intent to cause serious bodily harm, reckless endangerment, and felony murder. Examining these legal distinctions may assist us in determining charges against doctors practicing euthanasia.

Definition of Death

In order to discuss the legal issues involved in death and dying, we need to first define death. These general legal concerns about death ultimately entail deciding on a definition of death, which is where the metaphysical and the legal interface. The line between life and death is not always clear: some even say that living and being dead are part of a continuum. Some confusion has developed concerning the legal and medical definitions of death. Legal aspects of this debate have to do with when heirs should inherit, when insurance benefits should be paid out, when remarriage may be allowed, and when organs may be harvested. Lawyers depend on doctors to say when death has occurred, though it is often the nurse who is present and attending when a patient expires. For example, a person on life support is not dead. The question is: Should death be defined by doctors, or should the definition of death simply be acceptable to doctors?[3] The entire discussion of the determination of death raises the question of whether death should be determined by the medical profession. In the 1970s, the physician-philosopher Leon Kass raised the question whether definitions of death are medical and philosophical and should be determined by the law in a way that is acceptable to physicians. He based this on the fact that errors could lead to a disconnect between the law and medical knowledge.[4] The President's Council on Bioethics under George W. Bush reviewed this issue extensively in its report entitled "Controversies in the Determination of Death," as I discussed in chapter 3 above.[5]

The definition of death should not be confused with when it is desirable or permissible to withdraw or withhold treatment. This distinction is important when we discuss the withdrawal of treatment, because it is the illness, not the withdrawal, that causes the death. This distinction would seem to be one the courts would be wise to note when they review cases

---

3. Roger B. Dworkin, "Death in Context"; Alexander Morgan Capron, "The Purpose of Death: A Reply to Professor Dworkin," *Indiana Law Journal* 48 (Summer 1973): 623-46.

4. Dworkin, "Death in Context," p. 624.

5. "Controversies in the Determination of Death: A White Paper of the President's Council on Bioethics" (December 2008): www.bioethics.gov.

concerning withdrawal of feeding tubes, for example, which is a medical procedure. The way we die is important from the law's perspective. Is it by natural processes, or is it at the hand of another person, that is, without our consent or against our desire?

The complexity of the problem of who is alive and who is dead has increased. Prior to the Harvard Brain Death Criteria in 1968, the physician simply examined the patient to determine death; now she reads the EEG. The issue of who is alive and who is dead is literally a life-and-death question because of advances in transplant surgery and increased medical-legal culpability. The film *21 Grams* raised the question of whether death could be determined by the loss of twenty-one grams, perhaps indicating that a person's soul had departed, thus claiming that he was dead. However, if the soul is a spiritual and not a physical property, as Christian theology would assert, it would have no weight.[6] Putting this point aside, some pastors may worry whether the soul has truly departed the body. (See the link for an interesting summary of an early twentieth-century doctor who conducted experiments on the weight of the soul, which was the basis for *21 Grams*.[7])

6. http://www.21-grams.com/index.php (April 15, 2009). "'21 Grams' is a film directed by Alejandro González Iñárritu. It is a story of hope and humanity, of resilience and survival. Whether you fear death or not, it comes, and at that moment your body becomes twenty-one grams lighter. Is it a person's soul that constitutes those twenty-one grams? Is that weight carried by those who survive us? The lead actors in '21 Grams' are Sean Penn, Benicio Del Toro, and Naomi Watts. This film explores the emotionally and physically charged existences of three people over a period of several months. An accident unexpectedly throws their lives and destinies together, in a story that will take them to the heights of love, the depths of revenge, and the promise of redemption. College professor Paul Rivers (Sean Penn) and his wife Mary (Charlotte Gainsbourg) find their union precariously balanced between life and death. He is mortally ill and awaiting a heart transplant, while she hopes to become pregnant with his child through artificial insemination. Cristina Peck (Naomi Watts), having matured since her reckless past, is a beloved older sister to Claudia (Clea DuVall), a good wife to Michael (Danny Huston) and loving mother to two little girls. Her family radiates hope and joy. Much farther down the socioeconomic scale, ex-con Jack Jordan (Benicio Del Toro) and his wife Marianne (Melissa Leo) struggle to provide for their two children while Jack reaffirms his commitment to religion. A tragic accident that claims several lives places these couples in each other's orbit. In the aftermath, Paul confronts his own mortality, Cristina takes action to come to terms with her present and perhaps her future, and Jack's faith is put to the test. If spiritual equilibrium is to be regained by any one of them, it could come at great cost to the others. Yet the will to live, and the instinct to reach out to another person for support, remains ever-present among them all."

7. "Soul Man," *Snopes.com online* (internet resource for verifying and debunking rumors): http://www.snopes.com/religion/soulweight.asp (accessed Mar. 10, 2009).

How we define death can determine whether, concerning a given patient, we are discussing the termination of treatment, which would lead to death, or the continuation of treatment, which would prolong a life. "Just as there is no consensus about when conscious life begins, there is none about when it ends. Determining the precise time of death is, in fact, medically and scientifically impossible, says Atlanta cardiologist Michael Sabom. 'It used to be thought that the point of death was a single moment in time,' says Sabom. 'It is now thought that death is a process, not a single moment.'"[8]

Because we need some guidelines about when death has occurred, our society has developed various legal and social definitions of death to give us a sense of finality. The principal terms are:

> *Clinical Death:* Breathing and heartbeat have stopped. A person might still be able to be resuscitated with CPR or other means, depending on why the vital signs ceased and under what conditions. *Brain Death:* The lower brain, or brainstem, which controls automatic body functions, stops working. A person can be kept alive only with the help of life-support machines. The length of the period that the brainstem must be inactive before a person is declared legally dead varies from jurisdiction to jurisdiction. Complicating the issue, the same person can be considered legally dead if about to become an organ donor, but legally alive if not. *Persistent Vegetative State/Death of the Higher Brain:* The brainstem still functions, keeping the heart, lungs and digestive system working, but the sensing, thinking part of the brain has shut down. It may be possible to keep the body functioning for long periods with life-support systems. *Whole Brain Death:* Both lower and higher brain function have ceased.[9]

Some ethicists believe that a spontaneously breathing patient with a flat EEG is alive, and thus decisions about whether to keep her on the respirator would be considered prolonging life; for others, the patient is already dead. For example, bioethicist Robert Veatch believes that the patient would already be dead since neocortical activity is what decides the time of death. There are states — Maryland, Virginia, Kansas, and California — that have adopted irreversible coma into law. The official signs of death include the following:

---

8. Anita Bartholomew, "After Life: The Scientific Case for the Human Soul," *Reader's Digest,* August 2003, p. 125.
9. Bartholomew, "After Life," p. 125.

- No pupil reaction to light
- No response of the eyes to caloric (warm or cold) stimulation
- No jaw reflex (the jaw will react like the knee if hit with a reflex hammer)
- No gag reflex (touching the back of the throat induces vomiting)
- No response to pain
- No breathing
- A body temperature above 86°F (30°C), which eliminates the possibility of resuscitation following cold-water drowning.
- No other cause for the above, such as a head injury
- No drugs present in the body that could cause apparent death
- All of the above for twelve hours
- All of the above for six hours and a flat-line electroencephalogram (EEG, brain-wave study)
- No blood circulating to the brain, as demonstrated by angiography.[10]

Harvard Brain Death Criteria

Due to various definitions of death and the need of legislation to protect physicians from liability, especially transplant surgeons, the Ad Hoc Committee of Harvard Medical School proposed its definition of brain death in 1968 in a *Journal of the American Medical Association* article.[11] The Anatomical Gift Act in all fifty states uses these criteria. However, a transplant team cannot be involved in the determination of the death of a donor. The law has now created the category of a pool of nondead and dead metabolic tissue; the former group are left on the respirator so that the organs can be used later.

Here it is important to separate the question of the definition of death and whether a person is transplant material. The hospital should be a place of life, not death. A related question is: When do we stop using the word "person" and switch to the word "cadaver"? In a sense, this is the

10. "Death, Diagnosis," *The Free Dictionary:* http://medical-dictionary.thefree dictionary.com/Clinical+death (accessed Mar. 9, 2009). It should be noted that these signs are different from the neurological tests now being used to determine that death has occurred for legal purposes.

11. "A Definition of Irreversible Coma," Report of the Ad Hoc Committee of the Harvard Medical School to Examine the Definition of Brain Death, *The Journal of the American Medical Association* 205, no. 6 (Aug. 5, 1968): 337-40.

same question as when we refer to a "fetus" and when a "baby." Expectant mothers uniformly refer to their "babies" (before they are born), not their "fetuses." It seems that the term "fetus" is for legal purposes — that is, to delineate whether we have a protectable human life.

The main part of the body of interest in definitions of death is the central nervous system (CNS), which is associated with cerebral activity: voluntary, language, recognition and recall, memory and memorization, skilled motor activity, awareness-consciousness, electrical activity (EEG). The Harvard criteria are as follows:

1. *Unreceptivity and unresponsitivity.* There is a total unawareness to externally applied stimuli and inner need and complete unresponsiveness — our definition of irreversible coma. Even the most intensely painful stimuli evoke no vocal or other response, not even a groan, withdrawal of a limb, or quickening of respiration.

2. *No movements or breathing.* Observations covering a period of at least one hour by physicians is adequate to satisfy the criteria of no spontaneous muscular movements or spontaneous respiration or response to stimuli such as pain, touch, sound, or light. After the patient is on a mechanical respirator, the total absence of spontaneous breathing may be established by turning off the respirator for three minutes and observing whether there is any effort on the part of the subject to breathe spontaneously. (The respirator may be turned off for this time provided that at the start of the trial period the patient's carbon dioxide tension is within the normal range, and provided also that the patient had been breathing air for at least ten minutes prior to the trial.)

3. *No reflexes.* Irreversible coma with abolition of central nervous system activity is evidenced in part by the absence of elicitable reflexes. The pupil will be fixed and dilated and will not respond to a direct source of bright light. Since the establishment of a fixed, dilated pupil is clear-cut in clinical practice, there should be no uncertainty as to its presence. Ocular movement (to head turning and to irrigation of the ears with ice water) and blinking are absent. There is no evidence of postural activity (decerebrate or other). Swallowing, yawning, vocalization are in abeyance. Corneal and pharyngeal reflexes are absent.

As a rule the stretch of tendon reflexes cannot be elicited, that is, tapping the tendons of the biceps, triceps, and pronator muscles, quadriceps and gastrocnemius muscles with the reflex hammer elicits no contraction of the respective muscles. Plantar or noxious stimulation gives no response.

4. *Flat electroencephalogram.* Of great confirmatory value is the flat or isoelectric EEG. We must assume that the electrodes have been properly applied, that the apparatus is functioning normally, and that the personnel in charge is competent. We consider it prudent to have one channel of the apparatus used for an electrocardiogram. This channel will monitor the ECG so that, if it appears in the electro-encephalographic leads because of high resistance, it can be readily identified. It also establishes the presence of the active heart in the absence of the EEG. We recommend that another channel be used for a noncephalic lead. This will pick up space-borne or vibration-borne artifacts and identify them. The simplest form of such a monitoring noncephalic electrode has two leads over the dorsum of the hand, preferably the right hand, so the ECG will be minimal or absent. Since one of the requirements of this state is that there be no muscle activity, these two dorsal hand electrodes will not be bothered by muscle artifact. The apparatus should be run at standard gains 10μv/mm, 50μv/5 mm. Also it should be isoelectric at double this standard gain which is 50μv/5 mm or 25μv/5 mm. At least ten full minutes of recording are desirable, but twice that would be better. It is also suggested that the gains at some point be opened to their full amplitude for a brief period (5 to 100 seconds) to see what is going on. Usually in an intensive care unit artifacts will dominate the picture, but these are readily identifiable. There shall be no electroencephalographic response to noise or to pinch.

All of the above tests shall be repeated at least 24 hours later with no change.

The validity of such data as indications of irreversible cerebral damage depends on the exclusion of two conditions: hypothermia (temperature below 90 F [32.2 C]) or central nervous system depressants, such as barbiturates.[12]

In the past, the only criterion for declaring someone dead was when the heart stopped beating. The Harvard criteria permit — but do not require — death to be declared. The classic case is when the patient is on a respirator and in some senses still alive, but his kidneys can be removed. In these situations the family should not carry the responsibility of determin-

---

12. Task Force on Death and Dying, "Refinements in Criteria for the Determination of Death: An Appraisal," *Journal of the American Medical Association* 221, no. 1 (July 3, 1972): 48-53.

ing when to turn off the respirator, so the legal determination of death is enough. "The Harvard committee that Beecher subsequently chaired did not claim, in its ground-breaking 1968 report, that its new definition of death reflected some scientific discoveries about, or improved scientific understanding of, the nature of death. It was, instead, because the committee saw the status quo as imposing great burdens on various people and institutions affected by it, and as preventing the proper use of the 'lifesaving potential' of the organs of people in 'irreversible coma' that the committee recommended the new definition of death."[13]

Challenges to the Harvard Death Criteria

As medicine advances, there are a number of challenges to the Harvard Brain Death Criteria. Intensive Care Units (ICUs) have become increasingly sophisticated, so that it is possible for surrogate brain stems to replace respiratory functions, as well as hormonal and other regulatory activities of damaged neuraxis. For example, cardiac arrest in brain-dead patients is only inevitable if mechanical ventilation is removed. The *Journal of the American Medical Association (JAMA)* was one of the first to raise concerns.[14] The causes of concern were: (1) the problem of concepts and language with different views of death; (2) the difference between medical and legal death (the legal definition usually relies on physician's determination of death); (3) arbitrariness: it may not be true, for example, that it is reasonable to take twenty-four hours to confirm a flat EEG; (4) the determination of death is different from when it is permissible to withhold or withdraw treatment. Should we limit brain activity simply to the neocortex, as Veatch does?[15]

Others, such as Professor Kellehear, of the University of Bath in England, challenge it on more pragmatic grounds.

Professor Kellehear said this made the decisions potentially unsettling for the bereaved. He said: "Forty years ago, being dead used to be very

13. Peter Singer, "Changing Ethics in Life and Death Decision Making," *Society* (July/August 2001): 9.

14. Task Force on Death and Dying, "Refinements in Criteria for the Determination of Death," pp. 48-53.

15. Robert M. Veatch, "The Whole-Brain-Oriented Concept of Death: An Outmoded Philosophical Formulation," *Journal of Thanatology* 3, no. 1 (1975): 13-30.

simple — it was the point at which your heart stopped beating. Now death itself has been complicated by the fact that we can keep alive people who are brain dead almost indefinitely. Brain death is the point at which doctors can switch off machines or begin harvesting organs, but, to relatives, being brain dead is not the same as being a corpse. Corpses are not warm, they are not pink, they do not move, they are not pregnant — but a person who is brain dead can be all of these things." Professor Kellehear said there was little apparent difference to the untrained observer between a person who was brain dead and somebody who was asleep.[16]

Harvard Medical School's Robert Truog joined the chorus of the opponents of the Harvard Brain Death Criteria. "Indeed, some have concluded that the concept is fundamentally flawed, and that it represents only a 'superficial and fragile consensus.' In this analysis I will identify the sources of these inconsistencies and suggest that the best resolution to these issues may be to abandon the concept of brain death altogether."[17]

Truog provides a thorough analysis of how brain-dead patients may in fact retain some brain functions, so that brain-death criteria are plagued by internal inconsistencies. He goes on to reflect that using the cardiorespiratory standard would be better because the result would be the death of the entire brain and every organ. However, this creates a problem concerning whether organs could be harvested.[18] Truog proposes two alternative approaches to the whole-brain formulation: (1) higher-brain criteria where individuals who have permanently suffered the loss of all consciousness are dead; and (2) return to the traditional tests for determining death, that is, the permanent loss of circulation and respiration.[19] The advantage of adopting the latter is that it would eliminate objections based on religious grounds.

More recently, Peter Singer has entered into the debate: he is also a critic of the brain-death criteria and proposes irreversible loss of consciousness because it is at that point that we have lost everything we love. He repeats some of the earlier critiques that are based on new medical informa-

16. "Call to Revamp Death Definition," *BBC News online*, September 12, 2007: http://news.bbc.co.uk/2/hi/health/6987079.stm (accessed Aug. 13, 2009).

17. Robert D. Truog, "Is It Time to Abandon Brain Death?" *Hastings Center Report* 27, no. 1 (1997): 29-37.

18. Truog, "Is It Time?" pp. 29-37.

19. Truog, "Is It Time?" pp. 29-37.

tion because the function of dead brains can be replaced by machines, and bodily functions can be maintained for months or even years.[20]

Legal Perspectives on End-of-Life Choices

Landmark Cases

From the perspective of the law, definitions of death and prognosis of persistent vegetative state (PVS) from the medical profession, for example, are important, but the law is primarily interested in major precedent cases that may influence subsequent judicial rulings. Although there are a number of cases that have addressed issues concerning death and dying based on states' rights, one state's ruling is not binding on another. However, these rulings may be referred to and used by lawyers who represent the plaintiffs and defendants in similar cases. We will highlight a few of the most interesting cases. However, in some ways the fact that end-of-life decisions land in court is due to a failure of the medical system, the complexity of choices, and the absence of shared values on the part of the American public. We find a mix of perspectives in these cases; and in some of these cases, such as the preexistent condition of the patient (the mental retardation of Saikewicz), the presumed consent of the patient (Brother Fox), or the hope or lack of hope of a patient's recovery (Quinlan and Cruzan), the courts may have complicated rather than clarified what is better left as a private moral issue.

Karen Ann Quinlan: Withdrawal of the Respirator (1976)

This case prompted the adoption of "brain death" as the legal definition of death in some states and the adoption of laws recognizing "living wills" and the "right to die" in other states, as well as the formation of "bioethics committees" in many hospitals. In 1985, the New Jersey Supreme Court ruled that all life-sustaining medical treatment, including artificial feeding, could be withheld from incompetent, terminally ill patients, provided such action was shown to be consistent with the afflicted person's past wishes.

20. Singer, "Changing Ethics," p. 10.

On 15 April 1975, 21-year-old Karen Ann Quinlan passed out and lapsed into a coma after sustaining bruises which was never satisfactorily explained and ingesting tranquilizers "in the therapeutic range" and alcohol. Unable to breathe on her own, she was placed on a respirator. By the following autumn, Quinlan's family and doctors had given up hope of recovery. Her parents, Julia and Joseph Quinlan, were devout Roman Catholics who consulted their parish priest, Father Thomas Trapasso, and were told that they could, in good conscience, request that Karen be removed from the respirator. The request was made, but Karen's primary physician, Dr. Robert Morse, refused to end the artificial support. In the absence of any other means with which to execute what he believed to be his daughter's wishes, Joseph Quinlan went to court.

However, one week before the trial it was disclosed that Karen Quinlan did not have a "flat" electroencephalograph — a medical test which would have been evidence of a complete absence of brain-wave activity. She also was capable of breathing on her own for short, irregular periods, and had occasionally shown muscle activity which some doctors had described as voluntary. It immediately became clear that the trial would not center on New Jersey's definition of death; rather it would address the more complicated question of whether Karen Quinlan had a "right to die."[21]

The Quinlan formula arose out of the decision of the New Jersey Supreme Court that twenty-one-year-old Karen Ann Quinlan, who had accidentally lapsed into an irreversible coma for more than ten years, should be removed from life-support systems at the request of her parents. The grounds for this decision were in the realm of privacy, which included the right to refuse treatment; second, the role of the family as critical in such cases; third, the ethics committee responsibility to review the decision; and fourth, immunity against civil or criminal prosecution would be granted.

Judge Muir of the lower court of New Jersey denied the request of Joseph Quinlan to be the guardian of his comatose daughter in order to turn off the respirator. The grounds for his ruling were: (1) she was not legally dead, so there was a duty to continue life-saving treatment; (2) the state has an interest in preserving life; (3) there is no constitutional right to die by proxy consent; therefore, unplugging the respirator would be homicide.

21. "In the Matter of Quinlan — Further Readings": http://law.jrank.org/pages/13113/In-Matter-Quinlan.html (accessed Mar. 18, 2009).

This decision was overturned by New Jersey's highest court in an opinion by Justice Richard J. Hughes. This decision appointed Joseph Quinlan as Karen's guardian: in that capacity, he could give permission for her to be weaned from the respirator. This precedent meant that if someone were in a permanent vegetative state with no hope of returning to a cognitive, sapient state, life support may be removed without criminal liability. Hughes's grounds were that stopping lifesaving therapy and homicide are two different acts. The New Jersey court was impressed with the notion of "realm of privacy."[22] Hughes did not contest that Karen Quinlan was alive or establish that she had a right to die. The fact that she lived for nine years after being taken off the respirator is testimony to the fact that ceasing treatment and dying are not always synonymous.

One can find both good and bad news in the landmark Quinlan decision of 1976. The good news was: it provided a fundamental right to refuse medical treatment; it made no rational distinction between artificial feeding and other medical interventions; it provided a boost for the importance of durable powers of attorney and consultation with an ethics committee about a patient's prognosis. The bad news was the ambiguity of some of the categories that the decision established: Do incompetent persons (including those in PVS) have constitutional rights? Can individuals in a PVS be harmed? What does the U.S. Supreme Court think about the proper authority of the state and the family (in this specific case, treatment termination)?

Perhaps most telling in this case was the recognition of the importance for all people, no matter what their age is, to have an advance directive. The fact that Quinlan remained in a persistent vegetative state for so many years seems tragic. An interesting aside is that in the Terry Schiavo case, thirty years later, the absence of an advance directive also led to legal suits and tragic family rifts.

Joseph Saikewicz: Withholding of Treatment (1976)

Joseph Saikewicz, a ward of the state for fifty-three years who had an IQ of a three-year-old and no hope of recovery, was denied chemotherapy to treat terminal leukemia because the quality of life was judged too low to justify this "extraordinary" treatment. This decision was appealed but sustained by the Massachusetts Supreme Judicial Court, based on the "reason-

22. "Trends in Health Care," *Law and Ethics* (Winter 1993): 11.

able man" standard: the judge declared that, if he were Saikewicz, he would not want to live that way. The judge's ruling referred to the Quinlan case, though it is hard to see how Quinlan's vegetative, nonsapient life as a result of an accident and the mentally disabled state of Saikewicz, which was unrelated to his leukemia, are parallel. Furthermore, the chemotherapy was in itself not considered extraordinary, and the guardian agreed that it would be followed for a normal three-year-old. Hence, the judgment was not rendered in light of his disease, but was due to his state of mental disability.[23] One wonders whether such a two-tiered system of those with diminished autonomy and those with full autonomy respects persons equally, as I argued in the earlier chapter about the dignity and worth of all persons. However, the argument was also based on mercy: that Saikewicz would suffer for no purpose.

Brother Joseph Fox: Discontinuation of the Respirator (1981)

At eighty-three years of age, Brother Joseph C. Fox sustained an inguinal hernia and during surgery suffered a heart attack, which resulted in brain damage and put him in an irreversible coma. His friend of over twenty-five years, Father Philip Eichner, asked the hospital to discontinue the use of the respirator; but the hospital wanted a court decision. The court ruled that the respirator could be turned off on the following grounds: (1) medical: he was terminally ill, in an irreversible and permanent vegetative coma, and his prospects of regaining cognitive brain functions were extremely remote; and (2) legal: it was a judgment based on the fact that the patient himself would have made the same decision.[24]

Nancy Cruzan: Discontinuation of Feeding Tube (1990)

The Cruzan case is perhaps one of the most prominent cases with respect to the question of negotiated death, in which legal concerns took prece-

---

23. *Commonwealth of Massachusetts, Superintendent of Belchertown State School and Another v. Joseph Saikewicz*, 373 Mass. 728, July 2, 1976 — November 28, 1977, pp. 729-59.

24. *In the Matter of Philip K. Eichner, On Behalf of Joseph C. Fox, Respondent, v. Denis Dillon, as District Attorney of Nassau County, Appellant. Dorothy Storar, Respondent*, Court of Appeals of New York 52.Y.2d 363; 420 N.E.2d 64; 438 N.Y.S.2d 26 (1981); cert. denied, 454 U.S. 858, 102 S.Ct. 309 (1981).

dence over the suffering of an individual and her family. Nancy Beth Cruzan was in a persistent vegetative state after cerebral anoxia following an automobile accident in 1983. Though she was not terminally ill, the prognosis was that she would never regain a conscious existence.

Five years after the accident, Nancy's co-guardians requested that health providers discontinue gastrotomy feedings. The state hospital officials refused, so Nancy's parents sought court approval for the withdrawal of artificial feedings. A Missouri trial court granted authorization for withdrawal of artificial feedings, but the Missouri Supreme Court reversed that decision on the grounds that Nancy's wishes were not clear and thus did not outweigh the state's interest in the preservation of life. Without an advance directive, especially since she was not terminally ill, her informal conversations with family and friends that she would not want to be kept alive if not normal were insufficient.[25]

Finally, nine years later, the Cruzan case was ruled on by the U.S. Supreme Court on June 25, 1990.[26] In a five-to-four decision, the high court upheld the continued use of the feeding tube: the majority based its ruling on the premise of the protection and preservation of the life of an incompetent person, which trumped both the right of privacy and liberty interests. The majority noted that individuals have a *constitutionally protected liberty interest* in refusing unwanted care. "In Missouri's case, the Court held that requirement that the evidence of an incompetent's wishes regarding treatment withdrawal be proved by CCE [clear and convincing evidence] was permissible and that the state could determine that Cruzan's casual statements to family and friends did not provide CCE."[27] However, the Supreme Court did not require all states to use this procedural safeguard. In fact, decisions of individual justices suggest that the Court might require states to honor the decisions of properly selected surrogate decision-makers. The only thing binding in this Supreme Court decision was states' rights.

There was both good and bad news in the U.S. Supreme Court's ruling on Cruzan. The good news was that it established a fundamental right

25. Her parents also sought assistance from the Society for the Right to Die.

26. "U.S. Supreme Court to Hear First Right-to-Die Case," *Society for the Right to Die Newsletter* (Fall 1989): 1, 3.

27. "Courts and the End of Life — The Case of Nancy Cruzan": www.libraryindex .com/pages/3143/Courts-End-Life-CASE-NANCY-CRUZAN.html (accessed Apr. 7, 2009); "Cruzan v. Director, Missouri Dept. of Health," The Oyez Project, U.S. Supreme Court Media, *Cruzan v. Director, Missouri Dept. of Health,* 497 U.S. 261 (1990): http://oyez.org/cases/ 1980-1989/1989/1989_88_1503 (Apr. 7, 2009).

to refuse medical treatment, making no distinction between artificial feeding and other medical interventions; it also gave a boost to the importance of a durable power of attorney. The bad news was that incompetent persons (including those in a PVS) do not appear to have constitutional rights — and thus may be harmed. The Supreme Court's perspectives on the proper authority of the state (herein abortion and treatment termination) and the proper role of the family (herein abortion and treatment termination) are still unclear.

The final outcome of this case was decided by the Missouri courts in an appeal in 1990, when three friends came forward as witnesses that Cruzan would not want the continuation of treatment. Subsequently, her doctors terminated her treatment and allowed Cruzan to die.

Theresa "Terry" Schiavo (2005): The Tragedy of Family Conflicts

Theresa Marie Schindler was born on December 3, 1963, to devoutly Catholic parents, Robert and Mary Schindler. At 5:00 a.m. on February 25, 1990, her husband awoke to find her unconscious and not breathing. He called 911. When the emergency response team arrived, they found her in full cardiac arrest; on their seventh attempt to defibrillate her, they restored her heartbeat to a normal rhythm.

At first she remained in a coma, and after she emerged from the coma she remained in a generally unresponsive state for the next fifteen years. She experienced varying degrees of paralysis to all four limbs, inability to speak, inability to breathe unaided, and oculomotor deviation, also known as lateral gaze palsy. Patients with this "locked-in syndrome" may retain the ability to think and reason, but she was diagnosed with only reflexive responses. Most neurologists labeled her condition "persistent vegetative state."

Since Terry left no living will, her husband, Michael Schiavo, was her health care decision-maker. When Michael, after many years, announced his intention to terminate his wife's life support, Terry's parents went to court to challenge Michael's decision to stop treatment because they felt that everything should be done to sustain her life. Michael also filed a lawsuit for the insurance money, which some say was a conflict of interest since he was also making decisions about her care. The last few months of Terry's life and death were played out on national television. The Schiavo case has served to raise many issues, including those of dying in institutions, inconsistent views about life and death, and medical decision-making.

What kinds of treatment or testing were done? At her initial placement at Humana Northside Hospital in St. Petersburg, Florida, Terry's release sheet gives no record of her Glasgow Coma Scale, which ranks eye, verbal, and motor response. In early March, at the request of the Florida Department of Children and Families (which was seeking to get custody of Terry), she was seen by a neurologist; he noted that she had had no significant neurological testing in the past three years. Other doctors asserted that this neurologist's conservative Christian views might have biased his diagnosis, because he described her movements, vocalizations, and gazes as responses rather than as reflexive, which was contrary to all the other neurological opinions. Her parents also requested further testing, which the court denied at the request of Michael.

Could she have recovered? Vegetative patients whose brain injury was traumatic (a fall, an accident, an external mechanical event) are more likely to recover response than those, like Terry Schiavo, whose injury resulted from a lack of oxygen to the brain. Patients who emerge from a coma and show some response can later drop into a less responsive state. Some have speculated that Terry suffered from some kind of eating disorder because her potassium level was initially well below normal, even below what would normally be expected to cause cardiac arrest; but many things, including medications, diuretics, laxatives, and kidney disorders, could have led to the deficiency.

What were her wishes? Because she left no living will, what her opinions on this matter were and whether they aligned with those of the Catholic Church were a matter of hearsay. Her parents wished to follow their interpretation of the Roman Catholic Church's teaching, but as Glanville Williams had pointed out years earlier, prohibition imposed by religious belief should not be applied by law to those who do not share the belief.[28] In a newspaper interview about the significance of this case, I said: "Until we learn how to live, we cannot learn how to die." I also concluded: "Hearsay doesn't stand up in a court of law if there's conflict in families. What people don't understand about advance directives is that they aren't just about shutting off machines. Rather, they are to express your wishes to do everything you want done."[29]

28. Glanville Williams, *The Sanctity of Life and the Criminal Law,* Carpentier Lectures at Columbia University, 1956 (New York: Knopf, 1958), p. 312.

29. Bill Tammeus, "In Schiavo Tragedy, We Find a Hard Lesson," *Kansas City Star,* April 1, 2005.

The resolution of the Schiavo case was that Terry was disconnected from life support by the local court's decision on March 18, 2005, and she died of the effects of dehydration at a Florida hospice on March 31. Some deplore this as a case that went against decades of progress that had given individuals the freedom to control and limit medical interventions performed on them; but this criticism is muted by the fact that she did not express her wishes in writing.

The Schiavo case generated a great deal of misunderstanding about what is involved in these kinds of decisions. This involves refusal of treatment, not euthanasia. Bert Dorenbos, a longtime critic of euthanasia and abortion in the Netherlands and head of the organization Schreeuw om Leven (Cry for Life), emailed leaders of U.S. groups opposing the removal of tubes. He warned that if Terry Schiavo were allowed to die, her case would quickly open the door to legal euthanasia. He cited the 1990 case of a Dutch woman in a coma, Ineke Stinissen, who was allowed to die at her husband's request, with food and fluids withheld. Dorenbos said that that case "shifted the debate" and led to legalization of these practices in the Netherlands.[30]

An examination of the Schiavo case suggests that the legal status of patient autonomy is not as strong as previously thought. The Supreme Court has reiterated in many of its decisions the importance of our individual conscience determining our choices about death. Furthermore, American case law has recognized the right for medical choices since the 1914 case of *Schloendorff v. Society of New York Hospital.* "Every human being of adult years and sound mind has a right to determine what shall be done with his own body. . . ."[31] The problem with surrogate decision-makers is almost always when they disagree, as it was in the Schiavo case; when they agree, there are rarely legal problems, unless "clear and convincing evidence" (CCE) à la Cruzan is made the standard. In the end, what we are arguing for is the right to choose, which is the very purpose of the Bill of Rights. Lazzarini and others are alarmed that, "Sometimes overbearing intensity of moral conviction and a frightening willingness to impose a single ideological or religious code . . . can foreshorten our basic rights."[32]

30. Keith B. Richburg, "Death with Dignity, or Door to Abuse? Dutch Euthanasia Law Enjoys Wide Support, but Resistance Remains," *Washington Post,* January 4, 2004, pp. A1, A13.

31. Zita Lazzarini, Stephen Arons, and Alice Wisniewski, "Legal and Policy Lessons from the Schiavo Case: Is Our Right to Choose the Medical Care We Want Seriously at Risk?" *Palliative Supportive Care* 4, no. 2 (June 2006): 146-47.

32. Lazzarini et al., "Legal and Policy Lessons from the Schiavo Case," pp. 150, 152.

Legal Rulings on Physician Aid-in-Dying
(physician-assisted suicide)

Moving from cases involving withholding and withdrawal of treatment, we will examine the legal status of doctor aid-in-dying, popularly known as "physician-assisted suicide." The American public is divided over the issue of whether physician-assisted suicide should be legalized. After Attorney General John Ashcroft, during President George W. Bush's first term, failed in his attempt to overturn Oregon's law allowing physician-assisted suicide, other states — including Hawaii, Vermont, and California — proposed bills, all of which failed to get enough votes.[33] Part of the problem is understanding what exactly is at stake. As I pointed out in chapter 3, physician-assisted suicide is an imprecise and emotion-laden term that was unfortunate when Timothy Quill introduced it to differentiate it from euthanasia. If death is by the hand of a physician, à la Kevorkian, it is morally equivalent to active voluntary euthanasia. However, the three states that have approved what is called "death with dignity" or "aid-in-dying" — Oregon, Washington, and Montana — have only legalized the doctor's writing a prescription for a lethal dose of medicine, not the administering of it.

The principal debates have concerned Dr. Jack Kevorkian, who was imprisoned for repeated cases of physician-assisted suicide — actually euthanasia — since death was brought about by his own hand. In 1997 "Congress passed legislation barring taxpayer dollars from financing physician-assisted suicide. The U.S. Supreme Court ruled that mentally competent people who were terminally ill do not have a constitutional right to physician-assisted suicide, thus leaving that issue up to the states. Oregon voters affirmed the right to assistance in dying by passing for the second time its 'Death with Dignity Act.'"[34]

Oregon

Under Oregon's Death With Dignity Act, only competent adult state residents suffering from an incurable disease that would likely result in their

---

33. States such as Hawaii, which have proposed legislation legalizing physician-assisted suicide, have failed. Ben Taylor, CitizenLink editor, "Hawaii Assisted-Suicide Bill Defeated!" May 3, 2002: http://www.family.org/cforum/feature/a0020633.cfm (accessed Apr. 5, 2006).

34. "History of Hospice Care," National Hospice and Palliative Care Organization: http://www.nhpco.org/i4a/pages/index.cfm?pageid=3285 (accessed Aug. 13, 2009).

death within a six-month period are eligible for a lethal prescription to end their life. A patient's diagnosis must be confirmed by two independent physicians, and the patient must sign a written request for the prescription in the presence of two witnesses who attest that the patient is competent and acting voluntarily. Because of the misinterpretation and misrepresentation of this act, I will quote excerpts from the actual bill.

> "Informed decision" means a decision by a qualified patient, to request and obtain a prescription to end his or her life in a humane and dignified manner, that is, based on an appreciation of the relevant facts and after being fully informed by the attending physician.[35]
>
> Who may initiate a written request for medication? An adult who is capable, is a resident of Oregon, and has been determined by the attending physician and consulting physician to be suffering from a terminal disease, and who has voluntarily expressed his or her wish to die, may make a written request for medication for the purpose of ending his or her life in a humane and dignified manner in accordance with this Act.[36]
>
> The attending physician shall: (1) make the initial determination of whether a patient has a terminal disease, is capable, and has made the request voluntarily; (2) inform the patient of: (a) his or her medical diagnosis; (b) his or her prognosis; (c) the potential risks associated with taking the medication to be prescribed; (d) the probable result of taking the medication to be prescribed; (e) the feasible alternatives, including, but not limited to, comfort care, hospice care and pain control; (3) refer the patient to a consulting physician for medical confirmation of the diagnosis, and for determination that the patient is capable and acting voluntarily; (4) refer the patient for counseling if appropriate pursuant to Section 3.03; (5) request that the patient notify next of kin; (6) inform the patient that he or she has an opportunity to rescind the request at any time and in any manner, and offer the patient an opportunity to rescind at the end of the 15-day waiting period pursuant to Section 3.06; (7) verify, immediately prior to writing the

---

35. "The Oregon Death With Dignity Act," Section 1: General Provisions, No. 7, Oregon Department of Human Services: http://www.Oregon.gov/DHS/ph/pas/docs/statute.pdf (accessed June 3, 2010).

36. "The Oregon Death With Dignity Act," Section 2: Written Request for Medication to End One's Life in a Humane and Dignified Manner, No. 2.01, Oregon Department of Human Services: http//www.Oregon.gov/DHS/ph/pas/ors.shtml (accessed June 3, 2010).

prescription for medication under this Act, that the patient is making an informed decision; (8) fulfill the medical record documentation requirements of Section 3.09; and (9) ensure that all appropriate steps are carried out in accordance with this Act prior to writing a prescription for medication to enable a qualified patient to end his or her life in a humane and dignified manner.[37]

Oregon voters have, since 1997, twice supported a state law that supports physician-assisted suicide. Since 1997, more than 340 people — mostly afflicted with cancer — have used Oregon's measure to end their lives.[38] The Oregon studies are based on fewer than thirty cases, which hardly give sufficient empirical data. The data were obtained from physicians' reports, death certificates, and interviews with physicians. They compared persons who took lethal medications prescribed under the act with those who died from similar illnesses but did not receive prescriptions for lethal medications. Information on twenty-three persons who received a prescription for lethal medications was reported to the Oregon Health Division. During the first year of legalized physician aid-in-dying in Oregon, the decision to request and use a prescription for lethal medication was associated with concern about loss of autonomy or control of bodily functions, not with fear of intractable pain or concern about financial loss. In addition, they found that the choice of physician-assisted suicide was not associated with level of education or health insurance coverage.[39]

Attorney General John Ashcroft attempted to use the Federal Energy Administration (FEA) regulations to revoke doctors' licenses if they used certain drugs known to be lethal in certain doses. The U.S. Supreme Court affirmed the decision by the Oregon District Court in *Gonzales v. Oregon* in a six-to-three vote. The Supreme Court argued that the Controlled Substance Act (CSA) was not intended to hold authority over states' decisions. As a result, the Oregon Death With Dignity Act was upheld, and physicians in Oregon continued to offer aid-in-dying as an option for patients making decisions about end-of-life care. This decision came almost five years after Attorney General John Ashcroft brought the initial suit in November 2001.

37. "The Oregon Death With Dignity Act," Section 3, Safeguards, No. 3.01.

38. Associated Press, "Washington State to Allow 'Dignity' Deaths," *MSNBC on the web,* March 1, 2009: www.msnbc.msn.com/id/29454171 (accessed Mar. 2, 2009).

39. Arthur E. Chin, Katrina Hedberg, Grant K. Higginson, and David W. Fleming, "Legalized Physician Assisted Suicide in Oregon — The First Year's Experience," *New England Journal of Medicine* 340, no. 7 (Feb. 18, 1999): 577-83.

Washington

The Washington law, as of March 2009, makes physician aid-in-dying available only to patients who are over eighteen years, are judged competent, and have been judged terminally ill by two doctors and have six months to live. Patients must make an oral request and a written request that is witnessed by two people (submitted five days apart), one of whom must not be a relative, heir, attending doctor, or connected with a health facility where the requester lives. Another oral request must be made fifteen days later. Physicians must tell patients about options such as hospice and palliative care.[40]

This "Death With Dignity" bill, however, allows doctors, pharmacists, and hospitals to opt out based on grounds of conscience. Because of this option, apparently, very few people in Washington have been able to receive a physician's assistance in dying. "The U.S. Supreme Court ruled in 2006 that it was up to states to regulate medical practice, including assisted suicide, and Washington's Initiative 1000 was passed by nearly sixty percent of state voters in November."[41]

Montana

A Montana state district judge ruled in December 2008 that mentally competent patients with terminal illnesses have the right to physician-assisted suicide under the state's constitution. However, the judge gave no guidelines on the definitions of terminal illness and mental competence. The state's attorney general plans to appeal this decision, which was to take up to a year.[42] However, Montana allows physician aid-in-dying though there are cases under debate.

Other states prohibit physician-assisted suicide, and that is why the state of Michigan prosecuted Dr. Kevorkian. Michigan banned assisted suicide in 1998. The Kevorkian case involves a physician — Jack Kevorkian — who caused patients' deaths, that is, did not simply provide the means by which they died. Kevorkian was sentenced to ten to twenty-five years

40. "Washington State to Allow 'Dignity' Deaths."
41. "Washington State to Allow 'Dignity' Deaths."
42. Kevin B. O'Reilly, "Montana Judge Rejects Stay of Physician-Assisted Suicide Ruling," *American Medical News, amednews.com online*, January 29, 2009: http://www.ama-assn.org/amednews/2009/01/26/prsd0129.htm (accessed Apr. 15, 2009).

after being convicted in 1999 of second-degree murder in the death of Thomas Youk, who was afflicted with Lou Gehrig's disease. Kevorkian has said he assisted in at least 130 deaths but that not all of them were euthanasia. He was denied parole for health reasons several times and was finally released from prison on June 1, 2007.[43]

International Perspectives on the Legality of Physician-Assisted Suicide and Euthanasia

Since the debate from other countries may affect the American scene, it is helpful to look briefly at four of these nations where physician-assisted suicide or euthanasia is legal: Switzerland, the Netherlands, Belgium, and Luxembourg. Switzerland was much in the news in 2008-2009 because of the Dignitas Society. Assisted suicide is legal in Switzerland, but euthanasia is not. I discussed whether one believes this is a distinction without a difference in the preceding chapter.

The Netherlands

The title of the Dutch law is "Termination of Life on Request and Assisted Suicide Act." Approved in 2002, it is quite different from the "Death with Dignity" laws adopted by states in the United States. The Netherlands was the first country to allow active euthanasia and physician-assisted suicide. It is important to note that since the 1980s, doctors, guided by four side constraints, could practice physician-assisted suicide without being prosecuted, though it was still considered illegal.[44] The early reports from the

---

43. Kathy Barks Hoffman, "Jack Kevorkian Released from Prison," *The Independent,* June 2, 2007: http://www.independent.co.uk/news/world/americas/jack-kevorkian-released -from-prison-451426.html (accessed Apr. 7, 2009).

44. Jack Horgan, "Death with Dignity: Science and the Citizen," *Scientific American* (March 1991): 17. Holland's euthanasia guidelines:
  • The patient must repeatedly and explicitly express the desire to die.
  • The patient's decision must be well informed, free and enduring.
  • The patient must be suffering from severe physical or mental pain with no prospect for relief.
  • All other options for care must have been exhausted or refused by the patient.
  • Euthanasia must be carried out by a qualified physician.
  • The physician must consult at least one other physician.
  • The physician must inform the local coroner that euthanasia has occurred.

Netherlands were quite positive with respect to the absence of abuses, which seems to suggest that the side constraints in place reduced the danger of abuses. According to one report, an estimated 2,000 to 3,000 lives end by euthanasia and doctor-assisted suicide in the Netherlands each year.[45]

"In the Netherlands, physician-assisted suicide, which is widely discussed in the U.S., is not as popular as euthanasia. Of the 3,000 deaths in which a physician has played some kind of active role (total euthanasia and physician-assisted suicide cases per year in the Netherlands) 90 percent are euthanasia and only 10 percent (approximately 300 deaths) are due to physician-assisted suicide."[46] Finding accurate figures is not easy, but probably the best report to date is listed in the table on page 205. The drop in the number of deaths by euthanasia is attributed to better palliative care, the option of terminal sedation, and a better understanding of the use of morphine.

There have been a growing number of studies about the Dutch experience to determine whether abuses exist and how it is being practiced. Education for doctors has reduced abuses and overuse.

> In the Netherlands we currently offer between 60 and 80 hours of palliative care training each quarter year. . . . What is happening now is an interesting scenario. These same doctors who were trained to be the second opinion doctors in the case of a euthanasia request, are now saying that the more they know about palliative care and pain and symptom control, the less euthanasia they need to perform. Their knowledge has become a powerful tool to prevent euthanasia. For example, when the second opinion doctor goes in to see the patient and explains the options to him or her, it is quite possible that the GP and the patient may have never even heard of these alternatives. Once they understand their options, the patient and the doctor immediately choose something other than euthanasia. I think this power to offer alternatives is one of the very important motives for developing pallia-

45. Keith B. Richburg, "Death with Dignity, or Door to Abuse? Dutch Euthanasia Law Enjoys Wide Support, but Resistance Remains," *Washington Post,* January 4, 2004, pp. A1, A13.

46. "Evolution of Palliative Care in the Netherlands," An Interview with Zbigniew Zylicz, *Innovations in End-of-Life Care: An International Journal of Leaders in End-of-Life Care,* November 15, 2002: http://www2.edc.org/lastacts/archives/archivesNov02/intlpersp .asp (accessed Apr. 18, 2006).

Estimated frequencies of medical end-of-life decisions and continuous deep sedation in the Netherlands in 2005 and 2001 (death certificate study)

	2005		2001	
	Abs.	%*	Abs.	%*
Medical decisions on end of life:				
Euthanasia	2,325	1.7	3,500	2.6
Physician-assisted suicide	100	0.1	300	0.2
Ending of life without an explicit request of the patient	550	0.4	950	0.7
Intensified alleviation of pain or symptoms with hastening of death as a possible side effect	33,700	25.0	29,000	21.0
Abandoning potentially life-prolonging treatment	21,300	16.0	28,000	20.0
Continuous deep sedation:				
With medical end-of-life decisions†	9,700	7.1	8,500	6.0
Without medical end-of-life decisions	1,500	1.1	n/a	

* Percentage of all deaths
† Cases of continuous deep sedation in which a medical decision was taken with the shortening of the patient's life as a possible or intended consequence were, depending on the answers given by the physician, classified as abandoning life-prolonging treatment, intensifying the alleviation of pain or symptoms, or (rarely) as ending of life. These cases should therefore not be added to the total number of medical end-of-life decisions.

SOURCE: B. D. Onwuteaka-Philipsen et al., "Evaluation — Summary; Termination of Life on Request and Assisted Suicide (Review Procedures) Act," The Hague: ZonMw Programme on evaluation of legislation, part 23 (May 2007): 7-8.

tive care in this country. . . . Thus, the pressure on the shoulders of the GP has increased enormously, and the GPs said, "We are fed up with this pressure, we are not doctors anymore if we cannot offer alternatives to euthanasia." So I told them, "The more knowledge you have about good pain and symptom treatment, the better you can resist this pressure."[47]

In other words, if it is practiced "correctly" and only for patients *in extremis,* its morality is judged by these utilitarian arguments.

Conclusions from the Dutch experience are not necessarily applicable to the United States because that country's population is slightly less

47. "Evolution of Palliative Care in the Netherlands," An Interview with Zbigniew Zylicz.

than twice that of New Jersey, only about 16 million. In 1996 a major Dutch survey on euthanasia outlined the main statistical findings indicating whether voluntary euthanasia was under effective control in the Netherlands. The study concluded that, though there has been some improvement in compliance with procedural requirements, the practice of voluntary euthanasia and physician-assisted suicide remains beyond effective control.[48] In 2002, physician-assisted suicide became completely legal in the Netherlands. It comes as no surprise that one's perspective vis-à-vis these practices influences one's evaluation of the Dutch experience.

At the beginning of 1996, twelve cases were presented to a representative group of forty-seven members of the public prosecution in the Netherlands. Assessment varied considerably between cases and characteristics of the respondents, such as level of function, personal life philosophy, and age. The shared characteristics were the presence of an explicit request, life expectancy, and the kind of suffering. The most important feature that warranted holding an inquest was the absence of an explicit request by the patient and the variations in the inquests depending on the assessor.[49]

The law appears to enjoy support among the Dutch public and doctors, many of whom for years carried out such procedures in secret. According to the Dutch pro-life organization Cry For Life, there were 1,882 reported euthanasia cases in 2002, compared to 2,054 in 2001 and 2,123 in 2000. The source of their information is the Netherlands Health Ministry, and it is supplied by regional euthanasia committees, which combine euthanasia and the tiny number of doctor-assisted suicides. The Right To Die organization in the Netherlands cited 3,800 reported cases of euthanasia and doctor-assisted suicides in 2001, about the same as the 1995 figures. The numbers have held generally steady. However, with these discrepancies in numbers, the reporting methodologies are imperfect.[50]

New questions are now arising about euthanasia for newborns. "The Groningen Protocol, as the hospital's guidelines have come to be known, would create a legal framework for permitting doctors to actively end the life of newborns deemed to be in similar pain to adults from incurable dis-

48. Henk Jochemsen and John Keown, "Voluntary Euthanasia under Control? Further Empirical Evidence from the Netherlands," *Journal of Medical Ethics* 25, no. 1 (Feb. 1999): 16-21.

49. Jacqueline M. Cuperus-Bosma, Gerrit van der Wal, Caspar W. N. Looman, and Paul J. van der Maas, "Assessment of Physician-Assisted Death by Members of the Public Prosecution in the Netherlands," *Journal of Medical Ethics* 25, no. 1 (Feb. 1999): 8-15.

50. Richburg, "Death with Dignity, or Door to Abuse?" pp. A1, A13.

ease or extreme deformities. The guideline says euthanasia is acceptable when the child's medical team and independent doctors agree the pain cannot be eased and there is no prospect for improvement, and when parents think it is best. Examples include extremely premature births, where children suffer brain damage from bleeding and convulsions; and diseases where a child could only survive on life support for the rest of its life, such as severe cases of spina bifida and epidermosis bullosa, a rare blistering illness. . . . Groningen estimated the protocol would be applicable in about 10 cases per year in the Netherlands, a country of 16 million people."[51]

Belgium

The Belgian parliament approved a bill permitting euthanasia in 2002, making that country only the second one in Europe to legally give terminally ill patients the right to die. The vote came after two years of committee discussions. It defines euthanasia as an act practiced by a third party that intentionally ends the life of a person at his request. Under the bill, this can be practiced by doctors only on patients who have reached the legal adult age (eighteen in Belgium), and only at their specific, voluntary, and repeated request. The request must be written, and if the patient is not capable of writing, it must be written by another adult of his or her choice. A patient seeking euthanasia must be in a hopeless medical situation and be constantly suffering physically or psychologically. If the person is not in the terminal phase of his illness, the bill says, his doctor must consult a second doctor, either a psychiatrist or a specialist in the disease concerned. At least one month must pass between the written request and the carrying out of the act.[52]

A recent follow-up study was conducted in Belgium to investigate differences in the frequency and characteristics of these practices before and after the enactment of the law. "In 2007, 1.9% of all deaths in Flanders were the result of euthanasia, a rate that was higher than that in 1998 (1.1%) and 2001 (0.3%). In 1.8% of all deaths, lethal drugs were used without the

51. Toby Sterling, Associated Press, "Netherlands Hospital Euthanizes Babies," *newsmax.com,* December 1, 2004: http://archive.newsmax.com/archives/articles/2004/11/30/203858.shtml (accessed Aug. 13, 2009).

52. Reuters, "Belgium Approves Bill on Euthanasia," *Compassionate Healthcare Network,* May 16, 2002: http://www.chninternational.com/belgium_approves_bill_on_euthana.htm (accessed Apr. 15, 2009).

patient's explicit request, a rate that was lower than that in 1998 (3.2%) but similar to that in 2001 (1.5%). The rate of intensified alleviation of pain increased from 18.4% in 1998 and 22% in 2001 to 26.7% in 2007, and the rate of withholding or withdrawing life-prolonging treatment increased from 14.6% in 2001 to 17.4% in 2007."[53] It appears from this study that the legalization of euthanasia has provided better control of pain and only slightly increased the number of deaths by euthanasia.

Luxembourg

Luxembourg passed a bill legalizing euthanasia on March 17, 2009, to become the third European Union country, after the Netherlands and Belgium, that permits doctors to help patients end their own lives. There was a fair amount of controversy in a country where Roman Catholic values are strong, and most of the medical community originally opposed it. Its purpose is to alleviate the pain of terminal patients at their request, with the consent of two doctors.[54]

Switzerland

While physician-assisted suicide is legal in Switzerland, euthanasia is not. The difference is that in euthanasia the doctor takes a life by administering a lethal drug; in assisted suicide, one has to be able to physically carry out that final act on one's own.[55] In Switzerland a doctor is allowed to provide a patient who wants to die with lethal medication that the patient has to take by herself. The person must be mentally competent, and a second medical professional must confirm the diagnosis. DNR and advance directives are legal in Switzerland.

In the past few years, Switzerland has been under fire because of "suicide tourism" due to the Dignitas Society in Zurich. "The Dignitas

53. "Medical End-of-Life Practices under the Euthanasia Law in Belgium," *New England Journal of Medicine* 361, no. 1 (Sept. 10, 2009): 1119-21.

54. "Luxembourg Enacts Euthanasia Bill," *Medindia.net,* March 18, 2009: http://www.medindia.net/news/Luxembourg-Enacts-Euthanasia-Bill-48774-1.htm (accessed Apr. 15, 2009).

55. Mary Jayne McKay, "Switzerland's Suicide Tourists," *CBS News online,* July 23, 2003: http://www.cbsnews.com/stories/2003/02/12/60II/main540332.shtml (accessed Apr. 16, 2009).

clinic is near Zurich, Switzerland, and therefore operates under Swiss law, which, since 1940, has permitted assisted suicide provided it is done for altruistic reasons. It can be doctor-assisted hastened death, or non-doctor."[56]

> [Dignitas] takes advantage of Switzerland's liberal laws on assisted suicide, which suggest that a person can only be prosecuted if they are acting out of self-interest. The law on suicide states: "Whoever lures someone into suicide or provides assistance to commit suicide out of a self-interested motivation will, on completion of the suicide, be punished with up to five years' imprisonment." Dignitas interprets this to mean that anyone who assists suicide altruistically cannot be punished. Its specialist staff all work as volunteers to ensure there can be no conflict of interest. They engage in detailed discussion about whether the patient's determination to die falls within the legal boundaries, and whether it is indeed the declared will of the patient. Dignitas also provides a text for patients, which states their wish for assisted suicide in terms which cannot be misconstrued and which allows them to carry out their wishes even in the face of opposition, if necessary. Once the decision has been made, the patient travels to Zurich where he or she is taken to a Dignitas flat. The patient is given an anti-sickness drug 30 minutes before the lethal dose of barbiturate. A camera is set up to record the patient take the drug themselves — firm evidence that it was not administered by clinic staff. The barbiturate is a colorless solution, bitter tasting, and comes in a portion like a small glass of sherry. The dose is three times the normal lethal amount required, based on the patient's weight. The patient drinks it and then may take a sip of orange juice. Within five minutes they lapse into a coma, and the heart stops soon afterwards, apparently leading to a peaceful and painless death. The police are then called, a coroner comes, they question the witnesses and look at the video.[57]

The cases of those who come to Dignitas, as previously mentioned, have received considerable press. One of Britain's most respected conductors, Sir Edward Downes, and his wife, Joan, a choreographer and TV pro-

56. "How to Contact Dignitas in Switzerland," Weblog of Derek Humphrey, Founder of Hemlock Society, February 6, 2006: http://assistedsuicide.org/blog/2006/02/06/how-to -contact-dignitas-in-switzerland/ (accessed Aug. 12, 2009).

57. "Dignitas: Swiss Suicide Helpers," *BBC News online*, July 14, 2009: http://news.bbc .co.uk/2/hi/health/4643196.stm (accessed Aug. 12, 2009).

ducer, died in 2009 at Dignitas. The controversy was over the fact that Downes was blind and deaf but not terminally ill, though his wife was. Should they both have been given the means to commit suicide? Great Britain also decided to take no action against the family of 23-year-old Daniel James, who traveled to Switzerland to die after being paralyzed from the chest down in a rugby accident. "Last week, the House of Lords voted against an attempt by the former lord chancellor Lord Falconer to relax the law on assisted suicide. His amendment to the coroners and justice bill would have allowed people to help someone with a terminal illness travel to a country where assisted suicide is legal. . . . Some people fear that relaxing the law on assisted suicide would lead to an increase in cases, and put people at risk of being pushed into taking their own lives. Gordon Brown is against a change in the law."[58]

However, there has been a shift in Switzerland toward restricting the practices of Dignitas. The new side constraints would require: (1) a longer period of counseling to assure that the subject wanted to end his life; (2) that Swiss doctors who prescribe the deadly anesthetic meet the person on at least two separate occasions — to be sure of their wishes; (3) that patients need to prove they are suffering from a serious terminal illness, severe disability, or the after-effects of a serious accident; (4) that the mentally ill or clinically depressed would need a psychological assessment before receiving PAS; (5) that those under the age of twenty-five who are not experiencing severe physical suffering are ineligible; (6) that a maximum fee of 500 Swiss francs ($461) could be charged per assisted suicide, compared to Dignitas's usual charge of 6,000 Euros (about $7,900).[59]

Patient Rights Under the Law

In addition to the precedent cases are acts and legislation that have guaranteed certain rights and responsibilities of patients. Some are only state specific, while others are federal law.

58. Matthew Weaver, "British Conductor Dies with Wife at Assisted Suicide Clinic," *Guardian.co.uk,* July 14, 2009: http://www.guardian.co.uk/society/2009/jul/14/assisted -suicide-conductor-edward-downes (accessed Aug. 12, 2009).

59. Patrick Sawer, Kathryn Quinn, and Alexandra Williams, "Clampdown on Dignitas Suicide Clinic," *Telegraph.co.uk,* July 18, 2009: http://www.telegraph.co.uk/news/ worldnews/europe/switzerland/5857781/Clampdown-on-Dignitas-suicide-clinic.html (Aug. 12, 2009).

Patient Bill of Rights

Written by the American Hospital Association and approved by the American Medical Association in 1973 and revised in 1992, the Patient Bill of Rights sets forth certain rights that patients can claim during medical treatment and hospitalization (see Appendix C for a copy). It has yet to be passed by the U.S. Congress, despite several tries.[60]

Patient Self-Determination Act

The Patient Self-Determination Act of 1990 mandates that all hospitals and nursing homes have in place a mechanism for advising patients of their legal rights and options for refusing or accepting treatment if they are or become incapacitated. This translates into an advance directive in most situations.

> While the *Cruzan* decision received significant attention, the "Patient Self Determination Act" enacted by Congress on October 26, 1990, is perhaps more important in defining legal obligations concerning the right to die. This legislation imposes new responsibilities on providers designed to protect patients' rights.[61]

This law became effective December 1, 1991, and applies to hospitals, hospices, nursing homes, HMOs, and other health care facilities that receive funds from Medicare or Medicaid programs. However, some states (e.g., Oklahoma and Oregon) make certain presumptions, such as receiving food and fluids necessary to sustain life, or that food and fluids can only be withheld if, when competent, the patient has declared her wishes (e.g., Oklahoma and Missouri).[62] All states do recognize the right to refuse medical treatment, but if a person is comatose — in a persistent vegetative state — the courts may rule in the direction of treatment. The Patient Self-Determination Act does put new responsibilities on health care professionals.

60. "Health Care Law: Patients' Bill of Rights," American Bar Association Governmental Affairs Office, *American Bar Association online:* http://www.abanet.org/poladv/priorities/patients/ (accessed June 22, 2009).

61. Susan R. Huntington and Sigrid Fry-Revere, "Provider Responsibilities Under the Patient Self Determination Act," *Health Law Trends* (Winter 1991): 1-6.

62. "Patient Self-Determination Becomes Law of the Land," *Hospital Ethics* (Nov./Dec. 1990): 3; see also *Hospital Ethics* (Jan./Feb. 1991): 4-5.

Advance Directives

In addition to the particular legal rulings I have previously cited, there are other legal avenues by which patients may declare their wishes. Despite the legality of advance directives, fewer than 25 percent of Americans have completed an advance directive.[63] In a poll conducted by AARP, 36 percent of fifty to fifty-nine year-olds and 47 percent of sixty-plus-year-olds have completed a living will.[64] This is why one proviso in the 2009 draft of the U.S. health care reform bill will pay for a consultation with a doctor every five years to discuss advance directives (though it is not mandatory).

An advance directive is an "umbrella" term that refers to all written instructions about end-of-life health care choices. Its purpose is to make treatment preferences as unambiguous as possible. This is necessary for four reasons: (1) to assure medical decisions that are consonant with one's values, shorten the period of possible suffering, and improve outcomes for patients; (2) to avoid conflict or legal suits where ambiguous patient preferences exist, which the family, hospital, or state then have to try to interpret; (3) to lessen a family's anxiety about doing the right thing and a physician's burden of cessation of treatment without sufficient information; (4) to reduce high financial expenditures for unwanted treatment.

Advance directives (AD) may include detailed instructions concerning the types of treatment or nontreatment that are specified in particular circumstances. ADs usually include "Do Not Resuscitate" (DNR) orders or the refusal of artificial nutrition and hydration, dialysis, chemotherapy, or other life-prolonging procedures in the event of terminal illness, permanent unconsciousness, or mental incompetence. However, it does not necessarily refer to the cessation of treatment, but can request aggressive and prolonged treatment. To be legally binding, ADs generally need to be written and signed by competent persons and witnessed by two persons with nothing to gain from the individual's death. In lieu of detailed instructions,

---

63. Ruthie Robinson, Mary K. Eagen, and Tammy J. Price, "Innovative Solutions: Taking Advance Directives to the Community," *Dimensions of Critical Care Nursing* 27, no. 4 (July/Aug. 2008), Abstract: 154-56: http://journals.lww.com/dccnjournal/Abstract/2008/07000/Innovative_Solutions__Taking_Advance_Directives_to.3.aspx. "Despite the hope that traditional advance directives would ensure that patient preferences are honored, numerous studies have found that only a minority (20 to 30 percent) of American adults have an advance directive." Susan E. Hickman et al., "Hope for the Future: Achieving the Original Intent of Advance Directives," *Hastings Center Report* (Nov./Dec. 2005): S26.

64. "The Poll: Planning Ahead," *AARP Bulletin* (Jan.-Feb. 2008): 4.

a proxy decision-maker may be appointed, a durable power of attorney (DPA), to act when a person is unable to speak for himself. ADs are now legal in all fifty states of the union, and religious organizations, health care institutions, legal societies, and state agencies have sample forms. Some religiously worded forms can be ambiguous. However, most religious groups encourage people to register ADs, and they affirm the individual's right not to prolong dying, even as they oppose active euthanasia.

Some people confuse these health care requests with euthanasia, either direct or indirect (that is, physician-assisted suicide). The central issue at stake is choosing how to live while dying, not choosing death itself. A person weighs the benefits and burdens of a particular treatment and the quality of life that is acceptable. Care should be conveyed when a cure is no longer possible. Public support for AD is tied to the historical shift from dying at home, surrounded by loved ones, to dying in a depersonalized hospital setting. Due to the phenomenal advances in technological medicine, many times it prolongs dying and suffering rather than improving the last days of living. AD becomes a form of self-advocacy. It is a continuation of the patient's rights. Certain standards for making advance directives morally valid have been suggested. These include sufficient information about the procedure, competence on the part of the decision-maker, and involvement, where possible, of interested parties so that extrapolating to diverse circumstances can be discussed ahead of time. "Patient preference, stability, and consistency may be hard to measure but is an important aspect of clear advance directives."[65]

A growing number of physicians and policymakers are affirming the need to improve the way advance directives are written and implemented (see Appendix B for further information on ADs).

> In addition to a low completion rate, there are many reasons why traditional advance directives are less successful than originally hoped. These reasons include the following: (1) ... [T]hose who complete such documents generally do not receive assistance in understanding or discussing their underlying goals and values. (2) The instructions in these documents and the scenarios they provide for discussion are generally too vague. . . . (3) Vague instructions result in conversations that produce equally vague expressions of wishes, such as "Do not keep me alive

65. Abigail Rian Evans, "Advance Directives," in *New Dictionary of Pastoral Studies,* ed. Wesley Carr et al. (London: SPCK Publishing, 2002).

with machines" or "Let me die if I am a vegetable." (4) Once advance directives are completed, planning is typically considered finished. A systematic effort to reopen the conversation as a person's health declines is rarely made. . . . (5) Traditional advance directives are seen as a right of the patient, with little attention given to routinely integrate planning into the clinical care of patients. (6) Traditional advance directives are based on the assumption that autonomy is the primary mode of decision-making for most people. However, many people in the United States, particularly those from non-Western cultures, conceptualize the broader social network as the basis of treatment decisions, not the wishes and needs of the individual. . . . (7) Additional information about values and goals is important to assist surrogates in decision-making during stressful times. (8) Research suggests that many patients do not expect surrogates to rigidly follow their traditional advance directives, but rather intend for surrogates to exercise judgment to determine the course of care when there is insufficient information available or for extenuating circumstances.[66]

Some recent forms may answer some of these objections. "One well-known example is 'Five Wishes,' a document that incorporates a surrogate appointment with a range of wishes about medical, personal, spiritual, and emotional needs. . . . 'Let Me Decide' is a recently developed Canadian program with empirical data to support its effectiveness. . . . In La Crosse, Wisconsin, 'Respecting Choices' began in 1991 as part of a community-wide care planning system. . . . A study of the Respecting Choices program evaluated La Crosse County deaths over an eleven-month period (524 in all). Eighty-five percent of all decedents had some type of a written advance directive at the time of death. . . . The newer, more successful, clinically based advance directive programs share key elements: a facilitated process, documentation, proactive but appropriately staged timing, and the development of systems and processes that ensure planning occurs."[67]

State laws may vary as to the statutory options under advance directives, especially concerning the competence of the decision-maker. It is problematic whether clear and convincing evidence is needed to determine competence or lack of competence, since the courts have ruled in different ways.

66. Hickman et al., "Hope for the Future," pp. S26-S27.
67. Hickman et al., "Hope for the Future," pp. S27-S28.

Living Will

"A living will is a type of advance directive with instructions about health care treatment in the event of terminal illness. An explanation of one's values and beliefs that shape the instructions and how to deal with disagreements over its interpretation should be included. To be legal it needs to be written, dated, signed and witnessed by two persons with no vested interest in the person's death. However, laws vary worldwide regarding living wills. It is implemented when the person is no longer competent to express her desires and should be furnished to the attending physician."[68]

Ninety-five percent of the public has heard of living wills, up from 71 percent in 1990. Almost 30 percent now report having one, up from 12 percent in 1990.[69]

DNR (Do Not Resuscitate) Orders

A DNR ("do not resuscitate") order is a kind of advance directive in which a person says that health care providers should not perform cardio-pulmonary resuscitation (restarting the heart) if his or her heart or breathing stops.[70] There are various views concerning DNR orders. According to Lawrence Schneiderman and Roger Spragg, medical indications are the first priority.[71] If therapy would be futile, there is no moral obligation to continue (or to offer) therapy based on the patient's wishes; hence, patient autonomy is the second priority. Tom Tomlinson and Howard Brody also support this emphasis on medical indications in their analysis of DNR orders.[72] The discussion of DNR orders also raises the questions discussed earlier under the patient-physician relationship.

68. Abigail Rian Evans, "Living Will," in Carr, *New Dictionary of Pastoral Studies.*

69. Peter Steinfels, "Supreme Court Decision in Right-to-Die Debate May Signal Time Out," *New York Times, Death with Dignity National Center online,* February 11, 2006: http://www.deathwithdignity.org/news/news/nytimes.02.11.06.asp (accessed Mar. 13, 2006).

70. "Dictionary of Cancer Terms," National Cancer Institute: http://www.cancer.gov/Templates/db_alpha.aspx?CdrID=430481 (accessed Apr. 7, 2009).

71. Lawrence J. Schneiderman, Department of Family and Preventive Medicine; Roger G. Spragg, Department of Medicine, both of the University of California, San Diego.

72. Tom Tomlinson, Center for Ethics and Humanities in the Life Sciences, Michigan State University; Howard Brody, Director, Institute for the Medical Humanities, University of Texas Medical Branch.

Allan S. Brett and Laurence B. McCullough, for example, discuss the limits of the physician's obligations from patients' requests for useless or harmful interventions.[73] "Furthermore, CPR can be harmful if it interrupts a timely death. Without a modicum of potential benefit, the patient (or guardian if the patient is demented) has no right to expect this useless therapy. Administration of such therapy would be irresponsible. Therefore, caregivers should have no obligation to discuss this useless therapy. Time would be better spent discussing other therapies and plans, such as administration of intravenous fluids, enteral feedings, transfer to acute care facilities, etc., that may have potential benefit but might not be in the patient's best interest."[74] It is very difficult to measure the outcome of CPR. "There are no reliable national statistics on CPR because no single agency collects information about how many people get CPR, how many don't get it who need it, how many people are trained, etc. Many studies have examined CPR in specific communities. While they show varying rates of success, all are consistent in showing benefits from early CPR."[75] "Despite flaws, some studies do provide insight into survival rates and the factors that influence them. Three major reviews of 253 publications documenting 59,000 in-house resuscitation efforts between 1959 and 1992 show that the 15 percent worldwide average survival rate did not change significantly during this time period."[76]

David C. Thomasma (1939-2002), deceased professor of medical ethics at Loyola University of Chicago, however, took a somewhat different position: he declared that "beneficence should be the overriding principle, since demented patients are exempt from the principle of autonomy; they are dependent, not autonomous. The substituted judgment model offers a way of reconciling these views. In the absence of a living will or advance directive, a family member or legal guardian speaks for the patient. Their goal

73. Allen S. Brett, University of South Carolina School of Medicine and Center for Bioethics and Medical Humanities; Laurence B. McCullough, Center for Medical Ethics and Health Policy, Baylor College of Medicine.

74. Donald J. Murphy, "Do-Not-Resuscitate Orders: Time for Reappraisal in Long-Term Care Institutions," *Journal of the American Medical Association* 260, no. 14 (Oct. 14, 1988): 2098-99.

75. "Cardiopulmonary Resuscitation (CPR) Statistics," American Heart Association: http://www.americanheart.org/presenter.jhtml?identifier=4483 (accessed Aug. 13, 2009).

76. Abstract, "Forty Years of In-Hospital CPR," *NursingCenter.com,* January 2001: http://www.nursingcenter.com/library/JournalArticle.asp?Article_ID=481807 (Aug. 13, 2009).

is to express what the patient would have wanted based on previous discussions with the patient."[77] As I have noted earlier, however, presumed or proxy consent is seldom recognized in legal cases for withdrawal of food and water and even some other life-sustaining treatments even if futile.[78]

Conclusion

Having reviewed some of the court's rulings on end-of-life issues, we may still wonder how helpful the law really can be in what seems to be a personal arena. Not only do Americans no longer die at home; it may actually be that it is not until the courts declare them so that they are declared dead. Is this really where we want to be as a society? How can we change these growing legal entanglements concerning death and dying? Of course, we applaud the protection of the defenseless that the law provides, the decriminalization of the refusal of treatment, as well as the prosecution of those who would end life presumptuously. However, the growing number of these kinds of court cases concerning end-of-life decisions should prod us as a society to clarify our shared values in this area. It is important that pastors and faith communities do a better job of educating and supporting people on their last journey. However, the law also has a positive role and many excellent contributions to make: counseling, advising, clarifying, and protecting those who have no voice. But we should never look to the law to settle our moral dilemmas.

77. Murphy, "Do-Not-Resuscitate Orders," 2098-99.
78. Donald J. Murphy, Anne M. Murray, Bruce E. Robinson, and Edward W. Campion, "Outcomes of Cardiopulmonary Resuscitation in the Elderly," *Annals of Internal Medicine* 111 (1989): 199-205.

III. THE EXPERIENCE OF DYING

7. When Winter Enters Your Life: Pain and Suffering

When the great Rabbi Israel Baal Shem-Tov saw misfortune threatening the Jews it was his custom to go into a certain part of the forest to meditate. There he would light a fire, say a special prayer, and the miracle would be accomplished and the disaster averted.

Later, when his disciple, the celebrated Magid of Mezeritch, had occasion, for the same reason, to intercede with heaven, he would go to the same place in the forest and say: "Master of the Universe, listen! I do not know how to light the fire, but I am still able to say the prayer." And again the miracle would be accomplished.

Still later, Rabbi Moshe-Leib of Sassov, in order to save his people once more, would go into the forest and say: "I do not know how to light the fire, I do not know the prayer, but I know the place and this must be sufficient." It was sufficient and the miracle was accomplished.

Then it fell to Rabbi Israel of Rizhin to overcome misfortune. Sitting in his armchair, his head in his hands, he spoke to God: "I cannot even find the place in the forest. All I can do is to tell the story, and this must be sufficient." And it was sufficient.

Now that we have examined the various aspects surrounding negotiated death, we are left with the realization that they do not address the experience of dying — the pain, the suffering, the knowledge of a terminal diagnosis that can turn life upside down, the deep grief at the loss of a loved one, and the hunger to be cared for when all the medical procedures become futile. In these next three chapters I will explore these realities.

Contrast between Pain and Suffering

In any discussion of death, the question of pain and suffering surfaces. In fact, many of the supporters of euthanasia and physician-assisted suicide are not as interested in death as they are in eliminating the pain and suffering of those who are kept alive despite their tremendous suffering. We will discuss the reality of pain and its management in the chapter on hospice and palliative care. This chapter is principally about suffering, with some reference to the interaction between pain and suffering, and with some first-person accounts by those who have confronted these realities.

There are different types of pain and also an interaction between pain and suffering, which have many subjective aspects. Rafael Benoliel says that pain is a symptom to be managed and that suffering is the "all-encompassing experience of the person."[1] According to physician/bioethicist Eric Cassell, suffering results when a person perceives the threat of impending destruction and experiences severe distress associated with events that threaten the intactness of the individual.[2] Stanley Hauerwas observes that one's autonomy is often threatened by suffering; he likens autonomy to a person's having a narrative through which he makes suffering his own.[3]

Some researchers describe how suffering is one dimension of pain. The experience of pain is influenced by its cause, the patient's experience of a prior painful experience, and the meaning ascribed to pain in a particular culture. Suffering is an experience common to all of us, but we wish it were not so. "David Smith, a philosopher and ethicist, makes a significant distinction between pain and suffering. Pain is mainly a physical sensation. While suffering can be produced by intense pain, it is much more: 'suffering is associated with a disruption in the coherence and order that I perceive in the world.'"[4] Suffering is part of the lot of being human. To a great extent, the way we face suffering determines the kind of people we are. Miguel de Unamuno (1864-1936) wrote: "Suffering

1. Rafael Benoliel, "Foreword," in *Suffering*, ed. Betty R. Ferrell et al. (Boston: Jones and Bartlett, 1998), p. ix.

2. Eric Cassell, "The Nature of Suffering and the Goals of Medicine," *New England Journal of Medicine* 306, no. 11 (1992): 639-45.

3. Stanley Hauerwas, *Suffering Presence* (Notre Dame, IN: University of Notre Dame Press, 1986).

4. Abigail Rian Evans, *Redeeming Marketplace Medicine: A Theology of Health Care* (Cleveland: Pilgrim Press, 1999), pp. 91-92.

is the substance of life and the root of personality for only suffering makes us persons."[5]

"[P]eople in pain frequently report suffering from the pain when they feel out of control, when the pain is overwhelming, when the source of the pain is unknown, when the meaning of the pain is dire, or when pain is chronic."[6] Many cancer patients describe the experience as a gradual unwinding in that one layer of their lives is removed at a time. The altering of life's priorities intensifies the suffering, because now patients have limited time to live out their newly discovered priorities and life goals. Pain is also a very private, individual experience, yet we yearn to share it. Philip B. Helsel puts it this way:

> Nevertheless, if the person who is suffering will find a way to share that pain, in this very effort he can reconnect both with the body, which is the troubling source of pain and the outside world which can promise, if not physical relief, at least the comfort of communion. . . . In his treatment of pain, David Bakan (1968) describes how pain is the "ultimate of individual experience," and essentially "lonely," since its meanings are "private" and irreducible to broad categories. The difference between the tools available for treating pain and those at our disposal for understanding it is vast. The nature of medical discourse, the methodological canon of science which is highly conditioned by man's social nature forces one into the position of essentially denying the existence of pain in the contexts in which it occurs.[7]

Physical pain may lead to suffering, but emotional suffering may also lead to physical pain. For example, there are cases of children who die from lack of love. However, sometimes distraction and emotion can block pain. Pain also may play a positive role, for example, as a preserver of life, because it is a warning system to the body.[8]

Pain and suffering are different: physiological pain can be managed

5. Miguel de Unamuno, *Tragic Sense of Life,* trans. J. E. Crawford Flitch (New York: Dover Publications, 1954).

6. Cassell, "The Nature of Suffering," p. 641.

7. Philip Browning Helsel, "Simone Weil's Passionate Mysticism: The Paradox of Chronic Pain and the Transformation of the Cross," *Pastoral Psychology* 58 (2009): 57, 59.

8. John Hick, *Evil and the God of Love* (Hampshire, UK: Palgrave Macmillan, 1985), pp. 321, 328, 335.

with drugs, but suffering involves questions of life's meaning, value, and trustworthiness. Suffering may also have a communal component.[9] "If one member suffers, all suffer together with it; if one member is honored, all rejoice together with it" (1 Cor. 12:26). Because of the interactions of pain and suffering — since physicians deal mainly with pain management — we need others who address the issues of suffering.

Types of Pain

Discussions of pain date from some of the earliest written documents. Greek philosophers wrote extensively on the topics of pleasure and pain. Epicurus, Aristippus, Plato, Aristotle, and others recognized differences between two distinct classes of pain: physical — sensory or bodily; and mental — spiritual, nonsensory, or psychological. Rem B. Edwards says: "Typical examples of bodily pains are those derived from bodily lesions and infection — cuts, bruises, burns, cramps, broken bones, headaches, toothaches, stings, etc. Typical examples of mental pains are those disagreeable feelings involved in depression, anxiety, uncertainty, guilt, grief, boredom, sadness, sorrow, fear, anger, alienation, loneliness, etc."[10]

Physical

Edwards distinguishes between these classes of pain along phenomenological lines. In his book *Pleasure and Pains: A Theory of Qualitative Hedonism,* he argues that so-called bodily pains are those that belong to immediate subjective experience as being located in some fairly definite place or region of the body and are fairly easy to identify. However, when we are experiencing emotional or spiritual pain, the question *"Where* does it hurt?" has no clear meaning.

Pain is also closely associated with overall physical function and has an important impact: it can create or increase many physical symptoms, such as fatigue, anorexia, sleeplessness, constipation, and nausea. When

9. Bruce Epperly, *Can Suffering Be Redemptive?* (Clairmont, CA: Center for Process Studies, 1995).

10. Rem B. Edwards, "Pain and the Ethics of Pain Management," *Social Science and Medicine* 8, no. 6 (1984): 515.

pain is not controlled, symptoms may worsen; conversely, and as pain is brought under control, physical well-being may also improve.[11]

Mental

Mental pain can create bodily pain, as Rollo May has written: "Acute loneliness seems to be the most painful kind of anxiety which a human being can suffer. Patients often tell us that the pain is a physical gnawing in their chests, or feels like the cutting of a razor in their heart region, as well as a mental state of feeling like an infant abandoned in a world where nobody exists."[12]

Psychological/Spiritual

Psychological pain is related to anxiety and depression. When we feel as though we have loss of control, we can also feel useless. Pain can reduce overall pleasure and participation in the activities of life, and when pain is uncontrolled, people will remain at home. We need to do more to address the real pains of loneliness, loss of meaning, angst, despair, and the feeling of simply growing old and useless. Pain affects social roles, relationships, and sexuality — among other factors related to social well-being.[13]

Understanding spiritual pain is extremely important in providing care. The research of Keiko Tamura and colleagues shows how to answer the patient's fundamental questions. "More recently, the structure of spiritual pain has been examined. Murata elucidated the spiritual pain of people facing death as pain experienced as (1) a being founded on temporality, (2) a being in relationship, and (3) a being with autonomy. He found spiritual pain expressed as (1) meaninglessness and worthlessness of living; (2) emptiness, loneliness, or anxiety; and (3) worthlessness, dependence, or burden, respectively."[14] Pain has a tremendous influence on

11. Betty R. Ferrell and T. Borneman, "Pain and Suffering at the End of Life for Older Patients and their Families," *Generations* 28 (Spring 1999): 12-17.

12. Quoted in Edwards, "Pain and the Ethics," p. 515.

13. Ferrell and Borneman, "Pain and Suffering," pp. 12-17.

14. Keiko Tamura, Kazuko Kikui, and Michiyo Watanabe, "Caring for the Spiritual Pain of Patients with Advanced Cancer: A Phenomenological Approach to the Lived Experience," *Palliative and Supportive Care* 4 (2006): 190.

spirituality and religious beliefs, which can in turn influence our experience of pain. Pain creates a sense of anxiety and impending death for both patients and family members. Pain also creates a sense of hopelessness, the sense that all of life will be filled with pain. Furthermore, the loss of control can make us feel dependent, which creates anger and resentment. Family members, for their part, also experience pain, which they describe as "agonizing, excruciating, horrible, and overwhelming." While the patient experiences greater physical symptoms, families also suffer sympathetically when they experience the suffering of their loved one.[15] It is in the area of spiritual pain that we see most clearly how intertwined it is with suffering. In an earlier work I have expressed it this way:

> Suffering and physical pain are not always synonymous, but the false dichotomy created between mind and body has inhibited our easing of suffering. To address the question of suffering, we need an understanding of humankind in its entirety. Most generally, suffering can be defined as the state of severe distress associated with events that threaten the intactness of the person. The loss of hope may intensify this distress. Suffering for the Christian is incorporated into healing. Healing is akin to the unleashing of the explosive force inherent in the act of creation. It is a power in nature that can even use suffering for ultimate good and incorporates setbacks into the evolutionary process.[16]

Nature of Suffering

I have already noted the similarities between pain and suffering, but now I will highlight the distinctive nature and experience of suffering. Suffering is when "winter enters your life," says Pierre Wolff in his book *May I Hate God?*[17] Suffering is an anguish, a threat to who we are, to our composure, to our identity. Sometimes it is a spiritual response to a physical pain. Suffering may be subtle and slow, like growing old: we experience loss of energy, are no longer able to travel cross-country to see our family, and are not able to work. Suffering may be from a feeling of emptiness that results

15. B. R. Ferrell et al., "Pain as a Metaphor for Illness, Part II: Family Caregivers' Management of Pain," *Oncology Nursing Forum* 18 (1991): 1315-21.

16. Evans, *Redeeming Marketplace Medicine*, p. 94.

17. Pierre Wolff, *May I Hate God?* (Mahwah, NJ: Paulist Press, 1979).

from loss of loved ones by separation or death or the end of a relationship. Suffering may be a spiritual response to a physical pain. Fear of death permeates all experiences of suffering, which at its heart reflects humanity's vulnerability and creatureliness.

Although pain and suffering are interrelated, suffering can be analyzed separately. Suffering is unresolved pain. According to theologian William Strawson, there are several ways of looking at suffering (and not all of them are compatible): suffering is not real; suffering exists and is real but is not evil because good comes out of it; suffering is an inevitable and a natural part of the world based on human freedom.[18] Suffering is part of the lot of being human, and the way one faces suffering determines to a great extent the kind of human a person is.

Suffering is described as both in our control and beyond our control. There is a great deal of suffering we bring on ourselves: bad lifestyle choices, poor health habits, poor attitudes, disobedience to God, and alienation from others. These represent preventable suffering because, to a large degree, we can change the way we live and act. In *Redeeming Marketplace Medicine*, I report on some of those distinctions.

> The 1930 Lambeth Conference Committee Report drew an analogy between temptation and sickness. Temptation is an evil from which we are to ask deliverance; we are all to pray for deliverance. In the same way we are to struggle against suffering, but sometimes the will of God dictates that suffering is our path to deliverance. Some make a distinction between pain and disease; pain may be instructive but disease should always be eradicated. Perhaps more helpful is the observation of Jim Wilson of the Guild of Health, London, that there are two types of suffering: suffering which comes from disease rooted in evil and suffering which comes from opposing evil and its manifestations. The Christian is called to resist the first and embrace the second (p. 98).

Although modern medicine has been quite successful in curing an incredible range of illnesses, it does not have an adequate perspective to address the problem of suffering. When medical practitioners do address suffering, they are moving beyond the strict boundaries of their discipline, often with good motives and with good effects. However, what we need is a view of suffering that makes it a central part of the human experience and

18. Evans, *Redeeming Marketplace Medicine*, p. 95. Hereafter, page references to this work appear in parentheses in the text.

treats it in an integrated — not in an ad hoc — way. The problem this creates, of course, is that suffering does not lend itself to a clear, systematic, and integrated treatment.

> Suffering may be a natural consequence of a fallen world, but that does not mean God sends it as a deliberate punishment. Suffering may originate from things over which we have no control, such as earthquakes, wars, epidemics, or drunk drivers, or it may be global in nature, such as oppression, hunger, and powerlessness. God does not will everything that happens, but God wills something in everything that happens. Good may come out of suffering, but that does not justify it. The good news of the gospel is not just good news but the transformation that a life in Christ may bring; sharing suffering with Christ may redeem it. Christ himself experienced the ultimate pain of unjustified suffering, freeing us ultimately (p. 93).

Is suffering sent, permitted, or used by God? "Suffering may dismantle well-established beliefs. One may say, 'I don't understand anything about God anymore, why God allowed this, or whether God can do anything about it.' Ultimately, the Scriptures and Christ's life, as well as the lives of the saints, leave the questions of the *why* of suffering unresolved. We are left most often with the absence of God or, as Helmut Thielicke described it in his book of the same title, 'the silence of God'" (p. 94).

Bioethicist John Kilner has noted the two commonly accepted assumptions about suffering: "One is that suffering is an unqualified evil; the other is that suffering should be removed at all costs."[19] However, both assumptions are far removed from the biblical understanding in two ways: first, each view is too drastic and extreme; second, each is divorced from the other.

Even in the face of the mystery, we can rage and be angry at God. When we feel angry, bitter, helpless, or in despair, we need to be honest with God about our feelings. "In fact, it is much better expressing our anguish *to* God than talking resentfully *about* God to others. God can take on anger. Indeed he did take our anger and all our other sins when his Son died on the cross for us. He wants us to be honest with him and not to put on a pious mask when we approach him."[20]

---

19. John Kilner, *Life on the Line* (Grand Rapids: Eerdmans, 1992), p. 102.

20. David Watson, *Fear No Evil: A Personal Struggle with Cancer* (London: Hodder and Stoughton, 1984), p. 127.

"Suffering is a universal, inexplicable mystery. . . . Suffering may be caused by shame in a family, loss of job, poor health, bad lifestyle choices, a pessimistic worldview, permanent disability, loneliness, rejection, broken relationships and marriages, physical pain, or the tragic loss of a loved one. All these experiences produce suffering. David Smith's suggestion that genuine suffering is something that appears purposeless is an important observation, for in genuine suffering one's whole being stands on the precipice of dissolution. Suffering threatens our whole sense of self" (p. 92). It is part of the fabric of the world, but it is also intensely personal. Part of our dilemma is determining the suffering that we can do something about and accepting what is beyond our control. But we can always transform our suffering into a source of redemption.

Harold S. Kushner is wrong when, in *When Bad Things Happen to Good People*, he suggests that suffering is a sign of God's absence from the world.[21] However, suffering does raise the question of God's role in the world, and we do not want to eliminate God from history, as is the case in deist theology. As the story of Job shows, suffering is a mystery, but God's goodness ultimately triumphs. However, we cannot rush too quickly to that triumph (Evans, p. 93). One of the most important dimensions of suffering is the recognition that God is with us in our suffering. This affirmation, by its very nature, places suffering in the realm of the transcendent. It forces us to view events not in their immediate context but in the context of God and the evolution of the universe. Even when the winter of suffering seems to go on too long, there are small signs of God's presence (p. 94).

Martin Marty develops this theme in *A Cry of Absence*. He says that we cannot escape the winter of the heart that is at the core of the believer's struggle. Summer-style believers shun the doubter and offer a Christianity of cool comfort. Winter Christians often find themselves alongside atheists, living on the edges of doubt but still struggling to include a yes to God. Marty agrees with Karl Rahner that we need not eliminate a summer Christianity, but neither should it be allowed to have the only voice.[22] Richard Niebuhr expresses this struggle in terms of our suffering: "Because suffering is the exhibition of the presence in our existence of that which is not under our control, or of the intrusion into our self-legislating

---

21. Harold Kushner, *When Bad Things Happen to Good People* (New York: Avon Books, 1981).

22. Martin Marty, *A Cry of Absence* (San Francisco: HarperSanFrancisco, 1990).

existence of an activity operating under another law than ours, it cannot be brought adequately within spheres of teleological or deontological [obligation-based] ethics. Yet it is in response to suffering that many and perhaps all [persons] . . . define themselves, take on character, develop their ethos."[23]

Sources of Suffering

There are several sources of suffering. First, the suffering that results from our own sin. Second, suffering that comes from our broken world, that is, as part of the natural order; God is ultimately but not immediately responsible. Third, God is considered the source when suffering is used for educational and redemptive purposes. The latter is the theme of several Bible verses: "It was fitting that God . . . should make the pioneer of their salvation perfect through sufferings" (Heb. 2:10). The redemptive path of suffering or the vocation of suffering is described in Philippians 1:12-30, especially verses 29-30: "For he has graciously granted you the privilege not only of believing in Christ, but of suffering for him as well — since you are having the same struggle that you saw I had and now hear that I still have." Also, in 1 Peter: "Since therefore Christ suffered in the flesh, arm yourselves also with the same intention (for whoever has suffered in the flesh has finished with sin), so as to live for the rest of your earthly life no longer by human desires but by the will of God" (1 Pet. 4:1-2).

The Ante-Nicene Fathers, discussing the evil sources of sin, refer to numerous biblical passages. Christ speaks of "this woman whom Satan has bound" (Luke 13:16), and he speaks of unclean spirits (Mark 5:8). In working out the consequences of sin, Jesus refers to the fall of Jerusalem and the collapse of the tower in Siloam (Luke 13:1-5). "Sufferings caused by conflict with evil are most notably seen in Christ's life (Eph. 6:12)" (p. 95). Patristic evidence makes frequent references to evil as the source of suffering. "Justin Martyr speaks of God entrusting our care to angels who protect us from demons. Tertullian refers to both kinds of evil, evils of sin and ontological evil. Origen argues that God did not produce evil even though God can bring good out of it. If there is no sin there is no suffering, according to Tertullian.

---

23. H. Richard Niebuhr, quoted in Marsha D. M. Fowler, "Suffering," in *Dignity and Dying: A Christian Appraisal,* ed. John Kilner, Arlene B. Miller, and Edmund Pellegrino (Grand Rapids: Eerdmans, 1996), p. 48.

Clement of Alexandria sees it as a rod of discipline used by Christ. It is God's power that is required for suffering to have any efficacy" (p. 95).

God Uses Suffering

Several Bible passages seem to support the idea that God uses suffering for healing: victims of Pilate's massacre, the fall of the tower of Siloam (Luke 13:1-5), the death of the Gadarene swine, the cursing of the barren fig tree (Mark 5:11-13), and Paul's thorn in the flesh (2 Cor. 12:7-10). In the second instance, these people were killed because of the general sinfulness of humankind; in the third instance, the swine were driven to the sea by demons, not by Jesus Christ. In the case of Paul's thorn in the flesh, sometimes an answer to prayer for the removal of a thorn is not its extraction but its transformation. "Paul recognized the value of suffering in the hands of God. It is a way of correction, a means of purging from sin and strengthening of the good in humans, and sets our eyes on what is eternal. God is not the source of suffering but uses it as an instrument of God's will" (p. 98). It is clear, therefore, that when God permits or even causes suffering, it is only in order that it may be overcome, and that, in the overcoming, the evil of sin may be purged, the weak strengthened, and the strong perfected.[24]

Our understanding of sickness, suffering, and pain is influenced by how we as Christians understand new birth. If we agree with Evelyn Frost, it is salvation for the whole person — body, mind, and soul — and pain is to become transformed so that each organ can continue to act in harmony with the whole. In eternal life, sin, disease, and pain will all be gone. There are teachings in both the New Testament and the Ante-Nicene Fathers about the pain or loss that may be experienced when we come into conflict with evil. John refers to purging and pruning of the branch in order to be grafted back onto the trunk; Paul suffers all things as loss in order to gain Christ (Phil. 3:8). Peter sees the refining use to which bad suffering, in the form of persecution, can be turned (1 Pet. 1:7). Irenaeus refers to Paul's growing in the knowledge and grace of God through his thorn in the flesh.

All of these are ways of sharing in the cross of Christ, but this must always be done with faith in his resurrection. God always supplies the

---

24. Evelyn Frost, *Christian Healing: A consideration of the place of spiritual healing in the church of to-day in the light of the doctrine and practice of the ante-Nicene church* (London: A. R. Mowbray, 1940), p. 218.

grace to bear one's suffering. The church is called to throw out the ravages of sin and the suffering of body and spirit that it brings. The Ante-Nicene Fathers recognized that it was in the conquest of disease, not in submission under it, that the Christian's victory was won.[25]

Suffering as a Challenge to Personal Faith

As we strive to understand pain and suffering, it is instructive to read of others' struggles with these realities. David Watson, a famous British evangelist with a large healing ministry, wrote of the challenge to his Christian faith when he was confronting his painful dying of cancer, despite the fact that he was surrounded by prayers for healing. Reading his journal can help us see the testing of Christian faith while walking through the valley of the shadow of death: because God is with us, we need fear no evil (Ps. 23). For Watson, it was not just the cancer, but pain and other conditions that exacerbated his suffering. His story gives us a window into how persons of great faith can suffer, but also can eventually be victorious.

> During the last few months I have felt extremely vulnerable. Unexplained aches and pains all too easily appear sinister. For the last three months, for example, I have had increasing backache — a common complaint but something I have never known in my life. Has the cancer gone round to my spine? What exactly is going on? Both my doctor and specialist say that in their opinion it is purely muscular and postural. But the pain continues, especially when I am standing (as I often am), and I wonder why. Why *now*? It is an easy temptation to fear the worst.
>
> Then the tumor in my liver, which for the first time I could feel a few weeks ago, began to harden and became sore — so sore, in fact, that I could sleep only in one position. Again, what was going on? In one difficult week recently, my specialist thought that the tumor in the liver was definitely growing, but three days later my surgeon was sure that it was *not* growing — if anything slightly smaller and softer. During this period we had special times of prayer for my healing. They were always extremely helpful. The sore, hard lump is no longer sore (and much softer), but the pains in my back seem to get worse — for whatever reason.
>
> Walking by faith is rather like walking on a tightrope: at times it is

25. Frost, *Christian Healing*, pp. 225, 248.

exhilarating, but it requires only the slightest knock to make me feel insecure and anxious. In the last week or so I have been bothered more by asthma, which probably indicates an increased level of stress. I have also not been sleeping so well as before.

I mention all this, not to wallow in self-pity (I *still* believe that God is healing me) but to emphasize that the question "why suffering?" is far from theoretical. I am profoundly aware that many millions in the world are suffering much more acutely than I am, yet the pains and vulnerability are still there.

For those who believe in a good God, the dilemma is so acute that Rabbi Kushner concludes that God cannot be all powerful after all. Using the analogy of quantum physics where it seems that certain events happen in the universe at random, Kushner believes that there is "randomness in the universe. . . . Why do we have to insist on every-thing being reasonable? Why can't we let the universe have a few rough edges?" According to Kushner, God is not in control of everything, al-though he is on our side whenever bad luck dominates. Evil some-times finally prevails and is not always overcome by good. Kushner claims that God does not have the whole world in his hands, and therefore is not responsible for malformed children, for natural disas-ters, or fatal diseases. These simply lie outside his jurisdiction.

It is a neat theory, and it saves us from the unacceptable conclusion of blaming God for all the evil in the world. However, if God is not in ulti-mate control, he cannot truly be God. If there is no final justice, no even-tual triumph of good over evil, God is not the God who has revealed himself in the Bible and in the person of Jesus Christ. If there is some whimsical evil force greater than God, making God finite and limited, we live a futile existence in a meaningless world — as the atheist main-tains. If God is not God of all, he is not God at all. There is little hope for any of us, apart from resigning ourselves to a fortuitous mortality in a universe ruled by chance. We cannot ultimately be sure of anything ex-cept being at the mercy of unleashed and unpredictable evil.

However, the ringing conviction of the scriptures is that *the Lord reigns!* Even in the one supreme case of truly innocent suffering, the crucifixion of Jesus, God knew what he was doing. He had not lost control. As Simon Peter declared, all the rulers put together could do only what God had planned to take place (Acts 4:27ff.). At the time no one could see why such excruciating suffering should destroy the only sinless man that had ever lived, the Son of God himself. Later the disciples saw it as clearly as could be. "Christ died for our sins to bring us to God" (1 Peter 3:18). There on the cross Christ bore the penalty for our sin once for all, so that we might be reconciled to God. Nevertheless, although Christians down the ages have seen in Christ's sufferings the salvation of the world, what can we say about the myriads of others whose sufferings and death have never had any special significance, or none that we could discern?

James Mitchell in *The God I Want* once wrote angrily: "The value of a god must be open to test. No god is worth preserving unless he is of some practical use in curing all the ills which plague humanity — all the disease and pain and starvation, the little children born crippled or spastic or mentally defective: a creator god would be answerable to us for these things at the day of judgment — if he dared to turn up." Here is the bitter anger that many feel towards God when faced with senseless and hopeless suffering.

Interestingly enough we find many expressions of anger against God in the Psalms. The psalmist often reveals the deepest hurts of his heart, whether they are godly or not.

Death for the Christian, it is sometimes said, is like the old family servant who opens the door to welcome the children home. Although it would be a mistake to base our beliefs on the experience of those who have clinically died but later have been restored to life, it is worth noting that of those who were Christians nearly all speak of walking peacefully into a garden full of staggeringly beautiful colors and exquisite music (or some similar description), so that it was with great reluctance that they came back to earth again.

It never worries me that we are not able to grasp more clearly the true nature of heaven. We can understand something of which we have no firsthand experience only by describing something with which we are familiar. We are limited by language. But for those who know God and who are trusting in Christ as their Savior and Lord, there is nothing to fear, and it is sufficient to know that we shall be like him and perfectly with him. Nothing could be more wonderful than that. Never fear the worst. *The best is yet to be.*

When I die, it is my firm conviction that I shall be more alive than ever, experiencing the full reality of all that God has prepared for us in Christ. Sometimes I have foretastes of that reality, when the sense of God's presence is especially vivid. Although such moments are comparatively rare they whet my appetite for much more. The actual moment of dying is still shrouded in mystery, but as I keep my eyes on Jesus I am not afraid. Jesus has already been through death for us, and will be with us when we walk through it ourselves. In those great words of the Twenty-Third Psalm:

> Even though I walk through the valley
> of the shadow of death,
> I fear no evil;
> for thou art with me . . .[26]

The central struggle with respect to suffering is the theodicy question, as David Watson shows. We either come to the unacceptable conclusion of blaming God for all the evil in the world or, if God is not in ultimate control, God cannot truly be God. "If there is no final justice, no eventual triumph of good over evil, God is not the God who has revealed himself in the Bible and in the person of Jesus Christ. If there is some whimsical evil force greater than God, making God finite and limited, we live a futile existence in a meaningless world — as the atheist maintains. If God is not God of all, he is not God at all. There is little hope for any of us, apart from resigning ourselves to a fortuitous mortality in a universe ruled by chance. We cannot ultimately be sure of anything except being at the mercy of unleashed and unpredictable evil."[27]

Suffering for the Sake of Righteousness

In Christian theology we refer to suffering for righteousness' sake, sometimes being persecuted for our beliefs, which is suffering with a purpose. Paul refers to this in Romans: "I consider that the sufferings of the present time are not worth comparing with the glory that is to be revealed" (Rom. 8:18). This suffering for Christ's sake is a major theme elsewhere in Scripture (e.g., 1 Pet. 3:17; 4:13). Paul also distinguishes between suffering for the sake of the gospel and the "evil" from which God will rescue us (2 Tim. 4:5, 18). Suffering may be a result of one's actions or a result of the evil world in which one lives. Suffering may be an occasion for spiritual growth, but not always. If one remains faithful to God, God may bring good out of suffering, but that does not eliminate our suffering. In *The Wounded Healer,*

26. Watson, *Fear No Evil*, pp. 124-26, 168.
27. Watson, *Fear No Evil*, p. 125.

Henri Nouwen emphasizes that it is Jesus Christ's suffering, his sacrifice, that becomes the road to redemption: by his stripes we are healed.[28] So our wholeness may be wrapped up in our brokenness, an inversion of how we generally understand the world to work.

Another way of thinking about suffering is the why, the how, and the what of it. The "why" is the theodicy question — Job's question. The "what" is the response of a person to another's suffering, that is, compassion: what we can do to help someone else. The "how" of suffering is our response to it. In many respects, this may not be terribly helpful to the one who asks, "Why me?" or "Why is there suffering at all?" These are the fundamental questions of theodicy to deflect, not to resolve. Deflecting them is achieved by accepting the reality of "evil" and suffering and by searching for their possible implications for the healing enterprise. The place to start is the suffering of Christ: his suffering was at its greatest when he least deserved it. Thus God's greatest work may take place on the road through suffering.

Preparing for Suffering

Since all of us will suffer, we ask, What can we do about suffering in our life? Preparing ourselves for suffering is crucial. This begins with developing deep wellsprings of spiritual strength and insight. Memorizing Scripture verses as a daily part of our lives can enhance the depth of our faith. They will come as a source of grace. Ernest Gordon wrote of the Japanese prison camp in the valley of the Kwai, where a young man transformed the inhumanity of that camp by sharing the words of the Bible.[29]

I can remember as vividly as yesterday when, in 1963, I was arranging for the burial of my infant daughter in the interior town of Chapecó, Brazil, and the words of Psalm 1:3 came to me: "They are like trees planted by streams of water, which yield their fruit in its season." These words are on her tombstone. In addition to reading and meditating on Scripture, writing a spiritual journal can be therapeutic. Write your own book of Job, so to speak. This is part of accepting one's feelings. We should not judge our feelings since the object is to express them, to give them over to God.

28. Henri J. M. Nouwen, *The Wounded Healer* (London: Darton, Longman and Todd, 1994).

29. Ernest Gordon, *Through the Valley of the Kwai* (New York: Harper and Bros., 1962).

Keeping a journal, writing poetry, and other writing practices can be a kind of prayer.

Addressing Pain and Suffering

As we attempt to address the assaults on our being of pain and suffering, we need to call on the full armamentarium of medicine, religion, spirituality, family and friends, health care professionals, and God's power and grace.

"What we in America have done is to attempt to use our medical knowledge and medical power to 'tame the terror and eliminate the darkness' — which is suffering — from our lives. We have asked medicine to do something that is not its fundamental purpose. In its care of the body, medicine and its technology can dull the sword of disease or pain or even death, but it cannot, itself, either tell us where to 'draw the line,' or come to grips with the issue of suffering."

There are many levels of dealing with a patient's pain and suffering, but ministering to the family is extremely important. The family caregiver's experience of pain in advanced illness can be described as beginning with the caregiver's perceptions of the patient's suffering. "However, family caregivers' perspectives of pain vary dramatically and are influenced by many factors, including their own experiences with pain, their relationship to the patient, and culture."[30] The burden of caregiving and observing a family member's pain can lead to severe suffering in the caregiver. According to Wilson, Balszer, and Nashold, suffering is subjective and is based on the affective response of the one suffering and the one empathetically sharing the individual's suffering.[31] Ferrell and Borneman found that family caregivers often describe physical sensations when observing the pain of family members: "'She's hurting and it makes me cry. It's like a knife twisting in her.'"[32]

Family members are increasingly called on to care for their sick loved ones, a care that was previously done in hospitals or in-patient centers. Families need more education and training to do this because, unlike health care professionals, they are on call 24/7. Furthermore, families need

30. Marsha D. M. Fowler, "Suffering," p. 48.

31. W. Wilson, D. G. Balszer, and B. S. Nashold, "Observations on Pain and Suffering," *Psychomatics* 17, no. 2 (1976): 73-76.

32. Ferrell and Borneman, "Pain and Suffering," p. 12. Hereafter, page references to this essay will appear in parentheses in the text.

to have a respite-care plan in place to relieve them, as well as training from hospice staff and other palliative-care specialists (pp. 12-17). Studies have shown that information on pain management is not enough, since family members feel helpless and overwhelmed. In fact, they may deny the presence of symptoms as a means of coping with the situation or acknowledging that the disease is worsening. The presence of pain becomes a symbol of death and introduces existential issues that necessitate completely different treatment modalities.

A research study at the City of Hope National Medical Center "evaluated a structured pain education program in both elderly patients and family caregivers. . . . The educational program was successful in improving knowledge and attitudes about pain, as well as direct outcomes such as improved pain intensity and overall quality of life. The study also revealed the unmet emotional needs of family caregivers arising from the perceived burden of responsibility for the relief of a loved one's pain and suffering" (p. 14).

Ferrell and Borneman identify the critical role of family caregivers in pain management. "On a scale ranging from 0 (no pain) to 100 (severe pain), caregivers' mean rating of the patients' pain was seventy, while the patients' mean rating of their [own] pain was forty-five. On a similar scale, caregivers rated their own distress with the pain at seventy-eight. The data revealed that mood disruption for caregivers was most severe in the areas of anxiety, depression, and fatigue. Caregivers reported extreme fear that patients would become addicted to the pain medication and that they would experience respiratory depression and drug tolerance. Based on these concerns, caregivers tended to undermedicate the patient. At the same time, caregivers expressed feelings of helplessness in being unable to provide the patient with comfort. The caregivers also received virtually no instruction in the use of nonpharmacologic pain management" (p. 16).

Two studies in 1993 by Ferrell and colleagues explored the ethical dilemmas associated with cancer pain as well as how patients, family caregivers, and nurses found meaning through their pain. Patients, family members, and nurses reported similar issues about medications, pain, death, suicide, and euthanasia, and spiritual concerns. Family caregivers also had concerns about personal needs, spiritual and existential conflicts, and acceptance of imminent death. Nurses were concerned about relationships with physicians, patient and family, professional boundaries, interventions, personal decisions, religious issues, balancing of career and personal life, and professional limitations.

A study by Grande, Todd, and Barclay showed that often family caregivers and patients do not want to impose on health care professionals, so they only ask for help they feel entitled to, not what they need. However, family caregivers do look for more support and reassurance from health care providers while their loved ones are dying. "This combination contributes to a situation in which the family caregiver and the patient have many unmet emotional and physical needs. Studies already have identified the important role and educational needs of family caregivers and have begun to describe conflicts and burdens faced by caregivers. Caregivers' knowledge of pain management principles and techniques is an important area for additional study" (pp. 16-17).

Health care professionals can go a long way toward helping patients and their families manage pain, but addressing the accompanying suffering, as I have mentioned above, is a much larger task. They can help patients and family caregivers find meaning and, when possible, help ease their existential suffering. The issues of spiritual well-being and suffering require a collaborative approach. However, ultimately it is our response to pain and suffering that matters.

Responses to Suffering

There are a variety of responses to suffering. I will discuss several of them in the hope that they will be of help when we are in its clutches.

Confronting

Some Christians write of the importance of confronting suffering rather than passively accepting it. In her book *Hallelujah Anyhow!* Diedra Kriewald, whose husband was killed in a car accident on their honeymoon, says that we should name the pain, enter into the suffering, let go, and witness to the power of God.[33] But she admits that anger did not come easy to her.[34] Later she realized that God suffers with us through compassion — that her being angry, in the tradition of the psalmist, was not against God but could reveal faith.

---

33. Diedra Kriewald, *Hallelujah Anyhow! Suffering and the Christian Community of Faith* (New York: Women's Division, UMC General Board of Global Ministries, 1986), pp. 103-6.

34. Kriewald, *Hallelujah Anyhow!* p. 3.

Part of this confronting is inviting others to sit with us to accompany us in our suffering. We need to communicate our feelings, to let others know what we need and how we feel: not just in words, gestures, touch, or acts, but also in our need for silence. "If you would only keep silent, that would be your wisdom!" says Job to his friends (Job 13:5). Yet speaking out loud may be cathartic in itself for the sufferer. Letting others know what would be helpful is essential. Part of this communication is to express our real feelings, to vent anger and grief. Job is perhaps the best illustration of this (Job 3:5, 11-13; 7:13-16). Faced with all the catastrophes that befell Job, most people would curse God or commit suicide. Job's reaction, even in his bitterest times, was to believe in God and God's justice. As the drama unfolds, we read of the various stages of Job's emotions: numbness, uncertainty, rage, doubt, discouragement, hope, repentance, and vindication. Job is torn between believing that God is all powerful (and thus unapproachable) and trusting that God will answer him directly. He recognizes the gulf between himself and God, and he wants an arbitrator between them: "For [God] is not a man, as I am, that I might answer him, that we should come to trial together. There is no umpire between us, who might lay his hand upon us both" (Job 9:32-33). Later he adds "that one would maintain the right of a mortal with God, as one does for a neighbor" (Job 16:21). Job becomes an example, not so much of how to endure suffering, but of how to confront it. He rages against God and confronts his friends and wife about how unhelpful they are. However, even in his suffering he declares that his Redeemer (Vindicator) lives.

In *May I Hate God?* Pierre Wolff tells stories of two women whose anger was an important part of their healing process. The first woman was caring for a small child who fell from a fifth floor window and was killed. Her response was, "God, I hate you because you let this happen!" The second woman, whose son was killed in a car accident, rebelled against God and felt her faith disappearing. Wolff writes: "The Lord is certainly as saddened as she is right now: How could he accept such an accident caused by negligence and imprudence? And all of a sudden I understood that she was for us a witness to the sorrow of God. This was affirmed for me when I saw her engulfed in profound peace. I said to her, 'Do not accuse the Lord; he is probably thinking the same thing you are. Do not think you are against him; he is beside you, speaking through you; for our Father has also 'lost' a child.'"[35]

35. Wolff, *May I Hate God?* p. 37.

John Hick rejects Hume's idea of a world that was designed for the avoidance of pain. For example, if your hand went into the fire and did not get painfully burned, our environment would change too much and we would have a soft, unchallenging world. However, Hick does not believe that pain is a result of the Fall of mankind, though for some of us Romans 8:4 seems to suggest precisely that: "So that the just requirement of the law might be fulfilled in us, who walk not according to the flesh but according to the Spirit." However, Hick refers to the redemption of creation.[36] He says that suffering and pain are evil, but that ultimately the power of God overcomes the power of evil. Jesus Christ's death and resurrection show that to be true.

Transforming and Transcending

Karl Barth speaks of Christ's transformation of human suffering: "By His [God's] own suffering He has characterized our suffering as a token of life and not of death, as a token of His friendship and not of His enmity, as a token which is meant to awaken and maintain and not destroy our faith. It is the shadow of death under which our life stands, the shadow of the eternal death which Jesus Christ has suffered for us . . . it is a real and serious shadow — it is a token of life, eternal life. We are given time and space to believe in Him."[37] Scripture is also our source of strength. The stories of men and women in the Bible become a source of encouragement, insight, and comfort to us. The pages of the Bible are full of stories of the sufferings of God's people. The Psalms are in many ways a book of lamentations.

We can also speak of transcending suffering as Viktor Frankl does while writing out of the Holocaust experience.

> During his years in Nazi death camps during World War II, Frankl observed that the prisoners who exercised the power to choose how they would respond to their circumstances displayed dignity, courage, and inner vitality. They found a way to *transcend* their suffering. Some chose to believe in God in spite of all the evidence to the contrary. They chose to expect a good tomorrow, though there was little promise of one. They chose to love, however hateful the environment in which they lived.

36. Hick, *Evil and the God of Love*, pp. 343, 252.
37. Karl Barth, *Church Dogmatics*, vol. II, part 1, trans. T. H. L. Parker et al. (Edinburgh: T. & T. Clark, 1957), p. 420.

In other words, they refused to yield ultimate power to their captors and circumstances. Though the world was horrible to them, they identified with another world — a world inside themselves, over which they had some control. They affirmed that they were more than the product of their circumstances. As Frankl observed, these few people tried "turning life into an inner triumph" and so grew spiritually beyond themselves.

It became clear to Frankl that "the sort of person the prisoner became was the result of an inner decision, and not the result of camp influences alone." In the end he asserts: "The experiences of camp life show that man does have a choice of action. There were enough examples, often of a heroic nature, which proved that apathy could be overcome, irritability suppressed. Man can preserve a vestige of spiritual freedom, of independence of mind, even in such terrible conditions of psychic and physical stress." Frankl concluded that these prisoners transcended their circumstances because they found meaning in their suffering. "If there is meaning in life at all, then there must be a meaning in suffering. Suffering is an ineradicable part of life, even as fate and death. Without suffering and death human life cannot be complete."

It was this power to choose that kept the prisoners alive, Frankl noted. They directed their energies inwardly and paid attention to what was happening in their souls. They learned that tragedy can increase the soul's capacity for darkness and light, for pleasure as well as for pain, for hope as well as for dejection. The soul contains a capacity to know and love God, to become virtuous, to learn truth, and to live by moral conviction. The soul is elastic, like a balloon. It can grow larger through suffering. Loss can enlarge its capacity for anger, depression, despair, and anguish, all natural and legitimate emotions whenever we experience loss. Once enlarged, the soul is also capable of experiencing greater joy, strength, peace, and love. What we consider opposites — east and west, night and light, sorrow and joy, weakness and strength, anger and love, despair and hope, death and life — are no more mutually exclusive than winter and sunlight. The soul has the capacity to experience these opposites, even at the same time.[38]

The Spanish mystic John of the Cross (1542-1591) wrote about "the dark night of the soul," though in the English translation of *escuro* the

38. Gerald Sittser, *A Grace Disguised: How the Soul Grows Through Loss* (Grand Rapids: Zondervan, 1995), pp. 38-39.

richer meaning is lost. He defines it as a depressed spiritual state into which one slips and, turning to traditional remedies — emotional fervor, spiritual discipline, rational analysis, worship, service — finds in them absolutely no help and comfort. All props are stripped away.[39] It is similar to what Teresa of Avila (1515-1582) writes about in *Interior Castle*.[40]

The response to suffering deals with the "how" of suffering. What can we do in the face of grief, pain, loss, crisis, and sickness to cope and to grow? The great men and women of faith are those who have redeemed their sufferings, overcome adversity, and clung to hope in the midst of overwhelming odds. How we face suffering says more about us than anything else. In *A Grief Observed*, C. S. Lewis put it this way: "Bridge players tell me that there must some money on the game 'or else people won't take it seriously.' Apparently it's like that. Your bid — for God or no God, for a good God or a Cosmic Sadist, for eternal life or nonentity — will not be serious if nothing much is staked upon it. And you will never discover how high until you find that you are playing not for counters or for sixpences but for every penny you have in the world."[41]

When we are suffering, most often we need to confront it in order to bring healing into our lives. Trusting in God's power gives us the strength to face "the slings and arrows of outrageous fortune." From first to last we live with absolute confidence in the power of God. In this world, that means a conscious repudiation of dominating power. But every act of service always involves some measure of deprivation. And the Christian's service never succeeds — and never means to succeed — in freeing others entirely from their needs and weaknesses.

> In his need as well as in his service, the Christian must always affirm the opening statement of the Apostles' Creed: "I believe in God the Father Almighty." The almightiness affirmed here is not that of a transcendent God whose power consists in standing above the Son in some kind of superiority. It is not the almightiness of a God who dominates the universe, compels its obedience, and proves his supremacy by always getting God's own way. The almightiness affirmed here is that of the Father, which means that it is the almightiness of the one

---

39. Saint John of the Cross, *The Dark Night of the Soul: Songs of Yearning for God,* ed. Mirabai Starr (London: Rider & Co., 2002).

40. Saint Teresa de Avila, *Interior Castle* (Garden City, NY: Doubleday, 1961).

41. C. S. Lewis, *A Grief Observed* (New York: Seabury Press, 1963), p. 43.

who confers all God's own being and glory upon God's Son. Therefore, to confess, "I believe in God the *Father* Almighty," is to confess that I believe in the almighty powerfulness of God's self-communication and self-giving. It means that I renounce all awe and admiration for that which merely dominates. By this confession the Christian continues to serve in the face of affliction, until the time comes when the pretenses of demonic power are swept away.[42]

Sharing

An important way of sharing our suffering is to create a support community. This may consist of one intimate friend or a larger group that one can relate to on a deeper level. With such persons in our lives, we will not hesitate to call on them in our hour of need. This is a network that becomes a safety net. Sharing our burdens, pains, and secrets with a support group is sometimes the only way to bear it. Joining a Christian community for worship, study, fellowship, and service is important. Isolation, loneliness, and alienation simply intensify our pain. It helps to ease our pain when we are able to share it. This does not mean we should not have our own times apart and alone, but the sustenance of an ongoing group is crucial. When we confront suffering and we endure, we will find hope. What should characterize this faith community is shalom: wholeness, harmony, tranquility, well-being, friendship, and an openness to the needs of those who are suffering.

Amazingly enough, in joining in solidarity with others' suffering, we can gain strength. Too often it has been assumed that the person of faith lives with a kind of perpetual smile on her lips, a constant upbeat frame of mind. This is not true, of course, and nothing either in the New Testament or in Christian experience could justify such an attitude. The Christian rejoices with those who rejoice, but he also weeps with those who weep (Rom. 12:15). We are called not simply to notice those who suffer and to sympathize with them, but also to identify with their pain and in the deceptions about power in which they are entangled. In short, Christians have no secure and happy vantage point from which to view sorrow and pain. We are to share in the suffering of others.

42. Arthur C. McGill, *Suffering: A Test of Theological Method* (Louisville: Westminster John Knox Press, 1982), pp. 116, 118-19.

Sorrow comes when we experience the violation of some good. But the Christian does not treat this violation as the first word and last truth about life or it would turn into hate or despair. We know that the power that breeds such misery is now being exposed in its pretense, and that the sufferings of this present age are not worth comparing to the glory that God shall reveal (Rom. 8:18). Therefore, the Christian can know joy in connection with sorrow, but only because he knows the power of God is overcoming the power of evil. As Christians, then, we must not gloss over the negative element of sorrow and pain with the notion that joy is the single, all-embracing mood of the Christian life. The joy of life in Christ is a consolation for our sorrow as human beings; it does not remove that sorrow.[43]

In the words of St. Paul: "Blessed be the God and Father of our Lord Jesus Christ, the Father of mercies and the God of all consolation, who consoles us in all our affliction, so that we may be able to console those who are in any affliction with the consolation with which we ourselves are consoled by God" (2 Cor. 1:3-4).

Integrating

Part of developing character is integrating disappointments into the whole of life. Along with the pain one gains insights. Attributed to Augustine is the definition of virtue "as that which God works in us, without us." When one is open to God's grace, God refines the dross of experience into pure silver. Grace carries hope in her arms and bestows it as a gift in the midst of human despair. There is also at work the mystery of the dialectic: two opposite forces producing a synthesis. From the ruins of lives God builds bridges and walkways.

Furthermore, years of struggle and disappointment can deepen resolve and insight. Paul's conflicts and troubles gave him the occasion to write to the Corinthians that "we were so utterly, unbearably crushed that we despaired of life itself" (2 Cor. 1:8). But he did not completely despair: "Even though our outer nature is wasting away, our inner nature is being renewed day by day" (2 Cor. 4:16). The sense of hope in the midst of suffering is well reflected in the words of St. Francis de Sales:

---

43. McGill, *Suffering,* p. 116.

Do not look forward to the changes and chances of this life in fear; rather look to them with full hope that, as they arise, God, whose you are, will deliver you out of them. He is our keeper. He has kept you hitherto. Do you but hold fast to his dear hand, and he will lead you safely through all things; and when you cannot stand, he will bear you in his arms. Do not look forward to what may happen tomorrow; the same everlasting Father who cares for you today will take care of you tomorrow, and every day. Either he will shield you from suffering, or he will give you unfailing strength to bear it. Be at peace, then, and put aside all anxious thoughts and imaginations.[44]

Given the above understanding of the many facets of suffering, one may now examine how the response to suffering can become a key ingredient in our enduring it. Because of the belief that God participates in all human suffering, one may thus view suffering as an opportunity. It is an opportunity that goes well beyond the restoration of the status quo. The enigma one faces in thinking about this is that there is no clear answer to the questions: Opportunity for what? How does this relate to healing? The answers to both questions will reside in one's understanding of the purpose and meaning of existence. Healing, in this context, will refer to the realignment of oneself on the path God intended.

How does suffering contribute to healing? On the physical level, for the burn victim for example, the suffering produced by skin grafts may eventually lead to recovery — and is a necessary part of it. Furthermore, those who have endured suffering and integrated it into their lives have much to teach us about the meaning of life, as the following story reflects.

I met Lin some years ago when she came into my care as a student in counseling training in the Westminster Pastoral Foundation. She spent one full-time year and two part-time years with us. She was a telephone switchboard operator, and later training supervisor, in a city bank. Sometime later, in 1985, Lin rang me up. I had seen her *en passant* once since she had left our training center. Now she was ringing to ask if she could do more training — had I suggestions to make about what she could do?

We discussed this in detail, and then I asked her what other things she was doing. She had given up her switchboard work because she

44. Lillian Eichler Watson, ed., *Light from Many Lamps: A Treasury of Inspiration* (Wichita, KS: Fireside Catholic Publishing, 1988), p. 43.

was so busy with other things. She had set up a bereavement counseling unit. She was giving special attention to the problems of the disabled, especially in sexual matters. She was writing her second book. She was training to be a lay preacher and hopefully beyond that, to enter the ministry. It was a full life indeed, but you may feel you know of others as heavily committed. . . .

There is, however, more to tell about Lin. When she was born, prematurely, a medical accident involving the use of oxygen took place. As a result, Lin was cerebrally palsied. She did not have the use of the lower part of her body. At the age of 13, after years of intensive physiotherapy and operations on her legs, she was able to take her first steps. She has been able to get about to some extent on level surfaces with the help of her tripod sticks, but otherwise has to go everywhere in a wheelchair or by taxi.

When Lin was nine, she lost the sight of one eye — as a further consequence of that medical error — and at 14 she had a detached retina in the other, "good" eye. An operation to deal with that condition was unsuccessful and Lin has been blind since then.

It is in the light of all this — cerebrally palsied and blind — that her record represents "the magnificence of suffering." Consider the list of her achievements just mentioned: writing, counseling, teaching, preaching and training. It is an incredible list — and there will be more to add to it. What is relevant to the theme is Lin's statement that "the best things that have happened to me in terms of service have all taken place since I became blind." The journey has taken Lin *through* suffering to wholeness.

This, too, is the healing ministry at work. The physical miracles may not be possible — as Lin knows — but the road to wholeness sometimes does pass through suffering, and in doing so produces magnificent results. Lin's testimony is borne out by others who have suffered greatly. It may be wholly outside any possibility for us as ordinary people to be able to see in extreme pain an opportunity to "share in the suffering of our Lord." It takes someone far along the road to wholeness to express the healing ministry in such a way. What perhaps we can understand, even though it lies outside our own experience, is the moving tribute of the husband and wife who both found they had terminal cancer, but lived on beyond their medically estimated time:

> "We do not know whether we have been cured of our cancers, but we do know that through the whole experience we are much more whole than we ever were before."

Within that glorious statement there is in essence the true meaning of healing.[45]

Growth Through Suffering

Surprising as it may seem, suffering may bring spiritual growth and depth as well as redemption (Isaiah's suffering servant). First, it can be the occasion for the cultivation of hope. Romans 5 emphasizes the redemptive side of suffering, and the psalmist (Psalm 119:67) describes suffering as bringing us closer to God. This is not to suggest that we should seek suffering in order to grow spiritually. Rather, when suffering comes, the experience can bring with it something good for the sufferer. Hope is the first important ingredient in alleviating our suffering. I have investigated Romans 5 elsewhere: "In Romans 5, Paul alluded to three stages of spiritual development through suffering: endurance, character, and hope. First, we develop endurance, as some translations render this word. As we grow older we learn that anxiety does little good; everything cannot be done yesterday. Endurance is not merely passive but an attitude of acceptance and perseverance. Endurance manifests the spirit of overcoming the world, but this does not mean that one can avoid being depressed. 'We are afflicted in every way, but not crushed; perplexed, but not driven to despair; persecuted, but not forsaken; struck down, but not destroyed' (2 Cor. 4:8-9). In the depths of despair if we find God there, then there is nothing to fear."

Therefore, the basis of endurance is hope. Hope is actively awaiting that moment when it can spring into action; it is not passive resignation, but is determination to stick with a vision. And once we have endurance, it will produce character, and then character produces hope. I use the word "produces" here to describe the process of metal passing through fire so that every impurity is removed. "Through the tribulation of sudden illness, we are thrust back on the essentials in life; family and friends become more important than job or money. One of Søren Kierkegaard's major contributions was to challenge our preoccupation with the trivial and our failure to grasp the essential. We learn truth in proportion to our suffering. Because suffering throws the whole of human existence into turmoil, it be-

---

45. Denis Duncan, *Pastoral Care and Ethical Issues* (Edinburgh: St. Andrew Press, 1988), pp. 81-82.

comes the opportunity to perceive correctly, perhaps for the first time, the essentials of life."[46]

Christ has given us peace with God. He gives us access to God. The Greek word προσάγω *(prosagō)* is used to describe ushering a person into the presence of royalty, that is, entrée. This word also means harbor or haven, a place where ships come in, a haven of God's grace. We deserve wrath, judgment, and exclusion from God, as Paul tells us in the preceding passages, but instead we are given peace because of Christ's death and resurrection. Jesus has granted us entrée to divine favor. This peace is not simply a feeling but a fact, not an achievement but a gift. It is relationship with God — peace with God — that indicates pardon and acceptance.

The basis for our hope is that we share in God's glory. If we suffer with God, we will also be glorified with him. We are made in God's image, and one day we will be made perfect, so that when we see God face to face, we will be like him. God loved us while were yet sinners. This means that the ground of our hope is outside ourselves: it is not dependent on our having arrived at some perfect state. God loves us in the midst of our disobedience.

Our hope is based on the fact that Jesus puts us into a new relationship with God. We can quit our sin and become new creatures, what the Reformed theologians call justification and sanctification. All our hope stems from the fact that God loves us. God's love, however, does not mean a shelter from suffering and problems. We will still encounter trials, and it is in them that we see how our hope relates to our suffering and despair. God does not make a cosmic pet out of a person the minute she or he becomes a Christian. And God, our heavenly parent, does not protect us from suffering, so we cannot protect our children from all "'gainst goings." However, we are promised joy and growth through suffering. This is to be the hope of resurrection to which we are pointed. As Jürgen Moltmann suggests, we risk our life for a coming future that will not pass away.[47] On the one hand, we have the basis of our hope in God's work in Jesus Christ, while, on the other hand, we learn how suffering can help us to develop hope by producing patience (endurance), which in turn produces character, which in turn produces hope.

The great "men and women of faith" are those who have redeemed their sufferings, have overcome adversity, have clung to hope in the midst

46. Evans, *Redeeming Marketplace Medicine*, pp. 96-97.

47. Jürgen Moltmann, *Theology of Hope* (Minneapolis: Fortress Press, 1993).

of overwhelming odds. How we face suffering says more about us than anything else. The Christian faith proclaims that sin and sickness do not have the final word. God's goodness and plan for individuals in this world will ultimately prevail. Christ's life of service and sacrifice testifies to how the symbols of hope and healing are conveyed in the midst of suffering. Jesus, the Suffering Servant, identifies with those who are suffering.

Hope is the most important element to sustain us in life. The greatest suffering is when we have lost all hope. The 15,000 children in the Terezin concentration camp during the Nazi horrors should have lost all hope; indeed, only a handful survived. But somebody found their poetry when the camp was liberated. Later it was collected and used as the text for an oratorio, *I Never Saw Another Butterfly* (music by Charles Davidson). One of the poems found at Terezin, by a young boy, tells of his seeing one yellow butterfly as a spot of hope in that desolate camp. But it was the last one he would see there.[48]

---

48. Pavel Friedman, "The Butterfly," *Seven Poems, Seven Paintings: A Teacher's Guide to Selected Holocaust Poetry, Yad Vashem online:* http://www1.yadvashem.org/education/learningEnvironment/english/Poetry/poetry.htm (accessed July 8, 2009).

8. The Last Days: Caring the Hospice Way

An Affirmation of Those Who Care

I believe in people who care.
Even more, I believe in what these generous people offer others.
They bring caregiving down to its essentials:
    they offer not abstract ideas, but personal attention;
        not definitive answers, but reasonable assurance;
        not empty platitudes, but authentic hope.

I believe the work they do is both deceptively simple
    and unusually difficult.
For their task is to offer those who so need it
    something irreplaceable: their own humanness.
They bestow a priceless gift:
    only themselves, and all of themselves.
They approach the other holding out what they have to offer:
    their sensitivity, their belief, their dedication.
They bring into the open what they choose not to hide:
    their honesty, their woundedness, their compassion.

What these empathetic people do requires real courage,
    for they do not know how they will be received,
        or if they will be understood.
What they give requires great perseverance,
    for healing is a time-consuming process,
        and staying with others in their pain
            is an energy-draining experience.

249

But if these souls did not perform their roles in the way they do,
    then in a very real sense the Word would not be made flesh.
The Love would not be made visible.
And the Hope would not be made genuine.

Yet because such committed caregivers are among us,
    we know the world is not just a better place
        but ours is a better time and we are a better people.
We know that because those who truly care show us,
    day after day after day.

James E. Miller

Palliative Care

I write this chapter from the perspective of those who practice palliative care with the dying, especially those in hospice. This is not to suggest that cure should be downgraded or avoided. However, based on the patients' choices about how to spend their final days, weeks, and months — or a doctor's assessment that further treatment would be futile — palliative care becomes the order of the day. It is ironic that, whereas in centuries past care rather than cure was all that was possible, now with so many amazing cures and life-extending technologies available, when treatment is futile we wish for care. Many health care professionals are looking for the best ways of caring. Of course, palliative care "is not dependent on prognosis and can be delivered at the same time as treatment that is meant to cure you. The goal is to relieve suffering and provide the best possible quality of life for patients and families."[1]

The World Health Organization (WHO) defines palliative care as "an approach that improves the quality of life of patients and their families facing the problem associated with life-threatening illness, through the prevention and relief of suffering by means of early identification and impeccable assessment and treatment of pain and other problems, physical, psychosocial and spiritual."[2] Palliative care today is most commonly asso-

1. "What Is Palliative Care?" Center to Advance Palliative Care, *getpalliativecare.org on the web*, 2009: http://www.getpalliativecare.org/whatis (accessed May 19, 2009).
2. Kirsti A. Dyer, "What Is Palliative Care? A Definition of Palliative Care," *About.com on the web*, November 4, 2006: http://dying.about.com/od/hospicecare/f/palliativecare.htm (accessed May 19, 2009).

ciated with hospices, which have done much to shape end-of-life care; but palliative care is not the same as hospice care, since it can be given at the same time as curative treatment.[3] In many ways, hospice has revolutionized end-of-life care, first in England, then in the United States and other parts of the world.

A History of Hospice

The term "hospice" (from the same linguistic root as "hospitality") was used during the Crusades to describe a place of shelter and rest for weary or sick travelers on long journeys, as well as those who were seeking sanctuary from the wars. The earlier hospices in monasteries were places of care for the traveler, especially sick ones, where the treatment might consist of prayer, laying on of hands, food, and water — with perhaps some additional herbal remedies.

Hospice is a caring community, as is reflected in its other cognates: *hospital, hostel,* and *Hôtel-Dieu* were originally used interchangeably, but now quite differently. The Latin word *hospes* means both "host" and "guest," thus connoting a simple interaction. The medieval hospice, which operated throughout Europe, offered hospitality in its original sense of protection, refreshment, and fellowship. This movement really began when pilgrims were returning from Africa over 2,000 years ago. However, one must be careful not to overromanticize places such as Hôtel-Dieu in medieval times or health care in Victorian England. The latter was a terrible time and place for medical care: it was unhygienic and barbaric in many ways, and the dying poor were treated as objects. Sweet *caritas* became condescending charity dispensed by the righteous to the deserving.[4]

The modern hospice offers a space for the dying in which attention to detail, such as clean bedding and night clothes, being bathed, care of the bowels, skin, hair, and so forth — and being surrounded by loved ones —

---

3. "Palliative care is NOT the same as hospice care. Palliative care may be provided at any time during a person's illness, even from the time of diagnosis. And it may be given at the same time as curative treatment. Hospice care always provides palliative care. However, it is focused on terminally ill patients — people who no longer seek treatments to cure them and who are expected to live for about six months or less." "What Is Palliative Care?" Center to Advance Palliative Care.

4. Sandol Stoddard, *The Hospice Movement: A Better Way of Caring for the Dying* (New York: Vintage Books, 1992), pp. 2, 7-8, 59.

are very important.[5] It represents a shift away from a purely medical model of technological, interventionist procedures for the dying to a palliative care approach for the terminally ill. It was initially a movement on the fringes of the medical establishment that was run by a great number of volunteers. In the United Kingdom it was principally used for end-stage cancer patients. While this was also initially true in the United States, it embraced the care of persons with AIDS in the mid-1980s, and later those with dementia and other illnesses as well. In fact, dementia patients are increasingly in hospice. "A University of Iowa study on the response of caregivers to the end stages of dementia in patients who are enrolled in hospice has been published in *Death Studies*. The results showed four different 'caregiver portraits': (a) disengaged; (b) questioning; (c) all-consumed; and (d) reconciled. According to the researchers, 'Recognizing the differences in the ways that caregivers respond to the final stages of the disease will assist hospice and other providers in best meeting the needs of the caregivers.'"[6] Hospice's main aim is to control pain, and modern pharmacology has given us a wonderful selection of pain medications that can keep pain at bay.

The modern use of the term "hospice" was first applied to specialized care for dying patients in 1967, at St. Christopher's Hospice in a residential suburb of London. Today, the term refers to humane and compassionate care that can be implemented in a variety of settings: in hospitals, nursing homes, patients' homes, or freestanding in-patient facilities.[7] The original hospice at St. Christopher's owes its character to its founder, Cicely Saunders, who brought her nursing and medical skills and deep spirituality to its structure and shape. Though Saunders struggled in early childhood with parents who eventually divorced, she attended a college at Oxford that was a forerunner of St. Anne's College, and it was only when she discovered a calling as a wartime nurse that she found a meaning for her life. She was very competent and well liked by her nursing colleagues. However, serious back problems forced her out of nursing. She then qualified for a degree in public health as a medical social worker and worked

5. Stoddard, *The Hospice Movement*, pp. 132-33, 211; Balfour Mount, "Care of Dying Patients and Their Families," in *Cecil Textbook of Medicine*, ed. James B. Wyngaarden, Lloyd H. Smith, and J. Claude Bennett, vol. 1, 19th ed. (Philadelphia: Saunders and Co., 1992), p. 29.

6. *Mental Health Law Weekly*, July 18, 2009; *Death Studies* 33, no. 6 (2009): 521-56.

7. "Hospice: A Special Kind of Caring," National Hospice Organization brochure (1996).

with cancer patients. During all this time she was on a spiritual journey and was blessed to meet a strong group of evangelical Christians, who were instrumental in her conversion to Christianity. She attended John Stott's All Souls Church and searched for how she could best serve God.[8]

The 8,000 hospices around the world take their form from their contexts and staffs; thus, though the philosophy is the same, its execution varies. Hospice moved from the United Kingdom to the United States after Cicely Saunders visited the latter country. I met her in the 1970s at St. Luke's Hospital in New York City, where she was explaining the hospice philosophy, which was new to medical practice in the United States. The first U.S. hospice was in New Haven, Connecticut, in 1973, and it was based on the St. Christopher's model, under the direction of Dr. Sylvia Lack, a young physician from St. Christopher's.[9]

There are other important milestones in the history of hospice. In 1979, the Health Care Financing Administration (HCFA) initiated demonstration programs at twenty-six hospices across the country to assess the cost effectiveness, definition, and type of hospice care, and in 1995 it clarified the conditions of participation. In 1982, Congress included a provision to create a Medicare hospice benefit. The Civilian Health and Medical Program of the Uniformed Services (CHAMPUS) Hospice Benefit was also implemented in June 1995.[10] At present the Medicare and Medicaid hospice benefits consist of two ninety-day periods followed by an unlimited number of renewable sixty-day periods.[11] As *The Boston Globe* noted: "Just last year [2008], national regulators officially recognized hospice and palliative care as a board-certified specialty."[12] Hospice offers care to those suffering from a number of end-stage diseases, such as congestive heart failure, chronic obstructive pulmonary disease, renal failure, Parkinson's disease, late-stage Alzheimer's disease, and other life-limiting illnesses so long as steady decline can be documented.

8. Shirley du Boulay and Marianne Rankin, *Cicely Saunders: The Founder of the Modern Hospice Movement* (London: SPCK, 2007).

9. Stoddard, *The Hospice Movement*, pp. 134, 231.

10. "History of Hospice Care," National Hospice and Palliative Care Organization: http://www.nhpco.org/i4a/pages/index.cfm?pageid=3285 (accessed Oct. 22, 2008).

11. "Medicare Hospice Benefits," U.S. Department of Health and Human Services, Centers for Medicare and Medicaid Services (revised September 2008), p. 8: http://www.medicare.gov/publications/Pubs/pdf/02154.pdf (accessed June 2, 2009).

12. *The Boston Globe*, May 26, 2009, p. B4.

Statistics on U.S. Hospices

Understanding the number, size, and patient population in hospices can help illuminate their role in today's health care system. It will be interesting to observe how health care reform will affect the future profile of hospice. In 2007, the National Hospice and Palliative Care Organization estimated that approximately 39 percent of all deaths in the United States were under the care of a hospice program.[13] More than half of the 1.4 million patients who received services from hospice in 2007 were female. Four out of five hospice patients are sixty-five or older, and more than one-third of all hospice patients were eighty-five or older.[14] This estimate included:

- 930,000 patients who died under hospice care in 2007;
- 258,000 who remained on the hospice census at the end of 2007 (known as "carryovers"); and
- 222,000 patients who were discharged alive in 2007 for reasons including extended prognosis, desire for curative treatment, and other reasons (known as "live discharges") (p. 4).

Data from the National Hospital and Palliative Care Organization indicated that in 2007, 58.3 percent of hospice agencies were independent; 20.8 percent were based in hospitals; 19.7 percent were geared for home health care; and 1.3 percent were in conjunction with nursing homes (p. 8). According to regulations approved in December 2008, after initial certification, patients must be recertified every two months. When they are decertified, they need to be released to a nursing home or their own home or that of a family member. Part of the tightening of the regulations is because length of stay has been increasing for the average hospice patient. In contrast, some HMOs are paying for all the costs of resident hospice programs, which becomes a kind of long-term health care insurance.

Questions have been raised about whether hospice in fact saves money. A major study demonstrated that hospice services save money for

13. "NHPCO Facts and Figures: Hospice Care in America," National Hospice and Palliative Care Organization, October 2008, p. 4: http://www.nhpco.org/files/public/Statistics_Research/NHPCO_facts-and-figures_2008.pdf (accessed June 2, 2009).

14. "NHPCO Facts and Figures: Hospice Care in America," National Hospice and Palliative Care Organization, October 2008), p. 6: http://www.nhpco.org/files/public/Statistics_Research/NHPCO_facts-and-figures_2008.pdf (accessed Nov. 14, 2008). Hereafter, page references to this article will appear in parentheses in the text.

Medicare and bring quality care to patients with life-limiting illness — as well as to their families. Researchers at Duke University found that hospice reduced Medicare costs by an average of $2,309 per hospice patient. Furthermore, the study found that Medicare costs would have been reduced for seven out of ten hospice recipients if hospice had been used for a longer period of time. For cancer patients, hospice use decreased Medicare costs up to 233 days of care. For those who were not cancer patients, there were cost savings up to 154 days of care. While hospice use beyond these periods costs Medicare more than conventional care, the authors of the report said: "More effort should be put into increasing short stays as opposed to focusing on shortening long ones" (p. 11).

The average number of days that a hospice patient received care in 2007 was twenty days, and the mean survival was twenty-nine days longer for hospice patients than for those who were not. The largest difference in survival was in congestive heart failure patients, where the mean survival period jumped from 321 days to 402 days. Hospice use was also found to be higher for diseases that impose a high burden on caregivers, or diseases for which prognostic accuracy is easier to achieve. In fact, fewer than 25 percent of U.S. deaths are now caused by cancer, with the majority of deaths due to terminal chronic diseases. In 2007, the top five chronic illnesses served by hospice included: heart disease (11.8 percent of admissions), debility unspecified (11.2 percent), dementia (10.1 percent), and lung disease (7.9 percent) (p. 7).

The number of hospice programs nationwide continues to increase, from the first program that opened in 1974 to approximately 4,700 programs today. This estimate includes both primary locations and satellite offices. Hospices are located in all fifty states, the District of Columbia, Puerto Rico, Guam, and the U.S. Virgin Islands (p. 8). "In 2007, 70.3% of patients received care at home. The percentage of hospice patients receiving care in an in-patient facility increased from 17.0% to 19.2%. Hospices range in size from small all-volunteer agencies that care for fewer than fifty patients per year to large national corporations that care for thousands of patients each day. One measure of agency size is total admissions over the course of a year. In 2007, 79.4% of hospices had fewer than 500 total admissions" (p. 8).

The access of non-Anglo populations to palliative care and hospice care is of some concern. "Studies reveal that African Americans and other minorities are more likely than whites to want, and get, more aggressive care as death nears and are less likely to use hospice and palliative care services to ease their suffering. As a result, they are more likely to experience more medicalized deaths, dying more frequently in the hospital, in pain, on ventilators and with feeding tubes. Some experts believe that social and economic circumstances, along with religion, determine why terminally ill patients choose more aggressive treatment."[15]

Many physicians do not discuss hospice with their patients. "Clinicians reported discussing hospice with 45% of patients with cancer, compared to 10% with COPD [chronic obstructive pulmonary disorder] and 7% with HF [heart failure]. Apart from diagnosis of cancer, the factors most strongly associated with hospice discussion were clinicians' estimate of and certainty about patient life expectancy. . . . Clinicians' discussion of hospice independently increased the likelihood of hospice use."[16] Furthermore, many people do not choose hospice because they do not want to face the fact that they are dying. An article in *The Boston Globe* reported on a Harvard Medical School study that described this phenomenon well: "Americans tend to procrastinate when it comes to matters involving death and dying, but a Harvard Medical School study published yesterday finds that even many terminally ill patients and their doctors put off conversations about end-of-life choices. The study, one of the largest to date on the issue, found that only about half of the 1,517 patients with metastasized lung cancer who were surveyed had discussed hospice care with their physician or healthcare provider within four to seven months of their diagnosis. The vast majority of such patients do not survive two years." The article goes on to quote the head of the study: "'Patients who had unrealistic expectations about how long they had to live were much less likely to talk about hospice with their doctor,' said Haiden Huskamp, a Harvard Medical School associate professor and the study's lead author. The emotionally charged issue takes on growing urgency as an estimated 90 million Americans live with serious and life threatening illnesses. That number is expected to more than double over the next 25 years as baby boomers age, according to a recent report from the National Palliative Care Research Center."[17]

15. *Newsletter,* Global Action on Aging (March 12-16, 2007), email to author (Mar. 17, 2007).

16. *Cardiovascular Device Liability Week,* August 2, 2009; *Journal of General Internal Medicine* 24, no. 8 (2009): 923-28.

17. *The Boston Globe,* May 26, 2009, B4.

Hospice Around the World

The style of hospice internationally is influenced by the culture and economy of the country. Here are some facts provided by Help the Hospices, based in the United Kingdom:

- There are currently about 8,000 hospice and palliative-care services in 110 countries.
- Around the world, over one million people die every week.
- There are currently six million cancer deaths and over ten million new cases of cancer every year; that will rise to fifteen million by 2020.
- It is estimated that 100 million people could benefit from basic palliative care every year.

Information on the hospice situation in different countries helps to give us a global perspective. Although sub-Saharan Africa has twice as many deaths per 1,000 of population annually as North America does, it has only 1.5 percent of global palliative-care resources, compared to 55 percent in North America.[18] In China, with all family members working outside the home, in-home hospice is not possible; in Russia and Japan, tight living quarters make it impossible. In Ghana there is hesitance to pay if there is no cure, whereas in the Netherlands, which has universal insurance, economics is not an issue.

Characteristics of a High-Quality Hospice Program

The National Hospice and Palliative Care Organization (NHPCO) has created a consensus statement of optimal hospice care. It applies generally to those attracting 500 or more patients per year with diverse diagnoses. However, about 60 percent of hospices in the United States are small, attracting fewer than 100 patients per year. In-home hospice care is linked with the staff of an in-patient residence or hospice unit in a hospital or nursing home. The phenomenon of larger nursing homes having some "hospice beds" is not without its problems. In some instances, hospice creates addi-

---

18. "Bono and Sir Elton John Lend Support for World Hospice and Palliative Care Day," National Hospice Foundation, October 6, 2006: http://www.nationalhospicefoundation .org/i4a/pages/Index.cfm?pageID=110 (accessed Feb. 25, 2009).

tional nursing services, but if the regular nurses are still in place, there may be competing philosophies of pain management — on demand versus set hours. However, the family is grateful for "an extra set of eyes." Financial viability is a struggle for these hospices, and they find it harder to achieve all the characteristics listed below for a high-quality hospice program.

- Serves, above all, patients, families, and community, with sensitivity to different cultures, values, and beliefs
- Provides interdisciplinary teams of palliative-care experts trained to give competent, compassionate, highly skilled, state-of-the-art care to dying patients
- Has a small patient-to-worker ratio
- Is responsive twenty-four hours per day, seven days per week
- Elicits and responds to patient and family needs and wants — and encourages — involvement of patient's own physician
- Conducts outreach to the entire community, including the traditionally underserved
- Does not discriminate in accepting patients based on their need for more aggressive palliative therapies, such as chemotherapy and radiation
- Shows willingness to accept referrals early in the illness trajectory, regardless of reimbursement likelihood
- Has well-established, cooperative relationships with area hospitals and nursing homes
- Measures, monitors, and continuously improves its quality of care
- Produces accurate, reliable data about care, outcomes, and costs
- As part of a continuum of health care service, works as an advocate, educator, and role model for quality end-of-life care in its community
- Earns community support[19]

Hospice Philosophy

Hospice is more a philosophy and approach than a new specialty, though it has certainly shaped the palliative-care movement. The U.S. government also provides a formal definition of hospice in terms of health care reim-

19. Jennifer Matesa, "Hospice Care, Part I: A Policymaker's Primer on Hospice Care," *State Initiatives in End-of-Life Care* 11 (Aug. 2001): 4.

bursements and other benefits: "A program which provides palliative and supportive care for terminally ill patients and their families."[20] Some define it as a compassionate method of caring for terminally ill people. By its very nature, hospice is interdisciplinary and works from a team-based approach. It is different from the general medical model, because the physician has a somewhat minor role, usually involving the initial diagnosis and then medication to treat symptoms and pain. Where there are available family members, they are expected to play a major role. It is a medically directed, interdisciplinary, team-managed program of services that focuses on the patient/family as the unit of service. Hospice care is palliative rather than curative: it emphasizes pain and symptom control, and it enables a person to live his or her final days fully, with dignity and comfort, at home or in a homelike setting.

Here are some phrases that are used to define hospice: a caring community with the patient at the center; a community of highly trained people with various skills and medical competence, not a faith-healing group; services offered to the entire family, not just the patient; eligibility to all regardless of race, creed, color, or ability to pay.[21] An in-patient facility does not need to be linked to in-home hospice. One hospital chaplain and longtime pastor said about hospice: "In 1977, Josephina Magno came to northern Virginia and began what is now Capital Hospice. It is hard for me to imagine that for the first fifteen years of my ministry there was no such entity as hospice. I quickly recognized the value of this movement and saw it as a movement that has overlapping concerns and benefits with ministry. In the ensuing 25 years the churches that I served hosted bereavement groups; hospice speakers helped to equip deacons and Stephen ministers; I became an advocate with families for them to consider hospice for a loved one."[22]

The philosophy of hospice is reflected in its logo: "At its center, the hospice logo features a shining white light, symbolic of hope, life and love. Its outer circle represents the continuum of life, and the four lotus petals represent the physical, psychological, social and spiritual components of hospice care."[23] Care is something more than technique, skills, or training, and that is one of hospice's hallmarks. What is truly amazing about hospice is the loving environment that may actually make people feel happier than

20. Stoddard, *The Hospice Movement,* p. 189.

21. Stoddard, *The Hospice Movement,* pp. 166-69.

22. Graham Bardsley, Director of Pastoral Care, Virginia Hospital Center, in a phone interview with the author (May 30, 2009).

23. "Hospice: A Special Kind of Caring."

they did when they were well. When one is carried by love, everything else recedes into the background. Sandol Stoddard's book *The Hospice Movement* contains many stories about people in St. Christopher's hospice, stories that help us understand their joys and struggles. What strikes the reader is that what provides its unique character is hospice's emphasis on how to live while dying — with attention to small details. It's obvious that not every hospice is identical, however, so if there is more than one hospice available, it is important for the family to find one that reflects their values and the patient's values.[24]

Hospice is in some ways an anomaly in our health-care system. Its emphasis on care, when cure is no longer possible, means that it is not unusual for people to get better in the short run. In fact, when pain is held at bay, people may want to live longer; thus, for those who have given up on life, there is a new optimism and hope. Of course, the ravages of the person's disease may take over, and with it the inevitability of death becomes obvious. It is then that the medical knowledge of pain control is crucial.

The *knowledge* that pain will be controlled — as well as the actual control of pain itself — is what makes hospice so effective. The movement, even at the beginning, sought the control of pain. For example, during the fifteenth century, the Hôtel-Dieu in Beaune, France, used poppies to make opium, which they mixed with wine or other alcohol. Stoddard felt strongly that mind-altering drugs should not be used: "I do not think that religious experience as an orgasm of the mind can be very authentic when artificially induced" (pp. 116, 119). However, pain control is not hospice's only contribution; rather, it addresses the whole needs of the whole patient (p. 48). Competence, communication, and compassion are also key ingredients of hospice. Although hospice values the aftercare of family members, the staff is not compensated for bereavement care for the family, so aftercare is not totally realistic.

Spiritual care is central to hospice philosophy. Cicely Saunders says of hospice: "This is indeed a place of meeting. Physical and spiritual, doing and accepting, giving and receiving, all have to be brought together. . . . The dying need the community, its help and fellowship. . . . The community needs the dying to make it think of eternal issues and to make it listen" (pp. 10-11). These eternal issues that are so important to hospice are addressed in the foundational spiritual care, which is so much a part of hos-

---

24. Stoddard, *The Hospice Movement*, p. 222. Hereafter, page references to this work will appear in parentheses in the text.

pice. Pastoral and spiritual care in hospice is a series of perspectives more than of functions. Hospice patients on the whole are more open to deep conversations, sometimes motivated by the crisis of their dying. Spiritual care in hospice is described in a variety of ways. "[Glen] Dourdon writes of 'stories, symbols, rituals' which allow mourners to move from the fragmenting, alienating, and disorienting consequences of change to a renewed sense of wholeness." Hospice does not apply a general definition of pastoral care; rather, it is shaped by a particular patient.[25]

Some pastors may see hospice as competition for the spiritual care of their members if they come from a very ecclesiastically oriented, closed tradition. The functions of the pastor are quite similar to others on the hospice staff, that is, reducing fear, incarnating the love of God, and sharing God's peace. The model of companioning is frequently described this way: listening to the patient and not bringing up formulaic questions but letting the patient set the agenda. One pastor said, "I try to help people see God coming to us rather than pursuing God."[26]

One of the strengths of the hospice philosophy is the "total presence" of the staff, which is a gift in our distracted society. Henri Nouwen refers to being totally present as *alertia* and links it with hospitality.[27] As Christians, we recall Jesus Christ's words in Matthew: "[A]s you did it unto one of the least of these you have done it unto me" (Matt. 25:40). One of the best elements of hospice is its spiritual dimension, which could be at risk if government regulations interfere. Some even draw a parallel between hospice and church because of the way the community of staff, patient, family, and friends work together. There are some cautions to be raised about this analogy because, unlike a church, hospice does not have a defined membership, nor does it adhere to a set of beliefs. However, what knits hospice units together is their common commitment to the best possible care for the dying person.

The Future of Hospice

Those who have followed the growth of hospice in the last decade wonder about its future. Hospice is now in its fourth decade, and its future shape is evolving because of changes that have already occurred. One of the biggest

25. Paul Irion, *Hospice and Ministry* (Nashville: Abingdon, 1988), p. 20.
26. Irion, *Hospice and Ministry*, pp. 188-96.
27. Henri Nouwen, *Reaching Out* (Garden City, NY: Doubleday, 1975), pp. 55-56.

challenges that faced hospice in the 1980s was whether to accept persons with the HIV-AIDS. Fortunately, after some soul-searching and determining how the hospice model would best work for AIDS patients, the movement did welcome those sufferers with open arms. I remember a hospice volunteer calling me in the 1980s, early in the epidemic, asking how she could continue to volunteer at her hospice if they were accepting AIDS patients. She had called because her husband, on his deathbed, made her promise not to work at a hospice for fear she would get AIDS and transmit it to their granddaughter. Before all the medical facts were known about AIDS transmission, there was much fear abroad in the 1980s. One hospice director said that the greatest challenge for hospice in the future will be "to maintain the original philosophy and grassroots commitment of hospice while maintaining a position as a contributing member of the healthcare system. Hospices must maintain a balance between pragmatism and humanity if we expect to survive . . ." (Stoddard, p. 251).

Hospice Patients

As is reflected in the interviews later in this chapter, patients appreciate honesty about their condition. It is common for doctors not to be honest with patients about a terminal diagnosis — for fear the latter will lose hope. In a new, federally funded study, only one-third of terminally ill cancer patients said that their doctors had discussed end-of-life care with them. And new research has shown that the physicians are wrong in their assumptions: those patients who received information about their terminal diagnosis were no more likely to become depressed than those who did not. "They were less likely to spend their final days in hospitals, tethered to machines. They avoided costly, futile care. Their loved ones also were more at peace after they died. Doctors mistakenly fear that frank conversations will harm patients, said Barbara Coombs Lee, president of the advocacy group Compassionate Choices."[28] Convinced of such benefits and that patients have a right to know, the California Legislature passed a bill on August 20, 2008 (#AB2747), to require that health care providers give complete answers to dying patients who ask about their options.[29]

28. Marilynn Marchione, "Study Touts Honesty to Dying Patients," *The Virginian-Pilot*, June 16, 2008, p. 11.
29. http://info.sen.ca.gov/pub/07-08/bill/asm/ab_2701-2750/ab_2747_bill_20080903_enrolled.html (accessed July 8, 2009).

In another study of 600 terminally ill patients, only 7 percent developed depression.

> The new study is the first to look at what happens to patients if they are or are not asked what kind of care they'd like to receive if they were dying, said lead researcher Dr. Alexi Wright of the Dana-Farber Cancer Institute in Boston. It involved 603 people in Massachusetts, New Hampshire, Connecticut and Texas. All had failed chemotherapy for advanced cancer and had life expectancies of less than a year. They were interviewed at the start of the study and are being followed until their deaths. Records were used to document their care. Of the 323 who had died so far, those who had end-of-life talks were three times less likely to spend their final week in intensive care, four times less likely to be on breathing machines, and six times less likely to be resuscitated. About seven percent of all patients in the study developed depression. Feeling nervous or worried was no more common among those who had end-of-life talks than those who did not.[30]

Informed consent is key to the hospice approach to patients. Of course, the patient's physician is contacted to make sure she agrees that hospice care is now appropriate for this patient. The primary-care physician must write the initial order for hospice. (Hospices may have medical staff available to help patients who have no physician.) The patient will also be asked to sign consent and insurance forms stating that the patient understands that the care is palliative (that is, aimed at pain relief and symptom control) rather than curative. It also outlines the services available.[31]

When giving bad news, the physician should not have a set of fixed rules concerning whether "to tell" or "not to tell," but should have an openness to examining the patient's situation. "Communication that is insensitive in the interest of 'telling all' or evasive, falsely optimistic, or otherwise misleading in the interest of 'protecting' the patient generally risks seriously undermining long-range physician credibility."[32] Studies suggest that the majority of terminally ill patients are already aware that they are dying, whether or not they have been told; if they are told the truth, they are less afraid. The relating of "bad news" is usually a process, not an event, and

30. Marchione, "Study Touts Honesty," p. 11.

31. "20 Commonly Asked Questions," in the brochure "Hospice: A Special Kind of Caring."

32. Mount, "Care of Dying Patients and Their Families," p. 30.

needs to be done according to the needs of the patient. "The physician needs to be sensitive to all forms of communication: plain language ('I fear I may be dying'), symbolic language ('I keep dreaming of a long tunnel with a candle at the end and I am afraid someone is going to blow the candle out'), and nonverbal communication (depressed facial expression, excessive muscle tension). It has been estimated that eighty percent of communication is nonverbal."[33] Even those patients who do not ask questions may still have them. The physician may need to take the initiative because the ill person may be too vulnerable or uncertain to broach the subject. These conversations enable the person to prepare for her last weeks or months. Life review becomes a very important part of the hospice experience, and this may sometimes take the form of writing her own story, including its ending.[34]

Definitions of Family Important for Hospice Care

A central part of hospice is the incorporation of the family into patient care. The best place to start in hospice care, besides the patient, is with the family. An assessment of how the family members perceive their assets and challenges in coping with the situation with their dying loved one and what problems and resources they have is an essential part of the care plan. Some members may be stronger than others and can assist each other.[35]

The common ground of love and concern for the patient can help to overcome conflict when it exists in a family. Open communication among the patient's family members and friends is essential, so that fears, old wounds, embarrassment about discussing sensitive topics, or the mistaken urge to try to withhold vital information from each other can be addressed.[36]

What constitutes a family is not as straightforward as it used to be, and thus it is important for hospice staff to sort through the variables. "In an age of blended families, same sex parents, and vast geographic distances separating family of origin, the definition of what constitutes the family or who is considered a member is unique to each patient and family encoun-

33. Mount, "Care of Dying Patients," p. 30.

34. Irion, *Hospice and Ministry*, p. 39.

35. Robin McMahon, "Understanding Family Dynamics at End-of-Life," The Hospices of the National Capital Region, *Hospice Management Advisor* (March 2003): 3.

36. McMahon, "Understanding Family Dynamics," p. 4; M. Galazka and K. B. Hunter, "Hospice: Current Principles and Practices," clinical appendix in Sandol Stoddard, *The Hospice Movement: A Better Way of Caring for the Dying* (New York: Vintage Books, 1992), p. 343.

tered by the hospice team. The family who provides care may not be the same family who sits in the front pew at the funeral service or who inherits the deceased's estate." Who the patient regards as family may not be based on biological or marital connection. They can be same-sex partners, support group members, or lifelong friends with whom the biological family may be at odds.

In one hospice a staff member was working with the nontraditional family of a male patient that included his current wife as well as two of his three ex-wives as caregivers. It is the patient who determines who is family and gives permission to contact them and what information to provide. "A typical question when there are no caregivers present at an initial visit with a patient is, 'With whom shall I follow up after this visit?'" It is a truism that each family has its own culture in terms of communication, hierarchy, and beliefs about death and dying. Hospice staff need to care for the family especially when members clash. "Qualities of compassion, dedication, and respect that draw nurses, social workers, nursing assistants, chaplains, volunteers, and other front-line staff to hospice also enable them to make a difference in working with even the most complicated families."[37] Families also need to be educated about the hospice culture, for example, about staff roles, protocols, and so on.

A relationship with family members does not end when the patient dies; an interesting side benefit of hospice is the aftercare with the deceased's family. This emotional support helps them avoid future illness at a time of their greatest vulnerability.[38] Later in this chapter I will say more about the role of the family and their crucial part in the patient's care. I can speak at first hand of the importance of family in hospice: my two parents and a sister died in hospice. We played a crucial role as a family, though the medical circumstances were different in each case, due to geography, age, and hospice regulations.

Hospice Staff

It is the staff that gives hospice its life, meaning, and effectiveness. Hospice staff usually include nurses, physicians, social workers, psychologists and

37. McMahon, "Understanding Family Dynamics at End-of-Life," pp. 1-2, 5.
38. Stoddard, *The Hospice Movement,* pp. 152-53. Hereafter, page references to this work will appear in parentheses in the text.

counselors, clergy, art-and-music therapists, physical and occupational therapists, dietitians and nutritionists, pharmacists, and trained volunteers.[39] One of the principal strengths of hospice is its interdisciplinary team, all of whom, from their different specialties, work for the good of the patient. Many of them have a strong sense of vocation for this work, and they may even use religious language in describing their work. This was certainly true of Cicely Saunders, who experienced a religious conversion to Christianity as she was starting up a hospice. Saunders emphasized the importance for hospice staff of taking time to renew from within by means of prayer and celebration. The spiritual dimension must come from the core (Stoddard, p. 113). "'It is a spiritual thing' . . . because it is a way of life, really. It isn't just a job. And I don't mean spiritual because of the clergy who are involved" (p. 143).

Hospice staff members focus on the importance of giving patients the attention they need. This job is every bit as demanding as working in a hospital, but it involves different and more personal skills, along with medical expertise all the same. The sick are treated as persons, not patients — or as "the lung cancer in room 3" (p. 114). One of the challenges for hospice staff is the length of stay of particular patients. Patients who are in hospice for a matter of days leave staff without closure and time to be the most helpful, and patients who are there too long create a strain; therefore, it is important to establish an optimum time of stay. The skills needed to relate to the dying do not come easy, and they need to be individualized; that is, there is not a set way of doing this (p. 168). It is interesting that many members of hospice staffs, before they worked in hospice, have worked with the inner-city poor or on the mission field — so that this sense of mission stays with them. Staff members should have a sense of the spiritual dimension to life, though medical and nursing training is essential to hospice's success, as well as the presence of clergy. The entire family is involved both during and after hospice care, and art and music, special foods, and so on are considered part of hospice philosophy (pp. 190ff.).

The high number of volunteers at hospice provides much of its lifeblood. The nonhierarchal, relational staff structures are at the core of realizing the hospice model. As Stoddard visited hospices in the United States, she found that the common feature was that other health-care professionals took care of the hospice staff. Annual retreats provide opportunity to reflect on its work and build trust among team members (pp. 241-42). Pro-

39. Galazka and Hunter, "Hospice: Current Principles and Practices," p. 342.

tection against burnout is vital in hospice ministry. I remember in the 1980s holding workshops for hospice staff on coping with burnout. One of the realities was that some staff care too much. One hospice staff member remarked, "I won't get burnout out as long as I do not fight my feelings. Only resistance will wear you out." When asked what characterizes those who stay in hospice work, interviewees cited personal commitment to spiritual values and outgoing personalities who like helping others (p. 136).

Hospice and palliative-care staff and chaplains are a gift to the dying and their families. They reflect the caring side of medicine when a cure is no longer possible, and they provide hope, meaning, and comfort in the dying person's final days.

From the Bedside: Insights from Palliative Care Staff

Profile of Interviewees

The best way to understand patient palliative care is to talk with those who do it.[40] The following interviews conducted were of hospice staff at Wayside Hospice in Wayland, Massachusetts; professionals involved in end-of-life care in the Princeton, New Jersey, area; directors of pastoral-care services at Stanford University Medical Center, Stanford, California, and Pastoral Care, Virginia Hospital Center; and a palliative-care counselor at Robert Wood Johnson Medical Center, New Brunswick, New Jersey. Their dedication to the work, even in the face of growing bureaucracy and reorganization of the health care system, is amazing. Their clarity of purpose and concern for their patients is remarkable.

The following insights about palliative care were in response to the

---

40. All information provided from the author's interviews was summarized from the following sources: a focus group, Princeton Theological Seminary, April 2009, included a pastor, former chaplain, physician who is a hospitalist developing an ACE (Acute Care for the Elderly) unit, and the director of pastoral care at a continuing care community; chaplain, nurses, and social worker at Wayside Hospice, Parmenter Community Health Care, Wayland, Massachusetts, March and May 2009; a director of Spiritual Care Services, Stanford Hospital and Clinics, Stanford, California; a director of pastoral care, Virginia Hospital Center, Fairfax, Virginia; and counselor, Pediatric Oncology, Bristol-Myers Squibb Children's Hospital and Robert Wood Johnson University Hospital, New Brunswick, New Jersey. These views do not represent the official views of the individuals' institutions, but instead their own experiences.

author's questions used in individual interviews and focus-group discussions (see Appendix D). Considering the diversity of their backgrounds and positions, there was a surprising congruity in their answers. Some work only with the dying, others with those who are sick and will recover, and others with a healthy elderly population who may become terminally ill. Others, such as local church pastors, have conducted hundreds of funerals and accompanied the dying in their last journey. The purpose of these questions was to understand why they had chosen to work with the dying and how they found the experience. The areas addressed provide a window into the work of those at the bedside. Surely they are God's agents who bring healing to the spirit and emotions even when the body may no longer be cured.

The years of experience these people had of working with the seriously ill and dying ranged from one to forty-five years. They consisted of two physicians from major medical centers, a nurse/pastor and a pastor/hospital chaplain, three hospital chaplains, two hospice nurses, a social worker, and a pastoral-care director of a continuing care community. Some of the interviewees initially became involved in end-of-life care as part of their professional positions; but they are now in settings where this would be only part of their responsibilities. Others began working with the seriously ill and dying because they had a sense of personal or pastoral calling to do so. One person said: "This is a second career for me personally. My husband left our house one morning and never returned; he was killed in a car accident that day. He left me with our two young sons. I truly struggled with the idea that he died alone in that car without someone he loved there with him. This struggle led to my exploration into the dying process, bereavement, the afterlife, and of course my spirituality and that of our children. I needed desperately to know how to go on and how to help our children have faith that life is still good and worth living, even when we experience such a devastating event."[41]

Another person began working with this population because he recognized an unmet need while he was fulfilling his fellowship as an intern. Yet another person, due to her background in nursing, sought how she might integrate this with her current role as a pastor. One chaplain started this ministry thinking it would last a few years and found it so fulfilling he

41. Quotations by Karen Cambria, a counselor in the Pediatric Advanced Comprehensive Care Team, Pediatric Oncology, Bristol-Myers Squibb Children's Hospital at Robert Wood Johnson University Hospital, in an interview with the author (June 18, 2009).

is still doing it after forty years. Several found that hospice work provided more time for patient personal care and comfort with a smaller nurse-to-patient ratio than is the norm in most hospitals. Several observed that working in hospice, with its philosophical emphasis on pain management, enables staff to give necessary medication that would keep the patient comfortable and free of pain. Regardless of the route the interviewees took to serve the ill and dying, they all expressed feelings of purpose and fulfillment in doing it.

Joys and Challenges of Working with Seriously Ill and Dying People

The challenges for the interviewees varied, but a common theme was the importance of patient advocacy in the midst of competing claims. They found it frustrating to try to negotiate the patient's wishes in light of conflicting doctor and family desires. Their challenge was to try to support the patient's wishes or do what was best for them. For example, a major difficulty was doctors and family members who did not respect the patient's wishes. Although they may have been expressed through advance directives or verbally at the time, the treatment given was often futile. DNR and DNH (Do Not Hospitalize) orders for nursing-home residents sometimes are simply not followed. It was also frustrating when the treatment options presented did not represent a realistic view of what the patient and her family wanted or needed. This did not allow the patient and family time to adjust to the knowledge that death was imminent and to prepare for the end of her life. In other words, what constitutes a "good death" should be defined by the patient, and how the patient wants to live while dying, not by someone else's preconceived definition.

The challenges are somewhat different when one is working with dying children. Karen Cambria, the pediatric counselor, said: "I am not so sure there is one great challenge, but rather many that present themselves at different times during the process. I work in the pediatric oncology field, and my patient base is not just the child, but every member of his or her family who now live with cancer in their daily lives. I guess a strong challenge to me is helping parents be strong enough to make difficult decisions that are best for their children, not necessarily best for them. Part of my role is to help them integrate this disease into their life and encourage them to seek and know all the available options for their child. At the end of the day, whether their child lives or dies, they must have a sense of comfort that they did all they could to cure the child. Parents will continue to actively treat their child even when knowing there is no cure for their disease."

The challenges faced by hospital staff are to some degree influenced by where they fit into the structure of their institution. "I feel so honored, privileged to be a part of people's lives during such crucial times. So my challenges do not have to do with death and dying per se. The challenges and/or frustrations have to do, for the first time in my life, with serving in a large bureaucracy, a 350-bed hospital. As Stephen Covey says, 'The main thing is to keep the main thing the main thing.' Ostensibly patient care is the main thing. But in large bureaucracies, it is so very easy for other agendas to intrude and supplant 'the main thing.' So often turf issues, financial priorities, and so on preempt the real work of the hospital. It is not necessarily the case that people who work in hospitals have a passion for patient care. Kenneth Haugk asks the simple but pertinent question, 'Whose need is being met here?' Direct patient care is my passion. However, as the director of the department, I spend much of my time and energy in administration and program. In the church much time was spent in 'equipping the saints.' In the hospital, the recruitment and training of paid clergy, volunteer clergy, volunteer laity, and the provision of educational programs designed to help local clergy and hospital staff to be more effective requires a significant amount of time, energy, and imagination."[42]

A number of hospices are becoming larger and more administratively oriented; this is true of both not-for-profit and for-profit hospices. In 2007, 48.6 percent of providers reported not-for-profit tax status, and 47.1 percent reported for-profit status.[43] There is now a growing number of for-profit hospices, whose goal is to increase the census, hence marketing becomes important. Many of these hospices function like nursing homes for dementia patients. Paperwork, computer data entry, administration, and trying to work under growing economic constraints — "sitting at the computer filling out forms" — puts a strain on the staff. The hospice philosophy, which is at odds with bureaucratic structure, creates tension. Of course, administrative details such as filling out forms are also challenging for staff in other health care settings.

From an entirely different perspective, the greatest challenge inter-

42. Quotations by Graham Bardsley, Director of Pastoral Care, Virginia Hospital Center, in a phone interview with the author (May 30, 2009).

43. "NHPCO Facts and Figures: Hospice Care in America," p. 9.

viewees mentioned was whether everything possible had been done for a particular patient — what was called maintaining "a checklist in my mind of things to try when some things I have done for a particular patient don't work."

When contrasting the positive and challenging aspects of their work, the interviewees agreed that one of the greatest rewards of working with the seriously ill and dying was the privilege to assist those at the end of life. One participant said that "it was extraordinarily meaningful work." Another said, "It [was] a gift, a privilege to be with the dying." They relayed the joy of being allowed to accompany the patient on his journey to the end of life, the delight of a ministry of presence to assist patients and their families in making decisions about what is best for the patient. Still another participant expressed that his greatest joy was being an advocate for patients — to ensure that their wishes were executed.

The interviewees contrasted working in hospice to being in an ICU or hospital, where death is seen as a failure and where there is so much hubbub and whirring of machines that there is no time for reflection on spiritual matters and the meaning of death. The goal of hospice is a good death: one with emotional and spiritual peace. However, chaplains in medical centers also speak now of a renewed interest in spirituality, so one has to be careful about stereotypes. The acceptance of death allows one to choose the way to live while dying. In the hospital there is often avoidance by the staff of a patient when nothing more can be done; this is in stark contrast to hospice, where the whole raison d'être of the staff is caring for a patient when a cure is no longer possible. In other words, the goal is to help the most vulnerable, those who are on the edges of life, to focus on making their life meaningful for the days or weeks or months that may remain. These last days are not always negative, because staff members feel needed and can provide meaning to their patients. One staff member said, "I always feel that I have made a difference holding the hand of someone when they take their last breath."

Another blessing mentioned was helping the family feel less anxious and scared, thus in some ways reflecting God's love of the patients and families: being a presence of hope in the midst of the dying and helping them find peace and hope at the end of life. The fulfillment often comes with helping families navigate the difficult passage of losing a beloved child. Karen Cambria said: "My training and experience have taught me how to assess and help a family through the disease trajectory, whether to a successful cure or through the end-of-life process. Part of my role is to assess their coping skills and utilize appropriate modalities to assist them. Knowing that I can assist them in the care of their child is an amazing gift that I never lose sight of: assisting them, for example, to attend school or have a tutor, receive insurance benefits, confront emotional problems. I can provide information to parents and empower them to do what they have to do."

The Dying and Their Families

As I have reported, patient responses to their diagnoses are idiosyncratic. Graham Bardsley said: "As would be expected, there is a great range of responses to dire diagnosis. Some people are genuinely philosophical, others outwardly philosophical, some in great distress, outwardly and inwardly. I wouldn't say there is a pattern, but there are certain phenomena that I see rather frequently." Usually the patient's response is based on several factors: the patient's faith, personality, age, family, and how the patient lived his or her life. Older patients are ready to die, and some wonder why they are still around. For the younger patient, or those with children, it is much harder. Most patients realize that they have come to the hospice to die, and surprisingly they do not seem overly discouraged and do not refuse treatment that is offered to them. It is important to be clear that treatment here means ways of treating symptoms and is not curative — so that they can enjoy their last days. Of course, it is true that, in order to be in hospice, patients have already received a terminal diagnosis; thus it is unclear how they first received this news. Often older patients of deep faith accept their diagnoses and plan how they want to live out the rest of their lives. Younger patients often want more time; a few need someone with whom they can rail and cry. Each patient's response is unique, and the patients' values come through in conversations with them. For example, patients' responses to facing end-of-life decisions seem directly correlated to how they approach other areas of life. If they have been angry and grouchy when healthy, they continue in the same vein with a terminal diagnosis. Some patients want to sue the doctor or to be angry at everyone. Patients who exhibit a great deal of desire for control prior to their diagnoses usually want to have as much control as possible over their treatment options.

Patients who acknowledge their faith prior to their illness seem to continue their reliance on it at the end of life. In other words, if they always have had a strong faith and the support of a religious community, they are often more able to accept the status of being terminally ill. However, "patients and families sometimes espouse deep religious beliefs, but 'white knuckle' their way through the experience," as Graham Bardsley put it. "The belief in a wonderful afterlife does not always manifest itself in a peaceful passing, either for the patient or the family. Denial and faith are not the same thing." Often these patients and their families consult their spiritual leaders for guidance in making decisions about treatment options. They do not seem to make distinctions between the moral and religious; instead, the moral becomes the religious, or, at minimum, they do not struggle over what they label as moral quandaries. Some hospice staff indicated that faith is not always a solace: some folks are afraid to die because they believe that they will be judged by God and consigned to hell.

What the dying consider to be of great importance is giving them space to share their stories and experiences, an opportunity to ask questions, and even to confess and ask forgiveness of estranged family members — which can give them a sense of peace. Some remarkable changes are also seen by family members, for example, in the forgiving of another family member's alcoholism. Overall, the presence of the patient's family is helpful for the patient in facing her end-of-life transition. However, families have their own issues of grief and guilt that need to be addressed.

Another surprising observation is that most of the patients do not spend a lot of time trying to figure out when they are going to die. However, the human psyche can only take so much; hence, there is often a disconnect in people's minds between a terminal diagnosis and the fact that they are going to die. Many people do not fully realize or accept that death is imminent, which is itself a kind of self-protection. Of course, the experience for children is different, and even varies depending on age. Karen Cambria put it this way: "One interesting thing to note is that young children only know one thing, how to be a child. A diagnosis of cancer is not as big a deal to a seven-year-old as it is to a twelve-year-old or an eighteen-year-old. They go through many phases, of denial, anger, and acceptance, though in a more cyclical style. Younger children do not react as strongly to their impending death because they lack knowledge, experience, or insight. However, children realize that they are going to die, and preparation happens through conversations, such as, 'When we choose to treat, you may get well, or if you choose no treatment, you may die.' Some children go through treatment for their parents' sake, and the staff assures them that they will help support them. On very rare occasions children will talk about their death indirectly by saying, 'I am tired and I want this [treatment] to stop,' which means 'I want to die.'"

Some patients feel that they are of no value, that all purpose is gone. Therefore, it is psychologically important to give them a reason to wake up each day, and this can be a powerful tool. When pain is under control, there is more acceptance of the diagnosis, and thus one can find meaning in one's death. There are some unusual patients who do not realize that hospices care for dying people; in these instances their families tell them that the hospice staff is taking care of them until they feel better. Patients' families, their upbringing, education, and spiritual beliefs — all these influence their response to hospice.

Not all patients share what they believe or how they feel, but it is important to ask them. One can often determine a patient's value system by indirection. Being a "non-anxious presence" enables patients to open up about their deepest fears. For example, some do not want aggressive treatment, which is why they have come to hospice: choosing how they die is their highest value. Surprisingly, however, they may not necessarily connect this with the fact that refusal of treatment will shorten their lives. Understanding patients depends on knowing their past experiences. If they have been victims of abuse or trauma, they respond differently concerning how they want to die. For example, a former pilot whose plane went down during World War II was constantly reliving that trauma in his dying days. It is also extremely important to understand the culture of the patient. For example, one Asian patient came from a culture where it was believed that people should not die in bed, so hospice staff members placed pillows on the floor so that the patient could lie there. Others came from a culture that forbade people to die at home for fear of contaminating the house; so the patient was brought to the hospice to die. The hardest thing for patients is if they feel "sullied" by their disease, and thus lose hope and meaning.

In determining a patient's values, Karen Cambria said this: "It is the therapeutic relationship I develop with my patients and their families that always allows me to understand their value system. Time and trust are the most important elements toward learning about religious beliefs through conversations. They are more often about spirituality, not religion. Facing death and the process of dying is one of the last sacred rituals that we do." One head of pastoral care, C. George Fitzgerald, said: "When I walk into a room, if there are pictures on the walls, flowers, photos of family, this helps to elicit conversations about their life stories." As a chaplain — because of his long experience in patient care — Fitzgerald is generally the one to discuss advance directives with patients. Chaplains on his staff also practice ministry with the bereaved family members.[44]

The family members' responses to their loved one's dying may vary dramatically. Some actually want to run the treatment plan for the patient, that is, when he should be turned in bed, when he should get his medication for pain, and so on. Most families, however, trust the nursing staff to make the best assessment of the symptoms and administer medication and treatment when needed. A majority of family members want to be by the side of their loved one and will provide a round-the-clock presence by rotating it among the family members. Karen Cambria asks: "What is the involvement of families, especially when a child is dying? They are completely involved. They have been told from the point that no curative options are available what to expect and how we can assist them through the end-of-life process. This time frame is dependent on the length of the disease and uniqueness of each family. Occasionally, there are families who are either disruptive or unhelpful. If the patient is continuing to undergo some treatment, whether it is for emotional needs or palliative, the discussions center on the goals of the family."

Another issue discussed was whether an in-patient facility is better than at-home hospice care. This depends, to a large degree, on the family caregivers. In-home is more problematic because the quality of care that family members can provide is uneven, and the lack of a 24/7 support staff weakens it. However, as I have mentioned above, by far the largest number of hospice patients receive in-home care, which is much more cost-effective. If the patient has already been living in the home, the situation is far different from coming to live in an adult child's home for the first time.

Staff Relationships

Hospice staff members work together to assist the patient in determining his or her best options for care. Weekly staff meetings are the rule; of course, there are still staff members with their own agendas. Communication among staff about a patient is not always easy, because half of them use paper and the other half computers; so not all of the patient information is necessarily integrated into one chart. One finding was that the way

44. Quotations by C. George Fitzgerald, Director of Spiritual Care Service, Stanford Hospital and Clinics, Stanford, CA, in a phone interview with the author (June 25, 2009).

a doctor presented treatment decisions made a huge difference in the choices for families or patients. For example, if a "futile" treatment is presented as one last hope, but with small actual chance of succeeding, families may grasp for this one last chance, as opposed to listening to the doctor, who is really saying, "We have really done all we can for your mother, and now the best care is appropriate rather than more invasive procedures, which will only prolong her dying rather than enhance her living." Of course, the distinction between futile and reasonable depends on the condition of the patient. Often a medical center, for example, may promise a person with ALS (amyotrophic lateral sclerosis, or Lou Gehrig's disease) more than it can deliver for treatment efficiency. What might be helpful would be for physicians to receive training in "breaking bad news": this would be based on an assessment of the patient's values and personality by conversations with her, and these would guide the doctor on how best to approach these issues.

Another interesting finding is that some states spend considerably more on emergency room, intensive care unit (ICU), and hospital care costs during the last six months of life, with New Jersey being the top state. A concerted effort to work in a more integrated fashion in hospitals is underway. Because of medical errors, hospital staff members have crosscheck lists and work in a more collegial way. Staff members are shifting to multidisciplinary rounds so that all caregivers for a patient work collectively to determine what is best. In conjunction with the medical care, spiritual care is also provided for the patient. Graham Bardsley reflected on the influence of hospice on the hospital philosophy: "Hospice philosophy is the most biblical, wholistic philosophy in the West today. An integrated approach means that the patient is seen as a person, not a medical record number, a room number, a disease. The chaplain plays a major role in keeping this wholistic understanding visible in the hospice community. One of the great values of the hospice movement is that hospitals are now absorbing this philosophy and attempting to be more wholistic themselves."

The hospice structure has been called the more thoughtful side of health care; it has helped our culture accept death as a part of life. Therefore, staff members have a more unified focus and cooperative working style. For example, the staff at Wayside Hospice includes nurses, doctors, social workers, a chaplain and other clergy, administrative personnel, and volunteers. There appears to be good communication through biweekly meetings with the medical director and a cooperative spirit and communication with hospice nurses, nurses' aides, and volunteers. The volunteers perform the important role of bringing homemade goodies, cleaning, and buying groceries when needed. Surprisingly, the anticipated burnout of staff members because they do nothing but care for the dying becomes muted because their work is valued by patients and their families. Observations of colleagues can help an individual hospice nurse or social worker maintain some therapeutic distance with patients. However, one must be careful not to overromanticize the work of hospice staff members: they may sometimes withdraw from angry patients, and they also need personal space and time.

Interestingly, those who work with palliative-care teams in hospitals also find them working in a collaborative style. Graham Bardsley said: "In terms of a wholistic approach to patient and family care, this team 'gets it' more than any department in the hospital. The IDT (interdisciplinary team) meeting each week, which I experienced every Wednesday in hospice, I now experience every Wednesday at the hospital. I also work closely with the ICU department. The staff are fabulous in terms of patient and family care, and many of the staff are deeply spiritual. They were very receptive to working with GWISH (George Washington Institute for Spirituality and Health) in terms of integrating spirituality in our health care facility. Recently, the emergency department also opted to join the GWISH program." Karen Cambria expressed it this way: "Our PACCT team (pediatric advanced comprehensive care team) consists of physicians, nurses, nurse practitioners, chaplains, child life specialists, and of course counselors. We work very closely together, especially in end-of-life care, to make sure we are providing the very best of care, and our ability to communicate within ourselves is a key element in our being able to provide that care to our families."

Pastoral and Spiritual Care

Spiritual care is given in the same integrated fashion as medical care is. Caregivers, independent of their job description, may offer spiritual care. This includes all who come into contact with the patient — from the housekeeping staff to nurses' aides, nurses, and, of course, chaplains. This may be done through words of encouragement or prayer for patients — even occasionally a baptism. However, a distinction was made between spiritual care and pastoral care: the latter was thought to be reserved for the pastor/chaplain. In some instances, patients prefer their own pastors to the hospital or facility chaplain, though this may be the exception rather than the rule. The presence of the pastor/chaplain and those who offer spiritual care often gives patients hope to reach their recovery goals. Karen Cambria said: "Chaplains can provide enormous insight into how people make their most difficult decisions. We learned how to view each patient in the bed, their feelings of loss and their crisis of faith and its process in their decision-making. It also taught how to recognize my 'stuff' and how it can affect my effectiveness in the therapeutic process." The faith of those who realize death is imminent provides peace while they are dying. Patients who are not spiritual find solace in focusing on practical matters. These patients tend to draw on other areas of their lives. For instance, one patient found peace in his last days by making arrangements for his survivors, that is, caring for others.

Wayside Hospice has a part-time chaplain who is available to pray, read poetry, play music, read from Scripture, meditate, or do whatever brings the greatest comfort to the patient. She may also assure the patient that he has an opportunity to meet with clergy members, staff, or a spiritual person of his choosing. She considers herself an interfaith chaplain, so she does not wear any religious garb, such as a cross or a clergy collar. Spiritual assessment is mandated under hospice guidelines, but these assessments are often done through indirect questions, such as, "What are your joys and hopes?" "Do you belong to a religious community?" Many patients feel distant from God and do not use God language, so it is important to create an openness to spiritual discussion. The spiritual assessment is tied to gaining understanding of a patient's values, which, as I have observed above, is best done by building a relationship with a patient. The role of the chaplain is constantly evolving, and there is a lot of paperwork. But not all spiritual care is dependent on the chaplain or the volunteer clergy; often other staff members, especially nurses, may come from a spiritual place and belief in God.

Spiritual and religious needs and services in the hospice setting are not identical. "Some people are religious and not spiritual," says Graham Bardsley. "Some are spiritual and not religious; some are both. Intellectual assent to a codified set of doctrines does not provide one with the spiritual resources needed to cope with many of the challenges of life and death. Religion, beliefs about God, can be a substitute for a relationship with God. With the qualification that one cannot speak too definitively about such things, my experience tells me that the 'white knuckle' folks are often very religious, but not necessarily spiritual. To be 'religious' does not provide immunity from the seductions of the physiologically obsessed society in which we dwell. To be 'spiritual,' whether one is 'religious' or not, is an internal integration of one's trust in a power beyond oneself. Hospice is popularly associated with death and dying, but its basic focus is on living, not dying, on quality of life, and controlling pain, without which there can be no quality of life."

"Attention to the spirit during the dying process," says David McCurdy, "is more than an afterthought. Nurturing the spirit will not dispel the sorrow of death's parting, but it may sweeten that sorrow and help us find meaning in the parting."[45] Patients who are spiritual have an easier time than nonreligious patients. Of course, how one defines spirituality varies widely. Also, hospitals are interreligious and intercultural. Graham Bardsley said: "It is not uncommon for me to join hands with a Muslim, Orthodox, or Jewish family and lead them in a prayer for their loved ones and themselves. It is as though all the doctrinal tenets that divide become very much secondary to the fact that they are in crisis; they see me as a spiritual person who cares for them." There is a vividness of life and a hyper-"in-tuneness" of what goes on. As one patient expressed it, "Everything is so vivid to me now. I am looking at the birds and trees as if they are fully alive." One staff member said that the greatest comfort to the patient is the knowledge that God continues to care for him no matter what is happening to his body. It would be hard for many nurses to work in a hospice if they felt life ends "with the last heartbeat. . . . Spiritual comfort no matter [from whom] provides courage, hope and a feeling of peacefulness to patients and their families. No matter the religion or lack thereof, if a patient knows there is a power greater than herself overseeing each day, she has less of a sense of worry." Of course there are those who feel that God has abandoned them and are angry and depressed, as George Fitzgerald observed: "On the one hand, religion gives some people a sense of community — that they are no longer alone or isolated. However, religion can be a double-edged sword. For those who believe that if they keep praying they will get well and then do not, their faith can be shattered because it was not deeply grounded in the first place. Other religious people may not understand how modern medicine works and are thus reticent to fully embrace it." Religion is not an inoculation against pain and suffering, but it may provide comfort and meaning.

45. David McCurdy, "A Sweeter Sorrow," *Park Ridge Center Bulletin* (May-June 2001).

Summary of Perspectives

A major theme recurring during these interviews about care for the seriously ill and dying was that hospice staff members approach their work differently. The experiences of the interviewees were not uniform, but they all wanted to assist patients in finding peace at the end of their lives. For some patients, peace came through sharing their life stories. For others it came through confession and absolution (either giving or receiving). Others found peace in expressing their feelings to their loved ones. Overall, the patients needed to be able to express their feelings without guilt. In summary, all interviewees agreed that the best care for those who are seriously ill and dying is to allow patients to define what a good death is for them, and then assist them in achieving it.

9. Good Mourning: Loss, Grief, and Bereavement

Surprised by Joy

Surprised by joy — impatient as the wind
I turned to share the transport — Oh! with whom
But thee, deep buried in the silent tomb,
That spot which no vicissitude can find?
Love, faithful love, recalled thee to my mind —
But how could I forget thee? Through what power,
Even for the least division of an hour,
Have I been so beguiled as to be blind
To my most grievous loss? — That thought's return
Was the worst pang that sorrow ever bore
Save one, one only, when I stood forlorn,
Knowing my heart's best treasure was no more;
That neither present time, nor years unborn,
Could to my sight that heavenly face restore.

William Wordsworth (1770-1850)

Now that we have explored the pain and suffering of the dying and the care of those who will never recover, we will examine the realities of loss, grief, bereavement, and mourning. For those who remain alive after a death, grieving their loved ones is the reality. People do not pass from loss to bereavement as stages in the Eriksonian sense of the word, but as movements of the spirit.[1]

1. Erik Erikson (1902-1994) was a renowned psychologist who described the different ages and stages of human experience.

As we reflect on the interrelationships of these realities, we see that loss also brings suffering on an emotional and psychological level. Suffering brings grief, and grief may lead to a sense of bereavement. If we are bereaved, it is because we have lost something. Then we enter into a state of mourning.

As I suggested in chapter 7, pain may bring suffering that is both physical and psychological. One can have pain without loss if one is ill. For the absence of health is a kind of pain. Are these connections the same when someone is dying or if a loved one dies? In both cases there is loss, pain and grief, bereavement, and mourning — these are all intertwined. To add texture to these realities, we will include some first-person stories that provide a vividness to the experience of pain and loss.

There are many different losses in life. They include loss of a job, a home, relationships, health, memory, bodily function, a sense of future (for the dying person), or the life of a loved one. There are similarities among these losses, and many foreshadow the ultimate loss through death. This is why people who have lost something, even though the losses are different, can sympathize with each other. This was especially apparent at a conference sponsored by the Thanatology Society of New York City and the Department of Rehabilitation Medicine of Columbia Presbyterian Hospital in 1979, where persons with disabilities described their loss of a particular function as a kind of death.

Differences Among Loss and Grief and Mourning and Bereavement

Although grief and mourning, loss and bereavement are stages or trajectories in a process, we need to clarify their differences as well. Are bereavement and loss synonymous? According to the National Cancer Institute, bereavement is "a state of sadness, grief, and mourning after the loss of a loved one."[2] In other words, bereavement is the *response* to a loss. As we experience our sense of loss, we enter into a state of bereavement, then start grieving, and finally start mourning when everything comes together.[3] Grief and mourning are not the same experience, and if we are to

2. National Cancer Institute, "Bereavement": http://www.cancer.gov/common/popUps/popDefinition.aspx?id=CDR0000430476&version=Patient&language=English (accessed Mar. 20, 2008).

3. Alan D. Wolfelt, "Dispelling 5 Common Myths About Grief": http://thecare-foundation.com/griefwords/griefwords.html (accessed Oct. 6, 2004).

provide comfort and solace to those suffering loss, we must recognize this difference as very important.

Grief refers to our internal thoughts and feelings, for example, over the death of a loved one: in other words, it is the internal meaning given to the experience of bereavement, the normal process of reacting to a loss, which may be mental, physical, social, or emotional. These reactions may be felt in response to physical losses (e.g., a death) or to symbolic or social losses (e.g., divorce or loss of a job). Each loss means that the person has had something taken away. As a family goes through a terminal illness, many losses are experienced, and each triggers its own grief reaction. Mental reactions can include anger, guilt, anxiety, sadness, and despair; physical reactions can include sleeping problems, changes in appetite, or physical illness. Social reactions can include negative feelings about taking care of others in the family, seeing family or friends, or returning to work.

As with bereavement, grief processes depend on the relationship with the person who died, the situation surrounding the death, and the person's attachment to the deceased. Grief may be described as the presence of physical problems and constant thoughts of the person who died — including guilt, hostility, and a change in one's normal behavior. There is also anticipatory grief, which "occurs when a patient or family is expecting a death. [It] . . . has many of the same symptoms as those experienced after a death has occurred. It includes all of the thinking, feeling, cultural, and social reactions to an expected death that are felt by the patient and family."[4]

"*Bereavement* is the period after a loss during which one experiences grief and mourning occurs. The time spent in bereavement usually depends on how attached the person was to the deceased, and how much time was spent anticipating the loss."[5]

Mourning expresses outwardly the internal experiences of grief and loss, and it is influenced by the customs of one's culture. "Another way of defining mourning is to state that it is 'grief gone public' or 'sharing one's grief outside oneself.'"[6] Mourning is the process of adapting to the losses in our life where we acknowledge the pain of loss, feel the pain, and then live past it. How each of us mourns depends on our state of readiness and our

4. "Anticipatory Grief" in "Loss, Grief, and Bereavement database," National Cancer Institute: http://www.cancer.gov/cancertopics/pdq/supportivecare/bereavement/patient/allpages#Section_101 (accessed Mar. 20, 2008).

5. "Treatment," in "Loss, Grief, and Bereavement database."

6. Alan D. Wolfelt, "Dispelling 5 Common Myths."

perception of loss.[7] An interesting fact is that tears of grief contain antitoxins that regular tears do not.[8]

Grief and mourning are universal experiences, but our cultural customs, racial-ethnic identities, national setting, and society's rules for coping with a loss make a huge difference in our experience.[9] However, grief that we feel for the loss of a loved one, the loss of a treasured possession, or a loss associated with an important life change, occurs across all ages and cultures. The role that cultural heritage plays in an individual's experience of grief and mourning is not well understood. Attitudes, beliefs, and practices regarding death should be described according to myths and mysteries surrounding death within different cultures. There are also similarities among cultures. This is true even though different cultures have various mourning ceremonies, traditions, and behaviors by which to express grief. Helping families cope with the death of a loved one as health care professionals or even friends includes showing respect for the family's cultural heritage and encouraging that family to decide how to honor that person in death.

Important questions that should be asked of people who are dealing with the loss of a loved one include:

- What are the cultural rituals for coping with dying, the deceased person's body, the final arrangements for the body, and honoring the death?
- What are the family's beliefs about what happens after death?
- What does the family feel is a normal expression of grief and the acceptance of the loss?
- What does the family consider to be the role of each family member in handling the death?
- Are certain kinds of death less acceptable (e.g., suicide), or are certain kinds of death especially hard to handle for that culture (e.g., the death of a child)?[10]

7. Mary Lou Cappel and Susan Leifer Mathieu, "Loss and the Grieving Process — Death of Loved Ones," *Parks and Recreation* 32, no. 5 (May 1, 1997): 82-85.

8. Barbara LaRaia, "Gender Differences and the Health Benefits of Crying," *San Mateo Daily Journal*, January 12, 2006: http://smdailyjournal.com/article_preview.php?id =53397&eddate=01/12/2006 (accessed Jan. 20, 2006).

9. "Overview," in "Loss, Grief, and Bereavement database."

10. "Culture and Response to Grief and Mourning" in "Loss, Grief, and Bereavement database."

It is one thing to analyze the process of grief, loss, and mourning, and quite another to read true stories of those who have experienced that anguish. Nicholas Wolterstorff captures the depth of this loss in his account of his own grief after the sudden, tragic death of his young son.

Born on a snowy night in New Haven, he died twenty-five years later on a snowy slope in the Kaisergebirge. Tenderly we laid him in warm June earth. Willows were releasing their seeds of puffy white, blanketing the ground. I catch myself: Was it *him* we laid in the earth? I had touched his cheek. Its cold still hardness pushed me back. Death, I knew, was cold. And death was still. But nobody had mentioned that all the softness went out. His spirit had departed and taken along the warmth and activity and, yes, the softness. *He* was gone. "Eric, where are you?" But I am not very good at separating person from body. Maybe that comes with practice. The red hair, the dimples, the chipmunky look — that *was* Eric.

The call came at 3:30 on that Sunday afternoon, a bright sunny day. We had just sent a younger brother off to the plane to be with him for the summer.

"Mr. Wolterstorff?"

"Yes."

"Is this Eric's father?"

"Yes."

"Mr. Wolterstorff, I must give you some bad news."

"Yes."

"Eric has been climbing in the mountains and has had an accident."

"Yes."

"Eric has had a serious accident."

"Yes."

"Mr. Wolterstorff, I must tell you, Eric is dead. Mr. Wolterstorff, are you there? You must come at once! Mr. Wolterstorff, Eric is dead."

For three seconds I felt the peace of resignation: arms extended, limp son in hand, peacefully offering him to someone — Someone. Then the pain — cold burning pain. Gone from the face of the earth. I wait for a group of students to cross the street, and suddenly I think: He is not there. I go to a ballgame and find myself singling out the twenty-five-year-olds; none of them is he. In all the crowds and streets and rooms and churches and schools and libraries and gatherings of friends in our world, on all the mountains, I will not find him. Only his absence. When we gather now there's always someone missing, his absence as present as our presence, his silence as loud as our speech. Still five children, but one always gone. When we're all together, we're not all together.

It's the *neverness* that is so painful. *Never again* to be here with us — never to sit with us at the table, never to travel with us, never to laugh with us, never to cry with us, never to embrace us as he leaves for school, never to see his brothers and sister marry. All the rest of our lives we must live without him. Only our death can stop the pain of his death. A month, a year, five years — with that I could live. But not this forever. . . . One small misstep and now this endless neverness. . . . It's so wrong, so profoundly wrong, for a child to die before its parents. It's hard enough to bury our parents. But that we expect. Our parents belong to our past, our children belong to our future. We do not visualize our future without them. How can I bury my son, my future, one of the next in line? He was meant to bury me![11]

Types of Losses

There is no doubt that the loss of a loved one is the most shattering loss possible. However, the dying person also experiences the loss of who she or he is. Even if we recover, we realize that we will never be exactly the same person. When we experience grief, loss, and bereavement at the death of a loved one, we are reminded of other losses. Of course, the dying person is also reminded of other losses, as Tom Droege eloquently expresses it: "In its most basic sense death is simply the end of life. But it serves as well as a metaphor for all the endings, all the losses we experience throughout life. Not all endings are bad of course, but for the most part they are the dark side to life, the shadow side. The psalmist touches a chord of universal experience when he speaks of the 'valley of the shadow of death.' We cannot escape the shadow side of life, but we can celebrate in the shadows, often more richly and profoundly than in the pure celebrations of life, like marriage and birth."[12]

These include loss of health, loss of function, lost relationships, job

11. Nicholas Wolterstorff, *Lament for a Son* (Grand Rapids: Eerdmans, 1987), pp. 8, 14-16.

12. Thomas Droege, former director of the Center of Faith and Health, Carter Center, email to author (June 21, 1999).

loss, memory loss, loss of history, the loss of a sense of self-worth due to prejudice, the loss of home and property due to earthquakes, fires, hurricanes, and so forth. To a greater or lesser degree, these losses foreshadow the greatest loss — death. They can disproportionately affect us simply because they tear away part of the fabric of who we are. Loss makes us feel vulnerable and forces us to reevaluate our identity and sense of meaning in life. Some comments about each of these losses may help us understand them.

Emotional Loss

The loss of relationships through separation or divorce seems like a minideath. The loneliness can dominate us at first, creating a sense of emptiness, disconnectedness, an absence of someone who cares and someone to care for. The severing of human connections can make us feel like less of a person. These losses produce reactions similar to those at the death of a loved one. Divorce represents a lost relationship that one wanted but never had, or had but gradually lost. Though divorce may be a relief, one may still wish things had been different, that the lost years, bitter conflicts, and betrayal that led to the death of the marriage had never happened. Anger, guilt, and regret well up when we remember a disappointing past that can never be forgotten or escaped.

In an emotional loss, there is a "grief reaction with the same kind of somatic sensations — numbness, distress in the abdomen, drying of the secretions, palpitation, and loss of appetite."[13] There are the accompanying psychological sensations that are manifest in emotional distress, such as feelings of rejection, the withdrawal from the relationship, the separation from a familiar way of life, and the end to the personal relationships that were previously important. There may be either an inability to cope with life or feelings of guilt or blame. Anger and hostility in face of betrayal are common.

There is also a searing, violent emotional loss through posttraumatic stress disorder (PTSD), brought on by experiences such as war, rape, terrorist attacks, tsunamis, and so on. These crises can lead to a loss of inner peace and stability. "Research has shown that 20% or more of peo-

---

13. C. Charles Bachmann, *Ministering to the Grief Sufferer* (Englewood Cliffs, NJ: Prentice-Hall, 1964), p. 71.

ple exposed to traumatic events typically develop clinically significant psychological problems. Many more will experience less severe effects."[14] Soldiers, rescue workers, and those who care for the injured and bereaved after violent events such as the 9/11 attacks often find themselves having flashbacks of the experience, feeling a lack of closeness with their families, and experiencing severe physical problems. Some victims of PTSD are able to recover; others are not.[15]

There is also the loss of a generation, where the history and heritage is wiped out, a phenomenon that has been studied, especially with respect to the Holocaust. Not only the children and grandchildren have lost the generation of their parents and grandparents via the ovens of Auschwitz; but sometimes those who survived will never utter a word about that period of their lives. This can have the effect of their past not existing at all, which can be deeply wounding for successive generations.

Loss of Job

In a career-oriented, upwardly mobile society, the right job and the promotions that come with it can often represent the largest share of one's identity. Losing the ideal job through poor evaluations can be devastating; but when it comes as a result of downsizing, it is also not easy. Tough economic times take a psychic toll on a society that often manifests itself in physical as well as psychological symptoms.

Loss of Home

Losing one's home to natural catastrophes, such as hurricanes, earthquakes, or tsunamis, or due to conflicts that can wipe out a family, home, or community in a matter of minutes, is devastating. People are left with a sense of displacement. There are Hurricane Katrina survivors from 2005 who are still experiencing homelessness, and they have an ongoing sense of loss as though life will never return to what it was. Not only the physical

14. "Media Resources: Posttraumatic Stress, Violence and Disaster," The International Society for Traumatic Stress Studies: http://www.istss.org/terrorism/media.htm (accessed July 10, 2003).

15. "Media Resources: Posttraumatic Stress, Violence and Disaster."

house, but the destruction of mementos, furniture, and pictures may cause a feeling of losing one's history.

Loss of Memory

The gradual loss of memory — because of Alzheimer's disease, for example — is a cruel loss for the victim of the disease and for his loved ones. It is as if the person is slowly disappearing and becoming a stranger to himself and others. Family members often experience two losses: the loss of the person they knew and then his second physical death. Donald McKim writes that, in a society that values the rational above all else, losing our cognitive abilities may seem devastating. For some, there is the comfort that God never forgets, and also that we are held in the memory of our community.[16]

Loss of Bodily Function

The loss of health, even from minor illnesses, can threaten our sense of strength and vitality. We are first afraid that we will never recover again, or if we do, that we will be altered. This is even truer of permanent disability. At the conference on disabilities, the presenters with disabilities described their losses of seeing, walking, writing, eating, and other bodily functions in terms of loss, grief, mourning, and even death. They were grieving the loss of part of who they were.[17] However, the field of rehabilitation medicine emphasizes not the loss but the regained and retrained functions. For example, when we become overwhelmed by the needs of children with spina bifida or teenage quadriplegics, as J. A. Downey, retired chief medical head of rehabilitation at Columbia Presbyterian Medical Center, says, "[Y]ou should focus on what they can do, not what they cannot do. See the world through the eyes of the patient."[18]

Ruth Zerner, a historian, was struck with Guillain-Barré syndrome in her twenties. After being paralyzed and hospitalized for a year, she

16. Donald K. McKim, ed., *God Never Forgets* (Louisville: Westminster John Knox Press, 1997).

17. John Downey, Georgia Riedel, and Austin Kutscher, eds., *Bereavement of Physical Disability: Recommitment to Life, Health and Function* (New York: Arno Press, 1982).

18. Information shared on physicians' grand rounds of the hospital, Columbia Presbyterian Medical Center, 1979.

wrote the following about her experiences, which she says were not nearly as sharp as the loss of a loved one through death.

> For me death stands in a special relationship to the sense of complete physical loss, not partial loss. I can view partial physical loss as an intimation, a hint or foreshadowing of death (which we all face). Borrowing the words of St. Paul, one can view partial physical loss as "seeing through a glass darkly." But since I have been so close to death, I can testify only that there is an enormous chasm between the experience of dying and the experience of partial physical loss. No matter how much physical loss I experienced, the "I" was still there, the part of me that was continuous with my pre-illness, pre-hospital life. To lose physical powers or, I would imagine, even to lose a limb is qualitatively different from the experience of losing a loved one in death. Bereavement of physical loss for me does not parallel bereavement of a loved one. Something deep inside us dies with the person we love, making impossible the sharing of certain intimacies and understandings in this world. There is no real replacement. However, losing part of our physical capacities may leave us with inabilities and weaknesses, but it does not rob us in the same way that the death of a loved one does. The human mutualities possible with another person do not truly resemble the relationships we have with our limbs. As long as I retain my mental powers (and I realize that this is an important qualifying fact), the sense of myself as continuous with my previous experiences remains, regardless of my physical loss. I am still alive — to love and to relate to others, no matter how partial my body may be. To be alive is to have more than memories (such as the memories we have of a beloved who has died). Life includes the possibilities for expansion of relationships, for inner growth, and for new experiences in spite of physical limitations. "I" am still alive despite my physical loss. But my dead friend's "I" is gone, never to return in my lifetime. If one has discovered that human relationships are the most important aspects of life, such mourning for a beloved is the most profound and continuing form of grief. No sorrow I felt about my physical loss could come close to the experience of bereavement for another person whom I loved and who had died.[19]

19. Ruth Zerner, "Physical Loss and Survivorship in Spite of . . . a Patient's Perspective," in Downey, Riedel, and Kutscher, *Bereavement of Physical Disability: Recommitment to Life, Health and Function*, pp. 184-85.

Gradual Losses for the Dying Patient

The dying person is also grieving because she feels that who she is, is gradually disappearing. These gradual losses may be in some ways more difficult than death itself. If hospitalized, the patient is stripped of her clothes, jewelry, familiar surroundings, and choices of food and music. She is often subject to painful treatments, with their side effects, plus the suffering from the disease itself. No wonder many people want to get their dying over as quickly as possible! The following account by a doctor dealing with cancer captures the roller-coaster nature of serious illness. People who have a terminal illness still struggle with how to live while dying or perhaps recovering; it is the ambiguity of the situation that may be most difficult.

A lot of people find the Holidays difficult as well as stressful; I must admit that I'm one of those people. Both Mom and Dad died just before the Holidays, plus there were several deaths (including family members) just before these past Holidays. This made me realize that I had not really completed the grieving process regarding Mom's passing; likewise I had not completed the grieving process regarding myself and the sudden change of events that resulted in my life being turned around 180 degrees; (normally, I love roller coasters but this emotional roller coaster is the pits). Death is inevitable, but that does not ease the pain or the hodgepodge of emotions that surround it. I would venture to say that most people (me included) are not prepared to have their lives suddenly turned around 180 degrees; there is *so much* that we take for granted on a day to day basis; this includes how magnificently our brains work. Unfortunately, some people perceive any shifts in behavior or attitude that accommodates a new baseline as "negative thinking."

We all have plans. Stuff happens! Do you have a will; a living will or advance directive; power-of-attorney; and medical power-of-attorney? Who will care for your children if you cannot? This is called taking care of business! Regardless of age, life can throw you a curveball at any time. The past two to three years have been incredibly interesting as I have staggered and stumbled along this road with many bumps (and I don't mean the ones that can make skiing fun and challenging). As a pediatrician, I learned a lot about how people deal with trials and tribulations in the context of their own personal lives or those around them. How true the expression "it can make you or break you" can be.

You never really know how strong your faith is until it is put to the test. I have no idea where I'm headed but I do know that I am very blessed to be surrounded by patient and compassionate people who have kept me upright and picked me up when I do stumble and fall.

As for my medical status, I am considered stable as of mid-January. Prior to this, there were concerns; in fact, my surgeon wanted to do a brain biopsy after comparing the MRIs done in October and November to the one done in March of last year. However, after my MRI on January 9 and my office visit, he felt I looked better than expected and could be followed up with a future MRI. NO BRAIN BIOPSY! Therefore, my next MRI will be sometime in April. Life as a "dizzy broad" goes on! I continue to be sufficiently symptomatic such that I am still unable to drive (real bummer). Just getting through a simple day can be logistically difficult and frequently exhausting. All too often I try to do too much; I just can't seem to get the knack of pacing myself. I want to do something but I need a flexible work opportunity. Ideally, I'm looking for something that I can do from the house using the computer. Vocational rehab has been wonderful to me by providing software with the training to help me adjust to my visual challenges and poor coordination. There is also a vocational counselor who is assisting me in finding a work environment that will be a good fit. . . . I could do workshops, seminars, and/or mentoring depending on the level of involvement necessary. Even though I am still considered permanently disabled, I am trying to find something to do that will create a little income and make me feel useful. I am also trying to do a little volunteer work. Finding a work environment is proving to be more of a challenge than expected. Even though I'm cognitively intact, it is necessary for me to consider myself "retired" from clinical pediatrics; this has been a hard one for me; this was not how I envisioned my retirement. Talk about making major adjustments in thinking and financial planning, you better believe that it takes some brutal honesty; not easy!! Due to my low and unpredictable stamina, I would never be able to work enough hours to afford malpractice. If I do clinical pediatrics as a 100 percent volunteer, I might be able to afford the malpractice but there are a lot of bureaucratic and political issues to consider.

Being the fitness fanatic that I have been, I'm trying to get back in the groove of that with the hope of improving stamina, balance, and physical strength. Of course, I have these high hopes of cycling, swimming, and skiing again. Right now, I have to make do with my adult tricycle and walking on the treadmill. Thanks again for your prayers and support. By the way, it is okay to share this email with others who know me. Well guys, that's it for now; signing off![20]

For the terminally ill person there is also the impending loss of family and friends, as well as one's past life, which occasions grief. One thing that sometimes helps the dying is reminiscing: going over one's life in order to make sense of it. In a way, it is as if the dying person is writing her autobiography. According to Victor Marshall's research, many people conclude that their life was okay.[21] So do people who actually keep a journal, which also becomes a treasure to their family once they have died. For those too compromised by illness, a family member can do it.

However, death can be a final stage of growth. The question is, When someone is wracked with pain, how can he be said to be a disciple and be of service to others? Christian discipleship reaches its perfect fulfillment not in activity but in receiving rather than giving. It can be very difficult for the seriously ill and dying patient who can do nothing but wait: wait for family visits, wait for food, wait for nurses, wait for medicine. But waiting for others can engender a kind of openness that is very important.[22] Lucy Rose, of Columbia Seminary, wrote her final book, *Songs in the Night*, while she was dying of cancer. But first, her sermon on "The Man Born Blind from Birth" focused on how giving God the glory became the central focus of her dying. Second, her journal of reflections as the cancer entered her bones forms the message of her book.[23]

> It all began on a Monday back in June. I planned to work on my dissertation that day, but I decided to take a shower first. Then I thought while I was taking the shower that I would do one of those womanly things called "a self-exam"; and that is when I discovered the mass. I was too nervous to do anything on Monday. I hoped it would go away. On Tuesday I called around to find the cheapest mammogram in Atlanta. If you're interested, it's the DeKalb Medical Center. I was still

20. This story about a friend was sent to the author by a student at Princeton Theological Seminary in the "Death and Dying" class (2007).

21. Tony Walter, "A New Model of Grief: Bereavement and Biography," *Mortality* 1, no. 1 (1996): 14.

22. Brian Greet, "Dying in Hospice — A Time to Grow," Leveson Center Conference Paper #4, *A Good Death* (Temple Balsall, UK, 2002), pp. 21-24.

23. After a four-year struggle with cancer, Lucy Atkinson Rose died at the age of fifty on July 17, 1997, surrounded by friends and family at home.

hoping this mass would go away, so I let Wednesday go by. On Thursday I called and made an appointment for Friday.

I went and had the mammogram, and then they decided to do a sonogram also. I thought that was a bit unusual. The next thing I knew a very nice nurse was talking to me, but her badge said "Oncology." Now, I know that's a fancy name for cancer. Sure enough, the next week they told me it was cancer. I had a mastectomy, and now I'm in chemotherapy with my last treatment to be next Thursday. So I have only wisps of hair underneath this hat. Wigs are just too tight and too hot. I am told that my hair will come back, and that it may be curly when it does. So if you invite me back next year, you might not recognize me.

I tell you this story because I have found meaning in my experience this summer by laying my story next to the story in John 9:1-41, which I read and which Lisa told this morning.

Remember how the story goes. On seeing the man who was born blind, the disciples asked Jesus, "Who sinned? This man or his parents that he was born blind?" Now, if *he* sinned, obviously it was before birth — in the womb. Or perhaps it was his parents who were at fault and *he* was being punished. In those days sickness was interpreted as punishment for sin. So, who sinned?

In my own struggles with cancer I have read a few books. Not many. And each one assigns blame differently. One of the books implied that *I* was to blame. I hadn't eaten right; I hadn't exercised right; or I hadn't dealt with my stress properly. In fact, if I would begin eating right or exercising, I could heal myself. I even heard a TV advertisement on how to heal ourselves. Assigning blame to the person who suffers is still prevalent in our day.

Another book which I read assigned blame to our parents — not just my parents, but to that whole generation who through public policy and through neglect allowed carcinogens into our food and toxic waste to seep into our streams and pollutants to belch into our atmosphere and create a world where cancer is so prevalent. It is my parents who are to blame!

But notice how different it is to assign blame, on the one hand, and on the other to ask the question the disciples asked: "Who sinned?" *Their* question implies that God is at work — punishing sin, yes, but at least God is at work here. Whereas, in the modern day version of the question, there is *no hint* of God's activity, only "Who is to blame?"

So I found myself preferring the disciples' question — reworded to be "How is God at work here?" And Jesus' answer makes sense, for he said, "No one sinned, not this man, not his parents. This man was born blind *so that the works of God might be revealed in him.*"

Now in my own situation I knew that perhaps I had not lived a perfect life, and that there might be ways I could change my life for the better. And in fact I have tried to do some of that changing — and I know that we should do something about the pollutants and the toxic wastes and the carcinogens in our food. But this only underlines all those questions again; and Jesus' answer is, "God is at work — not a God who punishes but a God who *saves.*"

The entire Gospel of John is about a God who "so loved the world that he gave his only begotten son" — a God who sent his son into the world "not to condemn the world, but that the world through him might be *saved.*" So I began to interpret my experience of the summer as an opportunity for the God of love to work works of healing and saving — in my life.

Immediately after Jesus answered the disciples' question, he made mud of his spittle, put it on the man's eyes and sent him to the pool to wash. And he came back seeing. The people around asked, "Are you the man who used to beg? Are you the man who was born blind?" And he said, "Yes, yes, I am." But some of them said, "No. It's not him." And he kept saying, "Yes, yes. I am the one. And hear my story!" for now he has a story to tell — of God's work in his life. He said, "A man anointed my eyes and I washed and now I see." In John's Gospel he tells his story at least three times. And by the last time he has gotten it down to the fewest words — "I was blind and now I see." But he was still telling the story of God's work in his life. And I found the same thing true for my own life, as I looked for God's hand in it.

I'd like for us to go back to that Friday when I went home from the DeKalb Medical Center not knowing but feeling that I needed to get back into the Emory system and have an appointment with my own doctor. A cheap mammogram is one thing, but having your own doctor is another. So I went home that Friday afternoon and made an appointment with my doctor over at Emory. And then I worried, and then I prayed. Off and on the next days I spent a lot of time in silence and crying, wondering about what really mattered to me, wondering if this was a life-threatening experience. And in that quietness and through those tears I discovered three things about my life — three wishes: I wanted to see my little girl, who is 4 years old, grow up; I wanted to move into old age with my husband; and deeper than those wishes, was my yearning to give glory to God's name. *That* was what I wanted, even if I could not have the others. And I found myself giving each one of those wishes to God. I wanted so much to see my little girl grow up and I wanted to grow old with my husband by my side! How often I had put those two in God's hands when they went on a trip, or were driving around the town. I would say to God, "Take care of them. I want to be wrestling with you and to trust that you will bring me through this" — but I had never put *myself* in God's hands and said, "God, if something happens to me, can I trust you to raise my little girl? Can I trust you to give her another mommy who will love her as I do? Can I trust you to raise her to be a child of yours, to give wisdom to my husband and to those who love her? And the same with my husband, can I trust you to give him the love he needs and will you open a future for him without me? Can I?" And each time I would say, "Yes. I can trust you, God, because I have trusted you throughout my life. And this dissertation — I am committed to this dissertation. The ideas need to be out there in the world — but I can give it to you, God." And there came over me through the course of that weekend a profound sense of peace, so that on Monday and Tuesday I found myself working on the dissertation with a great deal of energy.

And then on Wednesday I was in the clinic all day — waiting and waiting — waiting on doctors, waiting for the results of tests. And the Holy Spirit gave me a gift. I found myself singing — not out loud — but singing a hymn to myself over and over again, and it wasn't one I had consciously chosen:

> Have Thine own way, Lord! Have Thine own way!
> Thou art the potter; I am the clay.
> Mold me and make me after Thy will,
> While I am waiting, yielded and still.
> While I am waiting, While I am waiting, yielded and still.

About three o'clock in the afternoon we were told that it *was* cancer, and that the surgeon had an opening the next day. So I said, "I want a mastectomy. And I want it tomorrow." I had time to go back home and call Columbia Seminary and my church and the community that is important to me in my own neighborhood. I knew that I needed to be uplifted on the wings of prayer by them. Not as though those loved ones would change God's mind, but that they were lifting me up and God was coming down and in the midst I would be sustained.

Those were good days. I felt buoyed up. I felt the presence of the Spirit with me. And then came the chemotherapy. Days of nausea, days of exhaustion — and slowly I found my spirit being ground down, depressed. I could no longer feel the buoyancy I had felt. I was discouraged, somewhat confused. And then, in preparing this sermon, I went back to the story about the man born blind. I was amazed. The biblical story does not have a happy ending. The man is thrown out of the synagogue.

Now think about that! He was not just being thrown out of church, but he was being excommunicated from the people of God forever. As a beggar, blind from birth, he had been on the margin of society — but he had been *on the margin*. He had neighbors, he had family. But now he is outside the circle completely. Would he still have a loving family? Would he still have neighbors to speak to him and give him a few pennies? What would he do now that he could see and was not blind anymore? He couldn't go back to begging. And think about the long moments, maybe hours between the time he was kicked out of the synagogue and the time that Jesus found him — in those hours I am sure he too felt confused and discouraged. And then Jesus found him and said, "Do you believe in the Son of man?" And he said, "Who is he that I may believe?" Jesus said, "I am he." And the man said, "I believe," and he worshiped him. And I too found that during those long, slow, empty days I could still believe, and worship.

I tell you these two stories today in order for you *to believe* through the stories of your own life — in order for you to look at your own lives and the experiences that you have, and to ask, "Is God at work saving, loving, reaching out to me, to the whole world?" And can you *believe* and *worship,* particularly through those long, slow, empty days of confusion and disappointment?

The Bible story invites us to tell our story of God's work, and to believe and to worship. Amen.[24]

Rose's testimony is a powerful one that reflects the power of strong Christian faith in the midst of a serious diagnosis. She died after a four-year struggle with her cancer, but she left behind an uplifting legacy of courage.

---

24. Lucy Atkinson Rose, *Songs in the Night: A Witness to God's Love in Life and in Death,* ed. Ben Lacy Rose (Decatur, GA: CTS Press, 1998), pp. 9-14. Used with permission. To obtain copies of this book, contact Vital Churches Institute, P.O. Box 18378, Pittsburgh, PA 15236 (tel. 412-246-4847): www.vitalchurchesinstitute.com.

Loss by Death

The ultimate loss is from the death of a loved one or even a colleague, which can remind us of our own vulnerability. The change to our everyday life is both dramatic and subtle. There is the gaping hole in our heart: the emptiness inside and the emptiness of the room where the person used to be — no one to talk to, no one sitting in his favorite chair. A sudden death is like a sharp arrow piercing the heart: the teenager on the way home from the prom killed by a drunk driver; the mother killed by a hit-and-run driver; the three-month-old only child dead of SIDS (sudden infant death syndrome). It is the finality of death that is unlike any other loss. The death of a child can remind us of the death of a parent, sibling, or even a grandparent. In other words, these past losses become intertwined and can actually intensify the current loss.

Response to Loss

Physical reactions to loss have been described as shock; emotional release; preoccupation with the deceased; symptoms of some physical and emotional distresses; hostile reactions; guilt; depression; withdrawal and repression of feelings, or just being exhausted; reentering relationships; resolution and readjustment. The difficulty of this description is that it sounds as if one passes through these emotions sequentially, whereas they may hit randomly.

Health care professionals have also described the variety of responses of the bereaved in the face of great loss:

- A feeling of tightness in the throat or heaviness in the chest
- An empty feeling in the stomach and loss of appetite
- Restlessness and a need for activity, accompanied by an inability to concentrate
- A feeling that the loss isn't real, that it didn't really happen
- A sense of the loved one's presence, like finding yourself expecting her to walk in the door at the usual time, hearing her voice, or seeing her face
- Aimless wandering, forgetfulness, inability to finish things that you started
- Difficulty sleeping, frequent dreams about the loved one

- A tendency to assume the mannerisms or traits of the loved one
- An intense preoccupation with the life of the deceased
- Intense anger at the loved one for leaving
- A need to take care of other people who seem uncomfortable in one's presence, but do not actually talk about the loss
- A need to tell and retell and remember things about your loved one and the experience of his death
- Crying at unexpected times[25]

There are also coping strategies for those suffering a loss: not a formula to follow, but effective coping methods, such as: exercising, keeping a journal, listening to music, reading inspirational books, going to a place of worship, getting a massage, calling a friend, volunteering, praying, visualizing or meditating, talking with a therapist, knowing who you are, and understanding grief.[26]

Sharing of Loss

The ability to share our losses can help us through the grieving process, though many people who have a loss never talk about it. Unfortunately, even religious beliefs may cause grievers to suppress their grief, thinking that this is what it means to be "good" Christians.[27] However difficult it is, sharing our loss can be healing. When we decide to communicate, we open up ourselves to the comfort and reality that someone else exists. We find people to empathize with us in the wake of crisis, pain, and devastation. The Jewish philosopher Martin Buber (1878-1965) speaks about the deep level of communication that involves developing a relationship that reveals who we are and who the other is. The deepest revelation, of course, is between God and us, in which our inner self is laid bare.[28]

For the sufferer, there are also times of complete silence, times when our emotions are so strong that words fail and we wish only to weep, to cry inwardly for comfort, when our body feels drained. Job's response to his friends' flawed and unhelpful theology was that their silence was more

25. Chaplaincy Department of Hennepin County Medical Center, "The Loss of a Loved One," p. 4 (a Hennepin County Medical Center handout sheet [Minneapolis, 1991]).

26. Dale Larson, *The Helper's Journey* (Champaign, IL: Research Press, 1993), p. 76.

27. Bachmann, *Ministering to the Grief Sufferer,* p. 14.

28. Martin Buber, *I and Thou* (New York: Scribner, 1958).

helpful. In the wake of sudden, violent death, especially when someone has lost a family member through suicide or a terrorist attack such as 9/11, there are such strong emotions that the bereaved cannot even hear our words.

Unfortunately, in North American society, people who grieve are too often encouraged not to mourn. We send messages — none too subtly — that people are to get on with their lives, keep busy, and not be consumed by grief. Hence people mourn alone and miss the comfort and support of loved ones. When we suffer great loss, we are in an unknown territory, and remaining silent may be all we can do. This silence may effect a kind of inner suffering as we come to terms with our loss. Eventually, if we are to heal, we must begin to speak about and share our grief so that we can mourn. In *A Grace Disguised*, Gerald Sittser — having suffered tremendous, multiple losses of loved ones — speaks powerfully of his continuous anguish.

> In the fall of 1991 Lynda was teaching a unit of home school to our two oldest children, Catherine and David, on Native American culture. She decided to complete the unit of study by attending a powwow at a Native American reservation in rural Idaho. So we piled our four children into the minivan on a Friday afternoon to drive to the reservation, where we planned to have dinner with the tribe and witness our first powwow. My mother, Grace, who had come to visit us for the weekend, decided to join us on the excursion. At dinner we talked with tribal leaders about their projects and problems — especially the abuse of alcohol, which undermines so much of what they were trying to accomplish. . . .

Sittser goes on to describe the dinner and the tribal dances that followed, and how much they enjoyed their time there.

> By 8:15 pm, however, the children had had enough. So we returned to our van, loaded and buckled up, and left for home. By then it was dark. Ten minutes into our trip home I noticed an oncoming car on a lonely stretch of highway driving extremely fast. I slowed down at a curve, but the other car did not. It jumped its lane and smashed head-on into our minivan. I learned later that the alleged driver was Native American, drunk, driving 85 miles per hour. He was accompanied by his pregnant wife, also drunk, who was killed in the accident.
>
> I remember those first moments after the accident as if everything was happening in slow motion. They are frozen into my memory with a terrible vividness. After recovering my breath, I turned around to

survey the damage. The scene was chaotic. I remember the look of terror on the faces of my children and the feeling of horror that swept over me when I saw the unconscious and broken bodies of Lynda, my 4-year-old daughter Diana Jane, and my mother. I remember getting Catherine (then 8), David (7), and John (2) out of the van through my door, the only one that would open. I remember taking pulses, doing mouth-to-mouth resuscitation, trying to save the dying and calm the living. I remember the feeling of panic that struck my soul as I watched Lynda, my mother, and Diana Jane all die before my eyes. I remember the pandemonium that followed — people gawking, lights flashing from emergency vehicles, a helicopter whirring overhead, cars lining up, medical experts doing what they could to help. And I remember the realization sweeping over me that I would soon plunge into a darkness from which I might never again emerge as a sane, normal, believing man.[29]

However, Sittser does go on to write about how he emerged from the searing pain and loss, and how God's grace was able to shine through this horrible tragedy. The pain of loss never goes away completely, but God is holding us in God's arms.

The Experience of Grief

As we experience loss we enter into grief, which involves how we feel about our losses. There is both expressed and unexpressed grief, and there is also anticipatory grief. If grief is repressed, it can affect our future emotional life in strange ways. The following true story of a woman in counseling illustrates this very clearly.

> "I held up beautifully during the entire time. The people who came, by the hundreds, to the funeral home all told the same story of what a really wonderful guy he was. He always wanted us to be independent, on our own. He wouldn't have wanted me to cry. It was Mother, however, who always told us to put on the front — not to show feeling. That, coupled with the fact that I had been listening to my husband's sermons on death, led me to believe that I had no right to cry. To cry

29. Gerald Sittser, *A Grace Disguised: How the Soul Grows Through Loss* (Grand Rapids: Zondervan, 1995), pp. 16-18.

would have been an admission to myself and others that I really didn't believe this immortality stuff my husband was spouting. . . ." She then began to review the "closeness" she had felt for her father, and how she could "go running home and tell him anything." He was, in her words, "predictable." "I could twist him around my little finger and get most anything I wanted." (It was in the next interview that she came back to the same feeling, as she reviewed her relationship with her father. She seemed eager to talk about it now that it was in the open and the tensions she had been experiencing and the pills she had been taking were drastically reduced. The tender moments that were recalled were of the storybook variety as she began to "idealize" her father to the counselor.) "I was his pride and joy — even though Mother wanted a boy." A fierce kind of competition arose between mother and daughter. "He would come and talk to me and he felt that he could talk to me. Mother resented this because he was treating me as an equal. . . ."

In the ensuing weeks, as she relived her relation with her father, tears flowed more freely and she began to feel more comfortable as a person. She also became pregnant. Though she had been having many miscarriages and felt a bit uneasy about this one, she began to develop more confidence. Things were going along in fairly good fashion until a parishioner hung himself, and all these feelings which she thought she had worked through in accepting her father's death came rushing back to the forefront. She even wondered if she, too, could take her own life. The thought of death again began to be a preoccupying factor, because at this time came the news that a cousin's two-year-old boy had leukemia. There was a strong identification with her cousin. She began to feel guilty and grateful, wondering what she would do if the roles were reversed. "But I began to realize that I could begin to be myself for the first time. I think I have worked beyond Father's death. I know it's all right to express emotion, and being myself is quite a relief. It gives me a sense of power I had not had before. . . . I realize that I never grieved properly for my father, and I know that I was feeling sorry for myself. . . . I am a sensitive person and soft-hearted in many ways. I guess underneath it all," she continued, "I hadn't accepted Father's death and this kept coming to the fore every time some event took place which challenged my security. . . ."

She began to get introspective as the pregnancy continued and the prospect of a new child began to take some of the edge off the old feelings that had always plagued her. She could even watch a play in which the father had no time for his boy. At one time she would have over-reacted. It amazed her a little to realize that after all this time (six months had elapsed from the time of the first interview) she had such feelings. She turned her attention, then, to resolving her relationship with her mother. She began to realize, further, that having been freed from the bondage to the past relationship with her father she could be a free person in her own right — a free, interacting being. When her father died her world had crumbled, but she never told anyone. These feelings were buried inside and never let out until she began to examine why she was having all these negative reactions in her interpersonal relationships.[30]

Anticipatory grief, a different form of grief, is especially apparent in the adult child–parent relationship. As parents age, become infirm, and their contemporaries die, their adult children begin to be concerned about eventually losing them. As Paul E. Irion notes, "Sometimes anticipatory grief expresses itself in what might be called 'disproportionate grieving' for the death of the parent of a friend. By indirection, this grief is for the death of the person's own parent which has not occurred."[31] As adult children become their parents' caregivers, parents may also be angry about the role reversal.

It is a truism that each person has his or her own way of handling grief. One's experience and background shapes one's response to grief. There is no one normal pattern. In a sense, we are renegotiating our lives, our relationship with God and with others, and we continue to relate to the deceased in a new way.[32] As various psychologists have analyzed the stages of grief, they sound similar to the responses to loss: shock/numbness, yearning and pining (anger and guilt), disorganization, and finally a shift to put life back together. As William Worden, a well-known grief therapist, has recognized, we need to accept the reality of the loss, work through to the pain of grief, adjust to an environment in which the deceased is missing, and emotionally relocate the deceased and move on with life.[33] This is

30. Bachmann, *Ministering to the Grief Sufferer,* pp. 68-69.

31. Paul E. Irion, *Nobody's Child: A Generation Caught in the Middle* (New York: United Church Press, 1989), p. 79.

32. Gerald Arbuckle, *Grieving for Change: A Spirituality for Refounding Gospel Communities* (New York: Continuum, 1991).

33. J. William Worden, "William Worden's Four Tasks of Mourning," Hospice of San Luis Obispo County: http://www.hospiceslo.org/lib_resourcecenter/articles/wordenstasks.html (accessed June 11, 2009).

conventional wisdom, but we need to learn to integrate those who are deceased into our present existence, not eliminate them from our life.

C. S. Lewis's classic *A Grief Observed,* though written about his wife Joy's death, is really a love poem to her. It is also an acknowledgment of how overwhelming grief can be even for a person of great faith.

And this separation, I suppose, waits for all. I have been thinking of H. and myself as peculiarly unfortunate in being torn apart. But presumably all lovers are. She once said to me, "Even if we both died at exactly the same moment, as we lie here side by side, it would be just as much a separation as the one you're so afraid of." Of course she didn't *know,* any more than I do. But she was near death; near enough to make a good shot. She used to quote, "Alone into the Alone." She said it felt like that. And how immensely improbable that it should be otherwise! Time and space and body were the very things that brought us together; the telephone wires by which we communicated. Cut one off, or cut both off simultaneously. Either way, mustn't the conversation stop?

Unless you assume that some other means of communication — utterly different, yet doing the same work — would be immediately substituted. But then, what conceivable point could there be in severing the old ones? Is God a clown who whips away your bowl of soup one moment in order, next moment, to replace it with another bowl of the same soup? Even nature isn't such a clown as that. She never plays exactly the same tune twice.

It is hard to have patience with people who say, "There is no death," or, "Death doesn't matter." There is death. And whatever is, matters. And whatever happens has consequences, and it and they are irrevocable and irreversible. You might as well say that birth doesn't matter. I look up at the night sky. Is anything more certain that in all those vast times and spaces, if I were allowed to search them, I should nowhere find her face, her voice, her touch? She died. She is dead. Is the word so difficult to learn?

I have no photograph of her that's any good. I cannot even see her face distinctly in my imagination. Yet the odd face of some stranger seen in a crowd this morning may come before me in vivid perfection the moment I close my eyes tonight. No doubt, the explanation is simple enough. We have seen the faces of those we know best so variously, from so many angles, in so many lights, with so many expressions — waking, sleeping, laughing, crying, eating, talking, thinking — that all the impressions crowd into our memory together and cancel out into a mere blur. But her voice is still vivid. The remembered voice — that can turn me at any moment to a whimpering child. . . .

This is one of the things I'm afraid of. The agonies, the mad midnight moments, must, in the course of nature, die away. But what will follow? Just this apathy, this dead flatness? Will there come a time when I no longer ask why the world is like a mean street, because I shall take the squalor as normal? Does grief finally subside into boredom tinged by faint nausea?

Feelings, and feelings, and feelings. Let me try thinking instead. From the rational point of view, what new factor has H.'s death introduced into the problem of the universe? What grounds has it given me for doubting all that I believe? I knew already that these things and worse happened daily. I would have said that I had taken them into account. I had been warned — I had warned myself — not to reckon on worldly happiness. We were even promised sufferings. They were part of the program. We were even told, "Blessed are they that mourn," and I accepted it. I've got nothing that I hadn't bargained for. Of course it is different when the thing happens to oneself, not to others, and in reality, not in imagination. Yes; but should it, for a sane man, make quite such a difference as this? No. And it wouldn't for a man whose faith had been real faith and whose concern for other people's sorrows had been real concern. The case is too plain. If my house has collapsed at one blow, that is because it was a house of cards. The faith which "took these things into account" was not faith but imagination. The taking them into account was not real sympathy. If I had really cared, as I thought I did, about the sorrows of the world, I should not have been so overwhelmed when my own sorrow came. It has been an imaginary faith playing with innocuous counters labeled "Illness," "Pain," "Death," and "Loneliness." I thought I trusted the rope until it mattered to me whether it would bear me.[34]

Of course, the rope did bear Lewis, but he helps us understand the depths of doubt that death can bring to our faith.

When a catastrophic death happens, we may, like Sittser, wonder whether we should try to know ahead of time what life holds.

My brother-in-law Jack challenged me to reconsider whether I really wanted that kind of power. He said that life in this world is an accident

34. C. S. Lewis, *A Grief Observed* (New York: Bantam Books, 1976), pp. 15-17, 41-43.

waiting to happen, and there is not much we can do about it. Common sense, of course, tells us to wear seatbelts, drive the speed limit, eat healthy food, exercise regularly, get sufficient rest, and make wise decisions. These good habits will minimize accidents but not eliminate them. Did I really want to know what was going to happen in the future so that I could protect myself from the accidents that inevitably and randomly occur in every person's life? . . . What I really wanted, he said, was to be God — an option obviously closed to me.[35]

What we need to accept is the unexpected nature of life, and we need to live in hope anyway. Sittser goes on to testify how God comforted him:

But I have found comfort knowing that the sovereign God, who is in control of everything, is the same God who has experienced the pain I live with every day. No matter how deep the pit into which I descend, I keep finding God there. He is not aloof from my suffering but draws near to me when I suffer. He is vulnerable to pain, quick to shed tears, and acquainted with grief. God is a suffering Sovereign who feels the sorrow of the world.[36]

It is God's victory in Jesus Christ's resurrection that can help us find our way out of our despair and loss.

Stages of Grief

As we read C. S. Lewis, we sense the unfolding and folding back of his grief. Some psychologists have described this experience as stages of grief. Following a great loss and the ensuing grief, there are certain psychological factors that need to be considered. Guilt and hostility are common factors in the face of what has happened. Grief has an ambivalent character: it is a place where we are alternately sad and angry. We feel keenly the separation from the person we love, and the hole in our heart is matched by the grief we feel between ourselves and the person we love.

When someone we love dies, our first reaction to that death is shock and denial. Of course, the degree of shock and emotional response varies greatly. The bereaved, experiencing different levels of shock, may weep silently or out loud. There can be a sense of denial or disbelief or immobility

35. Sittser, *A Grace Disguised*, p. 99.
36. Sittser, *A Grace Disguised*, p. 143.

that makes grieving difficult. This may be short-lived, but it is often followed by a longer phase of intense psychic pain. There may be a sense of hopelessness, anxiety, fright, and helplessness expressed in lethargy, hyperactivity, aggression, or regression. One may express anger toward the doctors, toward care-providers, or friends, or the deceased, or God. If there was no chance to say goodbye, we may feel guilt, shame, regret, or ambivalence. Some professionals who describe these stages say, "After the initial shock has worn off, and the fear, anger and depression have diminished, the bereaved enters into an adjustment phase."[37] This tidy description may seem a little too neat to many of us: as the first-person accounts in this chapter have shown, grief is neither neat nor uniform.

Mourning Is the Way We Process Grief

Many psychologists and counselors have created lists of how to face grief. However, grief does not lend itself to lists. Some of the comments are helpful, but they may best be processed with a counselor. The focus is to get in touch with our feelings, to open up to others, to move outside of our own needs, and to find ways to help others.[38] Experiencing grief through mourning is necessary, but it is different for each person.

Like Kübler-Ross's stages of dying, we seem to think that there are acceptable periods of mourning, and then we need to get on with our lives. A long enough time depends on the individual. A woman whose husband died two years ago said her friends told her, "You should have gotten over it by now." Her response was hurt and anger. Although we must beware of charting emotions and experiences of loss on a linear scale, there are certain observations from health care professionals and others about the so-called stages of grief. For those who are experiencing these losses, there may be some recognition of "stages." But we should beware of making them a checklist, because they may be more circular than linear.

One researcher asked eighty-five mourners to write a free essay in response to the question "What does the death of your loved one mean to you?" An analysis of the resulting narratives showed that nine unique

37. Cappel and Mathieu, "Loss and the Grieving Process — Death of Loved Ones," pp. 82-85.

38. Donna O'Toole, "Things You Can Do to Help Yourself Face Grief," in *Facing Change: Coming together and Falling Apart in the Teen Years* (Burnsville, NC: Compassion Books, 1995), pp. 23-30. See Appendix J for O'Toole's list.

meaning constructs emerged, the most prominent one being feeling the absence of the deceased. "A distinction was drawn between meaning categories referent to pain and suffering versus recovery and hope and between consequent/instrumental forms of meaning versus philosophical/existential meanings. Implications for additional study of the relationship between meaning constructs and bereavement adaptation were discussed."[39]

Comforting Those Who Mourn

Having read stories of those who have experienced tremendous loss, we know that it is important to find ways to bring comfort to the bereaved. We comfort through communication, which does not consist merely of words: it can be by way of a handshake, sitting with someone in silence, a gift or letter (either sent or received), a caress as a sign of tenderness. These acts can be of great comfort.[40] This is Nouwen's definition of hospitality marked by the virtue of *alertia:* being centered on and having an attentiveness and openness to the other.[41]

How do we comfort those who are mourning? In chapters 10 and 11 below, I will especially discuss how the faith community — pastor, chaplain, and faith community nurse — can really assist. Again we are instructed by Wolterstorff.

> What do you say to someone who is suffering? Some people are gifted with words of wisdom. For such, one is profoundly grateful. There were many such for us. But not all are gifted in that way. Some blurted out strange, inept things. That's OK too. Your words don't have to be wise. The heart that speaks is heard more than the words spoken. And if you can't think of anything at all to say, just say, "I can't think of anything to say. But I want you to know that we are with you in your grief."
>
> Or even, just embrace. Not even the best of words can take away the pain. What words can do is testify that there is more than pain in our journey on earth to a new day. Of those things that are more, the great-

39. Louis A. Gamino, Nancy S. Hoga, Kenneth W. Sewell, "Feeling the Absence: A Content Analysis from the Scott and White Grief Study," *Death Studies* 26, no. 10 (Dec. 2002): 793.

40. Pierre Wolff, *May I Hate God?* (Mahwah, NJ: Paulist Press, 1979), p. 10.

41. Henri Nouwen, *Reaching Out: Three Movements of the Spiritual Life* (New York: Image Books, 1975).

est is love. Express your love. How appallingly grim must be the death of a child in the absence of love.

But please: Don't say it's not really so bad. Because it is. Death is awful, demonic. If you think your task as comforter is to tell me that really, all things considered, it's not so bad, you do not sit with me in my grief but place yourself off in the distance away from me. Over there, you are of no help. What I need to hear from you is that you recognize how painful it is. I need to hear from you that you are with me in my desperation. To comfort me, you have to come close. Come sit beside me on my mourning bench.

I know: People do sometimes think things are more awful than they really are. Such people need to be corrected — gently, eventually. But no one thinks death is more awful than it is. It's those who think it's not so bad that need correcting. . . .

Some say nothing because they find the topic too painful for themselves. They fear they will break down. So they put on a brave face and hide their feelings — never reflecting, I suppose, that this adds new pain to the sorrow of their suffering friends. Your tears are salve on our wound, your silence is salt. And later, when you ask me how I am doing and I respond with a quick, thoughtless "Fine" or "OK," stop me sometime and ask, "No, I mean *really*."[42]

In addition to friends and family who can comfort us are professionals who are skilled in bereavement counseling. Seeking professional help is not a sign of moral weakness, a lack of faith, or abnormal grief, but rather a sensible way to assist us in the healing process.

Bereavement Counseling

As one constructs a counseling model for grieving individuals and families, there are conflicting approaches. There is little doubt that death is the most important event for a family. It is often the beginning of processes in the family that can continue for generations: both alienation and reconciliation can occur. Some family members will find new freedom, while others have to assume new responsibilities.[43] "The most important thing we

42. Wolterstorff, *Lament for a Son*, pp. 34-35.
43. Edwin H. Friedman, *Generation to Generation* (New York: Guilford Press, 1985), pp. 168-69.

can do for others who are grieving is to be patient and caring. The unsung heroes are those who care for a dying spouse. Actually, they may be sick themselves; the burden they carry may in fact be too great. Sometimes pastors hear, 'I just wish she would die.' Long-term chronic illness seems as if it will never end."[44] These wishes that the loved one die may also be related to her pain and suffering in the dying process.

Family systems theory helps us understand that sadness and pain over loss, difficulty in functioning, and the urge for replacement are all part of unresolved relationships. Communication about these issues among family members is key for the future health of the family members. Friedman gives two examples of family approaches to death and dying: one is of a man killed in a car crash, and each family member is afraid the others "can't take" seeing the mangled body; and another is of a mother dying of cancer, which provides the opportunity for her daughters to rethink relationships and life decisions.[45] Each family member's reaction to a dying loved one will be unique based on the life cycle of the family, what other losses are occurring as a result of this death, the course of the patient's illness, and the roles both the patient and the various family members have held in the family. "As we attempt to comfort and counsel those who are grieved, certain realities about the family are important. What was the place of the deceased person in the family? Was he the patriarch of the family or a young child who was seen as the hope of the family? Was the deceased the major financial support of the family or a precious caregiver? Was his or her illness frightening and protracted or sudden — without time for preparation? All of these factors influence the grief, loss, and mourning. There can be real fear of being without the parent in a kind of unsupported loneliness."[46]

The common wisdom about families' grief is "that the *purpose* of grief is the reconstitution of an autonomous individual who can in large measure leave the deceased behind and form new attachments. The *process* by which this is believed to be achieved is the working through and resolution of feelings. The psychological literature on grief is full of discussion of anger, guilt, depression, sadness and a whole range of feelings with which bereaved people may have to come to terms. These concepts of the pur-

44. Delores Kuenning, *Helping People through Grief* (Minneapolis: Bethany House Publishers, 1987), pp. 257-59.

45. Friedman, *Generation to Generation*, pp. 172-77.

46. Irion, *Nobody's Child*, p. 82.

pose and process of grief form much of the conventional wisdom, or what Wortman and Silver (1989) call 'the clinical lore,' of bereavement counseling."[47] As I discuss below, Tony Walter roundly criticizes this approach, challenging its validity.

The purpose of bereavement counseling is to help people focus on feelings.

> Counselors do this in two ways — either by asking the client to talk directly about their feelings, which actually entails a certain distance from feeling the feelings and may assist self-understanding. Or by asking about particularly traumatic events, such as the funeral, the retelling of which is likely to bring feelings directly to the surface and may assist catharsis. Whichever technique is used, the counselor's aim is to enable the client to clarify his or her feelings. Lendrum and Syme provide some basic loss counseling guidelines, which may be helpful. Restate in different words, and in clear and simple language, the literal meaning of the client's statements:

> > SUSAN: My husband was a fine man. His sudden death was a great shock. I still miss him terribly.
> > COUNSELOR: Your husband's unexpected death really shook you to the core. You still miss him terribly.[48]

This illustrates how the counselor can translate any objective statements about the deceased into how the bereaved is feeling.

Tony Walter does not follow conventional wisdom in bereavement counseling, that is, learning to live without the deceased family member. This conventional perspective is that after the strong emotional response of loss, the grief should turn to mourning. "These basic tasks of mourning include accepting that the loss happened, living with and feeling the physical and emotional pain of grief, adjusting to life without the loved one, and emotionally separating from the loved one and going on with life without him or her. It is important that these tasks are completed before mourning can end."[49] He points out that in the West the sense that the deceased is still alive is considered a temporary but perhaps necessary illusion before learning to live without the deceased. However, in other cultures it is the

47. Walter, "A New Model of Grief," p. 7.
48. Susan L. Lendrum and Gabrielle Syme, *Gift of Tears: A Practical Approach to Loss and Bereavement Counseling* (New York: Routledge, 1992).
49. "Treatment," in "Loss, Grief, and Bereavement database."

opposite. For example, the Shona have a straightforward and simple burial.[50] They do not hide the reality of death, meaning "that they quickly accept that the person has died physically [as] a necessary preliminary to the long-term welcoming of the deceased back as one of the ancestors. The dead person is lost and then re-found, rather than clung onto before being ultimately relinquished."[51] Some grief reactions are more complicated than others. "Complicated grief reactions require more complex therapies than uncomplicated grief reactions. Adjustment disorders (especially depressed and anxious mood or disturbed emotions and behavior), major depression, substance abuse, and even posttraumatic stress disorder are some of the common problems of complicated bereavement. Complicated grief is identified by the extended length of time of the symptoms, the interference caused by the symptoms, or by the intensity of the symptoms (for example, intense suicidal thoughts or acts)."[52]

Walter goes on to expand his theory that bereavement counseling usually abhors the person "stuck" in his grief because he is petrified of letting go of the dead person. The aim then is to give the bereaved the permission to let go. However, for Walter, learning how to *retain* the dead person in a healthy way should be the aim. This can be a liberating place where there is both a retaining and a moving on. "Members of modern Western societies need to know that they can keep those they have lost, and that one way to do this is to talk honestly about the dead with family, friends and neighbors who knew them" (p. 23). He then applies this view to his own experience at the loss of his father: his friend from the Shona culture encouraged him to hold onto his father and not let go. This means he could move from preoccupation of loss of the bereaved and concentrate on the character of the deceased (p. 9). "The purpose of grief is not to move on without those who have died, but to find a secure place for them. For this place to be secure, the image of the dead normally has to be reasonably accurate, that is, shared by others and tested out against them" (p. 20).

What is fascinating is that, for example, once a widow recovers from the first shock and grief, she can begin to experience joy in recalling memories, a process Jane Littlewood has described as "falling in love backwards." Though this process is described in texts such as the one by Parkes,

50. *Shona* is the name collectively given to several groups of people in Zimbabwe and southern Mozambique.
51. Walter, "A New Model of Grief," p. 9. Hereafter, page references to this work appear in parentheses in the text.
52. "Complicated Grief," in "Loss, Grief, and Bereavement database."

such women did not always find bereavement counselors validating their experiences.[53] Many bereaved parents and widows belong to self-help groups such as the Compassionate Friends and the National Association of Widows, which take a different view (Walter, p. 10).

This paradigm shift is a move away from generalizations about bereavement "to a more postmodern individualizing of loss and a rejection of grand theory." Counselors need to be aware of the diverse ways that clients grieve so they are not reducing their experience to "normal" grief or pathological grief. This more postmodern view can also use cross-cultural data not to justify a universally normal grief but to demonstrate diversity (p. 11).

Conclusion

In the end, what can we say about these troubling realities? In some ways there is little to say; in other ways there is a world of things to express — tears, cries, rage, disbelief, depression. We experience all the human emotions that are the opposite of joy and happiness when we face great loss. We can stay, listen, weep with those who weep, and remember Christ's words: "Blessed are those who mourn, for they shall be comforted" (Matt. 5:4). It is in our darkest hour, when we think that God has abandoned us, that we will find God at the bedside, the theme of the last section of this book.

53. C. M. Parkes, "Bereavement in Adult Life," *British Medical Journal* 316, no. 7134 (1998): 88.

IV. GOD AT THE BEDSIDE

10. Clergy at the Bedside

Prayer is the Soul's Sincere Desire

Prayer is the soul's sincere desire,
Unuttered or expressed;
The motion of a hidden fire
That trembles in the breast.

Prayer is the burden of a sigh,
The falling of a tear,
The upward glancing of an eye,
When none but God is near.

Prayer is the Christian's vital breath,
The Christian's native air,
His watchword at the gates of death;
He enters Heav'n with prayer.

Prayer is the contrite sinner's voice,
Returning from his ways,
While angels in their songs rejoice
And cry, "Behold, he prays!"

The saints in prayer appear as one
In word, in deed, and mind,
While with the Father and the Son
Sweet fellowship they find.

No prayer is made by man alone
The Holy Spirit pleads,
And Jesus, on th'eternal throne,
For sinners intercedes.

O Thou by Whom we come to God,
The Life, the Truth, the Way,
The path of prayer Thyself hast trod:
Lord, teach us how to pray.

James Montgomery (1771-1854)

As we move to the final section of this book, which is about God at the bedside as seen through the ministry of the faith community, the pastor, and the Faith Community Nurse (FCN), we are not suggesting that God was absent until now. God was accompanying us all along. So far we have considered the problems, realities, and challenges of dealing with death, loss, grief, pain, and struggle. We may wonder where God is in the midst of this, and we may turn to clergy members for sustenance and strength, hoping that they may have the answers we seek. A pastor's most important ministry may be with the sick and dying and their families. However, this ministry at the "edges of life," to borrow a phrase from Paul Ramsey, requires an understanding of a pastor's various roles and functions, as well as the nature of pastoral care itself.[1] The language I use here comes primarily from my Protestant tradition, though there is much about the subject that we may learn from our Roman Catholic, Jewish, and other faith colleagues.

According to a Gallup survey entitled "Spiritual Beliefs and the Dying Process," Americans are dissatisfied with dying in America. What people want is: death at home among close family and friends; recognition of the deeper spiritual dimensions of dying and death; and the assurance that their families will not be overburdened with caring for them while they are dying and will not feel neglected after they are gone. The Gallup findings suggest that people do not trust professional caregivers with the spiritual care and support they need in their dying days. Only 36 percent of respondents saw the clergy as providing broad spiritual support in their dying

---

1. Paul Ramsey, *Ethics at the Edges of Life: Medical and Legal Intersections* (New Haven: Yale University Press, 1978).

days. (Part of this is no doubt due to the shrinking number of church members.) Fewer than 30 percent look to physicians for spiritual comfort; 21 percent look to nurses for it.[2] Despite these findings, clergy still have an important calling to be with the dying, and I hope that this book will give them some more tools to use.

General Pastoral Care

Before we look at the specific roles of the pastor/chaplain in caring for the sick and dying, we need to understand what constitutes pastoral care. There are many models of pastoral care: client-centered, informal, clinical/ crisis, formal counseling, worship-based, and so forth. Carl Rogers says: "The essence of pastoral care is the giving of unconditional, positive regard to another."[3] You allow the person to speak to you as she describes her problem or situation, rather than rushing in and telling her what her problem is. "Oh, I see you look depressed. Is it your breast cancer?" That is not client-centered. Questions such as "What is wrong today? Is something bothering you?" are more client-centered. For some it may be worry about the young children for whom they will no longer be able to care, not primarily their impending death.

We might also note the difference between pastoral counseling and pastoral care. Counseling is a subset of pastoral care: it requires specialized training and certification. Counseling can be done in a one-on-one setting or in peer groups. After several meetings, pastors are best off referring parishioners to professionally trained counselors or therapists, especially if they detect serious mental-health issues. Pastoral care can happen in worship, informal conversations, or in other settings. It often happens in unexpected moments — which is often precisely how it happens with the very busy pastor — as in the few-word exchange when people are greeting the pastor after worship. For example, the pastor might ask, "How are you today, Mrs. Jones?" She may respond, "Well actually, things are absolutely horrible because my daughter was just diagnosed with leukemia." Obvi-

2. "Spiritual Beliefs and the Dying Process," Gallup Poll, 1997, quoted in Edwin R. DuBose, "Preparing for Death," *Park Ridge Center Bulletin* 21 (May-June 2001): 3-4.
3. Carl Rogers (1902-1987) was an American psychologist who was among the founders of client-centered therapy, which was applied to many other disciplines. It was based on unconditional regard and acceptance of the clients, allowing them to draw on their own resources for human growth. The therapist becomes a facilitator for the person's own growth.

ously the pastor cannot go into a long conversation with a line of people building up. However, in the few words exchanged at that moment, he or she can say, "This must be very difficult for you. I wish we could talk about this now. I will call you tomorrow and we can talk about this further. The church is concerned, and we are with you to help you with your daughter." This is pastoral care growing out of worship, where Mrs. Jones's heart was opened to feel free to share her deepest fears *en passant*.

The coffee hour after church is another one of the key moments for pastoral care, but it is generally done by Stephen Ministers, faith community nurses, or deacons, that is, it is pastoral care by lay leaders. It can be at a table in the fellowship hall, where there are books and literature that can help disarm the awkwardness of people bringing up deep subjects. Conversation over books can become an occasion for meaningful pastoral care.

Another model of pastoral care is the crisis-centered approach. The Clinical Pastoral Education (CPE) movement, begun by Anton Boisen and Seward Hiltner, followed a crisis model of pastoral counseling. Besides having an undue focus on crises, the CPE model can be dominated by the medical setting. Pastoral theology has always looked for a language of acceptability in the clinical setting, which it found in CPE. This has had the effect of transferring psychological vocabulary into the pastoral setting in the hope of gaining more respectability. It is not that CPE lacks important contributions to pastoral care; it is simply one among several models.

Another approach to pastoral care is linking it with worship, as Methodist bishop William H. Willimon does. He refers to the historical functions of pastoral care — healing, sustaining, guiding, and reconciling — and explains how each one of those functions can be carried out through worship. Historically, healing occurred by way of anointing and the laying-on-of-hands.[4] Reconciling takes place through the ritualized acts of forgiveness, confession, penance, and absolution. Sustaining takes place through the administering of the Eucharist (the Lord's Supper). There is a connection between the traditional features of worship and pastoral care; unfortunately, those two functions were separated during the Reformation.[5]

Pastoral care should not forget the pastor as person: the healing power of the presence of the pastors/chaplains. These may be the most important roles in the hospital setting, but clergy are often not given access to parishioners who are in the throes of medical procedures. One chaplain

---

4. William H. Willimon, *Worship as Pastoral Care* (Nashville: Abingdon, 1979), p. 31.
5. Willimon, *Worship as Pastoral Care*, pp. 33-35.

reported a situation where a mother of a young son who was dying was forced to stand behind glass with the pastor, both watching the procedures being done to her son, neither allowed to be with him in the last minutes of his life.[6] Death was not always medicalized in this way. Historically, death was overseen by clergy; furthermore, the early doctors were priests; faith communities founded and sponsored hospitals, and nursing and medicine were perceived as religious callings. During the Renaissance and Reformation, with the split between science and religion, medicine and theology went their separate ways.[7]

As I have mentioned above, the founding of CPE created a sub-specialty of hospital chaplains who had additional clinical training. Chaplains provide clinically oriented pastoral care in the medical center, integrating particular theory and techniques regarding the place of religion in health care with a commitment to the spiritual well-being of patients, their families, and staff. In many settings this has provided a place on the modern medical-care team for members of the clergy; at the same time, however, it has often had the result that parish priests, pastors, rabbis, and imams relegate the care of the dying to these professionals.

Before we examine the role of the pastor, allow me to make the important caution that the pastor needs to be aware of self-care: keeping healthy by exercise, diet, prayer, meditation, recreation, time with family and friends, and Sabbath rest. Staying fit and healthy makes it possible to continue to serve the dying. It is easy to allow the urgency and demands of the dying person and his family to overshadow everything else. Pastors are tempted to think that they are indispensable, especially if they try to go it alone. How to set boundaries and share this ministry is crucial. Pastors should learn the "art of the possible," to borrow Dale Larson's phrase.[8]

A related concern in self-care is recognizing what Kenneth Doka has called "disenfranchised grief." The chaplain's grief is not recognized or accepted, because the hospice chaplain or pastor is supposed to carry the grief for the community.[9] For those who cannot share or fully experience their own grief, burnout can result. Bringing in experts in areas that are

---

6. Student story in the author's "Death and Dying" class, Princeton Theological Seminary (Fall 2007).

7. DuBose, "Preparing for Death," pp. 3-4.

8. Dale G. Larson, *The Helper's Journey: Working with People Facing Grief, Loss, and Life-Threatening Illness* (Champaign, IL: Research Press, 1993), p. 85.

9. Philip Helsel, "In Memoriam: The Disenfranchised Grief of Chaplains and the Recovery of Memory," *Journal of Pastoral Care and Counseling* 62, no. 4 (Winter 2008): 331.

beyond a pastor's experience helps her do what she can without trying to handle what is beyond her capabilities. Knowing when — and to whom — to refer people with needs beyond a pastor's expertise is especially important. Because there are spiritual and psychological dimensions to these illnesses, in addition to the physiological and sociological ones, pastors may operate with the illusion that they can treat these cases, which may cause undue suffering and damage. Building a good referral network may be the most important contribution a pastor can make to the healing team.

Part of the tension for the pastor is deciding who is the client. The dying person, the family, the staff — even the institution where the patient resides — may be under the pastor's care. There is no doubt that conflicts in loyalties to these various constituents may arise, and deciding who is primary is not easy. For example, the husband of a long-term, seriously ill patient is finally worn out and says, "I just wish she would die." Modern technology has made it possible for people to become breathing corpses. Time is also an enigma for the dying person: it either goes too fast or too slow. There is a tension for many of the dying between wanting time to "prepare for death" and just wanting to die suddenly in their sleep. The pastor here is often torn between the family's needs and the patient's needs.

The role of the clergy with the sick and dying varies from one religious tradition to another. Here I will focus on Christian clergy, particularly those in the Reformed tradition. How can a pastor be equipped to fulfill this kind of role? Many physicians view clergy as part of the problem rather than bearers of healing. Clergypersons may sometimes bring more trouble than comfort to the dying person, for example, judgments of sin that result in guilt.

Eric Cassell has emphasized for physicians the importance of language as a tool in healing. How much more is this true for pastors! A pastor's training is almost entirely in words; touch is infrequent, and medicine and surgery are not available for her use. However, the pastor may need to cultivate more of a presence ministry, that is, simply standing by in the face of sickness and suffering when words are inappropriate.[10]

To be effective, the pastor — perhaps more than any other professional — must integrate the professional and personal. It is of little value to hear a message that is spiritually uplifting one day, and then see it vanish in the pastor's personal life and relationships the next day. Not only are the personal lives of pastors examples, but their experiences of life, suffering,

---

10. Eric Cassell, *The Healer's Art* (New York: Penguin Books, 1979), p. 128.

and sacrifice, as well as of joy, can be the basis for this support and sympathy in all seasons of life. Pastors, unlike physicians, have the opportunity to develop relationships with their parishioners at times other than crisis and sickness.

The Roles of the Pastor/Chaplain with the Ill and Dying

The following are some specific roles and forms of ministry of the pastor/chaplain in end-of-life care that may help to differentiate their role from that of other health care professionals. We might even refer to these roles as the healing means that are available to clergy, just as medicine and surgery are available to the physician. As the pastor practices these forms of ministry with the sick and dying, healing will be enhanced in the fullest sense of the word. Some of these roles are peculiar to the chaplain in a medical setting, but most of them are part of the calling of local congregational clergy. They include providing worship and the sacraments, which are sources of healing; praying and reading Scripture, which provide profound comfort; wrestling with the questions of theodicy and eschatology, which are paramount in patients' minds (why is God allowing their suffering?); giving meaning and hope, which can help restore purpose and confidence in the midst of dying; providing spiritual assessment and care, which helps remove roadblocks to healing.

Before examining traditional roles with the dying, I should note that clergy may be asked to provide pastoral care in the midst of catastrophic events and crises.

In what was perhaps the most devastating tragedy and loss of life ever seen in New York City, the clinical staff of The HealthCare Chaplaincy was on the scene at several of the city's hospitals, providing spiritual care and support to those who were injured, grieving the death of a loved one, or frantically searching for lost family and friends after the terrorist attack on the World Trade Center on September 11, 2001. In addition to their hospital-based ministries, the Chaplaincy's clinical staff volunteered 400 hours of time during the first ten days after the terrorist assault, and reached out to more than 10,000 people participating in a hundred prayer and memorial services, which the chaplains organized and conducted.

The Rev. Handro and other chaplains who were working in the

medical centers that day redefined the parameters of a "ministry of presence." "Much of what we did was not chaplaincy in the normal sense," he said. "We helped pass out bottles of water to people coming in off the street, and helped people wash the dust out of their eyes. I helped escort people who were either not injured or had already been treated to a waiting area upstairs because they had no safe way of leaving the hospital."

The Rev. Dr. Carolyn O. Yard, staff chaplain at The Burn Center at New York Presbyterian Hospital, had been at the World Trade Center herself that day. After running for her own life, she walked uptown in order to assist in managing the 22 patients injured in the explosion and admitted to the Burn Center. Chaplain Yard also mourned the loss of Father Mychal Judge, chaplain for the Fire Department of New York, who was among the first to die in the attack. "We were just about to do the dedicatory prayer together for the new playroom in The Burn Center," she said.[11]

This terrible tragedy brought forth caring, tenderness, and concern not only by chaplains but by police officers and other city officials and affected family members.

As one tearful chaplain said in a moment of regrouping at the SAIR team table at the armory, "I was praying with a family member who was grieving, and then all of sudden, she started praying for me. It really got to me."

At *ground zero,* Imam Zakat told victims and rescue workers, "I'm here to help," and asked, "What can I do for you?" They would say "Just hold me," he said. "I would hold them, or I would listen to them. You can't say that everything will be all right, because it won't be. But you can listen, and be there for them, simply be a human being. Be there, that's all you can do."[12]

Provide Sacramental/Liturgical Worship Resources

Traditionally, one of the most familiar roles of the pastor is as a worship leader and presider over the sacraments. It is one of the most powerful

11. "Chaplains Respond to World Trade Center Attack," News from the Healthcare Chaplaincy, *The Beacon* (New York, NY), Fall 2001: unnumbered pages.
12. "Chaplains Respond to World Trade Center Attack."

sources of healing for families of the seriously ill and their dying loved ones. Worship may prepare people for future crises and serious illness. There is an incarnational aspect to the sacraments, and spirituality and worship should engage the body, mind, and spirit. We do not throw our minds into neutral; our spirits do not float around unconnected, absent from our bodies. Real worship involves the whole person. The use of music, art, icons, candles, incense, and so forth may assist us in experiencing this more mystical dimension. Worship should have an air of mystery, and should not be simply a feel-good experience. Some worship is a type of "rah-rah" Christianity: it is too gimmicky when it simply uses contemporary symbols and experiences to jazz up the worship without understanding what underlies it. Worship needs to be grounded in real theology and substance.

The worship experience can be transforming, as Thea Bowman explains:

> If you go to a real Black Church, they promise you that you will have a good time in church. One reason why some of us go to church and stay so long is that we're having a good time. That means that if you are in sorrow you will find comfort and consolation. If you are in grief you will find someone to share your burden. If you are tired, you will find rest. If you are burdened, you will find relaxation and relief. If you've got a tear, you will find joy. An old lady says, "I go to church, I put my burden down at the door. I ain't no fool. I know I've got to pick it up, but I've got to get me some strength. I've got to get me some relief. In the time of sorrow, God will sustain me."[13]

When we bring our burdens to God and lay them at God's feet, we begin to experience that uplifting quality. It is not simply an escape from the world, but it equips and empowers us to go back into the world. That is worship at its very best. It is food for the soul.

Others describe the principal thrust of worship as the connection with God's love that we experience whether through the sacraments, the preaching of the Word, or simply the fellowship of other people. We need that fellowship of believers, particularly when we are lonely. However, one worship element, the passing of peace, may raise pastoral issues because some people feel alienated and are not ready for this ritual. When people

---

13. Thea Bowman, "Justice, Power and Praise," in *Liturgy and Social Justice: Celebrating Rites,* ed. E. Grosz (Collegeville, MN: Liturgical Press, 1989), p. 28.

are hurting in their own lives, it is difficult for them to reach out to others. Pastors need to be sensitive to this.

If true worship is happening, people should leave worship transformed. Unfortunately, many people think of worship as an opportunity to sit back and relax while the preacher expends him- or herself on their behalf. Many preachers encourage this behavior by their willingness to carry the entire burden. Worshipers, as well as the pastor, should be making their own active contribution to the worship of God throughout the service.[14]

Corporate worship often provides the context for the pastor's use of sacraments and rites for healing. In the words of Paul Tillich, worship happens when people touch the ground of their being.[15] The danger is that we make the transcendent into the commonplace, thereby stripping worship of its most important element — awe. Our response completes the act of worship and how it relates people to their call to ministry in the world. Liturgy not only has consequences for life, but life has consequences for liturgy. Christians should move from prayer and praise in the church to life and work in the world. "The two activities, properly understood, flow into each other, and reinforce each other to the greater glory of God. When the connection is broken both worship and witness suffer."[16]

General worship is also part of a pastor's armamentarium for the sick and dying. Liturgy provides people with an environment of meaning and gives pastoral care a corporate vision and transmits social forms of believing.[17] Believers have a vision as a collected community, and this creates an environment of belonging. The patient who is lifted up in prayer during worship can become part of this larger community of believers to which he belongs. The service creates an environment of history and memory. The memories are from the cloud of witnesses that surround us: those people who have experienced healing and whose testimony is especially powerful. On the other hand, people who have suffered great loss are able to go on living. These realities show how the church is a healing community as we are bound together in our brokenness as well as in our triumphs.

The historic role of the priest was a liturgical role. The connection

---

14. A. Daniel Frankforter, *Stones for Bread* (Louisville: Westminster John Knox, 2001), pp. 170-71.

15. Paul Tillich, *Systematic Theology* (3 volumes) (Chicago: University of Chicago Press, 1973).

16. Charles Price and Louis Weil, *Liturgy for Living* (New York: Seabury, 1979), p. 40.

17. Robin Green, *Only Connect: Worship and Liturgy from the Perspective of Pastoral Care* (London: Darton, Longman and Todd, 1987), pp. 1-19.

between worship and pastoring was automatically made because pastoral care was mediated through the sacramental functions of the pastor. Liturgy may be the role that thrusts clergy into the pairing of counseling and worship leadership.[18]

Understanding the interconnectedness between worship and pastoral care is important as we reflect on healing services and prayers for seriously ill persons and their families. Leslie Weatherhead refers to the healing service conducted by the pastor as a liturgy for service. We do not often think of that dimension. When the pastor conducts a healing service, whether it is at the bedside or in the context of a public worship service, it is to equip the patient for service. How can we interpret that? What form of service would this be for the person? For those who are healed it would be to go forth and serve others. In addition, the response of the congregation can also bring healing. Jesus often gave instructions to the persons he healed: go to the pool and wash, take up your bed and walk, go to the temple, and so on. Mainline Protestant denominations are beginning to embrace rituals for the dying. "There is growing use of brief services for the commendation of the dying, which were formerly found mainly in high liturgical tradition."[19] Families often respond positively to the commendation, since it gives patients permission to let go.

When we refer to the pastor's use of sacraments with sick parishioners, we usually think of the sacrament/rite of healing. The power of the rite of healing, as with the Eucharist and baptism, rests in its corporate nature: we are joined with one another as well as with Christ. We become the body of Christ during these moments. Rituals should be an integral part of the pastoral ministry to the dying and reflect the symbols of life and hope in the midst of death. These "rites of passage" may contain three phases: separation, transition, and reincorporation. Rituals can help people enter the mainstream of life as well as help them enter into their dying.[20] Rituals ideally arise from within our context of a broader and more comprehensive lived experience, which extends far beyond the fragile boundaries of the ritual itself.

The James 5 passage has traditionally been understood as the origin of the rite of healing. This passage principally addresses moral and ethical practices rather than precise theological formulations: "Are any among

18. Willimon, *Worship as Pastoral Care*, p. 26.
19. Paul Irion, *Hospice and Ministry* (Nashville: Abingdon, 1988), p. 208.
20. Willimon, *Worship as Pastoral Care*, pp. 102-6.

you suffering? They should pray. Are any cheerful? They should sing songs of praise. Are any among you sick? They should call for the elders of the church and have them pray over them, anointing them with oil in the name of the Lord. The prayer of faith will save the sick, and the Lord will raise them up; and anyone who has committed sins will be forgiven. Therefore confess your sins to one another, and pray for one another, so that you may be healed. The prayer of the righteous is powerful and effective" (James 5:13-16). In an earlier book, *The Healing Church,* I put it this way:

> A key term in this James passage is the reference to "elders" (or in the Roman Catholic tradition translated "priests," *presbyteros*). Palestinian Jews used the word "elders" *(zeqenim)* for those who handled sacred functions (m. Aboth 1:1), but the elders referenced here are linked with the Christian church with one of their specific functions being praying for the sick. An important dimension is the presence of the elders — not just the priest but a group of elders — as a sign of the love of the community. It seems no accident that the James passage refers to elders in the plural when giving the instruction for the administration of the anointing. Sickness and dying, then, are reintroduced within the community of believers. Hence, instead of the sick person being isolated, as modern medicine has done by removing the person from her community at a time when isolation is one of the biggest fears, she is put back into the center of the community.[21]

The shift to a group model of pastoral care may also reflect this concern.[22]

> At the time James was written, oil was commonly used for healing the sick in both the pagan and the Judeo-Christian worlds. In everyday life, oil was applied as a soothing lotion for athletes as well as perfume or ointment for the body. It was also used in the anointing of kings. Here its purpose was both to save *(sozein)* and to restore *(egeirein).* Most scholars argue that these terms indicate both bodily and spiritual healing. Since *egeirein* can also mean "to rise up on the last day" or "to

---

21. Abigail Rian Evans, *The Healing Church* (Cleveland: United Church Press, 1999), p. 4. Hereafter, page references to this work appear in parentheses in the text.

22. "Pastoral care in its larger meaning . . . involves the pastor in giving caring attention to concerns that reach beyond the individual to the community of Christians and to the larger society." Charles Gerkin, quoted in Philip L. Culbertson, *Caring for God's People* (Minneapolis: Augsburg Fortress, 2000), p. 2.

rise up from the sick bed," or both, the meaning cannot be determined from the context alone. The "saving and raising up" in James 5 refers to the integration of sickness within one's Christian life and bringing to bear the meaning of Christ's death and resurrection in the life of the patient. The anointing is a sign of the strengthening and comfort of Christ. The death of Christ, however, has meaning only in relation to the resurrection. Catholic scholars see a further link between the anointing of the sick with oil and the forgiveness of sins, which is certainly reflected in the text but not necessarily part of anointing by the bedside for Protestant clergy. This anointing can bring an infusion of power and healing force for a short time or simply sustain the person (p. 4).

The James passage emphasizes the saving of the sick with the prayer of faith, accompanied by anointing. Did James consider this anointing to be remedial or religious? According to Charles Gusmer, the James passage indicates that the elders, not those with special gifts of healing, exercise the general commission to heal. Was it a sacrament conveying sanctifying grace *ex opere operato* or a sacramental provision of supernatural means for the recovery of health? (p. 5)

If we consider this as a sacrament in the Roman Catholic sense, then it has a power of its own. However, Protestants refer to healing "services," not the *sacrament* of healing. In either case, they are instruments of God's healing power.

During the Carolingian Renaissance in the ninth century, the healing ministry was replaced by elaborate rites for the dying. They consisted of five parts: (1) visitation of the sick with the priest and family gathered around the bed in prayer; (2) confession of sin and absolution; (3) the sacrament of extreme unction; (4) the last Holy Communion, that is, food for the journey *(viaticum)*; and (5) the watch with the dying person and commendation of the departing soul. Although not all Christians may embrace all of these practices today, they provided an extended ministry to the dying person that also provided comfort to the patient's family.

In terms of liturgical responsibilities, it is more than the administration of the sacrament of healing. Offering communion can represent not only Christ's presence at the bedside, but also that of the gathered *community*, bringing comfort to the ill and their families as an inclusion in the larger body of Christ.

Pray and Read Scripture

Over several years, there have been a series of articles and polls about faith and healing and especially about the role of prayer — even by doctors. A *CBS This Morning* poll shows that more than three-quarters of people pray for the health of others and believe that prayer may help speed or cause healing, as well as other spiritual and religious practices.

> Sixty-three percent [of those polled] say doctors should join their patients in prayer to ask for help in curing an illness, if patients request it. However, a majority do not believe prayer should become standard medical practice. And younger people are much less likely than older folks to think prayer should be a standard part of care.

	Yes	*No*
Does prayer help healing?	80%	14%
Should doctors pray if asked?	63%	25%
Should prayer be standard?	34%	55%

> Sixty percent of Americans say they pray at least once a day. Two thirds say they pray for their own health, and 82 percent say they pray for the health of others. But praying for people they don't know is less common. Protestants are more likely to pray for people they don't know than Catholics are. The importance of religion in people's daily lives does not entirely account for their belief in the healing power of prayer or for their support of doctors praying. Even 59 percent of those who do not see themselves as especially religious agree doctors should pray with patients, if asked. But opinion on whether prayer should become standard practice is linked to education. Less than a quarter of college graduates think prayer should become standard, while 60 percent of those with less than a high school diploma think it should. Fewer people believe in the power of healing touch. Twenty-eight percent of Americans believe some people can heal with their touch. Twenty-two percent of those who say religion is extremely important in their lives say they have been personally healed through touch.[23]

23. "CBS Poll: Prayer Can Heal," *CBS News online:* http://www.cbsnews.com/stories/1998/04/29/opinion/main8285.shtml (accessed May 26, 2009). This poll was conducted among a nationwide random sample of 825 adults, interviewed by telephone, April 20-22, 1998.

These polls, if we can trust them, seem to prove that people want God at the bedside. However, this does not seem to match our extreme medicalization of dying. There has always been a strong expectation that clergy pray and read Scripture at the bedside of ill persons. This is especially true for longtime church members who have witnessed pastors praying with their family members. People need the deep resources of inspiration and intake that prayer provides at all times, but especially when people are gravely ill. As William James is purported to have written, "We should always be open to a great deep where the tides rise." In the midst of crisis, we are too overwhelmed as we search for inner strength and resources. When we are healthy we believe that, if we work hard enough or will something single-mindedly enough, it will come to pass. However, when we are gravely ill, we can only say, "Spirit of God, descend upon my heart and give me peace."

Although the pastor is more often praying for others, sometimes the pastor is the patient. My friend Rev. Deborah Brincivalli shared her experience of breast cancer with her congregation, the First Presbyterian Church of Burlington, New Jersey:

> Diagnosed with breast cancer in January, Rev. Brincivalli was on the last leg of her treatments, and had been declared cancer free. A firm believer in "practice what you preach," the 50-year-old had shared the diagnosis and every step of her treatment with her congregation. "We are a loving and caring faith community that relies on each other when times are good and when they're bad," she said in February, three days before undergoing a lumpectomy on her left breast. Together, Rev. Brincivalli and her church family have faced this challenge. They helped her heal; she helped them to understand. . . . But no get-well cards, thank you. Individuals coping with a serious illness would prefer greeting cards with messages such as, "Thinking about you" or "Praying for you," not get-well cards, which "can be devastating," said the pastor.[24]

The Bible has no lack of clarity as to when we should pray: "Pray without ceasing" (1 Thess. 5:17). Prayer should always be on the lips of clergy members. Prayer is a deep, interior attitude — not just saying prayers, but a habitual and constant highland and background of great liv-

24. Linda Wondoloski, "Burlington Township Minister Aims to Defeat Breast Cancer," *Burlington County Times Outlook*, October 23, 2005, D1.

ing. Pastors need to be constantly sending up prayers to God, so that they are not merely tuning in to their own inner voice, but the voice of God.

Before pastors visit the dying, it is important for them to prepare by saturating *themselves* in prayer, not just praying with the other person. One perennial question seems to be: How specific should prayer be, especially regarding a particular illness and diagnosis? There is nothing wrong with asking God to respond to a particular need. In fact, the writer of the book of James seems to urge this: "Are any among you suffering? They should pray" (James 5:13). It may be easiest to pray in desperate circumstances, but too often a feeling of desperation may block out the energy that can be released. In Philippians 4:6, Paul reminds us: "Do not worry about anything, but in everything by prayer and supplication with thanksgiving let your requests be made known to God." Especially when our requests are answered, clergy members need to remind others to give God thanksgiving and praise.

The prayer tradition of Jesus and Paul was continued in the early church. The elders came not simply to visit but to pray for healing, and to likewise encourage others to pray for healing. Therefore, when it is possible, the pastor should not come alone but should be accompanied by elders. The knowledge that a group is praying with us can have a tremendous healing power. Even if there is no physical recovery, there is always a spiritual and emotional blessing.

Teaching people how to pray is also an important part of the pastor's role. Prayer should bring us into accord with God's will rather than bribing God or begging for favors. We should not bargain with God — "If you heal me, I'll believe" — but trust and obey God. Prayer is no magic rite, but it often equips us to face problems. It provides no substitute for penicillin or physical therapy, but it can bring a change of heart, which medicine alone cannot do. Medicine eliminates the physical barriers inhibiting the body's own healing process, while prayer opens up our soul to God's grace. Medicine differs from prayer in that medicine can be administered without acknowledging God's power.

For the dying person and his family, the results of prayer are paramount in their minds, but those results are often equated with a complete physical recovery. One of the most important results of prayer is that it provides an openness to God and an acceptance of life's challenges and a belief that God is in control. "What then are we to say about these things? If God is for us, who is against us?" (Rom. 8:31) The answers we look for are not always the ones that God gives; we must trust in God while realizing that we live in a broken world. We may not receive a physical healing, but we may receive the healing of broken relationships or a reconciliation with a family member before we die.

Reconciliation and forgiveness sometimes is the most important need for a sick person. The pastor can gently broach this subject when she senses such a need. This is not an attempt to extract some deathbed confession; rather, it is asking, for example, "Is there someone in your family you especially want to see or talk with at this time?" Receiving or offering forgiveness may be the greatest gift to the terminally ill person.

Reading familiar passages of Scripture can also be of great solace to the seriously ill or dying person.[25] I know one woman who was in the hospital in the 1960s, hanging between life and death, who said afterwards that the greatest comfort was her pastor's reading to her from the Psalms when she herself could not speak a word.

Wrestle with Questions of Theodicy and Eschatology

The dying are focused in particular ways on questions about last things and the ultimate destiny of life: heaven and hell, good and evil, and God. Theologians label these questions of theodicy and eschatology, and many unanswerable ones loom as we near the end of life:

- Why is life so fragile? What is the meaning of my life? How will people remember me?
- How do I deal with pain and suffering?
- Should I fight death or embrace it? How do I prepare for the moment of my death?
- Why am I suffering?
- What is a good death?
- What will the hour of my death be like?[26]

These are but a few of the questions that dying people may ask their pastor. The goal is not to have predetermined answers, but to listen and respond. After all, people go to the physician to find out what is wrong with their

25. Ideas for some of this material come from Abigail Rian Evans, *Healing Liturgies for the Seasons of Life* (Louisville: Westminster John Knox, 2004).
26. "The Art of Dying Well," *Hungryhearts* 15, no. 2 (Summer 2006): 4.

bodies. Should pastors not be equipped to wrestle with hurting people concerning their spiritual anguish?One of the pastor's roles is to set theodicy questions within a larger framework, that is, to move them from the particular to the universal, proclaiming the universal truth in a concrete situation. These truths include the following: that each person has infinite worth; that illness is not necessarily a sign of sin; that when sin does cause illness, forgiveness is available; that death, though an enemy, has been conquered and need no longer be feared.[27] Furthermore, the pastor can provide a prophetic function that calls to mind the spiritual resources and theological truths about health, healing, and healers. Pointing to God's love as reflected in all healing is crucial, and it may include showing how even medical diagnosis, prognosis, and therapy may have Christological dimensions.

Since the pastor, unlike the physician, does not usually deal in categories of sickness, she is freer to clarify the individual nature of the person's illness. Medical statistics that only one in a hundred persons dies of a particular illness is little comfort if you are in the 1 percent. The pastor is oriented toward restoration rather than diagnosis, so she can move away from a statistical approach to illness. She is concerned with affirming the person's sense of worth in the face of the limitations and sufferings that come with illness. This task involves listening as well as speaking. How does the pastor do this? By calling us to remember God's actions in our lives and the world.

Theology here is connected with the love of God, not the judgment of God. There is no need for the dying to fear. Yet fear or grief can still ambush us, and pastoral caregivers must be ready to comfort at just that moment. Often what appear to be meaningless conversations can be quite profound theologically, but they do not follow clear theological lines. There may not be closure or resolution of the patient's fears, so we need to trust God to bless the encounter between pastor and patient.[28] A pastor may share stories of others who have faced similar illnesses or losses, and those can be particularly helpful to the suffering patient.

27. Robert A. Lambourne, "The Healing Ministry of the Church," lecture notes presented at University of Birmingham, Birmingham, England (n.d.), p. 1.
28. Derek Murray, *Faith in Hospices: Spiritual Care and the End of Life* (Cleveland: Pilgrim Press, 2002), pp. 29-59.

Give Meaning and Hope to the Dying

Visiting the sick may not be easy: the hospital context is rather off-putting, and even those who ordinarily have a lot to say fall strangely silent.[29] It falls to the pastor to bring realistic hope and comfort to the suffering — both to patients and their loved ones. It is surprising to learn how many American Christians have lost a sense of God's grace.

> A majority of Americans (56%), with most describing themselves as Christians, say that when they think about their death, they worry "a great deal" or "somewhat" that they will "not be forgiven by God." Half of all interviewees (51%) worry about dying when they are removed or cut off from God or a higher power. Such findings, from a 1998 Gallup Institute survey conducted for the Nathan Cummings Foundation and the Fetzer Institute ("Spiritual Beliefs and the Dying Process"), raise the question of whether Christians in the U.S. have an understanding of the Christian meaning of "grace," and suggest the need for more effective biblical teaching in Christian churches in this country.[30]

People can suffer almost anything if there is meaning attached to it, or they can at least feel that their life has meaning. Illness challenges that sense of meaning and dissipates hope. The pastor/chaplain may be the very one to rekindle meaning and hope in important ways. How precisely can he do this? Through conversations with the patients about what they value, and assuring them that they are of value. The frail elderly especially feel that they no longer have a contribution to make. Members of their family no longer seem to ask for their advice or share their secrets; often they talk *about* the elderly rather than *to* them. Part of pastoral care is educating family members on how to relate to their mother, sister, or spouse as they would when they were well — that is, avoiding paternalism and exclusion, since both extremes are equally dehumanizing.

Providing meaning and hope is a theme in St. Paul's writings, especially Romans 5. Here we sense the movement from endurance to character to hope, each one building on the other. In other words, hope is honed on

---

29. David Willows and John Swinton, eds., *Spiritual Dimensions of Pastoral Care: Practical Theology in a Multi-Disciplinary Context* (London: Jessica Kingsley Publishers, 2000), pp. 81-89.

30. "Have Christians Lost a Sense of God's Grace?" *Emerging Trends* 21, no. 1, Princeton Religion Research Center (Jan. 1998): unnumbered page.

the crucible of living, on the confronting of crises. Norman Cousins wrote: "Death is not the ultimate tragedy of life. The ultimate tragedy is depersonalization — dying in an alien and sterile area, separated from the spiritual nourishment that comes from being able to reach out to a loving hand."[31]

The pastor may be the conveyor of the symbols of hope and healing, relating to people as persons first, not simply as patients. They may bring the message that, despite our fragility, despite our being severely compromised in the face of illness, despite our brokenness, there is hope. This is the hope I highlighted earlier, in the chapter on pain and suffering. Hope has been scientifically proven to contribute significantly to the healing of people — not only from mental or spiritual illness, but also from physical illness.[32] This is not a hope built on ephemeral items; it is a hope that is grounded in the living God, the God who is Lord, Creator, and Savior.

Much has been written about the power of a positive outlook in one's recovery. Perhaps this is a placebo effect: that is, if you think you are going to get better, you probably have a chance of getting better. However, here I am referring to something slightly different. It is the presence of hope that is built on the belief that life has meaning beyond what is happening right now. The pastor may help foster that sense of hope in the dying person and his family.

In the medical center setting, when people are catastrophically ill, hope is rarely highlighted. This does not mean that the pastor simply says, "Well, you're going to get better. We're going to pray and everything is going to be just fine." Rather it is a hope grounded in the fact that God is in control.

As people face sickness and struggle to regain some wholeness, they are challenged to accept and overcome the undeniable fact of their fragility. Symbols of healing may involve sustenance in the face of pain and suffering: assisting people to live in the midst of their brokenness. Certain questions emerge: What is the ultimate concern? Where does one stand amidst the ambiguities of suffering? What does one believe about health and disease?

There are three possible answers. One is that the ultimate truth lies in despair and disintegration; there is no point in using healing resources. From this perspective, there is no sense in struggling against disease be-

31. Norman Cousins, *Anatomy of an Illness* (New York: Norton, 1979), p. 133.

32. Dale A. Matthews and Donna M. Saunders, *The Faith Factor: An Annotated Bibliography of Clinical Research on Spiritual Subjects*, vol. 4: "Prevention and Treatment of Illness, Addictions, and Delinquency," presented to the John Templeton Foundation (Rockville, MD: National Institute for Healthcare Research, 1997).

cause treatment is wrong and to be avoided. This may sound stark, but it is the logical outcome of promoting only the negative side of life. One sees it sometimes in patients who refuse useful therapy. Of course, refusal of treatment may be for other reasons, including a physician's assessment that further treatment is futile.

On the opposite side is the view that, although disease is real, the ultimate truth about the relationship between human nature and disease is that one must struggle against it. This is seen in the natural attempts to reject disease by the human body in its development of antibodies, and in the care and concern of the medical, nursing, and allied health professionals. Some medical personnel can also see when it is time to stop fighting. The final possibility is a middle-of-the-road, noncommittal path. Here disease and healing are equally important or unimportant. An attitude of indifference prevails.[33]

One thing that is absolutely certain is that conveying hope to the dying should not consist of platitudes or sermons. Often what people long for is ordinary conversation, talk where there is no sense of a religious agenda at work. However, astute clergy know how to interject a few key words that can lead to deeper conversations about hopelessness, fear, and so on. For example, a pastor may mention the situation of another person (without naming her) who is suffering, which can open the floodgates of sadness and anxiety of the person being visited.

It is noteworthy that young children who are dying are often more honest about their hopes and fears. Their ability to talk freely depends on caring staff members who let them know that they can be frank in their fears, while the staff at the same time provides a sense of realistic hope. For example, a boy with cystic fibrosis actually chose to leave home and live in a care home because he felt freer with the staff, not his parents, to explore his hopes and fears about death.[34]

Provide Spiritual Assessment and Care

Another form of ministry to the dying that the pastor can provide is spiritual assessment and care. The pastor is uniquely called for this responsibility; but she may need additional training to maximize her effectiveness.

33. Melvyn Thompson, *Cancer and the God of Love* (London: SCM Press, 1976), p. 73.
34. Francis Dominica, "The Terminally Ill Pediatric Patient," in *Health Care and Spirituality,* ed. Richard Gilbert (Amityville, NY: Baywood, 2002), p. 260.

Pastors may counsel people where spiritual roadblocks to healing may exist. In addition, they may put people in touch with their own inner resources for healing, opening them to God's power of healing and integrating them into a support and service community. The pastor, as the physician, must be totally trustworthy, entering into a covenant relationship similar to that of the physician. Trustworthiness, as well as constancy, is part of the counseling ministry.

Spiritual Care We often refer to spiritual care, but it cannot adequately be given without spiritual assessment. Spiritual care is a term that is much bandied about, but it is fast becoming a term devoid of meaning. It should include recognizing spiritual needs and a range of conditions from spiritual distress to disintegration. It is Christ, not the pastor, who leads us to a deeper spirituality.[35]

TYPES OF SPIRITUAL CARE Some of those who are dying are in the midst of a profound spiritual crisis.

> Caplan defines crisis as the period of "psychological upset which occurs as a person wrestles with problems which are temporarily beyond his capacity." The crisis of brain injury may unsettle previously held concepts about the meaning and purpose of life; deep spiritual distress and questioning may occur. The individual and family may ask profound theological questions of themselves and others, such as: Where is God now? Is there a God? Did God do this or let this happen? Why didn't God protect me? Am I so bad that I deserve this punishment? Some individuals and families apply premorbid religious conviction to this crisis with ease and confidence. Others may find their faith shattered, or they cling tenaciously to closely circumscribed life views. Whatever the coping mechanisms, these families are dealing with a crisis, "a devastating, absorbing experience which demands mobilization and utilization of all available resources."[36]

Offering spiritual care to a dying person can be a challenge. A patient should be encouraged to express what kind of spiritual care would be most

---

35. Kenneth Leech, *Spirituality and Pastoral Care* (Cambridge, MA: Cowley Publications, 1989), p. 5.

36. Barbara Frye and Lena Long, "Spiritual Counseling Approaches Following Brain-Injury," *Rehabilitative Nursing* 10, no. 6 (Nov.-Dec. 1985): 14.

helpful. For some it may be reading the Psalms or Rumi's poetry; for others, it is drawing pictures or praying.[37] Science, religion, and art all use symbols, and symbols may be the best way of understanding spirituality. Metaphors are used for experiences and give them shape. There are eight metaphors that Stanworth suggests: temporality, marginality, luminality, control, letting go, hero, mother, and stranger.[38]

SETTING OF SPIRITUAL CARE   One of the challenges in spiritual care is where it takes place. For example, in the hospital, where medicalization and bureaucracy hold sway, time for careful spiritual care is difficult to find. Members of the clergy are seldom viewed as part of the health team, and they are often pushed out of the room to make way for the doctor or nurse. Even those who recognize the importance of the clergy view their role as secondary. The real question for the clergy may be how they offer spiritual care throughout a person's life so that she will be prepared at the end of her life. However, spiritual care can also take place in informal or unexpected places.

STORIES OF EFFECTIVE SPIRITUAL CARE   John Nyberg, a Protestant chaplain, tells of working with a lapsed Roman Catholic patient who said she had no interest in spiritual or religious matters. In fact, she told him that there was no reason for him to visit anymore. He suggested that a Catholic sister, a chaplain, and a trainee begin to visit her, and she completely changed, opening up again to her Roman Catholic faith. At the end she wanted to be buried by the church. The point is that religion, even in its initially faintest form, can lead to spiritual reflection. Instead of avoiding discussions of religion, pastors should encourage patients to explore these questions, which may be just beneath the surface anyway.[39]

Furthermore, spiritual care is not reduced to the ministrations of clergy; it can be given by anyone who listens to the sick person's story and provides spiritual insight. Joyce Hutchinson's true story about her encounter as a lay volunteer with a dying homeless man illustrates this point.

Joyce met Henry while giving him chemotherapy for an hour every day. He was a man in his sixties who had lost his family and home to alcohol and now, full of regret, was nearing the end of his life. As he was dying,

37. DuBose, "Preparing for Death," pp. 3-4.
38. Rachel Stanworth, *Recognizing Spiritual Needs in People Who Are Dying* (New York: Oxford University Press, 2004), p. 100.
39. Dominica, "The Terminally Ill Pediatric Patient," p. 275.

Henry asked for a bottle of whiskey, and Joyce gave it to him so that he would not have to face alcohol withdrawal DTs (delirium tremens) along with everything else. Even though he scarcely had any money, he offered to pay her, which was very important to him. Instead, Joyce asked that he repay her with a favor. She asked that, when he got to heaven, Henry would say "hi" to her brother. He assured her that he would. Establishing this connection was certainly the beginning of pastoral care, because it is so important to provide some kind of common ground. Spiritual care is not a technique but a relationship.

Henry was eventually transferred to a nursing home because, medically speaking, there was nothing more to be done for him. Joyce visited him those last three days of his life, and he entrusted to her the distribution of his last possessions. With her help he outlined the following in a will: his overcoat was to go to a man in the rooming house, the few canned goods to the lady down the hall, and his last $15 was to be divided evenly among his three friends, including Joyce. His dying words were, "What's his name?" Joyce told him that her brother's name was Joe, and she was sure that he said hello to Joe in heaven.[40]

HARMFUL SPIRITUAL CARE   Unfortunately, there is also harmful spiritual care and religionless spirituality. The latter may be so devoid of content that it is really not much good and has faint chance of putting anyone in touch with the transcendent. "Harmful" spiritual care may consist of demanding deathbed conversions with threats of hellfire and damnation, or even requiring the signing of faith statements, the renouncing of Satan, or requiring rebaptisms.

Spiritual Assessment   Spiritual assessment is more quantitative, a science, whereas spiritual care is closer to an art. I am not suggesting that a formal assessment is always needed before spiritual care can be given. However, if we do assessments, we need to apply some rigor. One of the problems with spiritual assessment and care is a lack of clarity about the meaning of "spiritual" and "spirituality." The following discussion may seem a bit too clinical or analytical, but we should apply the same rigor here that we apply to the practice of medicine.

There are many definitions of religion and spirituality. Peter Speck offers some helpful ones:

40. Joyce Hutchinson, "What's His Name?" *Faith at Work* (Summer 2001): 14-15.

Spiritual relates to a concern with ultimate issues and is often seen as a search for meaning, and echoes Frankl's words, "Man is not destroyed by suffering, he is destroyed by suffering without meaning."

The spiritual issues may be expressed in questions such as, "Why should this happen to me? Why now? What have I done to deserve this — it doesn't seem fair. . . ." These questions are more spiritual than medical and may be directed at anyone who is nearby. When a person is trying to find some meaning within a particular experience they will look in many different directions, starting with the things which have helped them make sense in the past. It may be that the person has developed a philosophy of life which has always been able to give them the answers they searched for, and thus enabled them to cope. This philosophical approach may have had nothing to do with religion — in either its folk or its orthodox form. Others may express a belief in God which has never found expression and practice within an orthodox religion; but to which they look to "bring me through." The arrival of a clergyman may be seen as a God-given opportunity to vent one's wrath or to seek answers to these questions. The questions (and the ambivalence they may reflect) may not be expressed if the right relationship of trust has not been developed since "one should always be polite to vicars."

Religious relates more to the need to put into practice one's usual expression of spirituality. This may be expressed as the need to see a priest, to attend chapel, have time to meditate, receive the sacraments, etc.[41]

There are pros and cons to asking strictly religious questions, such as church affiliation, religious practices, and beliefs, which will overlook the deeper spiritual questions. Intake forms often include questions such as "What is your religion?" and "Do you want to see a chaplain?" This may miss perceiving the deeper fears and spiritual crises through which the patient is passing. The concern is that the chaplain, when simply visiting, may only address the religious issues rather than forming a deeper relationship that intersects with the existential issues. The spiritual dimension involves issues of self-esteem, purpose, and a set of goals and objectives in life. These can provide the necessary power and energy to bring change to a person's life specifically in treatment, recovery, and long-term health.

41. Viktor E. Frankl, *Man's Search for Meaning* (London: Hodder and Stoughton, 1987), pp. 30-31.

ELEMENTS OF SPIRITUAL ASSESSMENT   As a member of the healing team, the pastor/chaplain has special responsibilities for doing spiritual assessment, which can enhance the spiritual care given. The spiritual history is the foundational element of the spiritual assessment. In most cases, the chaplain will need to ask specific questions of a spiritual nature, respectfully listening to the person's description of his spiritual experiences, including the assessment of the developmental, psychodynamic, and therapeutic implications of the history presented. This approach is similar to the clinician's careful, nuanced listening for psychodynamic and relationship problems in her client's life. The inclusion of the spiritual elements of a person's earlier life is part of the larger goal of understanding the current role that spiritual factors may play in the onset — and possible amelioration — of the illness when physical healing is no longer possible, opening the door to spiritual healing.

This in-depth spiritual assessment should include the role of religion during the developmental years; the involvement in a religious community (in the past and present); the person's concept of God and the role of prayer and meditation in his or her life; specific values and beliefs held by the patient; and rituals specific to the patient's religious/spiritual tradition. Sometimes, when the person is too sick to talk, the pastor will depend on family members for this information. Because the terminally ill person is fighting for his life, physical needs are at the forefront; but for some, spiritual survival is even more important.

The chaplain should determine who was instrumental in teaching the patient about spirituality, and determine the nature of the patient's relationship with these individuals. In addition, does the patient currently see himself as religious/spiritual? This approach can help determine whether religion during the developmental years was helpful, harmful, or neutral. The chaplain should also investigate whether the individual is currently receiving support from a religious community, and whether there have been changes in his relationship to it.

One of the fundamental questions regarding belief is: "Do you believe in God?" and/or "How would you describe God and your relationship to God?" For the religious person, information gained from this line of inquiry may be as relevant as the person's views regarding his or her parents. An assessment of the role of prayer and devotional practices is also pertinent. For the religious person, a more extensive conversation about his or her beliefs is important because each tradition has values and beliefs that adherents perceive as essential. The meaning of illness and suffering, the moral and virtuous life, the healthy family, and sources of spiritual authority (e.g., Scripture, religious teachings, and doctrinal tenets) may all be relevant for assessment. Such core beliefs can powerfully determine how an individual behaves; if the pastor/chaplain does not inquire about them, it may undermine an entire treatment process.

Stemming from the patient's beliefs, there may be certain rituals and spiritual practices that are important. These may be part of childhood practices continued to adulthood, or they may be more recently acquired aspects of the person's life. Differences between parents and children — and between spouses — regarding the importance of participating in religious rituals, as well as other aspects of belief, should be assessed.

Spiritual Diagnostic Categories   An increasing commitment to provide wholistic care has encouraged diverse approaches to the conceptualization and understanding of spirituality. Spiritual assessment involves looking behind the surface questions or problems and operating from a perspective that counts the transcendent as important. As we attempt to chart spiritual health and illness, we need to begin a more specific analysis. I propose three definitions (or diagnoses) that may be helpful in assessing spiritual health: *spiritual well-being, spiritual needs,* and *spiritual illness.* An orientation to the definitions, characteristics, and indicators of these diagnoses allow for more effective assessments and interventions.

SPIRITUAL WELL-BEING   Spiritual well-being is not a state, but it is indicative of the presence of spiritual health in the person. Therefore, spiritual well-being is identified as behavioral expressions of spiritual health. As defined by the National Interfaith Coalition on Aging (NICA), spiritual health is "the affirmation of life in a relationship with God, self, community, and environment which nurtures and celebrates wholeness." Indicators include: a sense of peace, serenity, and harmony within one's person; reverence for life and a sense of purpose for one's life; acceptance of life's experiences and one's relationships as being meaningful and enriching.

SPIRITUAL NEEDS   Adam Stevenson says, "Understanding human needs is half the job of meeting them." Spiritual needs have been described as any factors necessary to establish and/or maintain a person's dynamic personal relationship with God (as defined by that individual) and out of that relationship to experience forgiveness, love, hope, trust, meaning, and purpose in life. Spiritual need is sometimes recognized, felt, and expressed by the in-

dividual, and sometimes it is not. A patient does not always recognize everything that is essential to her recovery, healing, or acceptance of death;
similarly, the patient does not always recognize and express her spiritual
needs. Being heard and understood is at the heart of spiritual need.

There are also the influences of family and other wider relationships
that affect a person's emotional development, influencing her ability to enter
into other relationships. Bonding in the early years is a particularly important event in forming the capacity of love, trust, and the ability to communicate effectively with others. As life unfolds for each person, there is a unique
and cumulative effect from the range of experiences she enters into — some
good and happy, others traumatic and distressing. Success or failure in marriage, bereavement or loss of any kind, and happy or unhappy family life are
all experiences that contribute to an individual's perspective on life and her
responses to people, events, and (especially) catastrophic illness. The nature
of support given during a period of bereavement or trauma can influence receptivity and the way one approaches adversity. Influences such as war, economic depression, social deprivation, and other historical or social happen-
ings may have deep effects on attitudes and one's outlook on life.

Abraham Maslow's hierarchy of human needs, which embraces
physiological needs, needs of safety, love and belonging, self-esteem, recognition, and self-actualization, is often applied in this area.[42] All of these
needs are exacerbated for the person who is in the midst of dying. Most
chaplains are familiar with this model. It allows the patient to set personal
goals on a level that can be achieved within her potential capacity, rather
than attempting to reach goals set by someone else. Another helpful approach is found in Jonathan Bradshaw's "Taxonomy of Social Need."[43]
Bradshaw bases his classification on criteria for recognition of need. He
uses four definitions: normative, felt, expressed, and comparative needs. A
normative definition of needs is set by a professional, and individuals who
fall short of having such needs met are defined as "in need." This approach
is liable to value judgments. An approach that is currently more acceptable
involves "consumer participation," and includes "felt need," which may, of
course, be similar to "wants." Therefore, felt need alone is not an adequate
indicator to aid our understanding.

Spiritual needs differ from one person to another, and thus individ-

42. Abraham H. Maslow, *Motivations and Personality* (New York: Harper, 1954).
43. Jonathan R. Bradshaw, "The Concept of Social Need," *New Society* 30 (Mar. 1972):
640-43.

ual expression and satisfaction of those needs varies. This may be through corporate worship within one's own faith or individual spiritual practices and disciplines. Whatever the need, it is important for chaplains to understand the true nature of the concept of spirituality and to make the widest kind of provision for addressing individual preferences and needs.[44] Of course, the pastor should accept the patient's spiritual needs as they are stated, rather than contradicting them.

CHARTING SPIRITUAL NEEDS   In summary, spiritual needs include lack of a healthy and loving relationship with God or a transcendent power; lack of healthy self-love; lack of the ability to give love to and receive love from others; lack of trust; lack of meaning and purpose in life. In order to determine spiritual needs, the chaplain/pastor should note the following areas in patients' lives:

- Their concept or view of themselves
- Their perception of what is happening to them
- Their hopes, fears, and natural support mechanisms
- Their support from family and friends
- Their relationships within the family
- Their own views and beliefs with respect to their situation
- Their stated religion or commitment to religious practice
- Their cultural background
- Their life experience
- Their natural defense and coping mechanisms
- Their openness and receptivity to help
- Their general state of health
- Their mental and emotional well-being.[45]

When we examine these areas, we need to ask both direct and indirect questions to determine real needs and not to lead the patient into predetermined, "acceptable" answers. In some cases the need for help may be hard to uncover because of people's defense mechanisms. The assurance of confidentiality and the development of trust and empathy will go a long way toward assuring honesty.

---

44. David J. Stoter, *Spiritual Aspects of Health Care* (London: Mosby International, 1995), pp. 5-7.
45. Stoter, *Spiritual Aspects,* p. 43.

DIAGNOSIS OF SPIRITUAL ILLNESS   If spiritual needs go unfilled, they may lead to spiritual illness. The diagnosis of spiritual illness may be either direct or indirect; assessment instruments are not always the best way to determine spiritual issues. Once we understand spiritual needs, we can recognize spiritual illness. With terminally ill patients, the irony is that the pastor may be so focused on their physical illness that she may neglect their possible spiritual illness. The following are five possible levels of spiritual illness: dismay, disillusionment, distress, despair, and disintegration.[46]

Spiritual dismay is the earliest stage of spiritual illness. It is characterized by fear or discouragement, apprehensiveness or alarm. A person confronts a problem or situation that he does not know how to solve, for example, a diagnosis of inoperable brain cancer. He has continuous worry about life and a tendency to expect bad outcomes. The dismay shows the earliest stages of anxiety, the fear of the unknown.

Spiritual disillusionment stems primarily from the loss of familiar constructs that give meaning to life's events and the transcendent elements of life. It most often appears when one's childhood faith cannot hold up to the realities of life. Often the theodicy question is behind this state, for example, "Why would a good God let my mother die in the prime of life?" The person may recognize the essential unfairness of life but not accept it. Disillusionment may manifest itself in a pessimistic or jaded view of life and may also occur from lost opportunities, unremitting stress, or minor tragedies.

Spiritual distress results from a diminishing of hope, meaning, and purpose in life: the feeling that life no longer matters, that no one cares or loves me, and that God is not caring for me. Victor Frankl has coupled this loss of meaning with the failure to survive, and stories about holocaust victims abound in this area. Spiritual distress has an edge of bitterness and sometimes fatalism. It is often coupled with a sense of betrayal, and it may be the result of a series of broken promises, unfulfilled dreams, or a sense of abandonment. It is also characterized by a desire to deny the psychic pain or blot it out.

Spiritual distress touches on the human spirit. It is a disruption in the life principle that fills a person's entire being and that integrates and transcends one's mere physical existence. This distress can result from a separation from a person's religious or cultural ties or a challenged belief and

---

46. I developed these categories based on conversations with Donald E. Capps at Princeton Theological Seminary (May 26, 2001).

value system. The characteristics of such distress can include: concern about the meaning of life and death and/or a belief system; anger toward God; verbalized conflict about beliefs; questions about the moral and ethical implications of a therapeutic regimen; description of nightmares or sleep disturbances; the assumption that illness is a punishment; altering behaviors or moods, evidenced by anger, crying, withdrawal, preoccupation, anxiety, hostility, and so forth.[47] Identifying spiritual distress is essential for developing a treatment and care plan for the seriously ill person. The first step of this plan is helping that person develop ways of critical self-care.

The change from spiritual distress to *spiritual despair* is usually marked by a more sustained state of the various markers under distress. The episodes of hopelessness become a chronic state that is often accompanied by clinical depression (this is not to suggest that spiritual despair necessarily causes or is equal to depression, but it may accompany it). A kind of lethargy toward everything and a loss of direction and purpose often exist. "If I am dying, how can anything matter" may be the thought process, which, of course, leads some to complete withdrawal, or even suicide.

Spiritual disintegration is parallel in the mental health area to a complete breakdown. All familiar constructs that give life direction and purpose are gone. God is absent, or worse, God is seen as an angry, punishing parent. Religious beliefs and practices are nonexistent, and life is characterized by generalized angst. Values are characterized by health-defeating and evil intentions and a total disregard for others. We note this in the dying person who hates and curses all family and friends, screaming obscenities at everyone within earshot.

CHARTING STAGES OF SPIRITUAL RECOVERY   How to move from spiritual disintegration to spiritual well-being is hard to analyze and even harder to accomplish. However, when someone has no more hope of physical recovery, spiritual restoration is still available. The following are some suggested stages that may be observed as the person moves from spiritual illness to spiritual well-being.

- Recognition of personal spiritual illness
- Acceptance of the importance of a spiritual dimension in life

---

47. This is a nurse's definition, developed from a guide by the North American Nursing Association: R. S. Flesner, "Development of a Measure to Assess Spiritual Distress in the Responsive Adult" (unpublished master's thesis, Marquette University, 1982).

- Rediscovery of a feeling of self-worth
- General sense of well-being, even in spite of illness
- Belief in a loving God (can one be spiritually well and deny God's existence?)
- Restoration of a sense that life, no matter how short, still has purpose
- Hope in God's future promise
- Restoration of broken relationships

At the end of our lives, spiritual wholeness may be what we most need as we move toward being fully in God's presence. In this chapter I have attempted to describe the importance of the pastor's ministry to the dying and their families. This is a holy calling because clergy, in a variety of ways, come to the bedside and give testimony to God, who is already present at the bedside. However, it is important, as I have suggested, for the pastor to work with other people of faith in this ministry. This is not a solo enterprise. Our next chapter will present one such model that can enrich the ministry to the dying.

11. Ministry to the Dying and Their Families: Faith Community Nurse and Pastor in Partnership

Watch Thou, Dear Lord

Watch thou, dear Lord,
with those who wake, or watch, or weep tonight,
and give thine angels charge over those who sleep.
Tend thy sick ones, Lord Christ.
Rest thy weary ones.
Bless thy dying ones.
Soothe thy suffering ones.
Pity thine afflicted ones.
Shield thy joyous ones.
And all, for thy love's sake.
Amen.

Saint Augustine (354-430)

Pastor/Chaplain and Faith Community Nurse as Brokers

As I observed earlier in this book, with the medicalization and depersonalization of end-of-life care, there is a need to empower the patient, give her a voice, and then broker the sometimes competing roles of health care professionals, family, and the patient. I am confident that this can be done effectively by the pastor and faith community nurse. In today's era of specialization, it is not easy to determine the best models for cooperation of professionals in end-of-life care. It is a key ingredient of collaborative models that the person be at the center; if she is no longer able to speak, a trusted person can express her wishes.[1] Of course, the latter role requires that that designee be acquainted with the person. In developing a general collaborative model in *Redeeming Marketplace Medicine,* I noted that the dying person needs to take the central role, which is not always easy for someone who is compromised by a serious and debilitating illness. However, through an advance directive, people are able to express their wishes when they are no longer competent, and it behooves the health care professionals to meticulously follow those directions. The family is usually the entity that assures that the sick person will be heard. However, family members may need to be supported by the pastor and the faith community nurse (FCN), because some are hesitant to question or challenge the health care providers. Of course, sometimes the family may ignore the ill person's wishes, so again the FCN and pastor may need to step in where possible.

The tendency of the dominant medical model is to divide up the person among specialists: social worker, doctor, nurse, chaplain, and so forth — with a certain hierarchy of command. A collaboration of healers will not happen unless someone is responsible for making that a reality. What is clear is that integration is needed in the midst of a growing specialized and dehumanized medical system and the dependency role of a "patient." The role of the nurse has always been crucial to providing wholistic care. Although bedside care must be done or supervised by a registered nurse, some tasks may be delegated. However, what can be delegated and to whom is regulated by state statute. In-hospital bedside care is primarily provided by registered nurses, who are assisted by licensed practical nurses. Nurses' aides are restricted in what they are allowed to do; but from the sick person's point of view, nurses' aides may be the ones whom they see the most. Unfortunately, nurses' aides are generally poorly paid and have minimal training. In addition, with the bureaucratization and demands of the current health care system, nurses' time is often consumed by administrative tasks and treatments rather than meeting the physical, spiritual, and psychological needs of the person.

A partnership of FCN and pastor can help fill the gaps of our current system and assure the best wholistic care possible in the last season of life. How do we define "the best care"? This is relative to the person's values and health needs. Health needs are different from medical ones, and though

---

1. Generally, we prefer to use the word "person" rather than "patient," since the latter denotes a passive role and dehumanizes, as Ramsey has so eloquently written in *Patient as Person.* Occasionally, in the medical setting, "patient" will be used.

the two may overlap, they are not identical. For example, massage, silence, therapeutic touch, prayer, reading, and music may contribute to one's health without being medically indicated. It is my hope that the pastor and FCN may be more in touch with these broader needs and be advocates for their inclusion. This brokering role requires a sensitivity to and awareness of who the person is, which may not be available to other health care professionals. The professionals' relationship to the patient is more closely circumscribed by predetermined expectations and procedures that are part of their job description — for example, replacing defective valves, delivering radiation treatments, performing brain biopsies, and so on.

The strength of the FCN is that, as an RN, she has been educated to help the person experience a "good death." The book of the official North American Nursing Diagnosis Association (NANDA), *Nursing Diagnoses, Definitions and Classification, 2009-2011,* has three diagnoses related to spirituality, three related to religiosity, and many others that relate to assisting a person as he moves through the process of a terminal illness. The nurses who care for the person before, during, and after medical procedures can address his spiritual, emotional, physiological, and educational needs and concerns. These nurses are aware of the healing that is supported by a variety of means and can work with the patient and his support system (family, friends, FCN, clergy) to meet their needs by way of alternative approaches.[2]

Because both FCNs and pastors have a more wholistic perspective on health and sickness and how to address the whole person, they are natural partners in the ministry with the dying. Grave illness separates us from all that is familiar and draws us closer to God, who calls us into being and back to God's full presence at the end of our life. Words of God's continual love and care for us in the midst of dying need to be declared. While mem-

---

2. Information provided by Peggy Matteson, professor and chair of the department of nursing, Salve Regina University, Newport, Rhode Island. She was chair of the task force for the ANA and HMA assigned to do the revisions of the *Scope and Standards.* She served on national nursing committees; was on a state Board of Registration and Nursing Education; was head of a B.S. Nursing Education Program, and held many positions with HMA. She is a practicing FCN who has ministerial standing within her denomination. Additional information for this chapter came from the Health Ministries Association (HMA) and the American Nurses Association (ANA), *Faith Community Nursing: Scope and Standards of Practice,* 2005. NANDA International, *Nursing Diagnoses, Definitions and Classification, 2009-2011,* 2nd ed. (Hoboken: Wiley-Blackwell, 2008). These standards are issued periodically for FCNs.

bers of religious groups and communities might be inclined to call on their respective clergy members in moments such as these, the medical establishment sometimes underestimates the importance of clergy. The basis for cooperation among pastor, physician, nurse, and social worker is that they are agents of God, who is the source of all healing. In the past, a faith/science dichotomy and a mind/body dualism have marked our age, and this has made cooperation more difficult. Now, however, we live in a post-Newtonian era that accepts a more integrated approach to health care, and pastors are learning how to translate spiritual resources into meaningful language and hard data.

David B. Larson, the now-deceased founder of the International Institute of Healthcare Research (IIHR), devoted much of his research to emphasizing the importance of cooperation among all health care professionals. His scientific studies about religion and health were a wake-up call to health care professionals. The IIHR cooperated with other research centers to determine the role of clergy in relation to the practice of psychology, surveying eight leading psychology journals from 1991 to 1994. Each article was reviewed to see if it contained statistics that examined "the role or use of religious professionals." The reviewers found that of the over 2,400 studies examined, only four [0.2%] assessed the role of the clergy in mental health.[3] This fact seems surprising when one considers that 25 percent of people who sought treatment for mental disorders did so from a clergy member, which is a higher percentage than those who consulted psychiatrists or general medical doctors (about 16 percent).[4] Beginning in 1996, the John Templeton Foundation awarded grants to psychiatric residency programs in the United States to address spiritual and religious issues in their formal training. They also provided a large part of the funding for the IIHR, which, unfortunately, no longer exists (since David Larson's death).

Precisely in end-of-life care can pastors help other health care professionals who may be wrestling with their own fear of death or guilt at losing a patient. The pastor needs to be sensitive and knowledgeable about the ethical dilemmas and other problems that surround those who are caring for someone who is seriously ill.

3. A. J. Weaver et al., "What Do Psychologists Know about Working with the Clergy? An Analysis of Eight APA Journals: 1991-1994," *Professional Psychology: Research and Practice* 28, no. 5 (1997): 471-74.

4. Philip Wang, Patricia Berglad, and Ronald C. Kessler, "Patterns and Correlates of Contacting Clergy for Mental Disorders in the United States," *Health Services Research* 38, no. 2 (April 2003): 647-73.

A collaborative style of the pastor may be further enhanced when there is an FCN on the church staff. The FCN provides a new model for bridge-building between the pastor/priest/rabbi and the physician, that is, between religion and medicine. I have been recommending that an FCN be on each congregation's staff to strengthen and enhance the role of the pastor for end-of-life care.

The History and Role of the Parish Nurse/
Faith Community Nurse

Having examined the concept of a partnership between clergy and the FCN, we must now understand a little more about the development of Faith Community Nursing from its early roots in parish nursing to its current status as a specialized nursing practice role.

"Faith community nursing is the specialized practice of professional nursing that focuses on the intentional care of the spirit as part of the process of promoting wholistic health and preventing or minimizing illness in a faith community."[5] An FCN is a licensed registered professional nurse who generally works on the staff of a local church or hospital related to that congregation. This is one of the newest nursing specialties, and clergy members can work as partners with FCNs to meet the health-related needs of faith-community members. With a focus on spiritual health, the FCN primarily uses the interventions of education, counseling, advocacy, referral, resources available to the faith community, and training and supervising volunteers. In addition, the FCN collaborates with nursing colleagues to have them provide the traditional services of nursing care. When another registered nurse is unavailable and an urgent need is present, the FCN, as a registered nurse, is responsible for both general and specialty nursing care.

The assumptions of nurses working in this specialty are: (1) health and illness are human experiences; (2) health is the integration of the spiritual, physical, psychological, and social human functions, promoting a sense of harmony with self, others, the environment, and a higher power; (3) a person can experience health even in the presence of disease or injury; (4) the presence of illness does not preclude health, nor does optimal health preclude illness; and (5) healing is the process of integrating the

---

5. Information in the next two paragraphs provided by Peggy Matteson (July 2009).

body, mind, and spirit to create wholeness, health, and a sense of well-being, even when the patient's illness is not cured.

History of the Parish Nurse Movement

Although Granger Westberg is the founder of the modern parish nursing movement in the United States, the streams feeding into this movement are diverse. The health care activities of the early Christian church, as well as the European models of parish nursing, such as the nineteenth-century German Christian Deaconesses (*Gemeindeschwestern*), provide the historical roots for faith community nursing. The deacons and deaconesses of the early church cared for the sick in their homes as one of the primary ministries of the church. Through the centuries men and women have felt that their calling to minister to the infirm is a vocation from God. St. Vincent de Paul, the great minister to the sick in seventeenth-century France, established societies of women of the church who banded themselves together with some simple rules to tend the sick and the poor of the immediate neighborhood. They called themselves the "servants of the poor."

These women can surely be considered forebears of contemporary parish nurses. In the mid-twentieth century, a nurse named Cummings described her role as a parish health counselor in a parish of about 3,500 families, which was believed to be the first program of its kind in the United States. It focused on the care of the chronically ill elders in the parish, education for home care of the ill, referral to community agencies, volunteer services, and home visitation.[6] "Many orders of women religious throughout the world extended their ministry into the broad community: Sisters of Mercy, Sisters of Saint Francis, Sisters of the Holy Cross, just to name a few."[7]

The idea for the Evangelical Deaconess Society began in the 1880s, when an evangelical pastor went to give communion to a critically ill parishioner and found her being cared for in her home by a Roman Catholic nun because the woman was too poor to get help from anyone else. This pastor became concerned about the situation. Recognizing the need for such care, he asked the St. Louis Evangelical Pastors' Association if they

---

6. Mary Elizabeth O'Brien, *Spirituality in Nursing*, 3rd ed. (Boston: Jones and Bartlett, 2007), pp. 336-37.
7. Information provided by Sharon Stanton (July 2009).

would institute a program to train the young women of their churches to care for the poor and the sick, as had the deaconess sisters of Germany. At an organizational meeting several months later, seventy people formed a new organization whose purpose was twofold: (1) to nurse the sick and exercise care for the poor and aged; and (2) to found and support a deaconess home where deaconesses could be educated and trained. A board of directors was elected, consisting of four pastors, four laymen, and four laywomen, as stipulated in the Articles of Association in 1889.[8] These deaconess sisters had a deep sense of a call to service; from the New Testament onward, the deaconess service has been considered a high calling.

Another historical strain leading to contemporary faith community nursing is that of the black church nurse. "Cleveland's black Baptist churches gained national prominence through nurses' programs and gospel music. In the 1930s, women from Mt. Sinai Baptist Church, who had been assisting members who became ill at services, began to perform nursing services for the community. Their activity helped inaugurate the church nurses' movement; in 1945 they were accepted by the Ohio Baptist Convention."[9] Black Baptist and black Pentecostal churches usually have an organization for church nurses or nurses' aides, women who are trained to keep members from injuring themselves in the enthusiastic and ecstatic phases of worship services. While not necessarily registered nurses, they filled an important role in the black church.[10] I have learned in my research that more and more of these nurses are now registered nurses, and they may also serve a health-education role in the black church. The mission of the National Black Nurses Association (NBNA) "is to provide a forum for collective action by African American nurses to investigate, define and determine what the health care needs of African Americans are and to implement change to make available to African Americans and other minorities health care commensurate with that of the larger society."[11] This organization has influenced the status of nurses in the black church.

8. Ruth W. Rasche, "The Deaconess Movement in 19th-Century America: Pioneer Professional Women," United Church of Christ website: http://www.ucc.org/about-us/hidden-histories/the-deaconess-movement-in.html (accessed Apr. 16, 2009).

9. "The Encyclopedia of Cleveland History: Baptists," Case Western Reserve University, July 10, 1997: http://ech.cwru.edu/ech-cgi/article.pl?id=B3 (accessed Apr. 16, 2009).

10. Charles Eric Lincoln and Lawrence H. Mamiya, *The Black Church in the African-American Experience* (Durham: Duke University Press, 1990), p. 88.

11. National Black Nurses Association, Inc.: http://www.nbna.org/ (accessed June 19, 2009).

In the late 1970s and early 1980s, Granger Westberg, a Lutheran minister, hospital chaplain, and author of the best-selling book *Good Grief,* developed the current concept of parish nursing. His vision grew out of his work forming Wholistic Health Centers in churches. This model included an interdisciplinary team of pastor, nurse, general practitioner, social worker, and dietician, who together delivered health care in a church building. However, it was expensive, and many of the services could not be reimbursed through third-party payment. Thus the more practical idea of the parish nurse was born. Parish nursing was originally developed as a partnership between Lutheran General Hospital in Park Ridge, Illinois, and six area congregations. It was conceived as having a nurse as part of the ministerial staff of a congregation for health promotion and disease prevention. Later, parish nurses were also connected with hospitals.

Since the specialty began with a handful of nurses, it is remarkable how it has grown. But it needs more paid national staff to give it real impetus. The number of FCNs in the United States still remains elusive, though the number cited has been over 10,000 since 2000. According to former Health Ministry Assocation (HMA) president Sharon Stanton:

> Accuracy would be available if State Boards of Nursing in the U.S. would include this specialty practice within their scope of practices. They do not and I think it is due to the fact that approximately sixty to seventy-five percent of FCNs are not paid employees. Add to that the number of retired RNs who have not kept their licenses up to date yet still call themselves parish nurses and continue to function in that role, according to them. The credentialing process, which not all FCNs will seek, is currently being developed under an HMA committee in collaboration with the American Nurses Credentialing Center (ANCC). Once this is secure, those numbers of credentialed FCNs will be attainable. There are so many unaccounted for doing a variety of programs identified as parish nursing, health ministry to caring ministries, health and wellness, etc. This is a movement which is still in a neophyte stage. The practice is becoming clarified but the ministry element is still fluid and unformed.[12]

12. E-mail from Sharon Stanton to the author (Oct. 28, 2008).

Formation of IPNRC and HMA

The International Parish Nurse Resource Center (IPNRC) was established as part of Advocate Health Care in Chicago in 1985, and it moved to the Deaconess Parish Nurse Ministries in St. Louis in 2002.[13] The annual Granger Westberg Parish Nurse Symposium, sponsored by the IPNRC, provides opportunities for continuing education and training in parish nurse concepts for clergy, parish nurses, and other health professionals.[14] IPNRC is a nonprofit business that develops and sells resources for parish nurses and others who do this work, and employees and volunteers develop and provide a wide range of products and services.[15] The IPNRC also provides outstanding educational events and curricula to support this growing specialization.

The Health Ministries Association (HMA) was founded in 1989 by attendees at the Westberg educational conference (including Granger Westberg and the author of this book) to advocate for the work of health ministers, parish nurses, and other professionals, such as seminary faculty and chaplains engaged in health ministries. The mission statements and the type of incorporation of the two organizations, IPNRC and HMA, were clearly different from their origins, but they work on parallel paths.

The HMA is a membership organization open to all those interested in promoting health and healing ministries in faith communities and churches. As such, the HMA membership elects its leaders, participates in developing and implementing strategic plans, works on developing the scope and minimum standards of practice for FCNs, and advocates for the specialty role in regulatory and policy arenas. The American Nurses Association has acknowledged HMA as the specialty membership organization

---

13. Some of the insights and information about faith community nurses and their organizations (when not otherwise noted) are based on interviews I have conducted with leaders in faith community nursing. These interviews were conducted during the spring and summer of 2009 with Sharon Stanton, Faith Health Partnership coordinator for Catholic Healthcare West in Arizona, and president of Health Ministries Association, 1999-2003, 2008-2009; Norma Small, teacher and consultant, Parish Nursing/Faith Community Nursing, Health Ministries, and Gerontology; Peggy Matteson, professor and chair, department of nursing, Salve Regina University, Newport, Rhode Island; Nancy Rago Durbin, director of Advocate Health Care Parish Nursing Ministry, Park Ridge, Illinois. Their individual views do not necessarily represent official positions of their respective institutions.

14. "History of IPNRC," International Parish Nurse Resource Center: http://www .parishnurses.org/HistoryofIPNRC_221.aspx (accessed Apr. 16, 2009).

15. Information provided by Peggy Matteson.

for Faith Community Nurses. HMA groups in various denominations, various foundations, and the IPNRC work together to strengthen the healing and wholeness of congregations.

HMA is interfaith in its mission and membership. While the vast majority of the members are Christian, many persons from the Jewish, Hindu, and Islamic faith communities are embracing this concept. Connection with the divine resonates with all major faith groups, and that is why HMA strives to integrate this truth in the practice of ministry.[16]

One of the FCN leaders, Carol Story, says that about twenty Christian denominations have helped to shape how health ministry and parish nursing function. "That means they decide what education is needed, how the programs will look regionally, by district, or by geographical location. It also might determine whether a salary or stipend will be paid, what the standards are, and what the congregation's needs are. I see this trend continuing and growing."[17] However, churches have not been the major shapers of this field.

Development of Faith Community Nursing

Many in health care first learned of this specialty practice of parish nursing when the first *Scope and Standards of Parish Nursing* was published by the American Nurses Association (ANA) and HMA in 1998. When a revision of that document was required, after the ANA adopted the new *Nursing: Scope and Standards of Practice,* more than 300 people were involved in the process. In 2005 the term was changed from "parish nurse" to "faith community nurse." Although an estimated 90 percent of FCNs are Christian, the old terminology was deemed too restrictive to be formally used as an all-inclusive title. It was also a confusing label, because some states have "parish nurses" known as "county nurses."

The ANA provides the venue and approval process for the development of a defined scope and a minimum standard of practice for each nursing practice specialty. For each practicing FCN, the *Code of Ethics for Nurses* (ANA, 2001), *Nursing's Social Policy Statement* (2003), *Nursing:*

16. E-mail from Sharon Stanton to the author (Oct. 28, 2008).

17. Carol Story, faculty coordinator of Puget Sound Parish Nurse and Health Ministries, Everett, WA, "The Changing Face of Parish Nursing," August 2005: http://www.pugetsoundparishnurses.org/parishnurse/resources/changing-face-of-pn.asp (accessed Aug. 15, 2008).

Scope and Standards of Practice (2004), *Faith Community Nursing: Scope and Standards,* and the rules, regulations, and laws of the jurisdiction in which they practice provide the framework within which FCNs must practice.[18] The label of the specialty, Faith Community Nursing, reflected the fact that this practice does occur within a variety of faith communities. The expected scope of practice for an FCN is defined and explicated. FCN is officially defined as "the specialized practice of professional nursing that focuses on the intentional care of the spirit as part of the process of promoting wholistic health and preventing or minimizing illness."[19] Advanced practices for nurses at the master's level are generally offered for different fields; hence public-health nursing or faith community nursing can be a focus.

As stated in *Faith Community Nursing: Scope and Standards of Practice,* the formal title for this specialty is Faith Community Nurse. However, within the faith community that they serve, they may be referred to as health-ministry nurse, health minister, congregational nurse, parish nurse, health and wellness nurse, and so on. This is consistent with the fact that different religious denominations call their faith-community leaders by different names, such as pastor, minister, reverend, priest, rabbi, imam, and so forth.

The key element that differentiates the FCNs from the public-health or community-health nurses is their focus on intentional care of the spirit. This is an important distinction, because *all* professional registered nurses are required to assess the physical, mental, and spiritual needs of their patients. But FCNs are educated about not only how to *assess* but also how to *respond to* the spiritual needs, and they learn that specialized intervention takes time. The FCNs call in other nurses, those who specialize in providing interventions that are more focused on physical or mental issues, to provide ongoing nursing interventions in those areas.[20]

An FCN must have a clear job description and professional coopera-

---

18. American Nurses Association, *Code of Ethics for Nurses with Interpretive Statements* (Silver Spring, MD: American Nurses Association, 2001); ANA, *Nursing's Social Policy Statement,* 2nd ed. (Silver Spring, MD: American Nurses Association, 2003); ANA, *Nursing: Scope and Standards of Practice* (Silver Spring, MD: American Nurses Association, 2004); Health Ministries Association and ANA, *Faith Community Nursing: Scope and Standards of Practice* (Silver Spring, MD: American Nurses Association, 2005).

19. HMA and ANA, *Faith Community Nursing: Scope and Standards of Practice* (2005).

20. Information provided by Peggy Matteson.

tion with the pastor to be effective in a faith community. However, one problem for FCNs is that — even after twenty years — most FCNs are unpaid. The question is whether this subspecialty will continue to grow and flourish if it continues as a principally unpaid specialty.

Roles of the Faith Community Nurse

A faith community nurse bridges two disciplines and thus must be prepared in and responsible to both. "Appropriate and effective practice as a FCN requires the ability to integrate current nursing, behavioral, environmental and spiritual knowledge with the unique spiritual beliefs and practices of the faith community into a program of wholistic nursing care. This is necessary no matter the level of education the nurse has achieved."[21] FCNs are actively licensed registered nurses who must follow the state's laws, rules, and regulations regarding the practice of nursing. How much direct interaction they have with each individual varies considerably from one FCN to another. However, FCNs in general do not administer treatment or medications requiring a physician's order. Doing the dependent functions — that is, following physicians' orders — may depend on the FCN's liability insurance.

"FCNs focus on helping the person (which can be an individual, family or the entire congregation) to achieve health, healing, and wholeness by implementing health promotion and disease prevention practices. Their goal is the wholistic health of the congregation. They must be caring, spiritually mature people who reach out to comfort, console, strengthen, teach and encourage the faith community. They must have: good communication skills; the ability to work with others within the congregation and the larger community; a demonstrated relationship with a faith community; and the time and desire to implement a health ministry program within their faith community."[22]

As I came to understand the different models of faith community nursing, I was significantly assisted by those I interviewed for insights into the work of FCNs.[23] However, not everyone interprets the role of the FCN

21. Wyoming Women's Health, "What Is Parish or Faith Community Nursing?" p. 4: www.wyowomenshealth.org (accessed Jan. 6, 2009).

22. Wyoming Women's Health, "What Is Parish or Faith Community Nursing?"

23. Peggy Matteson and Nancy Rago Durbin, "Questions and Answers About Faith Community Nursing," June 2007 (updated Sept. 2008). See Appendix H for the full document.

the same way, since matters "in the field" can vary a great deal. The FCN functions as a health educator, a health counselor, a referral agent, an advocate, and an integrator of spirituality and health. In discussing the roles of the FCNs even in one state — Nebraska — I have noted how much they can vary. Some congregations have paid FCNs on staff, while others have FCNs who volunteer their time as needed. Some organize health fairs and support groups, others serve as consultants as needed.[24]

Many agree that the key role is that of health assessor of the whole person, family, or community. Their educational role includes training volunteers; providing information about health promotion through health fairs, adult education classes (which may cover issues such as pain education), or community resources; and training lay leaders to do visitation of the sick. Some describe the spiritual role of the nurse as providing a prayerful presence, being an active listener, and giving spiritual care by addressing the deeper underlying questions of life and death. Advocacy is important in assisting people to navigate the health care system, to advocate for those who are marginalized both economically and educationally. Advocacy may also include clarifying to people their rights to health care and services. Accompanying someone to a medical consultation and helping that person come up with questions for the doctor is important. However, many FCNs train volunteers in a congregation to do this rather than doing it themselves.

FCNs should be listed in a church bulletin as members of the ministerial staff in order to verify their professional standing. FCNs may be paid or unpaid, and they should work in cooperation with the priest/minister/rabbi as part of the faith community's pastoral care team. Other health professionals (LPNs, retired RNs, social workers, health educators, physical therapists, physicians, etc.) can be recruited to partner with the FCN as a health-ministry team, which would develop a model to fully use the expertise of many valued health professionals who are already members of that faith community.[25]

A fundamental calling of the FCN is the transformation of congregations in helping them move to a more fully realized health and healing community. The foundation for this role is addressing the needs of the

24. Joyce Davis Bunger, "Faith Community Nursing," *Nebraska Nursing News* 24, no. 2 (Spring 2007): 13-15: http://www.hhs.state.ne.us/CRL/nursing/NursingSping2007.pdf (accessed Aug. 15, 2008).

25. Wyoming Women's Health, "What Is Parish or Faith Community Nursing?"

whole person, not as a psychotherapist simply addressing the clinical needs, but getting at the root problems. "The role of the FCN challenges us to remember that we function under 15 standards of practice, to name a few: collaborates with the patient, spiritual leaders, members of the faith community, and others; integrates research into practice; attains knowledge and competency that reflects current nursing practice; provides leadership in the practice setting."[26]

Education for Faith Community Nursing

An FCN must hold an active license as a registered nurse and should have specific education beyond the preparation to become an RN. There is no one standard curriculum to prepare faith community nurses: the minimum requirement is a program that encompasses the scope and minimum standards of practice presented in *Faith Community Nursing: Scope and Standards of Practice*. Some religious denominations require additional study in the beliefs of their denomination. The HMA is currently gathering information on these programs around the country. Two programs that have been cited as the most effective are one in North Dakota and another in Pittsburgh, run by the Sisters of Mercy. Other schools have had success by offering FCNs dual master's degrees with a theology school. An attempt to set up a master's program for FCNs at Georgetown University School of Nursing in the late 1980s, under the leadership of Norma Small and with my involvement, was short-lived. But now several M.A. programs are in operation, including ones at Azusa Pacific University in California, at North Park Seminary in Chicago, and at Luther Seminary in St. Paul. The difficulty with launching such specific master's programs is the lack of money and time, although more nurses (who are taking graduate work) are doing their theses and taking advanced practice in faith community nursing.

The theological and spiritual component of these educational programs seems to be uneven. The spiritual component needs to clarify that the FCN is not running a clinic in a church but is addressing underlying issues about health. The majority of the regional continuing education programs for FCNs are interfaith in design. A few methods for growing in the FCN role are: finding support networks; attending local (Renewal Day),

26. Story, "The Changing Face of Parish Nursing."

regional (Portland), or national conferences (HMA, Westberg Symposium); subscribing to national journals (such as the new *Health Ministry Journal*); and pursuing local theological education.[27]

The question of education is connected with the current movement for what is called "recognition," which may lead to certification. A task force comprised of HMA members, some of whom work for the IPNRC and those who represent other groups, is developing the process for recognition and then certification for individual FCNs. Rather than requiring a further degree, they will base recognition on a web-based portfolio that can eventually lead to recognition, then certification. Recognition then has to do with gathering certain documents in a portfolio following guidelines in *Faith Community Nursing: Scope and Standards of Practice*. By mutual agreement of the ANA and HMA, the process of certification is on hold.[28] One requirement for recognition and then certification is that the registered nurse must have completed a bachelor's degree in nursing.

Different Models of FCN

In looking at the long-term future of faith community nursing, I raise the question about which model is most effective — the hospital-based or the congregation-based one. The answer to this seems to depend on the position of who is providing the response. Those who work out of a hospital setting see the advantages of a better structure, the encouragement to document effectiveness, colleagues with whom to work, financial security, and continuity. However, if the health care system is under financial threat, the parish nurse program may be the first one to go. The concern of the hospital-based model is that its work will be controlled by the mission of the hospital rather than the goals and standards of Faith Community Nursing. In certain instances, the hospital views this position as a marketing tool for linking themselves with the community. There are also large amounts of administrative protocol that need to be followed to satisfy the hospital, which may regard FCNs more as visiting nurses and public-health nurses, not as part of a congregation.

Another aspect of FCN jobs is whether they should be paid or unpaid. Almost everyone agrees that all should be paid. Some volunteers may

27. Story, "The Changing Face of Parish Nursing."
28. Information provided by Nancy Rago Durbin.

consider themselves less accountable, though they are held to the *Standards of Scope and Practice* no matter whether they are paid or unpaid. However, without a clear job description, unpaid FCNs may very well be taken advantage of, and burnout is a danger. It is also difficult for an FCN to find the time for the research that is needed, and recognition as a professional is more difficult to achieve. At the heart of this question is whether the FCN is a member of a movement or an individual in a specific practice. The ANA certainly views this as a practice, not simply an informal movement. However, because it began with and has continued with over 80 percent volunteers, these distinctions may be hard to secure. For example, at a recent continuing education event for FCNs in Houston, only two out of the forty-five attendees were paid.

The plain fact is that a person in this position does not ask to be salaried, and often they are not. One approach to securing a salary is to outline a specific job description, to specify how many hours it will take, and to develop a plan in which the FCN can eventually become a paid employee. It may even be necessary for the FCN to say that she would resign if not paid. The salaries can vary dramatically, from being quite modest to being a living wage. It is also important for the nurse to have a succession strategy in place so that the position has ongoing security. Continuity is one of the difficulties with these positions. If a congregation starts with a volunteer or older retiree who wants to become an FCN, the position may only last a short time. When she retires as an FCN, then the position disappears as well. This may be one of the greatest challenges of this specialty in the future.

Parish Nursing in the United Kingdom

Parish nursing has expanded to different countries, including Australia, Canada, Korea, New Zealand, Swaziland, and the United Kingdom. I am especially familiar with the early roots of parish nursing in the United Kingdom: in the 1980s and early 1990s, I discussed this concept with Malcom Rigler, who now serves on the U.K. Parish Nurse Advisory Board. British parish nurses define themselves as "not a cure for sick parishes, not a private care plan for elderly vicars, not a strategy for giving injections and treatments, not even traditional nursing or health advice by people using church premises. It is churches of all denominations appointing registered nurses with community experience to promote whole person health care in their local communities, for people of all faiths and none, including an intentional focus on spiritual care."[29]

Parish nursing began formally in the United Kingdom in 2004 — to provide "whole person health care" through local churches. "Using a registered nurse with community experience, practical nursing skills are complemented by spiritual care. Like a National Health Service (NHS) nurse, parish nurses can meet health needs, offer health advice, and health education. Unlike NHS nurses, they can also offer pastoral visiting and prayer."[30] Fifty parish nurses formed an organization for training, support, and recourse for parish nurses. They saw their mission as supplementing the work of the NHS. The following organizations and individuals are named in their development:

> Dr. Malcolm Rigler and "Partners in Health," together with Anthony Collins Solicitors, organized the first conference and hosted and arranged the first few meetings of the steering group.
>
> The Barrow Cadbury Trust, which sponsored the first U.K. conference on parish nursing in 2001
>
> The Baptist Union of Great Britain's department for Training and Research in Mission, which offered an expense allowance for a specialist mission networker in parish nursing
>
> The members of the steering group, who shared the vision and worked together on it
>
> The curriculum development group, which has adapted and delivered the introductory training and is continuing to work on the possibilities of further educational pathways
>
> The Central Baptist Association, which has recognized the mission potential of parish nursing for all denominations and encouraged their regional minister/mission enabler to develop further this aspect of her work
>
> The memorial chapel fund of the English Speaking Union, which awarded to Helen Wordsworth their 2004 travel grant of £1800, and which enabled several nurses to visit parish nurses in America

29. Home page, Parish Nursing Ministries UK: www.parishnursing.org.uk (accessed May 12, 2009).

30. "Finding the Healing Touch," *The Baptist Times* online, November 1, 2007, pp. 10-11: http://www.exacteditions.com/exact/browse/354/377/3094/3/10 (accessed May 11, 2009).

The International Parish Nurse Resource Center, particularly Prof. Phyllis Ann Solari-Twadell and Rev. Deborah Patterson, for their encouragement

Guy and Carly Sears, who formed the company and enabled the necessary legal processes[31]

Parish nursing is viewed as supporting and assisting the National Health Service (NHS), because time is something the NHS cannot offer anymore, and time is the main thing that parish nursing can offer. "Hospital chaplains do great work," one parish nurse wrote, "but some people don't like visiting the chapel in hospital, and people don't stay in hospital very long these days. But they still need spiritual care when they leave hospital, which we can give. People have been amazed that we can help them in such an ongoing way. They really value it. . . . Parish nurse credibility lies in the accountability and confidentiality policies in place. They are governed by the same body as NHS nurses, and as such are easier for the medical profession to trust."[32]

Ministry in Partnership

In the preceding chapter I discussed pastors' ministry to the dying, and now I will examine their ministry in partnership with FCNs. This partnership provides an ideal bridge between the church and medical settings. In both cases, they may train others to expand their collaborative roles for ministry at the bedside. In addition, congregations without FCNs can use church members with gifts and training in this area. This is especially important for the frail and sick elderly who have no family nearby and are at the mercy of the staff's whims for their care. How can we address the idiosyncratic nature of care at the end of life? I would recommend having, where possible, a dual team of FCN and pastor/chaplain. It is clear that this model is quite limited because of the limited number of FCNs in the United States.[33] But we need to increase this number if we are going to change end-of-life care as we know it. The collaborative roles suggested

31. Home page, Parish Nursing Ministries UK: www.parishnursing.org.uk (accessed May 12, 2009).

32. "Finding the Healing Touch," pp. 10-11. To find out more, go to www.parishnursing .co.uk, or call Parish Nursing Ministries UK coordinator Helen Wordsworth: 01788 817292.

33. Sharon Stanton in an e-mail to the author (Oct. 28, 2008).

are: incorporate the sick person into a faith community; empower the patient; assist in health care decisions; teach and equip church members for a condolence ministry; and be a caring presence.

Incorporate the Ill Person into a Faith Community

Faith communities are strong places of support and advocacy for those who are dying. The challenge is to link the patient to the faith community. Perhaps in considering the pastor and FCN roles, the centerpiece should be equipping church members to correct the solo model, which is overemphasized in theological education. In this paradigm the church goes to the patient. Meeting the needs of the faith community constitutes a fundamental part of a congregation's ministry. "Religious activities and connections are associated with greater well-being and lower levels of pain among patients with advanced cancer. Religious involvement is associated with hopefulness and general life satisfaction."[34]

Pastoral care should also be a community endeavor.[35] Earl Shelp began the Care Team Ministry in 1985 to empower lay teams to care for those dying of AIDS. This gave witness to the communal nature of pastoral care, which need not be limited to ordained clergy, as Stephen Ministry affirms.[36] However, there are certain guidelines for caregivers of those who have lost a loved one that can be helpful: these have been listed as the "do's" and "don'ts" of caregiving.[37]

34. "Spirituality Plays Important Role in Chronic Illness and Dying," *Faith and Medicine Connection* 2, no. 4 (Summer 1998).

35. Earl E. Shelp, "Pastoral Care as Community Endeavor," *Park Ridge Center Bulletin* (May/June 2001): 7.

36. Stephen Ministries website: http://www.stephenministries.org (accessed Jan. 23, 2009). The Stephen Series is a complete system for training and organizing laypeople to provide one-on-one Christian care to hurting people in and around a person's congregation. The series also provides congregations with the structure, training, and resources to set up and administer a complete system for caring lay ministry (called Stephen Ministry) in the congregation. In Stephen Ministry, congregations, lay caregivers (called Stephen Ministers) provide one-on-one Christian care to the bereaved, hospitalized, terminally ill, separated, divorced, unemployed, relocated, and others facing a crisis or life challenge. Stephen Ministry helps pastors and congregations provide quality caring ministry for as long as people need it.

37. Delores Kuenning, "Some Do's and Don'ts for Caregivers," *Helping People through Grief* (Minneapolis: Bethany House Publishers, 1987), pp. 257-59. See Appendix I for Kuenning's list.

Concern, support, and the presence of others are very important in the healing process. The images of the Christian church in 1 Corinthians 12, Romans 12, and Ephesians 4 describe the *ecclesia* in terms of a body with many members, a ministry with many callings, a unified spirit with many gifts. The community both strengthens who we are and defines the *ecclesia*. A person in isolation can languish in loneliness and guilt; but the church provides a resource for liberating people from "exaggerated individualism" and the isolation that the medical system may create at the end of life. The church functions as a community of acceptance and hope to attest that we are more than our sickness and suffering. It can testify to the love and healing of God, which is available at all times, not just in moments of crisis. The power of forgiveness, communication, and companionship can often arrest or alleviate — even prevent — disease. As I have observed above, worship and the sacraments can help incorporate a sick person into a faith community.

Society may label certain illnesses and diseases as unacceptable or beyond our area of concern: we may find in this category those dying of AIDS, drug or alcoholism addiction, or failed suicides. Marginalized by virtue of their illness or medical condition, these sick people may not receive the top medical treatment or, in fact, any health care at all. Tragically, they are often ostracized by the church as well. But the church should become the voice for such powerless people, and it should provide concrete assistance and comfort to those dying from those conditions.

Empower the Ill Person

The goal of this ministry is to enhance the agency, knowledge, and comfort of the ill person, who then is assisted by the nurse, physician, family, friends, and other healers. Of course, this is not always the case. There are two possible erroneous responses to the person's weakened state: (1) to take control of decision-making for the person, or (2) to abdicate any responsibility, pretending that the sick person is the same as a healthy person. Neither option is appropriate. The person who is ill needs to take some responsibility as he is empowered to do so. We are called to be stewards of our bodies and the care of them, and to serve others — even in the midst of our dying.

It is evident that an individual's ability to be empowered is to a large degree determined by the kind of person she is. A person who has faced other crises courageously may react more optimistically to cancer than someone who has failed repeatedly in other challenges. Earlier success, however, does not guarantee victory. When illness no longer allows a person to continue in her job or even her role as mother or wife, there is a threat to who she is.

Persons may accept or reject the sick role as they can the dying role. Kübler-Ross's five stages of dying may seem somewhat artificial and confining: though people do go through denial, anger, bargaining, depression, and acceptance, they do not necessarily pass through these stages in a neat progression.[38] People die in as many different ways as they live: some may be quiet, patient, and resigned; others, who perhaps have been gregarious and outgoing, may fight to the last breath. Therefore, empowering people does not necessarily mean equipping them to orchestrate their own death, since some people may prefer a passive role; rather, it means freeing them to make the choice. One can even refer to empowering a comatose person by making sure that his wishes and advance directives are honored. There is, so to speak, a proxy empowerment by honoring the person's values and wishes.

The patient is not only a healer but also a teacher. As Cassell says, the subjective data from the person about his illness are as important as the scientific information about his disease.[39] As Michael Balint implies, the physician should release the doctor that is within the patient.[40] This is not only a recital of symptoms and perceptions, but also insights into how the person is experiencing his illness and what is most effective in addressing pain and other symptoms of the dying. For example, even a person with terminal cancer may be concerned about swollen feet.

However, people generally want to get well. Motivation to be well may stem from negative forces; that is, sickness creates a tension that people naturally wish to avoid. When pain becomes great — whether the source be emotional, physical, social, spiritual, or intellectual — it motivates people to change and moves them toward growth and wholeness.[41] The pastor/FCN can help to motivate and empower the person to achieve optimal health even in the midst of dying. In the midst of dying, one can recognize the importance of spiritual and emotional healing. The person

38. Elisabeth Kübler-Ross, *On Death and Dying* (New York: Macmillan Co., 1970).

39. Eric Cassell, *The Healer's Art* (New York: Penguin Books, 1979).

40. Michael Balint, *The Doctor, the Patient, and Illness* (London: International University Press, 1957), pp. 91-103, 252-66.

41. Nancy Tubesing, *Philosophical Assumptions* (Chicago: Wholistic Health Centers, 1977), p. 8.

may work to this end even as the body is wasting away, as Paul explains in 2 Corinthians 4:16: "So we do not lose heart. Even though our outer nature is wasting away, our inner nature is being renewed day by day."

Assist in Health Care Decisions

Another important role of the pastor/chaplain and FCN is to help sick persons and their families as they face difficult choices. But before assisting individuals in reaching decisions, it is important to educate the congregation and the community at large about end-of-life issues. One way of assisting in health care decisions is to provide educational events. One effective educational model was called Compassion Sabbath in Kansas City, Missouri. This was a community-wide interfaith project to help clergy and congregations address the spiritual, social, and psychological needs of dying people and their families. Eighty thousand church leaders and their congregants gathered to recognize the Sabbath by putting a spotlight on death and dying. Clergy preached to their respective congregations about ministering to seriously ill and dying people. Sunday school classes taught ways to have caring conversations with those near death. Others had discussion groups focused on advance directives and reading the book *Tuesdays with Morrie.*[42]

Compassion Sabbath "was a six-month program that began with an all-day conference for faith leaders in the community and culminated in an intensive three-day weekend — Compassion Sabbath itself — held in individual places of worship. In between, the committee offered several training workshops and educational materials about topics such as the role of healing rituals at the end of life, ideas for sermons and homilies, and information about community resources that help dying people and their families. . . . In fact, Rev. Robert Hill, senior pastor at the Community Christian Church in Kansas City, Missouri, calculates the program has actually affected 250,000 people through 'the ripple effect.'"[43]

The significance of this event was to train the clergy as well as their constituents. Clergy training in all faiths — like the training of other professionals — does not adequately teach faith leaders to deal with death and

42. Mitch Albom, *Tuesdays with Morrie* (New York: Time Warner Paperbacks, 2003).
43. Renie Rutchick, "Compassion Sabbath: Improving Ministry at Life's End," *Partnership for Caring* [newsletter] 2, no. 1 (Spring 2001): 1.

dying. They, too, say that they are uncomfortable and anxious in the face of death, and they feel unable to adequately tend to those going through one of life's most difficult journeys.[44] This clergy discomfort can be eased by an FCN, who has more experience in this area.

The role of FCN and pastor in helping patients and their families to make health care decisions is related to the previous point of empowering patients and brokering the relationship between the family and other health care professionals. Assistance can be given to execute an advance directive or explore the possibility of organ donation. Andy Gordon has created a very helpful list of things to review.[45] Probably the most important piece is getting in touch with the person's value system, which is what happens during conversations about health-care decisions. In the decisions about refusal and withdrawal of treatment, clergy and FCNs can counsel and assist the severely ill person in making choices about medical and palliative care. The long-term consequences of the decision are probably *the* most important element to take into account. Choosing palliative care generally means that one will be dead sooner, though that is not certain.

Three goals of medical care have been suggested: cure, stabilization of functioning, and preparing for a comfortable and dignified death. However, Hank Dunn, a hospice chaplain, asserts that the hard choices have little to do with medical, legal, ethical, or moral decision processes but are emotional and spiritual.[46] However, the ethical, moral, legal, and religious become the background or context for what may in the end seem merely emotional or spiritual choices. Choices may be most influenced by the totality of an individual's life experience. For example, if a person has cared for a dying loved one who had a slow and lingering death, she may be more inclined to vote for no aggressive treatment if she herself becomes terminally ill. Informed decisions are the best, because they hold up over the long haul; for it is living with our decisions at the end of life that matters.

It can take the burden off a family when the dying person's wishes are known. In the literature on the family there is much discussion of a terminally ill person's "letting go," or allowing her to die, which is sometimes refused by a spouse or adult child. Perhaps part of the problem is the very

44. Rutchick, "Compassion Sabbath," p. 1.

45. Andy Gordon, "End of Life Decision Making: A Guide for Caregivers," *The Journal of Pastoral Care and Counseling* 62, no. 4 (Winter 2008): 375-78.

46. Hank Dunn, *Hard Choices for Living People* (Herndon, VA: A & A Publishers, 2003), pp. 7-8, 10.

term "letting go," which is used to refer to stopping futile treatment and letting the disease run its inevitable course. Is this really the analogy we want to use? What is the alternative? Letting a person die sounds harsh; ceasing treatment sounds like abandonment. Perhaps an alternative expression might be "carrying out her wishes" — if and when those are clear. On the other hand, "enhancing the quality of the dying" means the absence of medical intervention, while medical intervention to keep pain at bay is the other option. For the person herself it may be the difference between "giving up" and letting go.

The pastor/FCN may counsel the person in making health care decisions as well as advocate for her right to make them. Interpreting traditions of the religious community may also be helpful. Supporting the decision-maker in the midst of all her doubts and anxieties is crucial. Many times one's personal views and the church's teachings may conflict; thus the pastor assumes a counseling role to help the person struggle through her choices. One must assist the person in clarifying her values and be a moral guide without being judgmental. Confidentiality is the hallmark of this relationship.

Part of the problem with contemporary medical ethics is that it attempts to fit various principles, axioms, rules, policies, guidelines for action, inductive products, and professional personal virtues into a decision-making scheme, along with institutional and social values, without understanding the nature of medicine and nursing itself. As Thomasma and Pellegrino point out, medicine in diagnosis and therapeutics involves values, some of which are ethical. All should be working together to bring about values, for example, the value of good health.[47] The goal is to bring about healing, compassion, care, and the restoration of personal self-reliance. Pastors and FCNs, in collaboration with the medical staff, ferret out resolutions for dilemmas. Knowing analogous cases is crucial. The approach should be that of a moral consultant rather than an ethics expert. In the end, it is important to realize that decisions can be messy and constantly evolving.

Knowing when and to whom to refer people with needs beyond one's expertise, whether it be a psychiatrist, psychologist, or thanatologist, is especially important. Here an FCN can assist with referrals, which is often part of helping people make decisions, for example, linking a person with various health care professionals and community resources in decisions

47. Edmund Pellegrino and David Thomasma, *For the Patient's Good: The Restoration of Beneficence in Health Care* (Oxford: Oxford University Press, 1988), pp. 62-63.

about euthanasia, such as the Society for the Right to Die. Pastors can do more harm than good if they are ill equipped to make assessments, and they should develop a network of community resources when they move to a community.

A Decision-Making Health Care Model

As in other health care situations, the life of the dying involves making thoughtful daily decisions that are commensurate with their religious beliefs and values.[48] The following is a decision-making model that families, pastors, hospital chaplains, counselors, FCNs, and others can use with their clients and parishioners who face difficult health decisions. Or the decision-maker can use it directly. It is not uncommon today for pastors — and especially chaplains — to be consulted about advance directives or organ-donation issues. We recognize that very sick people may need assistance in clarifying their choices, and even in some cases making them. However, the goal is to give them as much autonomy as possible.

This model is designed to assist in reaching sound health care decisions that are consonant with the dying person's values. The goal is to make the best out of tragic situations or complex health decisions, while outlining the various factors that comprise a decision. It incorporates intuition, emotion, and one's faith perspective, and it acknowledges the mystery and unknown nature of life. It takes into account the fact that not all decisions are clear-cut or made in a linear fashion. Real life is a lot more complicated. When belief in God is an important part of our lives, we should be assisted in understanding how our faith can play a practical part in decision-making. The pastor and religious counselor have a key role in getting this to happen.

Decision-making, of course, is not a one-time act but a process. Decisions need to be viewed in relationship to their long-term consequences and repercussions, their effect over a lifetime. We need to help people think through how they will deal with the ultimate consequences of their decisions, not only how their decisions affect them but how they affect their family. Our decisions have several components: the rational, that is, the facts and information; the emotional, or the feelings; the psychological,

48. The following is adapted from Abigail Rian Evans, *The Healing Church* (Cleveland: United Church Press, 1999), pp. 101-7. Used by permission; all rights reserved.

which is connected to our mental health and past emotional experiences; and the spiritual/ethical, our values and religious beliefs.

The model I wish to use is divided into four parts: *preparation, analysis, process,* and *resolution,* which is a description of the stages in decision-making. Of course, the kinds of decisions faced by the seriously ill vary considerably. They can range from the use of cardiopulmonary resuscitation (CPR) or food/hydration, to treatments specific to cancer, such as radiation, chemotherapy, or bone-marrow transplants. Each decision can come out differently, but the process in reaching it can be quite similar. Giving accurate medical information is crucial for the landscape to be clearly known. Take, for example, the use of CPR in the very ill and frail elderly, where the survival rate is less than 2 percent.[49] Furthermore, CPR could result in a prolonged and painful death if the patient suffers broken ribs or other complications. When filling out an advance directive or being a surrogate decision-maker concerning CPR, its ultimate effectiveness could be very important.

Preparation

In the preparation for assisting in decision-making, a person's theology and ethics about health forms the basis for helping her reach a sound decision. Of course, the patient may have already prepared herself for confronting the difficult choices. An individual's values are usually based on personal, family, community, and national values, which may impact the ultimate decision. Ethical principles such as beneficence and truth-telling may clash, and this may necessitate prioritizing them. However, it is not simply a case of selecting ethical principles, but establishing a foundational framework for understanding health, healing, and healers. The religious, spiritual, and transcendent dimensions are important, and guidance from one's relationship with God and beliefs about God, as well as one's religious denomination and its teachings, affect the kinds of decisions that need to be made. Prayer and Bible study may help put a person in touch with the transcendent.

When first meeting with a person facing a decision, it is important to help the person become self-aware. Our gender influences our self-

49. Dunn, *Hard Choices for Living People,* p. 16; for verification elsewhere, see Derrick H. Adams and David P. Snedden, "How Misconceptions Among Elderly Patients Regarding Survival Outcomes of Inpatient Cardiopulmonary Resuscitation Affect Do-Not-Resuscitate Orders," *Journal of the American Osteopathic Association* 106, no. 7 (July 2006): http://www.jaoa.org/cgi/reprint/106/7/402.pdf (accessed Feb. 11, 2009).

perception and mode of decision-making; cultural and racial identity and ethnic origin may also influence self-perception and determine one's loyalties and values.[50] For example, one can reflect on the contrast between the North American and Latin American understanding of self. For North Americans, individual autonomy may take precedence over relationships with other people; for Latin Americans, the opposite may be true, so that the extended family is central to the choices they make.

A person's sense of self-esteem is also part of the preparation prior to making a decision. How much confidence do we have in our own judgments? Do we understand ourselves as unique persons with dignity and worth? Do we recognize our fallibility as we struggle with a decision while maintaining a degree of self-confidence? We must learn to separate who we are from our skills or achievements, such as our physical prowess or our intellectual gifts in a particular job or position. If we fail to do this, our self-esteem will fluctuate with our performance and hurt our ability to make an autonomous decision.

The third area in preparation is helping people recognize how their life experience equips them to make particular choices. Each decision creates a life pattern, which helps us face problems. Therefore, when the next crisis occurs, we already have experience in making decisions that will contribute to our ability to handle the new situation. The development of moral character, as Aristotle suggests, results from the practice of certain virtues. Responsibility and accountability are part of this preparation.

Next, in preparing for a particular health decision, gathering information on the various health issues and conditions that affect us is helpful. If, for example, a person has colitis, prostate cancer, or brain cancer, gaining information on the physical symptoms and treatments available by reading medical research, talking to several practitioners, and exploring documented alternative cures leads to a good decision. As I have observed above, the dying person needs accurate information about usual end-of-life treatments, such as CPR, PEG (percutaneous endoscopic gastronomy) tube, or nasal-gastric (NG) tube. Most studies seem to suggest that the NG tube, if not used as a bridge to mouth feeding, only prolongs the dying.[51]

The last step in preparation — before the onset of a crisis — is to have a support community in place. We should pay particular attention to

50. Carol Gilligan, *In a Different Voice: Psychological Theory and Women's Development* (Cambridge: Harvard University Press, 1982).

51. Dunn, *Hard Choices for Living People*, pp. 17-28.

putting faith-community members in touch with others in the community who have faced similar decisions, so that the dying person will have friends and family who are knowledgeable surrounding them. This is particularly helpful to family members who may be designated as the surrogate decision-makers.

Analysis

Adequate preparation before confronting a problem makes for better choices. Filling out an advance directive while one is still healthy is easier than when one is dying, so much so that all pastors should offer their parishioners an opportunity to meet with them for this purpose. When we face an immediate need to make a choice, the first step is to analyze the entire situation. We do this by gathering the data — the medical information about the course of the disease, the symptoms, the prognosis, legal rights, the cost and financial assistance available — and then assessing the wisdom and expertise of the individuals giving us the information.

The second step of analysis is to assess the overall physical condition — that is, how our general health impinges on our decisions. For example, if a person has multiple physical problems, he might not risk heart surgery if diagnosed with terminal cancer. Determining the primary and secondary health problems is also important in selecting a course of treatment. For example, in treatment decisions about AIDS, often the opportunistic infections, not the AIDS virus itself, demand consideration in treatment plans.

The third step in analyzing a decision is understanding the context of the crisis. Addressing backache in a terminal cancer patient may not be about prolonging life, but about the quality of life. As surrogate decision-makers or even decision-makers for ourselves, we must learn to separate what is a good decision in an abstract sense from what is the right decision in light of the particular circumstances. When we assist someone in wrestling with various choices, it is important that we include the right people in the consulting and decision-making process.

Should children, as well as spouses, be consulted about decisions that are about life and death? Should patients be encouraged to consult multiple health care practitioners? Understanding the ethical issues that are part of different decisions is very important. We should distinguish between personal values and objective ethical standards because there is often a gap between theory and practice when we choose ethical principles. One

376

searches for ways to strike a balance between subjective judgment that any decision is right as long as it is an autonomous one and the perspective that all decisions should be subject to objective standards of right and wrong. The person's religious tradition and theology may affect the ranking of particular values. How do we assess the conflict between love and truth-telling in informing a fragile spouse about a six-month terminal diagnosis? The special relationship of a parent to her children may create decisions that are not in the best interests of her own health. In such a case, the well-being of another may trump one's own personal health.

As we analyze the pros and cons of a particular course of action, projecting the consequences is crucial. These consequences are multiple in nature, involving personal suffering, whether it is psychological, physical, or spiritual; vicarious suffering, which may be reproduced in family members or others; and the balance between loss and gain of function or health or longevity. In life-threatening choices, the consequences are even higher, and the secondary benefits for families who are afraid of losing income and pensions as a result of stopping treatment may influence their decisions.

In some situations there is an 80 percent chance of complete recovery, while in 20 percent of the cases death may be the outcome. People may exercise the freedom of autonomy and refuse a treatment that is in conflict with their value system, knowing that the refusal could shorten their lives. In Roman Catholic theology, the lesser of two evils determines the analysis of tragic choices. The choices are not necessarily between what is objectively good or evil, but are often about what is best for any given person in light of tragic choices.

After all this analysis, we should allow for the unexpected, miraculous recovery, for example, from a medically diagnosed terminal illness. If we decide to forgo a life-extending treatment, the faith factor is capricious, but pastors may help us remain open to the God of surprises.

Process

Moving from the analysis of the various dimensions of a decision, next is the specific process that can be followed to make the final decision. First, we should use our reason to assess the difference between the correct decision and the good decision. The correct decision may be medically correct; the good decision, on the other hand, must be ethically sound. The good decision is a combination of the best medical advice and the honoring of one's highest values. It is important to some people to understand the church's position on a procedure, as well as the medical information on the illness.

Reason without intuition, however, is sterile. Stereotypically, women may often trust their intuition over their reason; men call this operating on a hunch. But intuition may also help us get in touch with our conscience. The conscience becomes sharpened through life experience, and God can speak to us through it to guide us to the right choice. The conscience may provide a segue to prayer, meditation, and the revelation that comes from a sudden understanding of God's will in a situation.

We should then join reason and intuition with our emotions. If we make decisions only in a coldly rational way, they may not be the right ones. Some thinkers believe that problems worth solving cannot be solved objectively, suggesting that sound decisions also include an emotional dimension. If we agree with writers such as Albert Camus (1913-1960), our feelings and emotions toward ourselves and others may be the principal factors that sway us.

Helping people recognize that we are not autonomous individuals, but are part of a community that affects their choices, is key. Connecting the person with his or her community, friends, and family is important. For example, people in traditional cultures value consensus from their community very highly and seek it before they proceed with a decision.

The decision-making process may entail procrastination when we do not feel ready to make an immediate decision. Procrastination may be a temporizing step and is certainly better than total avoidance or denial. In other words, until we feel ready to proceed with a concrete decision, delay may give us the confidence to move ahead. In some cases, rationalization may be used to justify a decision that we know is wrong but have convinced ourselves is right because it is the one that we want to choose.

Resolution

The last part of this decision-making model is the resolution, or the implementing of a decision. Implementing a course of action may be gradual, not done in a single step. Once a decision is made, the pastor can help the person live with the outcome. Making a decision precludes living with paradox. These paradoxes need to be addressed through conflict resolution, where people can negotiate tradeoffs. I remember a parishioner at a church I served in New York City who had advanced diabetes and was told that, if she wanted to live, she had to have her leg amputated. She could not reach a decision because she wanted to both live and *not* have her leg amputated.

Teach and Equip Church Members for a Condolence Ministry

So far we have focused on the ministry to the dying, but the bereaved also need our care. Much of what I have said above about caring for the patient can apply to caring for the family. Families play a central role in the quality of life of the terminally ill, but the burden can be heavy. If the illness is short — one to three months — the experience is far different than for those who carry the burden of long-term caregiving. Sometimes this can amount to years for those with cancer who go in and out of remission, or persons with Alzheimer's disease, where the family experiences two deaths — the death of the person they knew and then the ultimate physical death.

When a loved one dies, our reaction may be to lament. Lament is an important pastoral tool: "[A] lament is a repeated cry of pain, rage, sorrow and grief that emerges in the midst of suffering and alienation."[52] It takes the brokenness of human experience into the heart of God and demands that God answer. It often has a note of hope that things will change. In Hauerwasian terms, we name the silences, thus helping us move forward.[53]

Theodicy for the Christian is not a crisis of faith but a crisis of understanding. Lament needs the context of a community to move a person from pain to joy, and it places pain within a framework of hope and new possibilities.[54] Lament is a gesture of resistance in the face of evil, and the church needs to recapture the importance of lamentation. It is crucial that friends accompany us in our sorrow, and clergy and FCNs can facilitate this. We can learn much from the Jewish tradition about comforting the mourners.

> This is the Mitzvah of comforting mourners. It is considered more important than visiting sick people, for it enables you to honor both the dead and the living. *Nihum Avelim* (comforting the mourners) can be

52. John Swinton, *Raging with Compassion: Pastoral Responses to the Problem of Evil* (Grand Rapids: Eerdmans, 2007), p. 104.
53. Stanley Hauerwas, *Naming the Silences* (Grand Rapids: Eerdmans, 1990).
54. Swinton, *Raging with Compassion*, p. 113.

on any of the Shivah days, but it is best, if possible, to visit after the first three days. During the first three days the mourner's grief is so great that he cannot really be comforted, and therefore usually only best friends and relatives are present at that time. On the visit it is not accepted to say hello to the mourner. You must wait for the mourners to turn to you, and only then should you try comforting them. There is nothing "right" or "wrong" to say, but instead it is advisable to listen to the mourner, who often feels the need to talk. The purpose of comforting mourners is not to make them forget their grief or ignore it, but to let them know that they have the support of their friends, and help them deal with their loss.[55]

Sometimes, however, lament means silence: our only response to extreme evil and suffering may be silence. Jesus spoke only seven words during the six hours he hung on the cross. Elaine Scarry talks about the unsharability of pain: in a sense, it renders us mute. Elie Wiesel also reflects this with respect to the unbearable burden of speaking of the Holocaust. The question is: How can we facilitate the movement from silence to speech in the throes of suffering?[56] FCNs and pastors may also teach and equip the church members to carry out the ministry to the bereaved.

A national British organization, Cruse Bereavement Care, concretizes what aftercare for families can be like. This group offers bereavement care that is based on Elijah providing the widow of Zarephath with the "cruse" of oil that never ran out. This signifies that Cruse will provide support as long as it is needed. Despite the derivation of its name, Cruse is a nonreligious organization and welcomes people of any belief — or none. Cruse exists to promote the well-being of bereaved people and to enable anyone bereaved by death to understand her grief and cope with her loss. Cruse's support, information, advice, education, and training services are free to bereaved people; many who volunteer are themselves widows or others who have lost loved ones. Founded in 1959, Cruse has 134 branches throughout the United Kingdom, and over 80,000 people make contact annually for assistance. This concept could be used in the United States, and church members could join this ministry.[57]

Another possibility as part of a condolence ministry is to establish a

55. "Shivah Call": http://www.judaica-guide.com/shivah_call/ (accessed Mar. 18, 2008).

56. Swinton, *Raging with Compassion,* pp. 96-97.

57. See Cruse Bereavement Care website: www.crusebereavementcare.org.uk.

friendship ministry. Friendship is an important aspect of pastoral care, especially in the face of grief and loss. Having an *aman cara* (spiritual friend) is very important for the grieving: it refers to the Celtic spiritual belief of souls connecting and bonding. Would this not be a concept that the church could rediscover for its bereavement ministry? Having someone who is committed to accompanying us on the road of sorrow is a great boon.

Timothy Jones refers to the importance of spiritual friends helping us to grow: "[E]very believer can benefit from a friend or mentor, a confidant, or prayer partner with whom he or she can freely discuss the trials and triumphs of living for and with God."[58] Proverbs 18:24 says: "Some friends play at friendship but a true friend sticks closer than one's nearest kin." They are companions in the soul's itinerary. They can take on the role of a mentor, a prayer partner who provides accountability for spiritual growth, or simply a friend who is open and listening. A spiritual friend need not be perfect, but should understand his own wounds that need to be healed.[59]

The ministry of *aman cara* could be started in churches by deacons; or a new cadre of leaders could be appointed for these responsibilities. Some training would be necessary, but the most important thing would be the choosing of those who are naturally gifted for this accompanying ministry. This could be akin to Christian listeners who were trained at the Acorn Healing Trust in Southern England: that is, laypeople who sit and listen to those who are sorrowing or in crisis or illness. They are not counselors but companions.[60]

It is also possible to care for someone else without that person's actually knowing it. "In actuality, if you choose to harbor the other in your heart and soul in a practiced way, it probably does not matter if you inform them or not. Somehow they will know."[61] However, it is not clear that this is always the case. People often feel abandoned and need the assurance that others still care.

Another powerful outreach is a prayer shawl ministry. It is a comfort ministry for individuals and families who are experiencing grief or for those who are undergoing a medical procedure. It offers them tangible evidence of the love of God. A group of committed women knit shawls for

---

58. Timothy Jones, *Finding a Spiritual Friend* (Nashville: Upper Room Books, 1998), p. 18.

59. Jones, *Finding a Spiritual Friend.*

60. Evans, *The Healing Church,* p. 22.

61. James Miller, *What Will Help Me? 12 Things to Remember When Someone You Know Suffers a Loss* (Fort Wayne, IN: Willowgreen Publishing, 2000), p. 24.

these families at no cost to the family. They begin each shawl with prayer, continue to pray for the individual during the knitting process, and offer a final ritual before sending the shawl to its recipient. The shawl ministry was begun in 1998 by Janet Bristow and Victoria Galo, and was born of their experiences at the Women's Leadership Institute at Hartford Seminary and their desire to minister to the spiritual needs of women. These women combined their spiritual training with their knitting ability to create a very practical ministry of care and comfort.[62] The important element of this ministry is to be as present as possible during the person's dying, but most important to go immediately to the family at the time of death. Naturally, one must determine how the family feels about visitors. Often families will say that they do not want visitors because they do not want to trouble anyone. Reading these signals is essential. The power of this prayer shawl ministry is illustrated by the following story after a plane crash.

> When Continental Flight 3407 crashed into a home in Clarence, NY in February, members of the prayer shawl ministry of First Presbyterian Church in nearby East Aurora sprang into action. Since beginning the ministry in 1998, church members had knitted more than 400 shawls to give to people facing death, illness or other tragedies. Red Cross Chaplain Beth Lenegan sent this response: "Bring more . . . as many as you can get." She said grieving family members loved the shawls. "They're wearing them in the lobby, at lunch, walking around. The prayer shawls are bringing so much comfort. It's amazing." "This is what the prayer shawl ministry is all about — bringing healing, hope and life again in this time of loss," she explains. "In a symbolic way these shawls have become means of grace, an open window to God's healing love."[63]

Be a Caring Presence

In his foreword to *A Manual for Ministry to the Sick,* Martin Dudley writes: "Christians are called to serve Christ in their neighbors. When we stand by a sickbed or attend the dying, we are to be there with the respect and the

62. All information taken from Prayer Shawl Ministry home page: http://www.shawlministry.com/ (accessed Feb. 20, 2009), and Janet Bristow, Shawl Ministry brochure (2005).
63. Presbyterian Church (USA), *Presbyterians Today* (May 2009): 8-9.

tenderness which is appropriate to being in the presence of Christ. There should be no room for any kind of exploitation of a person's vulnerability at such moments, but rather a note of gentleness and attention."[64]

Caring presence is based on mutuality. Compassion moves us toward companionship, and the root of companionship is the recognition of our mutual need. We are bound together by our mutual brokenness, our common need. Companionship springs from fraternalism, not paternalism, which means that the pastor and/or FCN become a companion particularly by training the congregation for this ministry, and thus does the body of Christ embrace the person in her need.

Paul defined interrelatedness in Galatians 6:2: "Bear one another's burdens, and in this way you will fulfill the law of Christ." This passage has a twofold thrust: (1) bear one another's burdens, and (2) carry your own load. So we are responsible for the problems and health of others, that is, the weight of their difficulties, but are also accountable for our own actions, which cannot be shifted over to someone else. Our companionship is rooted in this twofold injunction: individual accountability but community concern.

We are interconnected precisely because of our needs and shortcomings. Companionship is thus a reflection of how we care. Companionship involves a one-on-one relationship, a covenanting between two people — a presence and an availability. However, it is not in itself a sufficient expression of caring. Isolation and loneliness can cause suffering and even physical illness in the same way that a virus or an accident can. Caring may involve only listening and then silence; we do not need to fill the spaces with words. Silence allows the person to cry out in anger, pain, or doubt. Sitting down, holding her hand, and focusing on her is a form of caring.

Another aspect of this condolence ministry we will name "watch and pray" ministry. The power and reality of the cross is being reenacted as we confront illness. "Anxiety, therefore, may be a friend rather than an enemy in that its inner qualities may grasp people and allow them to live more fully and deeply."[65] Illness tests our "courage to be," in the Tillichian sense. However, we need to be careful not to overglamorize the suffering of illness. James Woodward introduces a very powerful concept of watching:

64. Martin Dudley, ed., *A Manual for Ministry to the Sick* (London: SPCK, 1997), p. xi.
65. James Woodward, "Befriending Illness," in *A Good Death*, ed. Alison and Colin Johnson, Leveson Paper #13 (Solihull, UK: Foundation of Lady Katherine Leveson, 2003), p. 6.

The spirit is particularly at work in our waiting, watching, and hoping. This theme is particularly illuminated theologically by the words of Jesus in the Garden of Gethsemane, "Watch with me." The word "watch" says many things on different levels, all of importance to us: there is both a kind of vigilance and a kind of guarding. The relatives and friends know their vulnerability and distress. They are close to those they love, and begin to understand what kind of pain the person experiences.[66]

Andy Gordon says:

Please remember that all patients do not show all of these signs [of dying]; many of these signs will be seen in some patients. The reason for the tradition of "keeping a vigil" when someone is dying is that we really don't know exactly when death will occur until it is obviously happening. If you wish to "be there" with your loved one when death occurs, keeping a vigil at the bedside is part of the process.[67]

There are a number of ways to be a caring presence. As a companion to the suffering person, you should let him tell you what he is experiencing and help him to move from destructive to constructive views of suffering. Understanding the dying person's views of self, God, others, and even the meaning of life can intensify the sense of a caring presence. The caregiver can move from apathy to empathy to sympathy.[68] Rabbi Stephen Roberts put it this way: "'I provided direct pastoral care to residents and to the firefighters, who, after struggling with the World Trade Center disaster, were trying to make some sense of a plane falling on their neighborhood.' He recalls spending over two hours with a family who was forced to move their belongings out of their home, which had been nearly destroyed. 'What it comes down to, in a situation like that, is knowing how to ask the right questions, and being able to listen.'"[69]

If the pastor/FCN is not an anxious presence in this encounter, then the time to engage will emerge, and real pastoral care at a deeper level may be possible. The pastoral care of the dying takes a lot of time and patience and ability to pick up subtle clues. Structured conversation is part of being

66. Woodward, "Befriending Illness," p. 7.
67. Gordon, "End of Life Decision Making: A Guide for Caregivers," p. 378.
68. Jeffrey A. Watson, *The Courage to Care: Helping the Aging, Grieving, and Dying* (Grand Rapids: Baker, 1992), pp. 167-70.
69. "Chaplaincy Staff Responds to Plane Crash in Queens," *The Beacon* (Winter 2001): unnumbered page.

a caring presence. Chaplains, pastors, FCNs, and other health care professionals — and even family — who sit by the bedside of a dying person, however, may feel that words fail. And they do. Therefore, using art to help a person access her feelings can be effective. This is especially true of emotional conflicts that tear us apart in the face of our dying, that is, leaving those we love. Some people may want to do art themselves — paint, write a poem, or sculpt — in order to find a mode of expression that is better than words. However, this may be difficult: those weakened by illness may no longer have the energy or inclination to engage in such activities.

It is true, however, that art in all its forms may help to reach across the chasm created by approaching death. A medical center in Redmond, Oregon, uses harpists, sculptors, and journal writers with their patients who are dying.[70] The arts can open up our senses, our memories, our creativities to deal with deep questions in ways that may be profound, safe, provocative, and comforting.[71] The pastor and others, such as the Ruth and Naomi Senior Outreach in Birmingham, Alabama, may use the arts to bring unexpected healing and comfort.[72] Giving photos, books, CDs, art supplies, and so on provides people with the opportunity to follow their own creativity, helping difficult and painful emotions to surface.

Music in its forms of requiems, hymns, chants, spirituals, elegies, blues, and laments can create the environment to ease the journey toward death. Choosing what music speaks to any given person may not be easy. One resource for this is the CD *Dancing with the Dead,* which has music relating to death and dying from a number of cultures.[73]

The use of literature about deep spiritual issues or others facing death can open up possible conversations with the patient. Mary Jane Moffat's *In the Midst of Winter* is an anthology of literature related to death and mourning, which includes poetry, fiction, nonfiction, and so forth.[74]

---

70. These approaches were presented by the Redmond staff at a Fetzer Institute Health Summit in 1999. Ruth and Naomi Senior Outreach in Birmingham, Alabama, uses a dog and harp music as they reach out to nursing-home residents and ill people: http://www.ruthandnaomi.org/.

71. Gail Henson, "The Art of Dying Well: Death and Spiritual Formation," *Hungryhearts,* PC(USA) (Summer 2006): 3. See also Sandra L. Bertman, ed., *Grief and the Healing Arts* (Amityville, NY: Baywood Publishing Co., 1999).

72. See the Ruth and Naomi Senior Outreach website: http://www.ruthandnaomi.org/.

73. Can be ordered through Ellipsis Arts: http://www.therelaxationcompany.com/.

74. Mary Jane Moffat, ed., *In the Midst of Winter: Selections from the Literature of Mourning* (New York: Vintage Books, 1992).

The Future of Pastor/FCN Partnership

The calling of FCNs and pastors to the bedside is a privilege and a challenge. Let us hope that these concrete recommendations for avenues of ministry will encourage this partnership. If the collaborative model between FCN and pastor is to develop and grow, a great deal of education and prayer is necessary. To build the credibility of the FCN, clergy must have a comprehensive understanding of the FCN's role and what the integration of faith and health means. Clearly, the program will be nothing other than a nurse in the church doing her or his own thing if that church's clergy do not examine the bigger picture of health ministry. The clergy need to be educated that this is not just one person's idea of a ministry of health in a particular congregation; it is making the entire congregation aware of the wellness of body, mind, and spirit.

On the FCN side, doing the groundwork is necessary: examining the culture of the congregation, doing a well-planned community assessment, and building a firm foundation to sustain this model. "What we want and need for healthy faith communities is to build the credibility of the FCN. How? First, by valuing one's worth as a professional working within a community of faith."[75] Spelling out a central and important role with the dying for FCNs will give the pastor/FCN partnership visibility and show its desirability for congregations. Every congregation and pastor will want an FCN to help in this most difficult aspect of pastoral ministry. What we need is a job description that wakes up the congregation to believe that they can't get along without an FCN.

Our vision is to transform the care of those who are ill and their families by drawing on the strengths and experience of each of these professionals and responding to the call to enhance end-of-life care.

75. Story, "The Changing Face of Parish Nursing."

12. Death Is Conquered: How Christian Faith Informs Funerals

For All the Saints Who from Their Labors Rest

For all the saints who from their labors rest,
Who Thee by faith before the world confessed,
Thy name, O Jesus, be forever blest:
Alleluia! Alleluia!

Thou wast their Rock, their Fortress, and their Might;
Thou, Lord, their Captain in the well-fought fight.
Thou, in the darkness drear, their one true Light:
Alleluia! Alleluia!

O blest communion, fellowship divine!
We feebly struggle, they in glory shine;
Yet all are one in Thee, for all are Thine:
Alleluia! Alleluia!

From earth's wide bounds, from ocean's farthest coast,
Through gates of pearl streams in the countless host,
Singing to Father, Son, and Holy Ghost!
Alleluia! Alleluia!

William W. How (1823-1897)

Introduction

This book began with reflections of life and death, followed by chapters on negotiated death concerning euthanasia, physician-assisted suicide, organ donation, and legal issues; it next examined the experiences of pain, grief, and loss; and finally, it looked at the role of health-care professionals and clergy who care for the dying. In this final chapter we will turn our attention to a Christian theology of death and how it informs the funeral service in the Reformed tradition. This is not a comprehensive Christian theology of death; rather, it is composed of some reflections on how this theology informs the church and its practices regarding death and dying. A special focus will be on the doctrine of the resurrection, which frames the focus of the service. Also, this chapter will discuss the importance of the church responding to the anguish of people in the face of the sorrow of death and dying.

Funeral Service as a Ritual

As I observed in chapter 2, funerals have changed both here and abroad. It is within this context that I will reflect on the Christian funeral and the doctrines that inform it. Funerals in America often lack the rites and rituals surrounding death and dying that truly offer opportunities for lament, grieving, anger, understanding, and acceptance. The assault to our psyche and spirit that the death of a loved one represents needs more than a brief funeral that surrounds this event. In Victorian times most people died at home, surrounded by loved ones; often they "lay in state" at home, so people at that time were more accustomed to death.

The rituals surrounding death and dying were also quite different in Old Testament times. Upon news of a death, there would be a period of fasting (Gen. 50:10; 1 Sam. 31:13; 2 Sam. 12:16-18). Mourners would wear sackcloth (Gen. 37:34; 2 Sam. 3:31; 13:31; 2 Kings 6:30) and offer sad poems and laments (Gen. 50:10; 1 Sam. 25). Grief was facilitated by artistic means, such as song (2 Sam. 1:17-27) and poetry (Lam. 1–5). Likewise, in the New Testament, the rites surrounding the last journey were important. The dead body was washed and wrapped in linen cloths (John 11:44), spices and ointments were used, and flowers were strewn (Luke 23:56; John 19:39-40).[1] The body was often carried on an open bier to the grave (Luke 7:14; Acts 5:10). This practice reminds me of my experience in Chapecó, Brazil, in the 1960s, where the bodies of children who had died were carried

---

1. Jeffrey Watson, *Courage to Care* (Grand Rapids: Baker Book House, 1992), pp. 44, 95, 57.

through the streets on a stretcher strewn with flowers. The body would then be laid out on the kitchen table and the community would gather to weep and wail together. Even if the body is not on view, it should be honored, as Tom Long reminds us.[2]

Dignity in dying has often been replaced by better medical treatment and longevity, but some wonder if the tradeoff is worth it. Dignity in the treatment of others is often gone, especially at the end of life. There is a certain depersonalization when we distance ourselves from death and want to get the funeral over with as quickly as possible. Once someone has died, we want to move on with our lives. However, as I suggested in the chapter on caring, hospice has brought the patient/person back to the home setting for as long as possible.

The practice of rituals can help us recognize the ongoing nature of grief and mark those passages and embrace the different stages of the bereavement process. The importance of these rituals forms part of Tom Long's critique of Jessica Mitford's *American Way of Death* (published about four decades ago), which vigorously criticized the funeral industry. Partly as a result of her criticism, the American public has become skeptical of any rituals surrounding burial and has robbed the church of its role.[3] In *The Funeral: Vestige or Value?* Paul Irion considers the place of rituals in marking the different parts of death.[4] These consist of: symbolic action, a ritual that marks an event; providing a comforting guide through difficult circumstances of facing the death of a loved one where we have lost any coherent narrative; rituals that bring us into contact with the power of the past so that our memories in some ways become a comfort; and finally, rituals that provide master narratives about the meaning of death.

Some theologians speak of the deconstructing of master narrative. The funeral is not the whole ritual: there is the wake and visitation, eating, and meeting the bereaved in their home. One can even think of a funeral as a rite of passage: it can be very complex, and the theology standing behind it differs substantially from one Christian church to another. For Presbyterians, it is not a rite of passage, but it marks the entry of the deceased into heaven for some African-American Christians, as Langston Hughes's poems so clearly demonstrate.[5] Black Baptist, Pentecostal, and

---

2. Thomas G. Long, "Why Jessica Mitford Was Wrong," *Theology Today* 55, no. 4 (Jan. 1999): 506.

3. Long, "Why Jessica Mitford Was Wrong," p. 499.

4. Paul Irion, *Funeral: Vestige or Value?* (New York: Arno, 1977), pp. 44-59.

5. Marian Gray Secundy, ed., *Trials, Tribulations and Celebrations: African-American*

Methodist services celebrate the transition into being in the presence of God. The journey metaphor is a powerful one and should not be lost. "Deprived of the ritual of a saint marching into glory, we replace it with a psychically useful notion of a good, or at least somewhat interesting person we will remember from time to time as life returns to normal."[6] Sometimes the funeral takes on the atmosphere of a revival, in which the focus is on those who are left behind who should take the opportunity to ensure their salvation.[7]

A Christian Theology of Death

Given the current dearth of funeral rites and rituals in the United States, the United Kingdom, and elsewhere, it is essential that, as Christians, we base funerals on a Christian theology of death. Do our practices reflect our theology? First, there is a paradox at the heart of the Christian faith: life is a gift and a trust to be enjoyed, and yet in death we are freed from pain and suffering and we enter fully into the joy of God. This is the tension to which Paul referred: "[W]e would rather be away from the body and at home with the Lord" (2 Cor. 5:8). "Jesus . . . did not face his death with the equanimity of soul that characterizes the death of Socrates. 'Now is my soul troubled,' cried out Jesus, 'And what shall I say? "Father, save me from this hour?" No, for this purpose I have come to this hour. Father, glorify thy name' (John 12:27-28). [8] Luke 22:42-44 records Jesus saying this: "Father, if you are willing, remove this cup from me. . . . In his anguish, he prayed more earnestly, and his sweat became like great drops of blood falling down on the ground." Or his final words in the Mark (15:34) account: "Eloi, eloi, lama sabachthani? My God, my God, why have you forsaken me?"

In the account we have of Jesus going to the tomb of his friend Lazarus, John tells us that Jesus was deeply moved in spirit and troubled; he

---

Perspectives on Health, Illness, Aging and Loss (Yarmouth, ME: Intercultural Press, 1992). This collection of poems and stories gives wonderful insights into African-American experiences of death and dying.

6. Long, "Why Jessica Mitford Was Wrong," p. 506.

7. Cleophus LaRue says this in referring to "many" black Baptist, Pentecostal, and Methodist churches as the seven major black denominations studied by C. Eric Lincoln and Lawrence Mamiya in *The Black Church in the African American Experience* (Durham: Duke University Press, 1990).

8. Ray S. Anderson, *Theology, Death and Dying* (Oxford: Basil Blackwell, 1986), p. 37.

wept on learning of Lazarus's death (John 11). But it was precisely at this moment of greatest sorrow that Jesus turned the situation around completely by his actions: he said, "I am the resurrection and the life. Those who believe in me, even though they die, will live, and everyone who lives and believes in me will never die" (John 11:25-26). Then Jesus raised Lazarus from the dead to show his power over death and to foreshadow his own resurrection.

Against the backdrop of the medicalization of death comes the cross, with all of its horror, which lifts up death and suffering as bringing life. However, there is also the warning that God does not send suffering so that we can grow spiritually; rather, God uses it to eventually bring good. This is the promise of Romans 8:28: "We know that all things work together for good for those who love God, who are called according to his purpose." This is an eschatological hope that may not be realized this side of the grave and is not a justification for glorying in suffering. What, then, is our vision? "Against the power of death the Christian church affirms with Paul that 'we live by the Spirit.' It has, by the gift of the same Spirit, whom Paul calls the 'first fruits' of God's good future, a better sense of an ending."[9]

We need to pass through the winter of death, which leads us to the spring of new life, just as we move from Good Friday to Easter. Death is indeed inevitable, the final enemy, but thanks be to Jesus Christ, who gives the victory over death. However, there is still an abrupt disconnect between physical life, death, and eternal life: it is not a seamless passage, but one marked by suffering and sorrow even in the midst of Christ's conquering of death.

Some theologians question whether there is a Christian theology of death per se. Ray Anderson, for example, believes that there is no clearly defined theology of death in the Bible. "The theme of death is expressed descriptively (as history), poetically (as lamentation and complaint), theologically (as the outcome of sin), and eschatologically (as overcome through the resurrection of Jesus Christ). Yet, there is no single 'theology of death' to be found as a thematic development."[10] What Anderson seems to be arguing is that, since resurrection is the central Christian theme, we are more interested in new life than in death.

9. Allen Verhey, "The Spirit of God and the Spirit of Medicine: The Church, Globalization, and a Mission of Health Care," in *God and Globalization*, vol. 2: *The Spirit and the Modern Authorities*, ed. Max Stackhouse and Don Browning (Harrisburg, PA: Continuum International Publishing Group, 2001), p. 108.

10. Anderson, *Theology, Death and Dying*, pp. 38, 41.

Anderson draws heavily on Karl Barth's views of death. Barth's central theme is that God is the Lord of death as well as the Lord of life. He says: "The New Testament Christian does not fear death. But he never hopes for it. He hopes for the one who has delivered him from death."[11] Our basic fear should not be of death but of God, who is our judge. Death is our judgment, but the ultimate judgment is satisfied in Christ's crucifixion. "Is not the end of our being in time as such an unequivocal negative pronounced over our creaturely existence?" (pp. 610, 595) "Death, as it meets us, can be understood only as a sign of God's judgment, hence it is the supreme evil" (p. 597). However, God's judgment is accomplished in the crucifixion of Christ (p. 605).

Nancy Duff observes: "According to Barth, the gospel compels us to both admit that we are dying and yet never to fear death. In admitting that we are dying, we are required to accept without qualification that when we are dead, we are *dead*. By the gospel account death involves no transmigration of the soul from one life to another, no simple transition from this state of life to that. With death, all possibility of a second chance in this world is gone. [12]

> Barth, therefore, claims both that death is a natural part of life *and* that it is not. Calvin holds that we must despise the world and long for the next *and* that we must not despise the world but enjoy the good fruits of creation until God determines that our time to die has arrived. Some people will interpret these claims by Calvin and Barth as out-and-out contradictions. To the complex conversation regarding assisted death, it will seem to some that Reformed theology can only add double-talk and more confusion!
>
> Barth, however, understood that if one is concerned with truth, one cannot appeal to simplicity, because "in every direction human life is difficult and complicated." Calvin and Barth affirm the seemingly contradictory claims that we are to both accept death willingly *and* resist death, because no simple formula regarding the proper attitude toward death will serve the truth.[13]

11. Karl Barth, *Church Dogmatics,* ed. and trans. T. F. Torrance and G. W. Bromiley, vol. III, pt. 2 (London: T. & T. Clark, 1960), p. 640.

12. Nancy Duff, "Reformed Theology and Medical Ethics: Death, Vocation, and the Suspension of Life Support," *Toward the Future of Reformed Theology,* ed. David Willis and Michael Welker (Grand Rapids: Eerdmans, 1999), p. 306.

13. Duff, "Reformed Theology and Medical Ethics," pp. 309-10.

Ray Anderson picks up yet another theme of Barth, that the New Testament continues the themes of the Old Testament that both body and soul are subject to death. There is no dualism between the immortal soul and the temporal body. Our hope for redemption from death lies in God alone, who is the Lord of both life and death. There is no personal immortality as an essential aspect of human beings. God's gift is of eternal life, with a unity of body and soul through resurrection from the dead.

One of the debates in Christian theology is whether biological death is a natural part of life. Theologians such as Helmut Thielicke argue that society should not "take away" from a dying person the right to die her own biological death in her own time. Thielicke says that the physiological experience of death cannot be anything more than a "sign or pointer" to what is now a problem: the death of the person. Death is a theological problem, not merely an anthropological one. Ultimately, it raises the question of one's relationship with God as well as to the structure of the community in which one has experienced personhood.

"Human death is quite different from the death of animals, even though it takes place through the same process. 'The opposite of human dying (executed in the medium of biological death),' says Thielicke, 'is life from God.' That there should be, for human persons, a biological death, which may be termed a 'good dying,' is problematic to this understanding of human personhood and death. One's natural death as a biological creature must be placed within a context of divine promise and hope for the continuation of life for death itself to be robbed of its power to destroy life."[14]

Relationship Between Sin and Death

One of the central issues in a Christian theology of death is the relationship between sin and death, that is, whether death is solely the result of sin. Ray Anderson argues that mortal and finite are part of our original form, and yet sin has caused death to enter as a threat to human personhood itself. The theological issue is whether human nature possessed some form of "natural immortality" before the fall of Adam, a heavily debated issue in the history of theology. The historical debates in the Christian church about death were often about the relationship between sin and death, the soul and

14. Anderson, *Theology, Death and Dying*, pp. 45, 50.

the body, and the doctrine of resurrection. One question is whether there would have been a physical cessation of life without "the fall."[15] Millard Erickson, for example believes that passages such as Romans 6:23, "The wages of sin is death," have been misused to support the linkage of physical death and sin, but nonetheless "physical death was not an original part of man's condition."[16] There are many theologians who can contribute to our understanding of these issues, and I will highlight a few of them.

Ambrose of Milan (339-397 C.E.), who represents a blend of Christian faith and Platonic philosophy, refers to three deaths: death to sin, physical death, and death of the soul by mortal sin. He reflects the Greek view of death as freeing the soul from the body, but he does not really have a full-blown view of the resurrection. His concern is for the life of the soul, which flourishes in death.[17]

Augustine (354-430 C.E.), influenced by Ambrose, understands the death of the body and soul as evils resulting from punishment for sin; unlike Ambrose, he embraces a doctrine of bodily resurrection. Augustine avoids the spirit/flesh dichotomy that misreadings of Pauline theology can create (pp. 43-45, 59-63).

Aquinas (1225-1274 C.E.) believed that the rational soul is nonmaterial and indestructible. By itself it does not constitute a human person, but it exists in its own right and is better off in the human body. In resurrection, the body must be raised for the soul to be complete. Death is both natural and unnatural, because death is due to the fallen nature of humans, which robs us of our immortality. However, it brings us to our eternal happiness (pp. 94-118).

Karl Rahner (1904-1984), a German Jesuit, uses Thomistic theology in conversation with a post-Kantian existentialism. He picks up Aquinas's discussion of the soul: that at death it becomes pancosmic. There is an aspect of death that is neutral rather than evil, but suffering and death contain an element of martyrdom. Ultimately, death is a human act: it is a dying to sin and physical life.

---

15. Dennis Hollinger, "Theological Foundations for Death and Dying Issues," *Ethics and Medicine* 12, no. 3 (1996): 61.

16. Millard Erickson, *Christian Theology* (Grand Rapids: Baker, 1983), p. 1170. Erickson believes that this passage — and passages such as Ezekiel 18:4, 20 — are really about spiritual death and not physical death.

17. David Jones, *Approaching the End: A Theological Exploration of Death and Dying* (New York: Oxford University Press, 2007), pp. 32-36. Hereafter, page references to this work will appear in parentheses in the text.

If we were to claim a Christian theology of death, it would be that death is an enemy. This is in sharp contrast to Greek philosophy as reflected in Socrates' words on drinking the hemlock: "Welcome, O friend death." Ray Anderson describes Barth's position on this subject:

> "He is the Lord of death," writes Karl Barth, "but this does not mean that He affirms it. As the Creator He affirms life and only life. . . . His control over death is exercised for the sake of life and not for the sake of death. 'Have I any pleasure in the death of the wicked,' says the Lord God, 'and not rather that they should turn from their ways and live?'(Ezek. 18:23, cf. 33:11)." From God alone, then, is there consolation, help and deliverance. Death can never be a consolation in and of itself, nor can death be considered to have meaning even when considered as a judgment of God. For God Himself is not ambivalent: He desires life, and not death and therefore death is never considered as having meaning or significance in itself.[18]

Was there an immortal soul before the Fall? The Augustinian and Calvinist tradition teaches that death entered as a result of the Fall. "Traditional Protestant theology, finding its roots in Augustine, and fortified by the thought of Calvin, has generally held that death was not a condition to which Adam was subject prior to the fall. In this view, death entered the human race only as a consequence of Adam's transgression. Though it was possible for Adam to sin, it was not possible for him to die. Both the Lutheran and Reformed traditions seem to follow versions of this tradition" (p. 51).

This position is refuted by some theologians, such as Paul Tillich, who denies that biological death resulted from sin; rather, sin caused a spiritual death (pp. 66-67). "A theological distinction is thus made between physical death as natural and spiritual death as unnatural, and caused by sin" (p. 53). Tillich believed that, from creation humans were mortal, and thus sin did not produce death. However, sin gave death its power, which is conquered only in participation with the eternal. The idea that the Fall has physically changed the cellular or psychological structure of humans (and nature) is considered by some, including Tillich, to be absurd and unbiblical. The latter does accept the creation of Adam as histori-

---

18. Anderson, *Theology, Death and Dying*, p. 41. Anderson refers to Barth's *Church Dogmatics*, vol. III, pt. 2, pp. 616-17. Hereafter, page references to Anderson's work will appear in parentheses in the text.

cal, because human nature is a product of the evolution of the biological species. Sin is not a biological event, but rather an existential paradox centered in the alienation of the human self from God, which is experienced as a lack of faith. The death spoken of in the Genesis account of creation and the Fall, therefore, is an existential and theological reality, not one that introduced physical death into the human race (p. 53).

Anderson interprets Barth as saying that there was in fact disease and death prior to human sin (p. 55). This seems to be an astounding interpretation when one reads in *Church Dogmatics:* "As man's eternal corruption, but also as its sign, death is not a part of man's nature as God created it. But it entered into the world through sin as an alien Lord" (Rom. 5:12, 14, 17; 1 Cor. 15:22).[19] God created the world and humans and said they were good. How could disease and death be considered good? There seems no ground for arguing for the imperfection of original human nature, because the need for Jesus Christ's death and resurrection is tied to the fact of our fallen nature.

It is difficult to follow Anderson's seemingly contradictory arguments that, from creation, death and disease were possible, and that decay and corruption were possible before the Fall. If this were true, what, then, would be the significance of the Fall?[20] Anderson argues that this is a necessary position if one does not believe in the immortality of the soul. However, it is precisely because of sin that we need a savior. Traditional Protestant theology seems clear on this point. "Christian theology holds, on the grounds of a biblical anthropology, that human persons are in no way created to be or to become immortal by their nature. Rather, persons created in the image and likeness of God live within the limits of a human nature bounded by mortality and dependent on God for the gift of immortal life through resurrection from the dead. The promise of immortality that was basically implicit in the Old Testament, with only occasional explicit citations, has been defined in the New Testament as personal and bodily resurrection from the dead" (p. 59).

19. Barth, *Church Dogmatics*, vol. III, pt. 2, p. 600.

20. Anderson, *Theology, Death and Dying*, p. 55. "Barth can thus argue that dying can be held to be intrinsic to human nature as originally created by God. Whatever corruption and liability to death there is in nature, including disease, are present in the world before there is sin. Yet, this empirical reality of human nature has no absolute power over Adam, because he is upheld as a human person in his human nature by the sovereign power of God as creator and Lord of life and death." So this means that there is no "pre-fallen human nature where none of the biological laws of decay and corruption as presently known apply."

Death as Punishment

In chapter 2, I examined several images of death, among them death as punishment and death as friend. I will now discuss these from a Christian perspective. Some theologians argue that death is both natural and intrusive, though in Genesis 3, death is viewed as punishment for primeval rebellion. However, for Christians, death is robbed of its powers; this elimination was anticipated in Hosea 13:14 and exegeted in 1 Corinthians 15:55-56 and Revelation 21:4.

In the New Testament the power of death first is broken by baptism (symbolically death, dying, and rebirth) in Romans 6:3, and discipleship in 2 Corinthians 4:11, 1 Peter 2:24, and Revelation 12:11. Even with death as punishment, there is also the theme of being pulled toward death. Paul reflects this in Philippians 1:23, but in this tension between staying in the body and being present with the Lord, he decides for now he is to be in this life. Christians need not fear death because nothing separates us from God (Rom. 8:38-39).[21] "Eternity is born in time, and every time someone dies whom we have loved dearly, eternity can break into our mortal existence a little bit more."[22]

Death as Friend or Enemy

There is a certain strain in Christian theology that refers to death as a friend. This is often a counterpoint to the medicalization of death and the technological advancements that seem to guarantee not much more than a breathing corpse. In these instances, physical death seems like a friend. Henri Nouwen and James Woodward, to name just two people, have written about befriending death.[23] Nouwen's emphasis seems at first to be with regard to a person's preparing herself and thinking about death, and he traces his view to James Hillman, originator of archetypal psychology, who spoke of this vis-à-vis embracing the totality of our ex-

21. Bruce Metzger and Michael Coogan, eds., *The Oxford Companion to the Bible* (New York: Oxford University Press, 1993), pp. 160-61.

22. Robert Durback, ed., *Seeds of Hope: A Henri Nouwen Reader* (New York: Image Books, Doubleday), p. 195.

23. James Woodward, *Befriending Death* (London: SPCK, 2005). This book has both practical resources and keen theological insights for the Christian confronting the death of a loved one.

perience. This acceptance of the dark and the painful can lead to an acceptance of death.

Furthermore, if we have not accepted death, we cannot live life to the fullest. Fear of death can rule our days so that our joy in living can be diminished. With all that said, however, death is a breaking-in of evil, a disruption, a sense of judgment, finality, loss, sadness, grief. But death can be a friend when disease ravages us. Here we advocate a "letting go" — allowing our disease to run its course. This does not necessitate a belief that death is a friend; rather, when our biological body is worn out, it is time to enter into a fuller life free of our physical body. Nouwen's insights on befriending death are based on allowing love to overcome death.

> But how do we befriend death? . . . I think love — deep, human love — does not know death. . . . Real love says, "Forever." Love will always reach out toward the eternal. Love comes from that place within us where death cannot enter. Love does not accept the limits of hours, days, weeks, months, years, or centuries. Love is not willing to be imprisoned by time. . . . The same love that reveals the absurdity of death also allows us to befriend death. The same love that forms the basis of our grief is also the basis of our hope; the same love that makes us cry out in pain also must enable us to develop a liberating intimacy with our own most basic brokenness.[24]

Is conquering or transcending death the same as befriending it? If we say that the sting and grief of death is removed by love, in that sense we may have befriended it. However, in the ultimate sense, for the Christian, death is an enemy to be conquered.

Hell and Future Punishment

One of the most difficult teachings of the Christian church concerns hell and eternal punishment. The contemporary Protestant funeral service is almost devoid of any reference to hell and eternal punishment. Surprisingly, however, forty-seven books on the concept of hell were published between 2005 and 2007, according to a Google search. There are certainly some people who fear hell, so it is important to understand this doctrine.

Traditional Reformed theology found in John Calvin — and in his

24. Durback, *Seeds of Hope*, pp. 189-90.

nineteenth-century interpreter Charles Hodge — certainly focused on hell and future punishment: there is no end to the blessedness of the elect and the punishment of the wicked (Matt. 25:41, 46). Calvin's main points are as follows: God, not people, judges our destiny, that is, who goes to heaven or hell; God's goodness and infinite mercy mean that all things are possible in terms of our destiny; who qualifies as a believer in Jesus Christ is not reduced to members of a particular ecclesiastical body; and God's time, that is, the concept of past, present, and future is different, so God's judgment should not be thought of as taking place immediately at our physical death.[25]

Hodge, however, clings to the doctrine of eternal punishment based on the eternal existence of the soul after death (though this view does seem to shade into the immortality of the soul): "[T]here is no repentance or reformation in the future world; that those who depart this life unreconciled to God, remain forever in this state of alienation, and therefore are forever sinful and miserable. This is the doctrine of the whole Christian Church, of the Greeks, of the Latins, and of all the great historical Protestant bodies."[26]

The crux of the debate is whether there is unending, relentless punishment or whether, after death, there is a chance to repent. Hodge seems to take a rather firm line against the universalist position that eventually all will be saved. Hodge addresses many of these issues head-on. He explores these questions in the following vein: he initially presents the arguments of the universalists, the first being that the purpose of punishment is reformation, so that should be the goal; the second point is that unbelievers will only be punished as long as they continue to sin, and thus punishment is not necessarily eternal. This belief argues that everyone will eventually repent and turn to God. Others suggest that their punishment will not necessarily be painful or that physical life will end everything, and thus there will be no pain; but neither will there be eternal life.

Hodge cites several passages used by the universalists.

"Therefore just as one man's trespass led to condemnation for all, so one man's act of righteousness leads to justification and life for all" (Rom. 5:18). This is made to mean, that as all men are condemned for

---

25. John Calvin, *Institutes of the Christian Religion*, book III, chapter 25, trans. John Allen (Philadelphia: Presbyterian Board of Christian Education, 1936), pp. 250-51.

26. Charles Hodge, *Systematic Theology* (New York: Charles Scribner's Sons, 1898), pp. 868-69.

Adam's offense, so all men are justified for the righteousness of Christ. The same interpretation is put upon the parallel passage in 1 Corinthians 15:22: ". . . for as all die in Adam, so all will be made alive in Christ." The same remark may be made in reference to other passages which Universalists rely upon. Thus in 1 Corinthians 15:25, it is said that Christ "must reign, until he has put all his enemies under his feet."[27]

However, Hodge goes on to refute the universalist position. Calvin and Hodge's position against the universalists is buttressed by a number of Scripture passages that speak of eternal punishment.

The sinners in Zion are afraid; trembling has seized the godless: "Who among us can live with the devouring fire? Who among us can live with everlasting flames?" (Isa. 33:14). In Isaiah 66:24 it is said of those who should be excluded from the new heavens and the new earth which the prophet had predicted, ". . . for their worm shall not die, their fire shall not be quenched. . . ." "Hell," however, "is of both worlds, so that in the same essential sense, although in different degrees, it may be said both of him who is still living but accursed, and of him who perished centuries ago, that his worm dieth not and his fire is not quenched." The prophet Daniel (12:2) says of the wicked, that "Many of those who sleep in the dust of the earth shall awake, some to everlasting life, and some to shame and everlasting contempt." In Luke 3:17 it is said that Christ shall ". . . gather the wheat into his granary; but the chaff he will burn with unquenchable fire." In Mark 9:42-48 our Lord says ". . . it is better for you to enter life maimed than to have two hands and go to hell, to the unquenchable fire . . . where their worm never dies, and the fire is never quenched."[28]

Hodge aside, there are a number of Christian theologians who disagree with this strict view of salvation. What about the future life of those who are not Christians? There is some discussion in 1 Corinthians 15:24 that, after an interval in which Christians reign with Christ, the rest of humankind will be saved. C. K. Barrett does not subscribe to this view. Does judgment or grace have the last word? he asks.[29] Hans Conzelmann agrees

27. Hodge, *Systematic Theology*, pp. 871-72.
28. Hodge, *Systematic Theology*, p. 875.
29. C. K. Barrett, *The First Epistle to the Corinthians* (London: Adam and Charles Black, 1968), pp. 355-56.

with Barrett on this point. "Since it is not the mythical schema that holds, but the Pauline transformation of it, 'all' does not mean all men altogether, but all who are in Christ. Paul is only concerned with the resurrection of believers, that is, 'Those that are Christ's' (Gal. 5:24; 1 Cor. 3:23)."[30]

Contemporary process theologians repudiate the Calvinists on this point of eternal punishment. Drawing on a different perspective of time based on quantum physics, they point to God's love of all people. The concept of past, present, and future is different for God. John Macquarrie concentrates on themes of hope, Christ's resurrection, and a universalism vis-à-vis eternal life.

> [He] submits his own third view, which is based on an analogy drawn from the self's ability to be aware in one instant of past, present and future. This is a way we can understand God's eternity. Appealing to Einstein and others in order to eliminate the necessity of a single succession of events and the metaphysical notion of an absolute present or universal now, he contends that both past and future can be equally present to God, à la Aquinas. If this is the case, then, it explains how God can heal and renew the ills of the past: God can redeem them. Macquarrie argues for a nondualistic yet consummate vision of the "single divine work of both creation and redemption." In God's infinite mercy and goodness all things are possible. "God judges, not people; we do not decide who goes to heaven or hell. Believers in Jesus Christ are not reduced to members of a particular ecclesiastical body."[31]

Prior to the process theologians, some have concluded that the great twentieth-century theologian Karl Barth did not believe in eternal punishment. These conclusions are based on several passages that refer to God's light shining from darkness (1 Pet. 1:3; Titus 3:5), that we are saved while we are yet in darkness. The argument is that since there can be no realm hidden from God, even in hell we cannot be removed from God. This is both a comfort and a warning contained in God's omniscience.[32]

Where do we stand, in the end, with the universalist claim? In terms of the funeral service, when we pastorally offer comfort to the Christian

30. Hans Conzelmann, *1 Corinthians* (Philadelphia: Fortress Press, 1976), pp. 269-70.

31. Ted Peters, "One Future," review of *Christian Hope* by John Macquarrie, *The Christian Century* (Jan. 31, 1979): 106.

32. Barth, *Church Dogmatics*, trans. Torrance and Bromiley, vol. II, pt. 1 (Edinburgh: T. & T. Clark, 1957), pp. 274, 538.

family of a deceased unbeliever, we can certainly assert that nothing is beyond God's power to bring people to God's self. It is not up to us to judge who can be saved either now or in eternity. A central point to remember is that the New Testament was more interested in the cosmological dimension to death than simply individual salvation. From this perspective, Jesus' raising of Lazarus from the dead had more to do with foreshadowing the promise of Christ's victory over death in general than it did with saving Lazarus.

Doctrines of Election, Eternity, and Heaven

In any discussion of eternal life and heaven, the question of who will be there arises. For Calvinists, this is the doctrine of election, which comes under discussions of predestination. In the twenty-first century the doctrine of election is scarcely mentioned in Presbyterian funerals. For Calvin, however, it was central, as it was in my own upbringing in the Orthodox Presbyterian Church. I was called a child of the covenant, which for me meant memorizing the shorter Westminster Catechism and not going to the movies on Sundays. However, on reflection, what was really being said is that I was one of the elect.

Calvin argues that salvation is only for the elect.[33] The person who believes in Christ passed out of death into life (John 5:24) — by joyfully preparing and waiting for eternity and the day of the final resurrection.[34] By our tribulations God weans us from excessive love of this present life. The miseries of this life make us long for the next one.[35]

The doctrine of the resurrection is also related to questions of eschatology and our understanding of eternal life. The Roman Catholic theologian Hans Küng explores the resurrection of Jesus in light of his ascension and the notions of heaven and hell. "Death," says Küng, "is a passing into God, is a homecoming into God's seclusion, is assumption into His glory." In the epilogue of *Eternal Life?* he asks the questions that must nag even those who have followed his arguments carefully: "What difference would it make?" "If I believe in eternal life," he answers, "then, in all modesty and all realism and without yielding to the terror of the violent benefactors of

---

33. Calvin, "Election in Christ," *Institutes of the Christian Religion,* book III, chap. 24.
34. Calvin, *Institutes,* book III, chap. 24.
35. Calvin, *Institutes,* book III, chap. 9.

the people, I can work for a better future, a better society, even a better church, in peace, freedom and justice — and knowing that all this can only be sought and never fully realized by man."[36]

Küng's doctrine of eternal life echoes Reformed theology, and that is not surprising given Karl Barth's influence on his theology. However, recognizing the mystery is essential. "Christian . . . statements about eternal life are only images of the unimaginable and that finite personhood loses all the limitations of the finite in the dimension of the infinite, beyond time and space."[37] We become, in a way, pure spirituality.

Many are keenly interested in teachings about heaven as a place of love and freedom from suffering. The word *ouranos* ("heaven") occurs 272 times in the New Testament, especially the phrase *basileia ton ouranon* ("the kingdom of heaven"), which is not a cosmological but a theological and soteriological term. Angels are seen as messengers and servants of God from heaven, and Paul writes of the bodily form of heavenly beings in 1 Corinthians 15:40. God created heaven and earth (Acts 4:24; 14:15; 17:24; Rev. 10:6; 14:7); heaven is God's throne (Matt. 5:34). 1 Peter 1:4 also refers to the inheritance of Christians in heaven, which is reflected in Philippians 3:20 as well. Barth gives us important insight into the nature of heaven: "Heaven in biblical language is the sum of the inaccessible and incomprehensible side of God, the creative correspondence to His glory, which is veiled from man, and cannot be described except at His initiative."[38]

The Doctrine of Resurrection

Putting aside for the moment the doctrine of election, we move to the question of the resurrection. The belief that Christ was raised from the dead by God, and therefore we will be raised, is an article of faith that we are better off not trying to prove scientifically. However, Oxford philosopher Richard Swinburne used Bayes's theorem to prove the probability of the resurrection to be 97 percent.[39] It is obvious that the doctrine of eternal

36. Hans Küng, trans. Edward Quinn, *Eternal Life? Life After Death as a Medical, Philosophical, and Theological Problem* (Garden City, NY: Doubleday, 1984), p. 232.

37. Hans Küng and Walter Jens, *A Dignified Dying*, trans. John Bowden (London: SCM Press, 1995), p. 14.

38. Barth, *Church Dogmatics*, vol. III, pt. 2, p. 453.

39. Emily Eakin, "So God's Really in the Details?" *The New York Times on the web,*

life is related to the resurrection, especially the resurrection of the body; so we do not reduce our future state to one of disembodied souls that are floating in space. This salvation is not just for the soul, but includes the resurrection of the body. When we die, our souls are present with Christ (John 12:32), but we wait for final glory until Christ comes again. The doctrine of the resurrection of the body is based on the body's being good, unlike the Manicheans' view that it is evil (1 Thess. 5:23). Our bodies are temples of the Holy Spirit (1 Cor. 6:15).[40]

The incarnation and resurrection are central to the gospel, the Christian church, and our life as individual Christians, as Thomas Torrance observes. The resurrection reinterprets reality. There is no doubt that this doctrine, more than any other, is of supreme comfort to those family members who have lost a loved one: that death does not have the final word is an astounding comfort, when you think about it. One of the important truths of Christian teaching is that the incarnation and resurrection of Jesus were antithetical to what religious people of their age believed about God. Therefore, these doctrines forced themselves on the church against the grain, so to speak. In a sense, this is also true for us today. This is not some mythologizing by the apostles, as Bultmann would have us believe, but a breaking into history by God.[41]

The radical nature of the resurrection is seen in the New Testament writers' search for adequate words, *anistemi* and *egeirō* (to "lift" or "raise

---

May 11, 2002: http://query.nytimes.com/gst/fullpage.html?res=9C06EEDF1F30F932A25756 C0A9649C8B63&scp=1&sq=so+god%27s+really+in+the+details%3F&st=nyt (accessed Jan. 30, 2008). "Given e and k, h is true if and only if c is true. The probability of h given e and k is 97 percent; in other words, the probability of the resurrection is 97 percent. The question is whether we follow the evidentialists, such as Swinburne, or the Reformed (Calvinist) epistemologists, such as Alvin Plantinga and Nicholas Wolterstorff. Epistemologists rely on Thomas Reid, an eighteenth-century Scottish 'common sense' philosopher, who argued that many legitimate beliefs are simply instinctual. . . . These scholars reject the evidentialist insistence on independent proofs. After all, they point out, the ability to distinguish good evidence from bad requires reason, but reason is considered a 'basic belief,' one that doesn't require additional evidence to be true. But if reason can be considered a basic belief, then so, too, say the Reformed epistemologists, can faith in God. . . . Some beliefs are simply self-evident. Most people know that 1 + 1 = 2 . . . their bodily state — like 'I feel dizzy' — without having to consult other sources. . . . [So] . . . we do believe lots of things that don't have publicly formulated arguments."

40. Calvin, *Institutes of the Christian Religion*, bk. III, chap. 25, pp. 253, 257.
41. Thomas F. Torrance, *Space, Time and Resurrection* (Edinburgh: Handsell Press, 1976), pp. 21, 74, 17-18.

up"). Christ's resurrection was unique, since Jesus was never to die again; thus it transcended the old conditions of life so that death has no ultimate domain. One of the key points here is that Christ was raised by God. "Paul grounds belief in Jesus' resurrection by God with his prior Pharisaic faith in a resurrection of the dead: Verses 15-16 remind us of the *18 Benedictions,* a version of which he may have known and recited in the synagogue."[42] The importance of resurrection faith for New Testament theology becomes clearer when one studies the use and meaning of the Greek verb for "to raise" and the Greek noun for "resurrection"; the verb that means "to raise" is *egeirō,* and from it we get "being raised" *(egēgertai)* (cf. Matt. 22:31; Acts 23:6; 24:15, 21; 26:23; 1 Cor. 15:12-19). The verb *egeirō* occurs frequently in Greek literature, but usually in the sense of "to rise" from sleep, "to make to stand," and (infrequently) "to raise" from the dead (cf. *Iliad* 24.551). The Greek noun for "resurrection" is *anastasis.*

As Torrance points out, it is important to make a distinction between Christ's resurrection and the disciples' experience of it. It is the *event* that is the primary fact, not the experience of it. One is reminded here of the pitfall of the British empiricist, where experience becomes the measure and reality is grounded in our experience of it rather than an objectively measured occurrence. Although Jesus Christ's resurrection is a historical event, it is actually more than this: a continuity of who Jesus Christ is, and, in turn, who we are.

When we reflect on Christ's resurrection, we see the triumph of light over darkness, good over evil; it has cosmic dimensions. There is a blending of the crucifixion and resurrection, which are two intertwined realities.[43] Resurrection is linked to God's forgiveness, which is surely a central message. The story of the paralytic's healing in Mark 2:1-12 and Luke 5:17-26 makes the connection between forgiveness of sins and restoration, that is, healing.

Jesus submits himself to death and nothingness, which is used for the reconciliation of the world with God. The Holy Spirit works through Jesus Christ to bring the world's salvation. The parousia is the fulfillment of the promise made in the resurrection. In John 14:18, Jesus promises not to leave us comfortless. The knowledge of God has come but not come; it is

---

42. James H. Charlesworth, "Individual Resurrection from the Dead and Immortality of the Soul," unpublished English manuscript later translated and published in French as "Résurrection Individuelle et Immortalité de l'Âme," in *Histoire du Christianisme: Anamnèsis,* vol. 14, ed. J. M. Mayer et al. (Paris: Desclée, 2001), pp. 505-51.

43. Torrance, *Space, Time and Resurrection,* pp. 32, 39, 47-48.

both present and future.[44] Resurrection and reconciliation are knit together: the bond of unity and love are forged as we become sons and daughters of God. Resurrection and redemption are also linked as the bodily resurrection, in a sense, puts an end to our corruptible bodies and fulfills the ultimate destiny of what it means to be human.[45]

Historical Evidence of the Resurrection

A point that both Barth and Torrance raise is whether the historical fact of the resurrection or the faith in the resurrection are more important. For Barrett, faith in the resurrection is not created simply by the discovery of the empty tomb.[46] Of course, Rudolf Bultmann, the Jesus Seminar scholars, and others challenge the historicity of the resurrection. Bultmann demythologizes the resurrection and interprets it as "the rise of faith in the risen Lord," not a historical event.[47] This position is contrary to Reformed theology, which argues that the belief in Christ's historical manifestation in the resurrection is not a "historicist" concept of history, but is history.[48] "Jesus Himself did rise again and appear to His disciples. This is the content of the Easter history, the Easter time, the Christian faith and Christian proclamation, both then and at all times." The Christian belief in Christ's resurrection is not some wishful thinking on the part of the disciples; in fact, quite the contrary, they had lost all hope. They went into hiding for fear that they might be the next ones to be crucified. It was Jesus' subsequent appearances and their experience of the risen Christ that turned their lives around.[49] Resurrection was central to the whole New Testament history and the birth of the Christian church.

We can, however, speak of the historical nature of the resurrection and still refer to it as a miracle. If we use Augustine's definition of miracle

44. Karl Barth, *Church Dogmatics,* vol. IV, pt. 1, pp. 299-309, quoted in John McTavish and Harold Wells, eds., *Karl Barth: Preaching Through the Christian Year* (Edinburgh: T. & T. Clark, 1978), pp. 213, 216, 262.

45. Torrance, *Space, Time and Resurrection,* pp. 69, 75, 82.

46. C. K. Barrett, *The First Epistle to the Corinthians* (London: Adam and Charles Black, 1968), p. 349.

47. Erwin Fahlbusch, Geoffrey Bromiley, David B. Barrett, eds., *The Encyclopedia of Christianity* (Grand Rapids: Eerdmans, 1999), p. 670.

48. Barth, *Church Dogmatics,* vol. IV, pt. 2, p. 335.

49. Barth, *Church Dogmatics,* vol. III, pt. 2, pp. 442-47, 448-54, quoted in McTavish and Wells, *Karl Barth,* p. 205.

as anything contrary to the *known* processes of nature, the resurrection is, in fact, a deeper revelation of nature and the created order that breaks through as a new understanding of God's world. We come up against the limits of our own knowledge and cannot judge God from some higher "scientific plane," but simply acknowledge that God is the creator of reality as well as of nature.

One might take a cue here from Celtic spirituality, which has a unique understanding of the relationship between the material and spiritual. There is not, in Celtic spirituality, a sharp divide between the two, which is one of our stumbling blocks in accepting the resurrection. The material exists for the sake of the spiritual; the material is a sacrament of our true homeland. Christians are called to live in tension between these worlds without rejecting either one, since both worlds were created by God. The world should be read "as a window on mystery." The shadow is what comes first, and afterwards the substance (Col. 2:17).[50] Of course, there is also a true reverence for nature. Note that the Celtic cross reflects the earth in its orb and the spiritual in its cross.[51]

Jewish Concepts of the Resurrection

Resurrection is the centerpiece of a Christian theology of death. As James Charlesworth so provocatively argues, it is not Christ who rose from the dead, but God who raised Christ. It was not some immortal part of Christ that lived on, but God who broke the jaws of death. Resurrection has its roots in Jewish teaching and is not simply a new doctrine. However, this is dramatically different from the Greek immortality of the soul, or the transmigration of the souls of Hindus, or our memory of the deceased continuing life.

Most Christians are not aware that our doctrine of the resurrection actually has strong Jewish roots. Charlesworth's research has helped to change that misperception. The Jewish view of the "raising up" of the dead to an immortal and blessed condition, and the Jewish theology of "forevermore," which may be superlative time and not unending time, provide this

50. Thomas O'Loughlin, *Journeys on the Edges: The Celtic Tradition* (London: Darton, Longman & Todd, 2000), pp. 45-47.

51. J. Philip Newell lecture, Princeton Theological Seminary Continuing Education Center, Feb. 25, 2009.

framework. The Jewish concept of individual resurrection contrasted to the Greek view of the immortality of the soul. Is this a kind of reincarnation in which the soul is reincarnated in another body later in time? Sometimes the Jewish teaching means that the soul moves to another existence, with the same individual in a different bodily form; perhaps the soul moves to the Island of the Blessed Ones. The latter concept is well known in Greek and Roman thought and shapes the Jewish/Christian document named *History of the Rechabites*.

Before C.E. 136, according to a number of literary sources, far more Jews believed in the resurrection of the body after death than in the immortality of the soul. This belief developed within early (or Second Temple) Judaism.[52] Barrett echoes Charlesworth's interpretation: "Jews, Paul among them, had immortality in their tradition as well as resurrection."[53] As Charlesworth puts it:

> According to Mark, Jesus taught the classic belief in the resurrection of the dead: "when the dead rise from the dead, they neither marry nor are given in marriage, but are like angels in heaven" (Mark 12:25). Jesus' resurrection belief aligned him with the Pharisees, who believed in the classic doctrine of resurrection (Mark 12:18-23; Acts 23:6-8). Jesus' concept is also parallel to that found in 2 Baruch and contains the belief (found in Daniel, some Qumranic compositions such as 1QH, 2 Baruch, and 4 Ezra) that the righteous will be like angels. The author of the Gospel of John adds a new dimension to the concept of resurrection. He clearly knows and affirms the belief, and it cannot be attributed to a later editor (see John 5:21, 28-29). What the Fourth Evangelist emphasizes is that Jesus provides immortality in the present, even though there will be a future resurrection. A key passage is this: "Very truly, I tell you, anyone who hears my word and believes him who sent me has eternal life, and does not come under judgment, but has passed from death to life" (John 5:24). When one believes in him, then one has "living water" immediately (John 4:14) and is "born anew [or from above]" (John 3:3-15). Thus, the Fourth Evangelist corrects the idea that resurrection is only a future hope or promise for the one who believes in Jesus.[54]

52. Charlesworth, "Individual Resurrection from the Dead and Immortality of the Soul," pp. 505-51.

53. Barrett, *The First Epistle to the Corinthians*, p. 347.

54. Charlesworth, "Individual Resurrection," pp. 505-51.

The Apostle Paul on the Resurrection: 1 Corinthians 15

There is no doubt that 1 Corinthians 15 is the *locus classicus* of the Christian faith regarding eschatology. In fact, so much is concentrated in this fifteenth chapter that Karl Barth wrote a whole volume on this single chapter.[55] It is one of the passages most frequently cited at Christian funerals. However, most pastors de-emphasize its central doctrine of sin and death — which create the need for resurrection — and instead concentrate on our resurrection. Since 1 Corinthians 15 is so central to the Christian faith, there are hundreds of commentaries, of which we will consult Barrett's, Thiselton's, Conzelmann's, and Barth's. Barrett and many commentators on Corinthians take at face value the claim that if you take out the resurrection, there is nothing left.[56] Thiselton says: "Justification by grace and the resurrection of the dead are two sides of the same coin."[57]

Barrett sets this classic passage within a historical context. Christ died for our sins according to the Scriptures, so this is a fulfillment of the prophecy that is terribly important in terms of historical continuity. The important points in this passage are that Christ died, was buried, and was raised. Barrett surprisingly asserts that God's raising of Jesus cannot be demonstrated by historical evidence. However, Paul's listing of the historical appearance of Jesus seems to be an attempt to substantiate that these events really happened. Since all of us inherit death from Adam as our destiny, we are born into a sinful world.[58] Christ's death has rectified the condition caused by human sin. Paul interestingly repeats many aspects of the death and resurrection of Jesus as a fulfillment of Scripture. In addition, this is a two-part process, the sting of death, which is mitigated by its being the gateway to God.[59]

The parousia is important in Paul's argument as those who are alive at Christ's second coming will not die, but the dead will also be raised. Of course, scholars generally conclude that Paul expected the parousia in his

55. A. Katherine Grieb, "Last Things First: Karl Barth's Theological Exegesis of 1 Corinthians in *The Resurrection of the Dead*," *Scottish Journal of Theology* 56, no. 1 (2003): 49-64. Of course, that book was published in 1924, and Barth had a great deal more to say on the subject in the subsequent *Church Dogmatics*.

56. Barrett, *First Corinthians*, p. 348.

57. Anthony Thiselton, *1 Corinthians* (Grand Rapids: Eerdmans, 2006), p. 254.

58. Barrett, *First Corinthians*, pp. 336, 353.

59. Thiselton, *1 Corinthians*, pp. 262, 273.

lifetime.[60] Here one has to pause and ask why a believing Christian has to go through death at all. Why not be lifted, like Enoch or Elijah, directly up to heaven? Why did God structure things as such? The emphasis of Paul is for the necessity of death as the condition of life and the discontinuity between the present and the future life. In the Greek, *sarx* ("state," or "flesh") and *sōma* ("form," or "body") are both used to describe our state; the two are not always synonymous.[61] Of course, God's plan is a mystery: "Eye hath not seen, and ear hath not heard what God has in store for us" (1 Cor. 2:9). The only thing we know for sure is God's amazing love and grace, which surrounds and embraces us. The waiting father in the parable of the prodigal son not only forgives the prodigal but also searches out the jealous older brother. God wants to bring all of us into the fold. Is this the answer to the universalist debate?

To summarize the insights from 1 Corinthians 15, there are five main points concerning the last things: (1) Christianity without resurrection is a lie; (2) because Christ rose from the dead, we will overcome death; (3) how we live is affected by our understanding of death; (4) at our resurrection we will have new bodies; and (5) our victory over death calls forth thanksgiving to God.

(1) *Christianity without resurrection is a lie.* If Jesus Christ has not been raised, then our preaching is nonsense and our faith is in vain. This is why, as believers, our central message is Jesus Christ crucified and resurrected. Jesus as a prophet, a moral teacher, or the kind man of Nazareth is not enough. The power of the gospel is in the resurrection. Much of this chapter is an argument about the absolute necessity of accepting Christ's resurrection or ours through him. Otherwise, all torture (v. 32 — wild beasts), restrained living (v. 33 — why not follow the Epicurean philosophy of "eat, drink, and be merry"?), and living the moral life are in vain. This passage also makes clear that without eternal life, how we live and the company we keep and whether we sin or not, is of no importance. That is why a belief in eternal life gives us more concern with the world's problems and how we live, rather than providing an escape from them.

(2) *Because Christ rose from the dead, we will overcome death.* Paul draws a typology between Christ and Adam. Adam brought death; death entered the world through sin; death is the natural outcome of our disobedience to God; death is the conclusion of sin. 1 Corinthians 15:56: The con-

60. Barrett, *First Corinthians*, pp. 380-81.
61. Hans Conzelmann, *1 Corinthians* (Philadelphia: Fortress Press, 1976), pp. 281-82.

nection between sin and death are clear, which gives death its extra sting. Death as enemy is linked to fallenness, sin, and divine judgment. The sting of death is gone with Christ's resurrection. Thiselton, quoting Cullmann, points out that Socrates faced death under the illusion that it was not to be feared; but under Christ, death *has* lost its horror.[62]

The fact of death is a constant reminder of our evil. Death is the movement of self-obliteration of humans. When we are dead, we are dead all over; we have no deathless substance, no soul breaking through the body's shell. If we did, there would be no need for Jesus Christ to have died and been raised for us. Christ conquered death, for God has put all things in subjection under his feet. The buried Christ will not stay dead: no sooner is the obituary written than the birth notice clamors to be read. This is the Christian's answer to death: Jesus Christ's resurrection. We are not immortal, but God has promised to resurrect us as God resurrected Christ.

(3) *How we live is affected by our understanding of death.* When we come to that last moment of this life, and death hovers over us, we are comforted by the knowledge that Jesus Christ has been there. How we live is affected by our understanding of death. If we are not afraid of death, we can face life without fear. In connection with baptism, it was a practice for early Christians to be baptized for others who had died without baptism — in order to assure their resurrection. We do not know how Paul felt about this practice, but he uses it as reflecting the centrality of a belief in the resurrection in understanding death.

(4) *At our resurrection we will have new bodies.* The resurrection of the body is the central message here: the natural body is sown, the spiritual body raised up (v. 44). The spiritual body is animated by God's spirit. This doctrine is tied to the analogy of the first and the last Adam. In fact, the last Adam, Christ, transforms the first Adam — that is, our body — from a material to a spiritual body, and so we become heavenly persons (v. 48). Paul's typology of a first and last Adam provides a corporate solidarity between them.

The kind of resurrected body we will have is a point of great discussion. Verse 38: God gives us a body *(sōma).* This body "includes a person's capacity to be identified, to relate to God, and to communicate with others in a 'public' environment." We are the same self, existing even though our body has gone through changes. The resurrected body, unlike the perish-

62. Thiselton, *1 Corinthians,* pp. 271, 289.

able body, is totally present to and open to the Holy Spirit. This is one of its unique characteristics.[63]

The popular belief among the Greeks of Paul's time was that our soul lived on and that the body, as the center of evil, died. However, Christians believe in the resurrection of the *body*. We will have a suitable body for a glorious life, not one of weakness, but power; not perishable, but imperishable. This is our comfort: that we are not absorbed in some great beyond, but we are allowed to continue as individuals. We will recognize our loved ones, as the disciples finally recognized Jesus in his resurrected body.

(5) *Our victory over death calls forth thanksgiving to God.* Christ has ruptured death's front line. He has enveloped us in his life so that what we normally call our life is but a small segment of the total life in God. "If you would indeed behold the spirit of death, open your heart wide into the body of life." When we die, we fall into the hands of the living one.[64] Death cannot separate us from the love of Jesus Christ. We have no fellowship with death, but community with God. When we believe that Jesus Christ died and was raised for us, the opposite of death is not physical life, but eternal life. When we weep here and say goodbye to a loved one, God is saying, "Hello, welcome into my presence." This reality brings forth thanksgiving to God.

Funerals in the Reformed Theological Tradition

Now that we have set forth a Christian theology of hope and resurrection, we can construct funerals that reflect this theology. In planning the Christian funeral, one should remember that, though death is the last enemy to be conquered, physical death may be a friend for those who are in extreme pain and suffering — those who long to leave this mortal earth. In addition, we experience the paradox of believing in the joy of the deceased to be in God's presence, while at the same time we weep over their loss to us. We are called to both resist and accept death. Death is the result of sin, but God is still Lord over death.

Given these ambiguities and paradoxes, caring for and counseling the dying and planning their funerals is — to put it mildly — a challenge.

63. Thiselton, *1 Corinthians*, pp. 280, 283.
64. Kahlil Gibran, *Visions of the Prophet* (Hertfordshire, UK: Wordsworth Editions, 1997), p. 50.

The bereaved are anxious, and they are eager to know where the loved one is. Some wonder if they are in hell. Some family members may even wish they were, if those members have experienced violence and abuse at the hands of the deceased. The pastor and/or caregiver should encourage forgiveness in these cases, so that the bereaved can be truly healed. All the issues of past relationships, for better or worse, surface at the time of death. But our theology is based on the promise that God, not humans, is in charge of our destiny, and thus comfort can be given at the funeral.

Preparation for the Funeral

Many people wait until their loved one is gravely ill or has died before they start thinking about the funeral. Ideally, preparation for a funeral should begin when those growing older are healthy and able to think through the issues surrounding death and dying. Reflecting on the meaning of death can often free us to live life more fully, unless it becomes a morbid preoccupation with death itself. It is important to read the funeral service that is specified in one's church tradition, and to have a meeting with the pastor to better understand the segments and meaning of the service. Christian services are not simply a question of personal preferences. However, there is latitude in the selection of biblical texts and music, service leadership, and who will share remembrances of the deceased. People often write their own obituary. The advance planning of a funeral takes a tremendous burden off the family, whose members are usually eager to do what their loved one would have wanted; difficulties arise when they do not know. With fewer Americans attending church, however, an increasing number of people have their initial meeting with a funeral home director, who may in turn contact a local member of the clergy who is available to conduct the service.

For the pastor's role in the funeral preparation, classes on death and dying, which include writing an advance directive and a funeral service, can be extremely helpful. Taking a group of interested people to a local funeral home can be very important in giving them a sense of ease and familiarity when later they need to officiate at a funeral service. In fact, encouraging every member to put his or her advance directive and funeral plans on file with the church is important (see Appendix F for a form for clergy use). Of course, changes and updates can continue to be made, and this may happen especially when someone falls gravely ill and has a different view of what is important in her funeral service. Sensitivity to bring up these discussions with a terminally ill person when it is appropriate and to listen closely to her wishes requires time, patience, and delicacy. If these conversations are with the pastor, the latter should seek to draw the family into the conversations, with the person's permission, so that there are no surprises. In the chapter entitled "Clergy at the Bedside" above, I discussed the pastor's and the congregation's role in the condolence ministry. The needs of families do not stop with the funeral; indeed, they may actually intensify after everyone else has gotten on with their lives.

Many pastors decry the trend in which funeral services seem to be moving from the church to the funeral home.

> It seems to me that one of the best times for ministry to a family is in the careful planning and conducting of a church service in honor of the deceased. In a church a true worshiping community can gather, songs of the faith can actually be sung (instead of taped music or hymns being played before or after a service in a funeral home), and the departed's life can be celebrated in a place that had real meaning for him or her. And while funeral homes may be familiar and comfortable settings, none of the above statements hold true for them.[65]

Funerals are one of the most difficult and important times of a pastor's ministry. People are thrown into emotional chaos and lean on the pastor to bring some order to the midst of this crisis. Every pastor will be called on to perform funerals, and every practicing pastor can recall a large variety of funerals — from the sublime to the ridiculous.

Families find solace in different rites and rituals. They need to cling to something familiar, whether it be music, Scripture, the presence of loved ones, or a church to which they have some connection. That can sometimes be a tangential connection. One church performed a memorial service for a young man in his twenties who, with his fiancé, had drowned in the tragic Baltimore Harbor boating accident. He had not attended that particular church in a decade, nor did the parents attend the church; but the son had been confirmed there. Seven hundred people packed into the church for a very moving service. According to the parents, the pastoral staff was a tremendous source of comfort. Through that service and pastoral comforting they reconnected with the church. The pastor used opera music and in-

65. Will Humes, pastor, First United Methodist Church, Pottstown, *One Thing I Know blog website*, "Churches Versus Funeral Homes," August 28, 2008: http://onethingiknow.net/2008/08/28/churches-versus-funeral-homes/ (accessed Dec. 17, 2008).

cluded Jewish perspectives as a way to incorporate the whole family, which had both Jewish and Christian members. It was a model of pastoral care, proclamation of the gospel, and hope and sensitivity to non-Christians.

Another memorial service was for a father whose children were estranged from him, and who really did not want to be there. Scattering ashes at the beach became almost a counseling session, as the family talked through its resentments as part of the service. Some would rage in anger at their deceased father, leave the service, and then be encouraged to return. It was a tumultuous experience, but the family later reported that it was ultimately very healing.

Then there are the funerals when the minister does not know the deceased. In one such service, the pastor kept mispronouncing the deceased grandfather's last name until finally a grandson stood up in the middle of the service and shouted, "Can't you even say his name right?"

A pastor of a Presbyterian church in a small farm community wrote about the graveside service of his most unusual funeral:

> The deceased was one of at least six children (same mother, several fathers). The mother died and the children were placed for adoption (at least the younger ones). I knew there was bad blood in the family, and I was told that "Lucky" had served several times in the state prison, so I picked three passages about forgiveness: a Psalm, Jacob and Esau, and part of Romans 8 (nothing can separate us from the love of God).

The principal complication in this service was that the deceased had a common-law wife who was not recognized by all the family; furthermore, his sister had married her sister's ex-husband, so obviously there were strains in the family. As if this were not enough, friends put interesting items into the casket during the service.

> Two packets of cigarettes. A bottle of Jim Beam. Two peacock feathers. Harley Davidson attire. Someone called for a cigarette lighter. No one had one. "Well," she said, "we buried [name] with cigarettes but no lighter. If we gave [name of deceased] a lighter, they could have a real good time." Someone went to their car and got a lighter. They were now all through, but someone asked "Did you put in that whiskey?" "Yes," his brother replied. "Has he drunk it up already?"[66]

66. George Robert Pasley, "For somber reflection," e-mail message to the author (July 17, 2000). Used with permission.

All these examples illustrate that contemporary Americans are looking to create their own rituals when they are absent from the church and society. Protestant Christians are somewhat impoverished in their rituals concerning dying, death, and burial. But there are now some attempts to respond to this need with books such as *Healing Liturgies for the Seasons of Life*, which has a number of liturgies to use at the time of serious illness, death, and dying.[67]

Presbyterian Funeral Services

In order to understand the funeral and its theology, let us examine the service of the Presbyterian Church USA. Its themes are a continuous narrative, so it takes place in the church building, the meeting place of the fellowship of believers. It is not a story about immortality; rather, it is about the death and resurrection of Jesus Christ, who conquered the last enemy, death, that we might have eternal life.

What is important is that the theology and funeral service should be consistent. Charles Bartow refers to the two pairs of master plots in Presbyterian services: the story of Jesus in remembrance and baptism, the dying and rising; the story of God, who comforts the afflicted (Ps. 107); the story of believers, that is, the grieving congregations — trouble, cry, comfort.[68] In examining the funeral rites surrounding the service itself, we can perceive its meaning and comfort and its importance as part of the Christian message. This is what families are looking for, and we can hope Christian ministers are providing it. However, we have all heard horror stories of pastors who even condemn the deceased to hell during the service, leaving the family in a paroxysm of grief. Behind a pastor's preaching and worship leadership of the funeral, he must be clear about his own theology and what he believes about the resurrection. This doctrine is central to the Christian funeral: clarity about its meaning will shape the whole service, which is why I have given an extensive exposition to it in this chapter.

The service as found in the *Book of Common Worship* contains the following elements: placing of the pall; sentences of Scripture; psalm,

67. Abigail Rian Evans, *Healing Liturgies for the Seasons of Life* (Louisville: Westminster John Knox Press, 2004).
68. Charles Bartow, lecture in author's "Death and Dying" class, Princeton Theological Seminary (Fall 2004).

hymn, or spiritual; prayer; confession and pardon; readings from Scripture; sermon; affirmation of faith; hymn; prayers of thanksgiving, supplication, and intercession; Lord's Prayer; commendation; and procession. The service should follow a narrative, but there are some choices that can address the needs of the family and friends and who the deceased is. This requires the discernment of the pastor. Music should carry the narrative forward and provoke awe. The casket should be situated east to west, since the early church spit on the devil to the west and bowed to God to the east. Prayers of confession and pardon address our collective guilt and shortcomings. The preaching of the Word through Scripture and interpretation is continued. The prayers of commendation close the service.

The question of the eulogy or remembrances is a difficult one, because the focus should be on God, not the deceased. Eulogies should be realistic — not full of praise or blame — and not overly long. Prayers of thanksgiving and intercession should always be offered, as well as of commendation. Music is important, and the officiating pastor should choose the hymns carefully.[69] Some ministers avoid referring to the deceased, but Tony Walter has a somewhat different interpretation:

> Though still accounting for only a tiny fraction of ceremonies, humanist funerals have received considerable publicity in the UK in the last few years, this publicity typically contrasting humanist funerals which recount the life of the deceased with those religious funerals which do not. Some religious funerals, however, also recount the life lived and many clergy as well as humanists now see this as a good, though far from a universal, practice. The theory developed in the present paper implies that recounting the life of the deceased is not a secular alternative to religious ritual, but a social-psychological necessity in a late modern society in which identity is fluid and self referential.[70]

Preaching should be on the meaning of resurrection: a sermon to the glory of God that gives strength to the living. Preaching can be a form of pastoral care, so that the relationship started when the pastor visited the bereaved can form part of the sermon. However, it should not simply be a

---

69. Bartow, lecture on funerals in author's "Death and Dying" class, Princeton Theological Seminary (Fall 2004).

70. Tony Walter, Richard Bragg, Mark Pryce, and Janet Eldred, "A Good Funeral," *A Good Death*, Leveson Papers #14 (Solihull: Foundation of Lady Katherine Leveson, 2003), pp. 21-22.

retelling of the family's grief, but a retelling in light of Christ's resurrection. For example, the pastor should make the reality of death clear, while discovering the hope in Christ, especially indicating that their lives are not ended but will go on.

The sermon is central to the Christian service, not just to Presbyterians. Even Schleiermacher's sermon at his son Nathanael's grave, amidst his own deep personal anguish, did not neglect to proclaim the omnipotence of God even in the face of death.[71] "As an act of counseling, it uses this proclamation to help the living to relinquish their claim on the dead." Donald Capps shows how this sermon can be divided into four parts: identification of the problem, reconstruction of the problem, diagnostic interpretation, and pastoral intervention.[72]

The beginning of the sermon may be the most important part as it sets the tone, not a eulogistic one but one that points people to the hope found in God in the face of death. One should not speak of details of the death; but one may wish to refer to it, for example, if it occurred suddenly, or after a long illness. It is not appropriate to try to psychoanalyze people's feelings; but one can use those feelings to move to theological insights. The sermon should be a clear message about the resurrection, not an attempt to answer the theodicy question. It can acknowledge the grief that people are experiencing and help them face the reality of death. However, in the midst of their grief, one can also point beyond it to Christ's comfort. This does not mean family and friends should "get over their grief," or that Christians should not be sad because there is the hope of eternal life. After all, Jesus wept at Lazarus's death, and he was the one who said, "Blessed are those that mourn for they shall be comforted" (Matt. 5:4).[73]

The service should also include extensive Scripture, especially passages that resonate with the family, and those emphasizing that suffering and death are not eternal. God is faithful in God's unconditional love,

71. Friedrich Daniel Ernst Schleiermacher (1768-1834), German theologian and philosopher known for his impressive attempt to reconcile the criticisms of the Enlightenment with traditional Protestant orthodoxy, was also influential in the evolution of higher criticism. He casts a long shadow in practical theology. The Neo-Orthodoxy movement of the twentieth century, represented most prominently by Karl Barth, was in many ways an attempt to overturn Schleiermacher's influence.

72. Donald Capps, *Pastoral Counseling and Preaching: A Quest for an Integrated Ministry* (Philadelphia: Westminster Press, 1980), pp. 146-47.

73. Some of these insights were provided by Charles Bartow in a lecture to author's "Death and Dying" class, Princeton Theological Seminary (Fall 2004).

which overpowers death. Any personal element should be reflective of the family and the wishes of the deceased.

Aftercare

With the central focus of most churches on the funeral service, what happens afterwards is often left to chance. It is even difficult to find the right word to describe pastoral care after the funeral service. The *Book of Common Worship* seems to have no particular instructions. Might we call this "Good Mourning," or a "Ministry of Condolence"? Families are generally supported by the Christian community during the illness and at the time of the funeral, but afterwards the pastor and church members have no particular rites or rituals to frame their relationship with the mourners. Women's groups often organize the delivery of casseroles — which should not be underappreciated — or the forming of a telephone tree, or even the writing of cards (this is normally done during the illness, but condolence cards after a death are also common).

The Jewish custom of "sitting shiva" is a rite for aftercare from which Christians can learn. "Shiva" *(shiv'a)* is the Hebrew word for "seven." In Judaism it refers to the seven-day mourning period that begins immediately after a funeral and is observed at the home of the deceased. This Jewish custom is based on the Genesis passage that shows Joseph mourning his father, Jacob, for a week. "Sitting shiva" refers to the low stools customarily used during this period of mourning. These seven intense days help survivors face the reality of a loved one's death, and help them move from mourning to living. This rite can be adapted by Christians: I witnessed an Anglican who had grown up Jewish "sitting shiva."

Funerals for Suicide Victims

Funerals are always difficult, but some are more difficult than others. Since we discussed suicide and physician-assisted suicide earlier in the book, it may be worthwhile to comment briefly on funerals for suicide victims. Probably one of the most difficult funerals is for a suicide victim because of the shock, guilt, disbelief, and anger the family and friends are experiencing. How could he do it? Why did he? What drove him to that state of desperation? This can become even more complicated if the pastor knows a deep secret about the situation that led to the suicide, and only the pastor and his immediate family learned about it after his death. For example, a beloved elder of the church, successful and seemingly happy, "borrowed" several thousand dollars from his business account at the bank to use for personal items. The president of the bank called him in and told him he would have to be fired, and that triggered his suicide. These kinds of situations present a landmine to the pastor: she now wonders what she can say to comfort a distraught family and an unknowing congregation without divulging confidential information. One thing that seems clear is that a funeral for a suicide victim should have the same dignity, hope, and Christian message as for any other kind of funeral. The person who died is still loved and will be missed.

Saying the wrong thing in a sermon can have tragic repercussions, as reflected in the following true story.

> The death of an 86-year-old man, who had been in failing health for five years, would ordinarily not be a source of great distress. A clergyman officiating at the funeral in such a situation could scarcely be expected to recognize his role as one of momentous consequence. It was, however, to our family, in an agonizing drama which occurred recently.
>
> Our experience, as rare as it was tragic, is worth presenting to other clergymen in the hope that another family may be spared the anguish which has come to us.
>
> The man who died was my father-in-law, a grand old man, sharp to the end, but racked with the multiple infirmities expected for a man his age. The spirit was still willing, but the flesh was just not able. For the funeral there was the usual gathering of the clan, most of us total strangers to the dedicated young minister performing the service. There was no way that he could have known that among the mourning relatives was a 16-year-old boy, my son, Paul, experiencing his first direct contact with death. This boy had been struggling for several years with the not uncommon problems of searching for personal meaning in this confusing world. He was abnormally introverted, lonely, discouraged. He had been going to a psychiatrist, who had been unsuccessful in helping him to learn to react to the world with confidence, with humor, with joy. Our fervent prayers that God would somehow break through the armor with which our son had surrounded himself were unanswered.

In short, our young son was shackled in the depths of depression clinging to life by his fingertips. He was "tired of living, but feared of dying." It did not occur to us at the time and, of course, was unknown to the minister, how the funeral service would affect Paul's delicate balance. We thought the service was beautiful. There were the usual profusion of flowers, and cheery comments by so many of the relatives. "Doesn't he look peaceful." "His suffering is over." This theme was emphasized in the minister's reassuring remarks, "He has entered into eternal rest; he has gone to a blissful new life; he has found peace. . . ." It certainly did not cross the mind of that minister, just as it doubtless does not occur to any other minister performing a funeral service, that he was helping to confirm the shaky resolve of an impressionable, depressed young man to take his own life. Five days later Paul did just that while my wife was still staying with her mother and he was home alone after school. He left a note reassuring us that now he would be all right. This was a rare situation, one which you will probably never encounter, but you cannot know how fragile, disturbed individuals may chance to be influenced tragically by your best intentioned sermons or discussions. Certainly the bereaved must be comforted, but death need not be held up as the great *desideratum*, the wonderful escape from this world's torment. I hope now that the reassurances of that minister are true for our son, but no words can ease the burden which we, the living, must bear.[74]

Conclusion

The funeral service — better called a witness to the resurrection — should reflect both faith and hope, which are intricately interwoven and buttressed by the presence of God's grace. The doctrine of hope is essential to a Christian theology of death, which undergirds the funeral service. How serious illness and the specter of death can teach us about what matters in life is illustrated by so many stories. Lucy Rose, deceased professor at Columbia Theological Seminary, wrote of the power of 2 Corinthians 4:7-18 to speak to her in the midst of her dying from breast cancer in the prime of life. She wrote in her journal: "It is clear to me that grace — as an extraordinary power from God and not from me — is keeping me from feeling

74. Anonymous, "A Serious Theological Question," *Monday Morning*, August 1973, pp. 4-5.

crushed, driven to despair, forsaken, or destroyed. Someone said to me on the phone, 'You must be devastated.' 'No,' I said, 'Grace,' I thought."[75] Her unswerving faith sustained her through her dying.

Tom Droege, former director of the Faith and Health Center at Emory University, wrote and spoke about living under the shadow of death:

> A year and a half ago I was diagnosed with multiple myeloma . . . a bone marrow cancer that has no known cure. . . . I had a heightened sensitivity to everything around me. I became much more aware, much more mindful, much more appreciative of every day, every hour, every moment, and much more likely to celebrate life than ever before. . . . A transformed life is a gift of God, above all, nothing that you can make happen, but it's not automatic. When entangled by the cords of death, one option is to shut the door of our soul in bitterness and anger, and I know myeloma patients who have done that. But you can also open your hands to receive what God has to give you then and perhaps only then. The gifts I'm most aware of are spiritual growth and the support of family and friends.[76]

Ultimately, the power of the resurrection is seen in changed lives, as Lucy and Tom and the countless thousands whose lives have been changed by the death and resurrection of Jesus Christ bear witness. The funeral service is ultimately a witness to the resurrection, that is, God's power over death.[77]

75. Lucy Atkinson Rose, *Songs in the Night: A Witness to God's Love in Life and in Death,* ed. Ben Lacy Rose (Decatur, GA: CTS Press, 1998), p. 19. Used with permission. To obtain copies of this book, contact Vital Churches Institute, P.O. Box 18378, Pittsburgh, PA 15236 (tel: 412-246-4847): www.vitalchurchesinstitute.com.

76. Thomas Droege, Emory University, e-mail to author (June 21, 1999). Used with permission.

77. Colin Brown, ed., *New Testament Theology,* vol. 3 (Exeter, UK: Paternoster, 1978), pp. 302-5.

Epilogue

The Dying Christian to His Soul

Vital spark of heav'nly flame,
Quit, oh, quit, this mortal frame!
Trembling, hoping, ling'ring, flying,
Oh, the pain, the bliss of dying!
Cease, fond Nature, cease thy strife,
And let me languish into life!

Hark! they whisper; Angels say,
Sister Spirit, come away.
What is this absorbs me quite,
Steals my senses, shuts my sight,
Drowns my spirits, draws my breath?
Tell me, my Soul! can this be Death?

The world recedes; it disappears;
Heav'n opens on my eyes; my ears
With sounds seraphic ring:
Lend, lend your wings! I mount! I fly!
O Grave! where is thy Victory?
O Death! where is thy Sting?

Alexander Pope (1688-1744)

Death has been a very difficult subject to consider, bringing as it does the grief and loss, pain and suffering, changed lives, as well as the loneliness and sadness. We began this book with the question, "Is God still at the bedside?" I hope that the reader has discovered that the answer is a resounding "yes." As the words on Carl Jung's door, and later on his tombstone, declared: "Bidden or not bidden God is present." As we reflect on the lives of so many people of faith who have faced death in confidence and hope of God's eternal love, we can see that God's grace is sufficient. We rejoice in the comfort that this brings. We acknowledge the pain and suffering, the guilt and loss of each person, the dedication of physicians, nurses, auxiliary health care professionals, pastors, chaplains, and others. The bravery of patients and their families, the gifts of modern medicine, and the caring of faith communities — all these give witness to God's loving presence in the face of the horror of death. Death does not have the final word; God has the final word. Death reminds us that, even as we walk through the valley of the shadow of death, we need not fear, because God has gone before us not only to comfort us but to prepare a place for us in God's loving presence.

As C. S. Lewis wrote, Christians never say goodbye, but rather "I will see you later." This is the promise that we have been given: death is the passageway to eternal life, where we will bask in God's loving presence.

> Then I saw a new heaven and a new earth, for the first heaven and the first earth had passed away, and the sea was no more. And I saw the holy city, the New Jerusalem, coming down out of heaven from God, prepared as a bride adorned for her husband. And I heard a loud voice from the throne saying, "See, the home of God is among mortals. He will dwell with them as their God; they will be his people, and God himself will be with them; he will wipe every tear from their eyes. Death will be no more; mourning and crying and pain will be no more, for the first things have passed away." And the one who was seated on the throne said, "See, I am making all things new." Also he said, "Write this, for these words are trustworthy and true." (Rev. 21:1-5)

APPENDICES

A. Resource Organizations Addressing End-of-Life Issues

Aging with Dignity
P.O. Box 1661
Tallahassee, FL 32302
Tel: 800-562-1931
www.agingwithdignity.org

Alzheimer's Association
225 North Michigan Ave., Fl. 17
Chicago, IL 60601-7633
Tel: 800-272-3900

American Association of Retired Persons (AARP)
601 E St. NW
Washington, DC 20049
Tel: 888-687-2277
www.aarp.org

American Association of Suicidology
5221 Wisconsin Ave. NW
Washington, DC 20015
Tel: 202-237-2280
www.suicidology.org

American Foundation for Suicide Prevention
120 Wall St., 22nd Floor
New York, NY 10005
Tel: 212-363-3500
Toll Free: 888-333-AFSP
Fax: 212-363-6237
Email: inquiry@afsp.org
www.afsp.org

American Hospital Association
One North Franklin
Chicago, IL 60606-3421
Tel: 312-422-3000
www.aha.org

Association for Death Education and Counseling (ADEC)
60 Revere Dr., Suite 500
Northbrook, IL 60062
Tel: 847-509-0403
Fax: 847-480-9282
Email: adec@adec.org
www.adec.org

Bereavement Services
Gundersen Lutheran Medical Center
1910 South Ave.
La Crosse, WI 54601
Tel: 608-791-4747
www.gundluth.org/bereave

Caring Connections
http://www.caringinfo.org/stateaddownload
From this website any advance directive can be downloaded from any state in the U.S.

Center for Bioethics and Human Dignity
2065 Half Day Road
Deerfield, IL 60015
Tel: 847-317-8180
www.cbhd.org

Center for Death Education and Bioethics
Gerry Cox, PhD and
Tim Gongaware, co-editors
Illness, Crisis and Loss
Soc/Arc Dept.
435 Wimberly Hall
1725 State St.
La Crosse, WI 54601-3742
Tel: 608-785-6784

Center for Good Mourning
Arkansas Children's Hospital
1621 W. 10th St., Slot 690
Little Rock, AR 72202
Tel: 501-364-7000
http://www.archildrens.org/communityoutreach/centermourning/
supportgroups.asp

Centering Corporation
Dr. Marvin and Joy Johnson
1531 N. Saddle Creek
Omaha, NE 68104
Tel: 402-553-1200
Fax: 402-553-0507
www.centeringcorp.com

Choice in Dying
1035 30th St. NW
Washington, DC 20007
Tel: 202-338-9790 or 800-989-9455
Fax: 202-338-0242

Compassion and Choices (formerly the Hemlock Society)
P.O. Box 101810
Denver, CO 80250
Tel: 800-247-7421
www.compassionandchoices.org
Committed to providing information regarding options for dignified death and legalized physician aid in dying. To strengthen our ability to serve the terminally ill, and forward aid-in-dying laws across the country. To learn more about the choice-in-dying movement and Compassion and Choices' Client Support Program, legal and legislative advocacy work, and educational outreach programs, visit: www.compassionandchoices.org.

The Compassionate Friends
P.O. Box 3696
Oak Brook, IL 60522-3696
Tel: 877-969-0010
Fax: 630-990-0246
Email: nationaloffice@compassionatefriends.org
www.compassionatefriends.org
Contact: Patricia Loder, Executive Director

Cremation Association of North America
401 North Michigan Avenue
Chicago, IL 60611
Tel: 312-245-1077
www.cremationassociation.org

Cruse Bereavement Care
P.O. Box 800
Richmond
Surrey
United Kingdom
TW9 1RG
Tel: 020 8939 9530
Fax: 020 8940 1671

Death With Dignity National Center
520 SW 6th Ave., Suite 1030
Portland, OR 97204
Tel: 503-228-4415
www.deathwithdignity.org

Dignitas
Postfach 9 — CH 8127 Forch, Switzerland
Tel: +41-44-980 44 59
Email: dignitas@dignitas.ch
www.dignitas.ch

Dougy Center for Grieving Children
P.O. Box 86552
Portland, OR 97286
Tel: 503-775-5683
Fax: 503-777-3097
www.dougy.org

Duke Institute on Care at the End of Life
Dr. Richard Payne, Director
Duke University Divinity School
2 Chapel Drive
Box 90968
Durham, NC 27708
Tel: 919-660-3553
http://www.iceol.duke.edu/
The Duke Institute on Care at the End of Life has available an annotated bibliography of articles on spirituality at the end of life, with articles from 1998-2008. This bibliography is always being updated and expanded. Go to http://www.iceol.duke.edu/resources/bibliography.html to download a copy.

Elisabeth Kübler-Ross Foundation
Ken Ross
President
EKR Foundation
P.O. Box 6168
Scottsdale, AZ 85261
Email: info@EKRFOUNDATION.ORG
EKR Foundation.Org

Exit
(formerly known as the Voluntary Euthanasia Society of Scotland, or VESS)
Director: Chris Docker *(Law and Ethics in Medicine)*
17 Hart Street, Edinburgh EH1 3RN, Scotland, United Kingdom
Tel (International): +44-131-556-4404

GriefNet.org
http://www.rivendell.org/

GriefWorks
P.O. Box 912
Auburn, WA 98071-0912
Tel: 253-333-9420
www.griefworks.org

Help the Hospices
34-44 Britannia St.
London
United Kingdom
WC1X 9JG
Tel: +44 (0) 20 7520 8200
www.helpthehospices.org.uk

Hospice Association of America
228 7th St. SE
Washington, DC 20003
Tel: 202-546-4759
www.nahc.org/haa/

Hospice Education Institute
3 Unity Square, P.O. Box 98
Machiasport, ME 04655-0098
Tel: 800-331-1620 or 207-255-8800
www.hospiceworld.org

Hospice Foundation of America
2001 S St. NW, #300
Washington, DC 20009
Tel: 202-638-5419
Email: hfa@hospicefoundation.org
www.hospicefoundation.org

The International Association for Near-Death Studies
2741 Campus Walk Avenue, Building 500
Durham, NC 27705-9978
Tel: 919-383-7940
www.iands.org

The International Society for Traumatic Stress Studies (ISTSS)
60 Revere Dr., Suite 500
Northbrook, IL 60062
Tel: 847-480-9028
Fax: 847-480-9282
Email: istss@istss.org
www.istss.org

King's College Centre for Education about Death and Bereavement
King's University College at the University of Western Ontario
266 Epworth Ave.
London, ON
Canada N6A 2M3
Tel: 519-433-3491 or toll free 1-800-265-4406
Fax: 519-963-0973

Living/Dying Project
P.O. Box 357
Fairfax, CA 94978-0357
Tel: 415-456-3915
www.livingdying.org

The M.I.S.S. Foundation
(Mothers in Sympathy and Support)
P.O. Box 5333
Peoria, AZ 85385
Tel: 623-979-1000 (local and international)
1-888-455-MISS (toll-free in U.S.)
Fax: 623-979-1001
Email Contact: Founder, CEO, Joanne Cacciatore, PhD, MSW, FT
drjoanne@missfoundation.org
www.missfoundation.org

National Association for the Terminally Ill
P.O. Box 368
Shelbyville, KY 40066
Tel: 866-668-1724
www.terminallyill.org

National Funeral Directors Association (NFDA)
13625 Bishop's Drive
Brookfield, WI 53005
Tel: 800-228-6332
www.nfda.org

National Hospice and Palliative Care Organization (NHPCO)
1700 Diagonal Rd., Suite 625
Alexandria, VA 22314
Tel: 703-837-1500
Fax: 703-837-1233
www.nhpco.org
J. Donald Schumacher, President and CEO
Galen Miller, Executive Vice President

Samaritans
P.O. Box 9090
Stirling, FK8 2SA
United Kingdom
Tel: +44 08457 90 90 90
www.samaritans.org

Society of Military Widows
5535 Hempstead Way
Springfield, VA 22151
Phone: 703-750-1342
Fax: 703-354-4380
Email: naus@ix.netcom.com
www.militarywidows.org

Survival Research Network
www.survival-research.net/

TAPS (Tragedy Assistance Program for Survivors), Inc.
2001 S St. NW, Suite 300
Washington, DC 20009
Tel: 800-959-TAPS
Fax: 202-638-5312
www.taps.org

The William Wendt Center for Loss and Healing
4201 Connecticut Ave. NW, Suite 300
Washington, DC 20008
Tel: 202-624-0010
Fax: 202-624-0062
Email: info@wendtcenter.org
www.wendtcenter.org
Contact: Susan M. Ley, Executive Director

Willowgreen
James Edwin Miller
10351 Dawson's Creek Blvd., Suite B
Fort Wayne, IN 46825
Tel: 260-490-2222
Fax: 260-497-9622
Email: jmiller@willowgreen.com
www.willowgreen.com

World Federation of Right to Die Societies
http://www.worldrtd.net/

B. Information on Advance Directives

Caring Connections

Caring Connections, a program of the National Hospice and Palliative Care Organization (NHPCO), is a national consumer engagement initiative to improve care at the end of life. Caring Connections tracks and monitors all state and federal legislation and significant court cases related to end-of-life care to ensure that all advance directives are up to date. See http://www.caringinfo.org/stateaddownload to download an advance directive from each state in the United States. Some are geared to specific needs.

Five Wishes

Five Wishes was designed by the Commission on Aging with Dignity, which is a private, nonprofit organization founded in 1996 to affirm and safeguard human dignity and to promote better care of the dying. Living in Mother Teresa's home for the dying in Washington, DC, as a full-time volunteer inspired Aging with Dignity's founder, Jim Towey, to develop *Five Wishes*. A revised version was created with the help of the American Bar Association Commission on Legal Problems of the Elderly.

Five Wishes meets the legal requirements in 35 states and the District of Columbia. It has become America's most popular living will because it is written in everyday language and helps start and structure important conversations about care in times of serious illness. It was introduced in 1997 and originally distributed with support from a grant by the Robert Wood Johnson Foundation, the nation's largest philanthropy devoted exclusively to health and health care.

To use *Five Wishes* as a legal document in those states that accept it, go to http://www.fivewishes.org/catalog/ or you can write them at P.O. Box 1661, Tallahassee, Florida 32302, 1-888-5-WISHES (or 1-888-594-7437); it can be ordered for $5.00.

Crista Nursing Center: Guidelines Regarding Life-Sustaining Treatment

Beth Spring and Ed Larson, *Euthanasia: Spiritual, Medical and Legal Issues in Terminal Health Care* (Portland, OR: Multnomah, 1988), pp. 201-4.

Advance Directives for Health Care

Norman L. Cantor, *Advance Directives and the Pursuit of Death With Dignity* (Indianapolis: Indiana University Press, 1993), pp. 149-53.

C. A Patient's Bill of Rights

American Hospital Association

MANAGEMENT ADVISORY

A Patient's Bill of Rights was first adopted by the American Hospital Association in 1973. This revision was approved by the AHA Board of Trustees on October 21, 1992. It sets forth certain rights that patients can claim during medical treatment and hospitalization. In the health care reform bill of 2010 a new patient's bill of rights under the Affordable Care Act was made law (see HealthCare.gov).

Introduction

Effective health care requires collaboration between patients and physicians and other health care professionals. Open and honest communication, respect for personal and professional values, and sensitivity to differences are integral to optimal patient care. As the setting for the provision of health services, hospitals must provide a foundation for understanding and respecting the rights and responsibilities of patients, their families, physicians, and other caregivers. Hospitals must ensure a health care ethic that respects the role of patients in decision-making about treatment choices and other aspects of their care. Hospitals must be sensitive to cultural, racial, linguistic, religious, age, gender, and other differences as well as the needs of persons with disabilities.

The American Hospital Association presents *A Patient's Bill of Rights* with the expectation that it will contribute to more effective patient care and be supported by the hospital on behalf of the institution, its medical staff, employees, and patients. The American Hospital Association encourages health care institutions to tailor this bill of rights to their patient community by translating and/or simplifying the language of this bill of rights as may be necessary to ensure that patients and their families understand their rights and responsibilities.

Bill of Rights

These rights can be exercised on the patient's behalf by a designated surrogate or proxy decision-maker if the patient lacks decision-making capacity, is legally incompetent, or is a minor.

1. The patient has the right to considerate and respectful care.
2. The patient has the right to and is encouraged to obtain from physicians and other direct caregivers relevant, current, and understandable information concerning diagnosis, treatment, and prognosis.

   Except in emergencies, when the patient lacks decision-making capacity and the need for treatment is urgent, the patient is entitled to the opportunity to discuss and request information related to the specific procedures and/or treatments, the risks involved, the possible length of recuperation, and the medically reasonable alternatives and their accompanying risks and benefits.

   Patients have the right to know the identity of physicians, nurses, and others involved in their care, as well as when those involved are students, residents, or other trainees. The patient also has the right to know the immediate and long-term financial implications of treatment choices, insofar as they are known.
3. The patient has the right to make decisions about the plan of care prior to and during the course of treatment and to refuse a recommended treatment or plan of care to the extent permitted by law and hospital policy and to be informed of the medical consequences of this action. In case of such refusal, the patient is entitled to other appropriate care and services that the hospital provides or transfers to another hospital. The hospital should notify patients of any policy that might affect patient choice within the institution.
4. The patient has the right to have an advance directive (such as a living will, health care proxy, or durable power of attorney for health

care) concerning treatment or designating a surrogate decision-maker with the expectation that the hospital will honor the intent of that directive to the extent permitted by law and hospital policy.

Health care institutions must advise patients of their rights under state law and hospital policy to make informed medical choices, ask if the patient has an advance directive, and include that information in patient records. The patient has the right to timely information about hospital policy that may limit its ability to implement fully a legally valid advance directive.

5. The patient has the right to every consideration of privacy. Case discussion, consultation, examination, and treatment should be conducted so as to protect each patient's privacy.

6. The patient has the right to expect that all communications and records pertaining to his/her care will be treated as confidential by the hospital, except in cases such as suspected abuse and public health hazards when reporting is permitted or required by law. The patient has the right to expect that the hospital will emphasize the confidentiality of this information when it releases it to any other parties entitled to review information in these records.

7. The patient has the right to review the records pertaining to his/her medical care and to have the information explained or interpreted as necessary, except when restricted by law.

8. The patient has the right to expect that, within its capacity and policies, a hospital will make reasonable response to the request of a patient for appropriate and medically indicated care and services. The hospital must provide evaluation, service, and/or referral as indicated by the urgency of the case. When medically appropriate and legally permissible, or when a patient has so requested, a patient may be transferred to another facility. The institution to which the patient is to be transferred must first have accepted the patient for transfer. The patient must also have the benefit of complete information and explanation concerning the need for, risks, benefits, and alternatives to such a transfer.

9. The patient has the right to ask and be informed of the existence of business relationships among the hospital, educational institutions, other health care providers, or payers that may influence the patient's treatment and care.

10. The patient has the right to consent to or decline to participate in proposed research studies or human experimentation affecting care

and treatment or requiring direct patient involvement, and to have those studies fully explained prior to consent. A patient who declines to participate in research or experimentation is entitled to the most effective care that the hospital can otherwise provide.

11. The patient has the right to expect reasonable continuity of care when appropriate and to be informed by physicians and other caregivers of available and realistic patient-care options when hospital care is no longer appropriate.

12. The patient has the right to be informed of hospital policies and practices that relate to patient care, treatment, and responsibilities. The patient has the right to be informed of available resources for resolving disputes, grievances, and conflicts, such as ethics committees, patient representatives, or other mechanisms available in the institution. The patient has the right to be informed of the hospital's charges for services and available payment methods.

The collaborative nature of health care requires that patients, or their families/surrogates, participate in their care. The effectiveness of care and patient satisfaction with the course of treatment depends, in part, on the patient fulfilling certain responsibilities. Patients are responsible for providing information about past illnesses, hospitalizations, medications, and other matters related to health status. To participate effectively in decision-making, patients must be encouraged to take responsibility for requesting additional information or clarification about their health status or treatment when they do not fully understand information and instructions. Patients are also responsible for ensuring that the health care institution has a copy of their written advance directive if they have one. Patients are responsible for informing their physicians and other caregivers if they anticipate problems in following prescribed treatment.

Patients should also be aware of the hospital's obligation to be reasonably efficient and equitable in providing care to other patients and the community. The hospital's rules and regulations are designed to help the hospital meet this obligation. Patients and their families are responsible for making reasonable accommodations to the needs of the hospital, other patients, medical staff, and hospital employees. Patients are responsible for providing necessary information for insurance claims and for working with the hospital to make payment arrangements, when necessary.

A person's health depends on much more than health care services.

Patients are responsible for recognizing the impact of their life-style on their personal health.

Conclusion

Hospitals have many functions to perform, including the enhancement of health status, health promotion, and the prevention and treatment of injury and disease; the immediate and ongoing care and rehabilitation of patients; the education of health professionals, patients, and the community; and research. All these activities must be conducted with an overriding concern for the values and dignity of patients.

The Affordable Care Act passed in 2010 contains a new Patient's Bill of Rights with regulations issued by the Department of Health and Human Services that will help children (and eventually all Americans) with preexisting conditions gain coverage and keep it, protect the choice of doctors, and end lifetime limits on the care consumers may receive (www .healthcare.gov/law/about/provisions/billofrights/patient_bill_of_rights .html).

D. Author's Questionnaires

© *2009 Abigail Rian Evans*

Interview Questions for Palliative Care Staff

1. Why did you go into work with the seriously ill and dying?
2. How long have you been doing it?
3. What is the greatest challenge in your work?
4. What is the most fulfilling aspect of your work?
5. How do your patients respond to their diagnoses? Is there a pattern, or is it totally idiosyncratic?
6. How can you best determine a patient's value system vis-à-vis end-of-life care?
7. What is the involvement of families?
8. Do you find all the staff in your setting working in an integrated fashion, or does each one stay within his or her particular sphere of specialty?
9. What does pastoral palliative care look like? Does the whole team participate or only the chaplain?
10. How important is the chaplain to the hospice or hospital philosophy?
11. What is the role of religion and spirituality in recovery and quality of life while dying?

Interview Questionnaire on Views of Death and Dying and Health Care Decision-Making

Abigail Rian Evans © 2009

Instructions

1. State purpose of interview: to help us better understand how people actually make health care decisions and their views on death and dying.
2. Assure confidentiality.
3. Indicate that interviewees need answer only those questions they desire to answer.
4. Provide an overview of the interview process and indicate time limitations in answering the questions. Determine ahead of time how long you think the interview will take.

Profile

Sex
☐ Male
☐ Female

Age _____

Family Status
☐ Single
☐ Married
☐ Divorced
☐ Widowed

Your Occupation _____

Religious Affiliation _____

Current Health Status ☐ Excellent
                                ☐ Average
                                ☐ Poor

PART I: *General Health Care Decision-Making*

1. Do you think, when faced with a serious illness, you should make decisions:
   ☐ Immediately
   ☐ After evaluation
   ☐ Delay
   ☐ Ask someone else to make them

2. Does the seriousness of the illness make a difference about how you make a decision?

3. Are health care decisions:
   ☐ Medical
   ☐ Moral
   ☐ Both

4. Rank the following influences on your value system in order of priority. (Please rank the following, 1 being most important, 5 being least important.)
   ☐ Religious tradition
   ☐ Family
   ☐ Cultural/Racial
   ☐ Professional Code
   ☐ Societal

5. What factors are most important in reaching a decision? (Please rank the following, 1 being most important, 10 being least important.)
   ☐ Emotion   ☐ Assessment
   ☐ Intuition   ☐ Consultation
   ☐ Reason   ☐ Faith
   ☐ Conscience   ☐ Prayer
   ☐ Knowledge   ☐ Church position

6. Would you want to be fully informed about the implications of your health condition? _____

_____

_____

_____

7. How do you evaluate health care treatment options?
   ☐ Read information
   ☐ Consult doctor
   ☐ Talk with family
   ☐ Talk with friends
   ☐ Pray
   ☐ Other _____

_____

_____

8. If your answer to no. 6 is "pray," what do you pray for? _____

_____

_____

_____

9. Does your belief in God affect your decisions?
   ☐ Not at all
   ☐ Moderately
   ☐ Highly

10. Does your religious community have teachings/positions on health care decisions and end-of-life decisions?
    ☐ Yes
    ☐ No
    If yes, what are they? _____

_____

_____

_____

11. Is the process or the result of a treatment more important? _____

_____

_____

_____

12. Do you find the distinction between ordinary and extraordinary treatment meaningful? _____

    _____

    _____

    _____

13. Who would you consult before making a major health care decision?
    - ☐ Family (relationship)
    - ☐ Friends
    - ☐ Pastor/Clergy
    - ☐ Co-workers
    - ☐ Religious community
    - ☐ Other _____

14. If your health care decision affects other persons, about whom should you be most concerned? (rank in order of priority)

    _____

    _____

    _____

    _____

15. If you were incapacitated, whom would you choose to make health care decisions for you? (Please rank the following, 1 being most important, 7 being least important.)
    - ☐ Doctor
    - ☐ Family member (e.g., spouse, child, etc.) _____

        _____
    - ☐ Pastor/Clergy
    - ☐ Lawyer
    - ☐ Friend
    - ☐ Religious community
    - ☐ Other

16. Do you consider life itself, or the quality of life, more important?

    _____

    _____

    _____

17. How do you regard death?
    ☐ Welcomed
    ☐ Feared
    ☐ Prelude to eternal life
    ☐ End of existence

18. Do these answers depend on your health status? _____

    _____

    _____

    _____

19. Is it better to make a wrong decision or no decision? _____

    _____

    _____

    _____

20. Have you made a living will or other advance directives?
    ☐ Yes
    ☐ No

PART II: Perspectives on Death and Dying

21. To the best of your memory, how old were you when you were
    first exposed to death (such as a funeral, a viewing, a graveside
    service, etc.)?
    ☐ Under 5 years of age
    ☐ 5 to 10 years of age
    ☐ 11 to 17
    ☐ 18 to 29
    ☐ 30 or older

22. To the best of your memory, by the time you were 30 years of age,
    approximately how many significant people in your life had died?
    ☐ None
    ☐ 1 or 2
    ☐ 3 to 5
    ☐ More than 5

23. To the best of your memory, how many significant people in your life died between your ages of 20 and 30?
    ☐ None
    ☐ 1 or 2
    ☐ 3 to 5
    ☐ More than 5

24. When you were a child, how was death talked about in your family?
    ☐ Openly
    ☐ As though it were a taboo subject
    ☐ Awkwardly — only when necessary
    ☐ I don't recall any discussion

25. Which approach reflects your response when someone you know has a terminal illness or has a spouse who has a terminal illness?
    ☐ I go out of my way to be supportive.
    ☐ I have a tendency to avoid having to interact with the person(s).
    ☐ I feel uncomfortable around the person(s), but as long as the subject does not come up, there is generally no problem.
    ☐ I try to treat the person(s) the same as I always did before.
    ☐ I have never known anyone dealing with a terminal illness.

26. I think about my own death or of the death of those within my household —
    ☐ Daily, or several times a week
    ☐ Once a week or once a month
    ☐ A few times each year
    ☐ Only when I have to
    ☐ I never contemplate death
    ☐ I consciously try to avoid the topic of death

27. If you could choose, when would you die?
    ☐ At birth
    ☐ In youth
    ☐ In middle age, in my "prime"
    ☐ Just after the "prime" of life
    ☐ In old age
    ☐ Never

28. If you had a choice, what kind of death would you prefer?
    ☐ Tragic, violent death
    ☐ Sudden, but not violent death
    ☐ Quiet, dignified death
    ☐ Suicide
    ☐ Homicide victim
    ☐ In my sleep
    ☐ There is no appropriate kind of death
    ☐ Other (specify) _____

    _____
    _____
    _____

29. If you chose the third answer for no. 28, what do you mean by "quiet, dignified death"? _____

    _____
    _____
    _____

30. What efforts do you believe should be made to keep a seriously ill person alive?
    ☐ All possible efforts (transplants, surgery, kidney dialysis, etc.)
    ☐ Efforts that are reasonable for that person's age, physical condition, mental condition, and pain level
    ☐ After reasonable care has been given, a person should be permitted to die a natural death.
    ☐ Any and all care is completely up to the ill person, provided he or she is functioning enough to make a decision. Physician-assisted suicide should be an option.

31. To what extent do you believe in life after death?
    ☐ Strongly believe in it
    ☐ Tend to believe in it
    ☐ Uncertain
    ☐ Tend to doubt it
    ☐ Am convinced it does not exist
    ☐ Simply not an issue for me

32. If you believe in life after death, which view(s) most closely
approximates your own? Check any that apply.
☐ Immediately after death I will be with God.
☐ When I die, all of me dies; but when Christ returns, I shall be
resurrected.
☐ I cannot explain; it is just a mystery.
☐ My body will die, but my soul will be at peace somehow and
somewhere.
☐ After I die I will go to some kind of timeless resting place until
some dramatic moment in history, when everything will be
new.
☐ My spirit will roam creation, and I will "visit" people still living
and perhaps visit with loved ones who have died.
☐ I will be in some kind of torment.
☐ I will be in some kind of painless, timeless limbo.
☐ All I know for sure is that I will be judged; the rest depends on
the judgment.
☐ None of the above

33. What does death mean to you? Check any that apply.
☐ It is the final stage (or process) of life.
☐ It is the beginning of a new life.
☐ It is the great enemy.
☐ It is a welcome friend.
☐ It is neither an enemy nor a friend; it just is.
☐ It is inevitable, so it really doesn't matter what I think of it.
☐ It means I cease to exist, period.
☐ I don't know.

34. This questionnaire/interview —
☐ made me feel somewhat anxious or uncomfortable.
☐ made me think about my own death.
☐ had no effect on me.
☐ frustrated me, because I found the questions annoying and/or
the choices too limiting.
☐ Other (specify) _____

_____
_____
_____

E. End-of-Life Decision-Making Guide for Caregivers

The following list is from a fact sheet available online from www.caregiver.org. It suggests the following as a list of topics that should be in "the talk." These are specific issues related to the end of one's life. They include:

- Whom do you want to make decisions for you if you are not able to make your own, both on financial matters and health care decisions? The same person may not be right for both.
- What medical treatments and care are acceptable to you? Are there some that you fear?
- Do you wish to be resuscitated if you stop breathing and/or your heart stops?
- Do you want to be hospitalized or stay at home, or somewhere else, if you are seriously or terminally ill?
- How will your care be paid for? Do you have adequate insurance? What might you have overlooked that will be costly at a time when your loved ones are distracted by grieving over your condition or death?
- What actually happens when a person dies? Do you want to know more about what might happen? Will your loved ones be prepared for the decisions they may have to make?

"Most people decide to select the person who will inherit their money when they die to also serve as their health care agent. . . . Be aware

---

Andy Gordon, "End of Life Decision Making: A Guide for Caregivers," *The Journal of Pastoral Care and Counseling* 62, no. 4 (Winter 2008): 375-76.

that this may present conflicts of interest or trust issues. The person acting as a health care proxy ought to possess a certain degree of sophistication and experience with care planning. . . . Third, a health care agent needs to be a person of strong character and resolve, who can keep a cool head when the pressure is on. She must often make life-rendering decisions after completely assessing the risks and benefits of certain procedures or changes in care planning. . . . Fourth, it is vital that the person acting as the health care proxy is one who pays strict attention to details and demands accurate information. Finally, if possible, health care agents will be the most effective if they live nearby so they can meet face-to-face with the care team members when discussing care planning decisions."

F. Parishioners' Instructions and Information for Clergy

(Please fill in all spaces that apply)
This is to be filed at Church Office

Full name: _____

Maiden name: _____

Address: _____

_____

Birth date: _____

Place of birth: _____

Preferred funeral director: _____

_____

I have/have not planned my funeral: _____

I desire viewing: _____

Organ donation arrangements (Yes or No): _____

If yes, where made: _____

_____

I have signed a living will: _____

Developed by Rev. Dr. Deborah G. Brincivalli, Executive Presbyter, Presbytery of West Jersey, Haddon Heights, NJ. Used with permission.

I desire to be buried (place): _____

_____

I desire to be cremated — ash disposal as follows: _____

_____

_____

In lieu of flowers, I desire that donations be made to: _____

_____

I desire my funeral/memorial service to be at the church/funeral home
with the following being my preferences: _____

_____

_____

Scripture readings: _____

_____

Music/hymns: _____

_____

Prayers/readings: _____

_____

Persons to notify upon my death:

Name: _____
Address: _____
Phone/email: _____

Name: _____
Address: _____
Phone/email: _____

Name: _____
Address: _____
Phone/email: _____

Names of persons who could/should be asked as pallbearers (for a
funeral service) or as ushers at a memorial service: _____

_____

_____

_____

Suggested obituary notes: _____

_____

_____

_____

_____

_____

- -

Church office use:

Membership number: _____

Date of membership: _____

Date ordained as elder: _____

Date ordained as deacon: _____

Date of marriage: _____

Other involvement: _____

Executor name and address: _____

Lawyer name and phone/e-mail: _____

Safe deposit box and location: _____

Valuable papers information: _____

Armed Forces: dates of service: _____

Serial number: _____

Military funeral: _____

Discharge certificate located: _____

Member of clubs and organizations as follows: _____

_____

_____

_____

_____

_____

Other information for my obituary:

Survivors' names: _____

_____

_____

_____

Pallbearers: _____

_____

_____

Other information for my survivors: _____

_____

_____

_____

_____

Signed: _____

Date: _____

Some suggested Scripture passages:

Job 19:23-27a
Psalm 23
Psalm 42:1-7
Psalm 46:1-7
Psalm 90
Psalm 118
Psalm 121
Psalm 130
Psalm 143
Isaiah 25:6-9
Isaiah 61:1-3
Matthew 11:25-30
Matthew 25:1-13
Luke 12:35-40
John 5:24-29
John 10:27-29
John 11:21-27
John 12:23-26
John 14:1-6
Romans 5:1-11
Romans 5:17-21
Romans 6:3-9
Romans 8:31-35, 37-39
1 Cor. 15:12-26
1 Cor. 15:51-57
1 Peter 1:3-9
Revelation 7:9-17
Revelation 21:2-7

Suggested Hymns:

Hymn of Praise:

"Praise to the Lord, the Almighty"
"For the Beauty of the Earth"
"Now Thank We All Our God"
"Joyful, Joyful We Adore Thee"
"Immortal, Invisible, God Only Wise"

"All Hail the Power of Jesus' Name"

Hymn of Dedication:

"The Lord Is My Shepherd"
"How Great Thou Art"
"When Peace Like a River"
"Be Still, My Soul"
"Abide with Me"
"Near to the Heart of God"

Hymn of Repose

"For All the Saints"
"O God, Our Help in Ages Past"
"Blessed Assurance"
"God of Grace and God of Glory"
"The Church's One Foundation"
"Lift High the Cross"

This is but a partial list. Feel free to borrow a hymnbook from the church to look over hymns to determine your favorites and the ones that express your faith in God.

Prayers and Readings

The Lord's Prayer
"Footprints"
Any creed of the church

Others are available. Readings for funerals should be discussed with the pastor to determine the appropriateness for the service.

G. U.S. Organ Donors by Organ and Donor Type, 1997 to 2006

	1997	1998	1999	2000	2001	2002	2003	2004	2005	2006
All Organs										
Total	9,539	10,362	10,861	11,918	12,688	12,819	13,285	14,154	14,491	14,756
Deceased	5,480	5,793	5,824	5,985	6,080	6,190	6,457	7,150	7,593	8,024
Living	4,059	4,569	5,037	5,933	6,608	6,629	6,828	7,004	6,898	6,732
Kidney										
Total	9,017	9,761	10,110	10,982	11,566	11,878	12,226	12,972	13,269	13,616
Deceased	5,084	5,339	5,386	5,489	5,528	5,638	5,753	6,325	6,700	7,180
Living	3,933	4,422	4,724	5,493	6,038	6,240	6,473	6,647	6,569	6,436
Pancreas										
Total	1,328	1,464	1,635	1,706	1,820	1,873	1,773	2,017	2,046	2,027
Deceased	1,322	1,462	1,628	1,699	1,816	1,872	1,770	2,017	2,044	2,026
Living	6	2	7	7	4	1	3	—	2	1
Liver										
Total	4,687	4,935	5,200	5,397	5,626	5,656	6,004	6,642	7,012	7,304
Deceased	4,601	4,843	4,947	4,997	5,106	5,294	5,682	6,319	6,691	7,017
Living	86	92	253	400	520	362	322	323	321	287
Intestine										
Total	74	80	97	90	115	113	126	172	189	187
Deceased	72	78	95	87	115	112	122	166	184	184
Living	2	2	2	3	—	1	4	6	5	3
Heart										
Total	2,426	2,447	2,316	2,284	2,276	2,223	2,120	2,096	2,220	2,276
Deceased	2,426	2,447	2,316	2,284	2,276	2,223	2,120	2,096	2,220	2,275
Living	—	—	—	—	—	—	—	—	—	1
Lung										
Total	874	817	835	861	936	945	990	1,092	1,287	1,330
Deceased	836	764	777	825	887	920	961	1,064	1,285	1,325
Living	38	53	58	36	49	25	29	28	2	5
Donation after Cardiac Death										
Total	78	75	87	117	168	189	268	391	561	645

Notes

Includes only organs recovered for transplant.

The number of transplants using living donors may be different from the number of living donors. This is because there is a small number of multi-organ living donors and multiple donors for one transplant. For example, a living donor might donate a kidney and pancreas segment; or two living donors might each donate a lung lobe for one transplant procedure.

A donor of an organ divided into segments (liver, lung, pancreas, intestine) is counted only once for that organ.

A donor of multiple organs is counted once for each organ recovered.

Donors after cardiac death are included in the deceased donor counts as well and are counted separately on the last line.

Source: OPTN/SRTR 2007 Annual Report as of May 1, 2007.

H. Faith Community Nursing:
Scope and Standards of Practice (2005)

Why has the document outlining our specialty nursing practice changed?

There have been dramatic changes in health care and the profession of nursing during the past decade. The American Nurses Association responded with updated versions of the three documents that provide the foundation of our practice: *The Code of Ethics for Nurses with Interpretive Statements* (2001), *Nursing's Social Policy Statement,* 2nd ed. (2003), and *Nursing: Scope and Standards of Practice* (2004). The organization and content of these documents, as well as the evolution within our specialty altered the format and content of the scope and standards of our practice.

Could you share some examples of the changes you are referring to?

The practice of all registered nurses now includes many of the concepts we previously claimed as unique to our specialty. "The art of nursing embraces dynamic processes that affect the human person including, for example, spirituality, healing, empathy, mutual respect, and compassion. These intangible aspects foster health. Nursing embraces healing. Healing is fostered by compassion, helping, listening, mentoring, coaching, teaching, exploring, being present, supporting, touching, intuition, empathy, service, cultural competence, tolerance, acceptance, nurturing, mutually creating, and conflict resolution" (*Nursing: Scope and Standards of Practice,* 2004, p. 12).

[First edition was entitled *Scope and Standards of Parish Nursing Practice* (1998).]

- Understanding that a patient is an interconnected unity, every nurse in any nursing intervention must consider physical, mental, social, and spiritual factors.
- All nursing practice, regardless of specialty, role, or setting, is fundamentally independent practice.
- For consistency and brevity in ANA documents, the term *patient* is used to refer to all recipients of nursing care. In your practice you may still use terms such as client, individual, congregant, resident, family, group, community, or population.
- The term *practice* refers to the actions of the nurse in whatever role the nurse fulfills, including direct patient care provider, educator, administrator, researcher, policy developer, or other.

Now that the document is called *Faith Community Nursing: Scope and Standards of Practice* what do I call myself?

Within your practice site you may choose to call yourself a FCN or continue to use whatever term you have used in the past, such as parish nurse, congregational nurse, health ministry nurse, or health and wellness nurse.

How does *Faith Community Nursing: Scope and Standards of Practice* affect my practice?

As a licensed registered nurse, you first meet the practice requirements of your state law, rules, and regulations. Then the three foundation documents guide the application of your professional skills and personal responsibilities. *Faith Community Nursing: Scope and Standards of Practice* further delineates the unique, additional scope and standards of practice of our specialty.

Where does the statement "no hands-on care" appear in this document?

That phrase was not in the *Scope and Standards of Parish Nursing* (1998) and it doesn't occur in the current document.

In an effort to help differentiate parish nursing from other nursing specialties, early authors of parish nursing described the role as unique and different from other nursing specialties. The actual quote many people refer to states: "This nursing role does not embrace the medical model of care or invasive practices such as blood drawing, medical treatments, or maintenance of IV products" (*Parish Nursing: Promoting Whole Person*

Health within Faith Communities, ed. M. McDermott and P. A. Solari-Twadell, 1999, p. 3). Many have interpreted that statement inaccurately to mean that PNs were forbidden or not allowed to perform "hands-on care."

In reflecting upon the original statement, it would be best perhaps to consider what the Scope and Practice of FCN does allow: it is to provide the intentional care of the spirit, and as such, demands of the FCNs an intentional partnership/collaboration with their nursing colleagues and other health care professionals to meet the patients' acute and long-term needs.

In the recently released book *Parish Nursing: Development, Education, and Administration* (ed. M. McDermott and P. A. Solari-Twadell, 2005), Chapter 3, "Uncovering the Intricacies of the Ministry of Parish Nursing through Research," P. A. Solari-Twadell writes: "The outcomes of recent research have profound implications for the way that the ministry of parish nursing practice is understood. For the first time, the parish nurse role, which was speculated as being more complex than the seven functions, can be understood more fully. Perhaps it would be more accurate to describe the functions of the parish nurse role as follows:

- Care that supports physical functioning
- Care that supports psychological functioning and facilitates lifestyle change, with particular emphasis on coping assistance and spiritual care
- Care that supports protection against harm
- Care that supports the family unit
- Care that supports effective use of the health system
- Care that supports the health of the congregation and community" (p. 21).

Faith Community Nursing: Scope and Standards of Practice does not prohibit the FCNs (who are first and foremost registered professional nurses) from practicing within their state as licensed registered nurses, where they must meet the practice requirements of their state law, rules, and regulations. The three foundational documents of the profession, guide the application of their professional skills and personal responsibilities. *Faith Community Nursing: Scope and Standards of Practice* further delineates the unique, additional scope and standards of practice of our specialty.

Why is there a description of Advanced Practice Faith Community Nursing within this document?

The new format prescribed by ANA is to include all levels of practice within one document.

Expectations for advanced practice faith community nurses became necessary because more nurses with advanced practice degrees are practicing this specialty. Although state laws, rules, and regulations vary, many hold registered nurses with advanced practice degrees to a standard of practice that reflects their additional education.

I do many of the things listed under the measurement criteria of an Advanced Practice Faith Community Nurse. Does that make me an APFCN?

No. Your practice as an FCN will evolve, with mentoring and education, from novice to expert, enabling you to meet measurement criteria now required of an advanced practice nurse. However, for designation as an advanced practice faith community nurse you must meet the legal definition of an advanced practice nurse in your state of practice, the measurement criteria for a FCN as well as an APFCN.

When the term "reimbursement" is used in *Faith Community Nursing: Scope and Standards of Practice* does that mean third-party reimbursement?

No. It refers to seeking payment for the professional services of a Faith Community Nurse in the same manner as others who provide professional services within a faith community are paid. Being able to earn a salary would enable more nurses to devote more time to the care of congregants.

Will this document increase the amount of paper work that I have to do?

No. The requirements for documentation remain the same. Refer to your state's laws, rules, and regulations for clarification.

Please explain the timeline and process of the review and revision.

- Notice of review and revision of the scope and standards document was provided through information outlets of American Nurses Association (ANA), Health Ministries Association (HMA), the International Parish Nurse Resource Center (IPNRC), and other groups that connect with parish nurses.

- The ANA contracts with the HMA, which conducted the review and wrote the document. [HMA, the national professional membership organization for parish nurses, had co-written the first edition with ANA in 1998 that made parish nursing a recognized specialty.]
- The review process and the estimated time frame for this work were announced by HMA.
- HMA requested volunteers for the Working Group through three announcements in the newsletter and at networking meetings. All who follow the process to respond and volunteer their services are contacted. The extent of the project and the time frame being required by ANA is explained.
- The Working Group was established and announced. The majority were experienced parish nurses, several parish nurse coordinators. Several were actively involved with the IPNRC and the development of the curriculum for parish nurses and coordinators.
- The Working Group worked from February 15th to July 28th drafting *Faith Community Nursing: Scope and Standards of Practice.*
- August 2nd through September 10th draft was posted on the HMA website for review and written comment.
- Announcements of posting were made by ANA and HMA. HMA sent a blast e-mail to every e-mail address in system. Each addressee was asked to pass the announcement along to anyone who might be interested. Announcements were sent directly to other organizations and educational programs for further distribution. The use of multiple avenues was an effort to circumvent the block of information caused by filters and "black-listed" words by some electronic servers.
- The Working Group reviewed the written comments and re-worked the draft.
- October 20th the revised draft was sent to ANA. The Committee on Nursing Practice Standards and Guidelines reviewed for consistency with foundation documents and made recommendations.
- Once approved, the document was sent to the ANA Congress on Nursing Practice and Economics. The Congress then either approved or returned the document to the Working Group identifying unmet criteria and requesting additional information or changes in the document.

- Per contract with ANA this process was completed by December 31, 2004.
- The document entitled *Scope and Standards, Faith Community Nursing* was made available June 2005.

I. Some Do's and Don'ts for Caregivers

DO:

Acknowledge the loss with a call, card, or letter (letters can be read and reread). By writing a letter you are "offering handwritten hugs where human arms cannot reach." If possible, go to visitation or attend the funeral. Your presence means you care.

Simply say, "I'm so sorry" or "Words fail me" or "I share a bit of your grief."

Remember, a sympathizing tear, a warm embrace, an arm around the shoulder, a squeeze of the hand convey your sympathy. Words aren't always necessary.

Give the mourner permission to grieve.

Listen nonjudgmentally to the grieving person's thoughts and feelings.

Allow the grieving person to talk about the deceased loved one.

Ask open-ended questions such as "What happened?" Open-ended questions invite the grieving person to express him- or herself.

Tell them you'll remember them in your prayers.

Offer practical assistance.

Share a pleasant memory or words of admiration for the deceased with the grieving person.

Source: Delores Kuenning, *Helping People through Grief* (Minneapolis: Bethany House, 1987), pp. 257-59.

Remember them on the painful holidays, especially the "firsts."

Remember that grief is long-lasting.

Remember that you are a vital part of the grieving person's support system. Never underestimate your role as a caregiver.

Remember that usually the most difficult time is 7 to 9 months after the death.

Remember to extend condolences to forgotten mourners: grandparents, siblings, stepchildren, aunts and uncles, cousins, friends — anyone who was especially close.

Remember that nothing you can say will stop the grieving person's pain.

DON'T:

Avoid the grieving person because you don't know what to say.

Say, "Don't cry" or "Be brave." This may cause the grieving person to repress sad feelings.

Use clichés, trite statements, or euphemisms. Avoid statements such as "He's at rest," "Be glad it's over," "Time heals all wounds," or "The Lord knows best."

Be afraid of tears. Grieving persons seldom forget those with whom they've shed tears.

Say, "I know how you feel." Each person's grief is unique, and no one can totally understand another's grief.

Make statements or ask questions that induce guilt or affix blame. There is always some unfinished business and guilt associated with the death of a loved one.

Change the subject when the grieving person talks about his or her loved one.

Tell the grieving person his or her loss is God's will. Most grieving persons are troubled by that statement, but are too polite to say so. Avoid any of the following statements:

- Sooner or later He is going to get you.
- He will get you in the end.
- God had numbered his days, and when they ran out, God took him.
- I don't understand why he had to die, but God doesn't make mistakes.

469

- God must have needed another bud for his rose garden.
- You never know when the Lord's going to snatch you from this world, do you?
- God knows best. He won't put any more on you than you can bear.

Try to answer the question, *Why?*

Discount the loss of a baby or child by reminding grieving parents they can have other children or be glad they have other children.

Attempt to minimize the loss of a baby through miscarriage, stillbirth, or early infant death. Parents experience the death of their dreams and hopes for the future embodied in their wished-for baby. The age makes little difference; their pain is just as great.

Encourage the grieving person to "get over it" because of your discomfort with his or her depressed state.

J. Things You Can Do to Help Yourself Face Grief

by Donna O'Toole

1. Keep a diary of your feelings. Read it over once a month to see how things are changing.
2. Get physical. Find a way to let off steam that won't hurt someone else or get you in trouble.
3. Throw balls hard at a wall, then run to catch them. Do it until you get real tired.
4. Don't be surprised or feel guilty if you can't or haven't cried. Feelings are natural. They will take their own course.
5. If someone asks you how you feel, try to be honest. Don't say "I'm fine" if you're not.
6. Go for a long walk beside a river or stream or someplace else in a natural setting.
7. Find a good listener, then share your thoughts and feelings.
8. Get smart. Ask the school librarian to help you find books on the topics of your loss.
9. Write to a pen pal and tell that person everything. If you don't have a pen pal, make one up and write the letter anyway.
10. Help someone else who has a need.
11. Ask your school counselor about tutoring help if you are having trouble keeping up in class.
12. Make a new friend, and do something new with that person.
13. Call up an old friend, and work on the car with him or her. Or bake cookies together.
14. Rent a bunch of funny videos and have a laugh marathon.
15. Remember, grief takes time. The questions and concerns you have right now may take some time to get answered.

Selected Bibliography

Aiken, Lewis R. *Dying, Death, and Bereavement.* Mahwah, NJ: Lawrence Erlbaum Associates, 2001.

Ainsworth-Smith, Ian, and Peter Speck. *Letting Go: Caring for the Dying and Bereaved.* London: SPCK, 1982.

Albom, Mitch. *Tuesdays with Morrie.* New York: Time Warner Paperbacks, 2003.

Annas, George. "Physician Assisted Suicide: Michigan's Temporary Solution." *New England Journal of Medicine* (May 27, 1993): 1573-76.

Aries, Philippe. *Western Attitudes toward Death from the Middle Ages to the Present.* Translated by Patricia M. Ranum. Baltimore: Johns Hopkins University Press, 1974.

"Assisted Suicide and Euthanasia: Christian Moral Perspectives." *The Washington Report.* Harrisburg, PA: Morehouse Publishing, 1997.

Bachmann, C. Charles. *Ministering to the Grief Sufferer.* Englewood Cliffs, NJ: Prentice-Hall, 1964.

Bansemer, Richard F. *Getting Ready for the New Life: Facing Illness or Death with the Word and Prayers.* Minneapolis: Augsburg Fortress, 2004.

Battin, Margaret P., Rosamond Rhodes, and Anita Silvers, eds. *Physician Assisted Suicide: Expanding the Debate.* New York: Routledge, 1998.

Bolton, Iris. *My Son . . . My Son . . . : A Guide to Healing After Death, Loss or Suicide.* Atlanta: Bolton Press, 1983.

Bouma, Hessel, et al., eds. *Christian Faith, Health, and Medical Practice.* Grand Rapids: Eerdmans, 1989.

Bowling, Carolyn S., and Jeffrey W. Wilder. *Ya Got People: Helping People with Developmental Disabilities Deal with Grief, Bereavement and Loss.* Angus, ON: Diverse City Press, 2003.

Braham, M. *Ministry to the Sick and Dying.* Bloomington, IN: 1stPress, 2002.

Brown, Hugh, and Kristine Gibbs. *Euthanasia — A Christian Perspective.* London: St. Andrew's Press, 1995.

Buckman, Robert. *How to Break Bad News: A Guide for Health Care Professionals.* Baltimore: Johns Hopkins University Press, 1992.

Callahan, Daniel. *What Kind of Life? The Limits of Medical Progress.* New York: Simon and Schuster, 1990.

Cantor, Norman L. *Advance Directives and the Pursuit of Death with Dignity.* Bloomington: Indiana University Press, 1993.

————. *Legal Frontiers of Death and Dying.* Bloomington: Indiana University Press, 1987.

Cassell, Eric. "The Nature of Suffering and the Goals of Medicine." *New England Journal of Medicine* 306, no. 11 (Mar. 18, 1992): 639-45.

Chapman, Christine. *In Love Abiding: Responding to the Dying and Bereaved.* Edinburgh: Hodder and Stoughton, 1995.

Charlesworth, James H., et al. *Resurrection: The Origin and Future of a Biblical Doctrine.* Edinburgh: T. & T. Clark, 2006.

Churn, Arlene H. *The End Is Just the Beginning: Lessons in Grieving for African Americans.* New York: Harlem Moon, 2003.

Clark, Sandra M. *No One Dies Alone.* Eugene, OR: Sacred Heart Medical Center, 2003.

Cobb, Mark. *The Dying Soul: Spiritual Care at the End of Life.* Philadelphia: Open University Press, 2001.

Cohen, Cynthia, ed. *Casebook on the Termination of Life-Sustaining Treatment and the Care of the Dying.* Bloomington: Indiana University Press, 1988.

Collins, Mary, and David N. Powers, eds. *Pastoral Care of the Sick.* Philadelphia: SCM Press/Trinity Press International, 1991.

Consumers Guide for Planning Ahead: The Health Care Power of Attorney and the Living Will. Washington, DC: U.S. Government Printing Office, 1992.

Corr, Charles A. *Death and Dying, Life and Living.* 5th edition. Florence, KY: Wadsworth Publishing, 2006.

Daher, Douglas. *And the Passenger Was Death: The Drama and Trauma of Losing a Child.* Amityville, NY: Baywood, 2003.

Davies, Betty. *Shadows in the Sun.* Philadelphia: Brunner/Mazel, 1999.

Dickinson, George E., Michael R. Leming, and Alan C. Mermann. *Dying, Death, and Bereavement,* 11th Annual Edition. Guilford, CT: Dushkin/McGraw-Hill Publishing Co., 2009.

Downey, John A., Georgia Riedel, and Austin Kutscher, eds. *Bereavement of Physical Disability: Recommitment to Life, Health and Function.* New York: Arno Press, 1982.

DuBois, Paul M. *The Hospice Way of Death.* New York: Human Sciences Press, 1980.

Du Boulay, Shirley (with additional chapters by Marianne Rankin). *Cicely Saunders: The Founder of the Modern Hospice Movement.* London: SPCK, 2007.

Dyck, Arthur. "Physician Assisted Suicide: Is it Ethical?" *Trends in Health Care, Law, and Ethics* (Winter 1992): 19-22.

Enright, D. J. *The Oxford Book of Death.* New York: Oxford University Press, 1983.

Episcopal Church, Diocese of Washington, Committee on Medical Ethics. *Assisted Suicide and Euthanasia: Christian Moral Perspectives: The Washington Report.* Harrisburg, PA: Morehouse Publishing, 1997.

Epperly, Bruce G. *A Holistic Vision of the Human Adventure at the Edges of Life.* St. Louis: Chalice Press, 1992.

————. *At the Edges of Life.* St. Louis: Chalice Press, 1992.

Evans, Abigail Rian. *Healing Liturgies for the Seasons of Life.* Louisville: Westminster John Knox Press, 2004.

Fitchett, George. *Assessing Spiritual Needs: A Guide for Caregivers.* Minneapolis: Augsburg Fortress, 1993.

Fowler, Gene. *Caring Through the Funeral: A Pastor's Guide.* St. Louis: Chalice Press, 2004.

Friedman, Edwin H. *Generation to Generation.* New York: Guilford Press, 1985.

Gamino, Louis A., and Ann T. Cooney. *When Your Baby Dies Through Miscarriage or Stillbirth.* Hope and Healing Series. Minneapolis: Augsburg Fortress, 2002.

Gilbert, Richard. *Finding Your Way After Your Parent Dies.* Notre Dame, IN: Ave Maria Press, 1999.

Greyson, Bruce. *Journal of Near Death Studies.* New York: Human Sciences Press, 1998.

Griffith, W. *Lessons in Caregiving for the Dying; More Than a Parting Prayer.* Valley Forge, PA: Judson Press, 2005.

Harvey, John Collins, and Edmund D. Pellegrino. "A Response to Euthanasia Initiatives." *Health Progress* (March 1994): 36-39, 53.

Harwell, Amy. *When Your Friend Gets Cancer.* East Sussex, UK: Highland Books, 1987.

Hauerwas, Stanley. *Naming the Silences: God, Medicine, and the Problem of Suffering.* Grand Rapids: Eerdmans, 2005.

Heinz, Donald. *The Last Passage: Recovering a Death of Our Own.* New York: Oxford University Press, 1999.

Hilton, Bruce. *First Do No Harm: Wrestling with the New Medicine's Life and Death Dilemmas.* Nashville: Abingdon, 1991.

Hoffacker, C. *A Matter of Life and Death: Preaching at Funerals.* Cambridge, MA: Cowley, 2003.

Holloway, Karla F. C. *Passed On: African American Mourning Stories.* Durham: Duke University Press, 2002.

Holtkamp, Sue. *Wrapped in Mourning: The Gift of Life and Donor Family Trauma.* New York: Brunner Routledge, 2001.

Howell, David. *The Pain of Parting: Understanding the Grief Journey.* Bramcote Nottingham: Grove Books Ltd., 1993.

Humphrey, Derek. *Let Me Die Before I Wake: Supplement to Final Exit.* Junction City, OR: Norris Lane Press, 2002.

Illich, Ivan. *Medical Nemesis.* New York: Calder and Boyers, 1976.

Irion, Paul. "Changing Patterns of Ritual Response to Death." *Omega* 22: 159-72.

Irish, Jerry A. *A Boy Thirteen: Reflections on Death.* Philadelphia: Westminster Press, 1975.

Jackson, Edgar. *Understanding Grief: Its Roots, Dynamics, and Treatment.* Nashville: Abingdon, 1985.

Jones, David. *Approaching the End: A Theological Exploration of Death and Dying.* New York: Oxford University Press, 2007.

Justice, William G. *Training Guide for Visiting the Sick: More Than a Social Call.* New York: Haworth Press, 2005.

Kierkegaard, Søren. *The Sickness Unto Death.* New York: Penguin Books, 1989.

Kilner, John F. *Life on the Line: Ethics, Aging, Ending Patients' Lives, and Allocating Vital Resources.* Grand Rapids: Eerdmans, 1992.

Kramer, Kenneth P. *The Sacred Art of Dying: How World Religions Understand Death.* New York: Paulist Press, 1988.

Kriewald, Diedra. *Hallelujah Anyhow! Suffering and the Christian Community of Faith.* New York: General Board of Global Ministries, United Methodist Church, 1986.

Kuenning, Delores. *Helping People through Grief.* Minneapolis: Bethany House, 1987.

Kushner, Harold S. *When Bad Things Happen to Good People.* New York: Avon Books, 1981.

Lammers, Stephen, and Allen Verhey, eds. *On Moral Medicine: Theological Perspectives in Medical Ethics.* Grand Rapids: Eerdmans, 1987.

Leech, Kenneth. *Soul Friend: Spiritual Direction in the Modern World.* New Revised Edition. London: Darton, Longman and Todd, 1994.

————. *Spirituality and Pastoral Care.* Cambridge, MA: Cowley Publications, 1989.

Lendrum, Susan, and Gabrielle Syme. *Gift of Tears: A Practical Approach to Loss and Bereavement Counseling.* New York: Routledge, 1992.

Levine, Stephen. *Who Dies? An Investigation of Conscious Living and Conscious Dying.* Garden City, NY: Anchor Press/Doubleday, 1982.

Lewis, C. S. *A Grief Observed.* New York: Bantam Books, 1976.

Loewy, Erich. "Advance Directives and Surrogate Laws." *Archives of Internal Medicine* (Fall 1992): 1973-76.

Long, Thomas. "The Funeral: Changing Patterns and Teachable Moments." *Journal of Preachers* 19, no. 3 (Easter 1996).

Lynch, Thomas. *The Undertaking: Life Studies from the Dismal Trade*. New York: W. W. Norton, 1997.

Lynn, Joanne, ed. *By No Extraordinary Means: The Choice to Forgo Life-Sustaining Food and Water*. Bloomington: Indiana University Press, 1989.

―――. *Sick to Death and Not Going to Take It Anymore! Reforming Healthcare for the Last Years of Life*. Los Angeles: University of California Press, 2004.

Mansell, John S. *The Funeral: A Pastor's Guide*. Nashville: Abingdon, 1998.

May, William F. *The Physician's Covenant: Images of the Healer in Medical Ethics*. Philadelphia: Westminster, 1993.

―――. *Testing the Medical Covenant: Active Euthanasia and Health Care Reform*. Grand Rapids: Eerdmans, 1996 (reprinted, 2004, by Wipf and Stock, Eugene, OR).

McGill, Arthur. *Suffering: A Test of Theological Method*. Philadelphia: Westminster, 1982.

Miller, James E. *How Can I Help? Twelve Things to Do When Someone You Know Suffers a Loss*. Fort Wayne, IN: Willowgreen Publishing, 1994.

―――. *When You're Ill or Incapacitated When You're the Caregiver*. Fort Wayne, IN: Willowgreen Publishing, 1995.

Miller, Sue. *The Story of My Father: A Memoir*. New York: Alfred A. Knopf, 2003.

Ministry to the Sick: Authorized Alternative Services. Cambridge: Cambridge University Press, 1980.

Misbin, Robert I., ed. *Euthanasia: The Good of the Patient, the Good of Society*. Frederick, MD: University Publishing Group, 1992.

Moessner, Jeanne Stevenson. *A Primer in Pastoral Care*. Minneapolis: Fortress, 2005.

Momeyer, Richard W. *Confronting Death*. Bloomington: Indiana University Press, 1988.

Munday, John S., and Frances Wohlenhaus-Munday. *I Wasn't Ready*. Ocean City, MD: Skipjack Press, 1991.

Nowack, JoAnne Chitwood. *My Gift: Myself — A Step-by-Step Guide to Becoming a Grief and Bereavement Volunteer*. Student Manual. Beaverton, CO: Border Mountain, 2001.

Nuland, Sherwin B. *How We Die: Reflections on Life's Final Chapter*. New York: Vintage Books, 1994.

Oates, Wayne E., and Charles Oates. *People in Pain Guidelines for Pastoral Care*. Philadelphia: Westminster Press, 1985.

O'Brien, Mauryeen. *Praying Through Grief: Healing Prayer Services for Those Who Mourn*. Notre Dame, IN: Ave Maria Press, 1997.

O'Donovan, Oliver. "Karl Barth and Ramsey's 'Uses of Power.'" *Journal of Religious Ethics* 19, no. 2 (Fall 1991): 1-30.

Oliver, Samuel. *What the Dying Teach Us: Lessons on Living*. New York: The Haworth Pastoral Press, 1998.

Orr, Robert. "Why Doctors Should Not Kill." *Christian Medical and Dental Society Journal* (Spring 1993).

Osterweis, Marian, Fredric Solomon, and Morris Green, eds. *Bereavement Reactions, Consequences, and Care.* Washington, DC: National Academy Press, 1984.

Pohier, Jacques, and Dietmar Mieth, eds. *Suicide and the Right to Die.* Edinburgh: T. & T. Clark, 1985.

Quain, Kay D., and Jack Coyle. *Surviving Cancer.* Kansas City, KS: Sheed and Ward, 1988.

Ramsey, Paul. *Ethics at the Edges of Life.* New Haven: Yale University Press, 1978.

Reich, Warren. "Speaking of Suffering: A Moral Account of Compassion." *Soundings* (Spring 1989): 83-108.

Ritchie, George G., and Elizabeth Sherrill. *Return from Tomorrow.* Old Tappan, NJ: Fleming H. Revell, 1978.

Rose, Lucy Atkinson. *Songs in the Night: A Witness to God's Love in Life and in Death.* Edited by Ben Lacy Rose. Decatur, GA: CTS Press, 1998.

Rosenbloom, Dena, et al. *Life After Trauma: A Workbook for Healing.* New York: Guilford Press, 1999.

Saunders, Cicely, Mary Baines, and Robert Dunlop. *Living with Dying: A Guide to Palliative Care.* Oxford: Oxford University Press, 1995.

Secundy, Marian Gray, ed. *Trials, Tribulations, and Celebrations: African-American Perspectives on Health, Illness, Aging and Loss.* Yarmouth, ME: Intercultural Press, 1992.

Singh, Kathleen D. *The Grace in Dying: How We Are Transformed Spiritually as We Die.* San Francisco: HarperSanFrancisco, 2000.

Sittser, Gerald. *A Grace Disguised: How the Soul Grows Through Loss.* Rev. ed. (new preface and epilogue). Grand Rapids: Zondervan, 1995.

Smith, David, and Robert Veatch, eds. *Guidelines on the Termination of Life-Sustaining Treatment and the Care of the Dying.* Bloomington: Indiana University Press, 1987.

Sölle, Dorothée. *The Mystery of Death.* Minneapolis: Fortress, 2007.

Speck, Peter. *Being There: Pastoral Care in Times of Illness.* London: SPCK, 1988.

Spring, Beth, and Ed Larson. *Euthanasia: Spiritual, Medical, and Legal Issues in Terminal Health Care.* Portland, OR: Multnomah Press, 1988.

Stiller, Brian C. *What Happens When I Die? A Promise of the Afterlife.* Colorado Springs: Piñon Press, 2001.

Stoddard, Sandol. *The Hospice Movement: A Better Way of Caring for the Dying.* Updated and expanded ed. New York: Vintage, 1992.

Stout, N. *The Joy of Being a Bereavement Minister.* Totowa, NJ: Resurrection, 2005.

Stringfellow, William. *A Second Birthday.* New York: Doubleday, 1970.

Thompson, Melvyn. *Cancer and the God of Love.* London: SCM Press, 1976.

Tolstoy, Leo. *The Death of Ivan Ilych.* New York: Bantam Books, 1987.

Truog, Robert. "Is It Time to Abandon Brain Death?" *Hastings Center Report* 27, no. 1 (1997): 29-37.

Uhlmann, Michael M. *Last Rights: Assisted Suicide and Euthanasia Debated.* Grand Rapids: Eerdmans Publishing Company, 1998.

Vander Zee, Leonard J. *In Life and In Death: A Pastoral Guide for Funerals.* Grand Rapids: CRC Publications, 1992.

Veatch, Robert M. *Death, Dying and the Biological Revolution: Our Last Quest for Responsibility,* rev. ed. New Haven: Yale University Press, 1989.

Verhey, Allen. "The Spirit of God and the Spirit of Medicine: The Church, Globalization, and a Mission of Health Care." In *God and Globalization,* ed. Max L. Stackhouse (with Peter Paris). Harrisburg, PA: Trinity Press International, 2000.

Watson, David. *Fear No Evil: A Personal Struggle with Cancer.* London: Hodder and Stoughton, 1984.

Weatherhead, Leslie D. *Life Begins at Death.* Nashville: Abingdon, 1969.

Webb, Marilyn. *The Good Death: The American Search to Reshape the End of Life.* New York: Bantam Books, 1997.

Weir, Robert F., ed. *Physician Assisted Suicide.* Bloomington: Indiana University Press, 1997.

Wolterstorff, Nicholas. *Lament for a Son.* Grand Rapids: Eerdmans, 1987.

Wolff, Pierre. *May I Hate God?* Mahwah, NJ: Paulist Press, 1979.

Worden, William J., and William Proctor. *Personal Death Awareness.* Englewood Cliffs, NJ: Prentice-Hall, 1976.

Index of Names

Index of Subjects